Welcome to law school. These outlines are designed to help y
law school, One L year.

In this booklet are outlines for all of the major classes typically offered as first year law school
classes. These are the same outlines that I used to ace the One L year, updated to reflect recent
changes in the law. They are not meant to supplant any course of study or the development of
your own study guides or outlines, but merely aid you in learning and remembering the volumes
of information you will need to pass your One L exams. Good luck!

This booklet contains outlines for the following subjects:
• Contracts
• Constitutional Law
• Civil Procedure
• Property
• Torts

CIVIL PROCEDURE

Personal Jurisdiction

I. **General Jurisdiction**

a. *Pennoyer v. Neff* – the state has power over people and property inside its boundaries. Gives us the first 3 fingers of in personam jurisdiction test

    i. Presence

        1. D is physically found w/in the bounds of the state/territory

        2. Corporation is "present" at principal place of business as well as where substantial operations take place

    ii. **Domicile**

        1. Usual place of abode (can only have one)

        2. Determined by (a) intent of individual to make a location a permanent home (b) facts indicating that the party had physically located there

        3. Domicile of corporation is place of incorporation

    iii. **Actual consent**

        1. D is given proper service of process and appears in court

b. **Rule 12**

    i. implied consent (finger 4 of in personam jurisdiction test)

    ii. If D appears (and does not file special appearance) and failed to raise Rule 12(b) defense, then D waives right to that defense

        1. Special Appearance – allows D to appear to object to Jurisdiction, w/o letting appearance establish presence or actual consent (which could be basis for personal jurisdiction)

        2. Collateral attack – when D makes an attack on a previous judgment for lack of jurisdiction – can only be raised if D had not already raised the attack on jurisdiction or waived the defense of lack of jurisdiction under Rule 12

    iii. All 12(b) defenses must be grouped together and filed together

    iv. Rule 12(b) defenses

        1. Lack of jurisdiction over subject matter

        2. Lack of jurisdiction over the person

        3. Improper venue

        4. Insufficient process

        5. Insufficient service of process

        6. Failure to state a claim upon which relief can be granted

        7. Failure to join a party under rule 19 FRCP

II. **Specific jurisdiction**

a. Must have **minimum contacts** with the forum

b. **Cause of action must arise out of those contacts** or are connected to those activated in the forum state

    i. Functions – protect D from burden of a distant forum, ensure balance of federalism, Due Process Clause may divest state of jurisdiction

c. **Full Faith and Credit** – states must honor each other's judgments, unless the original state lacked jurisdiction – judgments are entitled to FFC only if rendering court has jurisdiction

    i. 28 USC § 1738 - extends FFC for fed. Judgments to states & state judgments to fed.

    ii. 28 USC § 1963 – allows a monetary judgment from one fed. dist. to be "registered" in another fed. dist in order to enforce it

d. *International Shoe Co. v. Washington* – WA brought suit against Shoe, a DE corp. w/ office in STL, to recover taxes owed. Shoe had temporary sales ppl living in WA, and sold orders there of substantial monetary value. Process served to salesman and STL offices.

    i. *HOLDING*: **systematic and continuous activities of Shoe in WA meets min. contacts test and claim was arising out of WA contacts**

    ii. *RULES* – maintenance of suit must not offend "traditional notions of fair play and substantial justice" under Due Process and

        1. Reciprocity – had D availed himself of the "benefits and protections of the laws of the forum state?"

        2. Quality and Nature of the Contacts – casual or isolated occurrences not enough, quantity not determinative, a single act can suffice

e. *McGee v. International Life Ins. Co.* - CA beneficiary (P) of the decedent's life ins. Policy sued the out-of-state ins. Co. (D) for nonpayment. D refused to pay. D's only contact with CA was the premium notices it mailed to the P, the CA resident.

    i. *HOLDING:* it is sufficient for Due Process that the suit was based on a contract with had substantial connection with that state. Unilateral act of a consumer can't pull a corp. into jurisdiction, corp. must "**purposefully avail itself.**"

f. *Hanson v. Denckla* – Donner a PA resident bought a trust from bank in DE, she moved to FL and died. C/A – trust is invalid under FL law, FL does not have jurisdiction over the trust

    i. *HOLDING*: no jurisdiction over the DE bank in FL. **Unilateral act of Donner going to FL.** DE bank did not purposefully avail itself to FL law

        1. *Unilateral activity of those who claim some relationship w/ a non-resident D cannot satisfy requirement for contact w/ the forum state*

    ii. **RULE: for min. contacts must show reciprocity and that by some act the D has purposefully and voluntarily availed itself of the privilege of conducting activities w/in the forum state, thus invoking the benefit and protections of its law**

        1. Purposeful availment- D must have made a deliberate choice to relate to state in some meaningful way before D bears burden of defending there.

g. *Shaffer v. Heitner* – shareholder derivative suit. P had one share of stock in Greyhound, sued directors of the Corp. Sequestered the stock and Stock options. Tired to get in rem jurisdiction by attaching the D's shares of stock and options.

    i. **HOLDING:** all assertions of state court jurisdiction must meet minimum contacts test. There are not enough contacts btwn D's and the forum state to satisfy minimum contacts

    ii. **RULE:** quasi in rem jurisdiction is absorbed into in personam jurisdiction. (*Harris v. Balk* "attachment jurisdiction" qualifies as quasi in rem and is subject to constitutional test)

    iii. **True In Rem** – jurisdiction against the property itself- recover limited to the property itself. Must be attached prior to filing and meet one of the 5 fingers

h. *World Wide Volkswagen Corp. v. Woodson* – P sues NY distributor and a dealer in OK for burn injuries in an OK accident. D's did no business in OK. The unilateral activity of the P to take the D's car to OK.

    i. **HOLDING: Test for non-resident D – (1) did D purposefully avail himself to forum state and then (2) reasonably foresee he could be hailed in to court in that forum**

    ii. **STREAM OF COMMERCE TEST – the forum state does not exceed powers under Due Process if it asserts personal jurisdiction over a corp. that delivers its products into the stream of commerce with the expectation that they will be purchased by consumers in the forum state**

        1. **Does apply when D delivers product into the stream with the expectation that they will be purchased by consumers in the forum state not just FROM the forum state**

2. **D's actions must be purposeful and directed toward s the forum state.** Simply because goods find their way to forum state does not make someone liable for entering it into that stream. Unilateral act of consumer cannot draw corp. in to personal jurisdiction (*Hanson*)

i. *Gray v. American Radiator* – Titan Valve in OH made valve, Am. Radiator in PA made hot-water heaters; Gray's hot-water heater explodes b/c of valve.

    i. **RULE: since Titan knew there valve would be used on radiators it is expected that they could be hailed in to court in any forum which the valves were sold**

j. *Keeton v. Hustler Magazine Inc.* – suit for liable, Hustler magazine distributed nationally

    i. **Single Publication Rule – P does not have to bring 50 different suits for libel, just one, heard in one court**

    ii. **HOLDING:** since the libel was arising out of all 50 states minimum contacts met

k. *Calder v. Jones* – article published defaming P, court claims jurisdiction in CA b/c the focal point of the article was CA and person claiming remedy was CA resident

    i. **Effects Test -** specific personal jurisdiction can be established if the D's intentional act, even if committed outside forum state, is expressly aimed at the forum state

        1. **Knowledge by itself cannot establish purposeful availment**

    ii. **General jurisdiction is determined at time of law suit**

    iii. **Specific jurisdiction is determined by the time that the claim arose**

l. *Burger King Corp. v. Rudzewicz* – D's opened a BK franchise and went under, P sues for breach of contract in FL. D's claim no contacts with FL only BK in MI where they operated

    i. **HOLDING:** franchise dispute grew directly out of a contract which had substantial connection with FL. D reached out beyond MI for purchase of a long-term franchise and benefits that would arise from affiliation with BK

        1. **Contracting with forum state pulls you into that state's jurisdiction**

    ii. **Contracts Rule: - if contract exists minimum contacts determined by – (1) prior negotiations (2) contemplated future consequences (3) look for relevant contract terms (4) overall course of dealing btwn the two parties**

    iii. **Jurisdiction Rule: court must balance fair play and substantial justice with minimum contacts**

m. *Asahi Metal Industry Co. v. Superior Court* –man has motorcycle accident sues manufacturers ChengShim in CA who impleads Asahi (both foreign companies) man settles, leaving only Asahi and ChengShim

    i. **HOLDING:** exertion of jurisdiction over Asahi exceeds Due Process

    ii. **RULE for fair play and substantial justice – (1) burden on D (2) forum state's interest (3) P's interest in obtaining relief (4) interstate judicial system's interest (5) shared interest of the several state is furthering substantive social polices**

    iii. **Must use Due Process b/c it is a right Rights can be waived but constitutional framework or structure cannot be waived. Personal jurisdiction can be waived therefore it is a right derived from the 14th amendment Due Process Clause**

n. *Pavlovich v. Superior Court* - P founded website that allowed DVD burning. P knew that sharing the program was illegal but never knew the company he was ripping off has its principal place of business in CA

    i. **HOLIDNG:** in order for a state to exercise specific personal jurisdiction over a foreign D, must show that D has minimum contacts related to the claim such that fair play is not offended

        1. **Application of Calder's effects test – only question is whether D knew that his tortious conduct may harm industries in CA. No express aiming**

o. *Perkins v. Benguet Consolidated Mining Co.* – During WWII D moved operations from warzone to Ohio. C/A arose from activities distinct from activities in OH

   i. HOLDING: D carried on in OH <u>continuous and systematic</u> supervision of the necessary limited wartime activities of the company

p. *Helicopteros Nacionales De Columbia S.A. v. Hall*

   i. HOLDING – claims against helico did not arise out of or are related to activities in TX, contacts w/ TX not continuous and systematic

   ii. RULE – mere purchases or annual trips even if occurring at regular intervals are not enough to warrant a states assertion of personal jurisdiction in a C/A related to those transactions, trips or other insignificant activities

   1. When a company's activities are so substantial in the forum that the company is deem present. Activities must be systematic and continuous

q. *Kulko v. Superior Court of Ca, City and County of San Francisco* –exercise of long arm jurisdiction over absent parents is unreasonable b/c it would discourage reasonable visitation

r. *Burnham v. Superior Court* – man visits children in CA is served with divorce papers. Does Due Process allow CA jurisdiction over non-resident who was personally served?

   i. HOLDING: Physical presence in the state was purposeful availment, thus satisfies minimum contacts. Presence jurisdiction exists & personal service of process

   ii. Personal prescience jurisdiction (general jurisdiction applies to corporations), tag/transient jurisdiction exists here – mere presence and service of process

   iii. D cannot be lured into jurisdiction, kidnapped and drug across state lines, tricked into being present, legally induced as by a lawsuit or criminal trial.

   1. EXCEPTION: state has power over anyone who appeared in pending action

s. *Carnival Cruise Lines, Inc. v. Shute* – Shute went on a cruise and was injured sued in WA, forum clause on the ticket said suits must be litigated in FL courts

   i. HOLDING: inclusion of forum-clause is reasonable b/c it limits forums D could be sued, dispels uncertainty and keeps fairs low. Forum-selection clauses are subject to judicial scrutiny for fundamental fairness. P was given notice of forum-selection clause and given opportunity to reject the contract but accepted when bought ticket

   ii. Forum Clause Not enforceable is – (1) not freely bargained for (2) create additional expense for one party or (3) deny one party a remedy

<u>NOTICE</u>

I. Notice

a. *Mullane v. Central Hanover Bank and Trust Co.* – Bank set up a common trust fund with several beneficiaries. Unknown number and place of residence of beneficiaries. Provided notice to beneficiaries though local newspaper. Mullane claims insufficient notice

   i. HOLDING: newspaper sufficient b/c parties interest were unknown and had unknown residences

   ii. Three Types of Beneficiaries

   1. Class 1 – missing or unknown – newspaper notice good enough

   2. Class 2 – conjectural or future – newspaper notice good enough

   3. Class 3 – property in the state – newspaper notice not sufficient mail required b/c they had names and addresses of beneficiaries

   iii. TEST FOR SUFFICENCY OF NOTICE

   1. Notice must give recipients an opportunity to present objections

2. Conant of the notice must reasonably apprise recipient of what's at risk
3. Recipients must get the notice in a reasonable time – must also be calculated so as to be likely to reach the individual
4. Notice by publication can be sufficient if it meets the test but is insufficient if the parties were of known resident

II. **RULE 4** - Summons for Personal and In Rem jurisdiction
   a. **4(d) Waiving service- simplifies and minimized cost. Carrot and stick approach**
      i. **"Carrot" – if you waive service of process, you have 60 days instead of 20 after request was sent to file answer/pre-answer motion (i.e. from post-marked date)**
      ii. **"Stick" = if you decline to waive process you bear the cost of the service of process**
   b. 4(e) -Serving an individual w/in a judicial dist. of the U.S. – serve under state court service of process rules or in hand service, at usual place of abode, or deliver a copy to process agent
   c. 4(f) - Serving an Individual in a foreign country
   d. 4(g) - serving a minor or incompetent person
   e. 4(h) - serving a corp. partnership or association – corps. often designate an individual to receive service of process
   f. 4(k) - Territorial limits of effective service – can always tell long-arm stat. b/c it always has min contacts test in the wording
      i. MO Long-Arm Stat reached to full extend of Due Process
      ii. 4(k)(1)(a) – **Borrowing Rule** – borrows long-arm stat. of the court where the fed. dist. court sits (i.e. Western Dist. Court of MO borrows MO Long-Arm Stat.) – fed courts have the same jurisdictional reach for service as the state courts
      iii. 4(k)(1)(b) – **Bulge Rule** – allows for effective service is 4rd party is joined under rule 14 (impleader) or rule 19 (compulsory joinder of 3rd party) and served in judicial dist. of U.S. – must be w/in allowed 100 mile radius from the place summons issued
         1. Only necessary if there is otherwise not personal jurisdiction over D
         2. **Widely suspected that buldge rule is unconstitutional – not consistent w/ Due Process**
      iv. 4(k)(1)(c) – **Federal Interpleader Rule** – allows nationwide service of process.
      v. 4(k)(2) Federal Claim outside State-Court Jurisdiction – must be federal claim, D not subject to jurisdiction in any state courts of general jurisdiction, and exercising jurisdiction is consistent with Due Process and Constitution
      vi. 4(l) – Proving Service – offer sworn affidavit on receiving service
      vii. 4(m) – **Stale Summons Rule** - time limit on service summons only good for 120 days

LONG ARM STATUTES

I. **Long-Arm Stat.** – a state statute or rule must authorize a court to exercise power over the D. w/o such a state court cannot exercise power over the D regardless of what the constitutional rule dictates
   a. *Gibbons v. Brown* – Gibbons (D) is passenger in car driven by Mr. Brown, in an accident in Canada, sues in FL. 2 yrs later Mrs. Brown sues Gibbons in FL, claiming P

availed herself of FL b/c of prior law-suit with Mr. Brown

     b. *HOLDING:* D's prior suit in FL should not keep her from challenging jurisdiction in a separate suit, even it if arises from the same subject matter

     c. **RULE – to obtaining jurisdiction over a non-resident requires – (1) P alleges sufficient jurisdictional facts to bring D w/in coverage of long-arm stat and (2) sufficient minimum contacts are shown**

VENUE, TRANSFER AND FORUM NON CONVENIENS

I. Venue

     a. Venue flows solely from statutory sources – state cases and fed. questions

     b. Venue statues are either mandatory or discretionary

     c. **28 USC § 1391 – Venue Generally**

          i. **A corporate D is deemed for venue purposes to reside where it is subject to personal jurisdiction**

          ii. **Must find a place where D is subject to personal jurisdiction**

          iii. **§1391(b) – prevents domestic D's from being sued in unreasonable venues**

          iv. **§1391(b)(3) – venue whenever a D "may be found" in that dist.**

          v. **§1391(d) – applies to alien corps. subjecting them to suit in any judicial dist.**

     d. *Dee-K Enterprises, Inc. V. Geveafil Sdn. Bhd.* - two American purchasers of rubber thread sue several foreign manufacturers and distributors of the thread alleging a conspiracy to restrain trade and fix prices

          i. **HOLDING: court found due process satisfied by D's appointment of exclusive U.S. sales agents and customizing its product for U.S. market**

          ii. **Footnote 24 – when both foreign and domestic D's §1391(b) must be satisfied for domestic D's or else §1391(d) could be used to gain venue over foreign D's then use §1391(b)(3) as a loophole to attach domestic D's**

          iii. **RULE: To obtain personal jurisdiction, (1) must point to a stat. (usually long-arm stat.) or rule that authorizes service of process over D and (2) rule or service must comport with Due Process**

II. Transfer

     a. 28 USC 1631 – gives Court enough power to transfer to a jurisdiction where there is venue and power

     b. **28 USC 1401 - transfer among federal judicial districts – applies only to fed. courts allowing them to move cases around the country**

     c. **28 USC 1404 – even if the case has been transferred, the judge must apply the law that would have been applied if the case had not been transferred b/c venue was proper**

     d. **28 USC 1406 – court has no jurisdiction from the start so it must dismiss or transfer the case to a district or division in which the claim could have been brought**

          i. **1404 & 1406 only apply to federal, if in state court use Forum Non Conveniens**

ii. **If claim is brought in Fed Dist w/o jurisdiction they can § 1631 transfer to a dist that has jurisdiction or quash the motion – gives courts w/o jurisdiction some power**

III. **Forum Non Conveniens** – power of the courts to hear a case

    a. Common law inconvenient forum – court may decline to exercise jurisdiction even if they possess it

    b. *Piper Aircraft v. Reyno* – Airplane manufactured in PA crashed in Scotland. Reyno commenced wrongful death claim in CA against Piper and Harzell (propeller co.)

        i. *HOLDING:* case should be filed in Scotland b/c could join additional parties like state of dead pilot. D wants to prove pilot error.

        ii. **FNC allowed if there is an alternative forum available w/ jurisdiction**

        iii. **Gilbert Test- Public and Private interests make the chosen forum appropriate**

            1. Private – parties have an interest in having the case litigated in the most convenient forum

            2. Public – courts may have an interest in avoiding burden of excessive caseload hearing cases unrelated to their state

            3. Best to use **Lex Loci Delicit** – law where the wrong occurred

            4. State interest analysis- which state has greatest interest in problem

SUBJECT MATTER JURISDICTION

I. **Federal Question Jurisdiction**

    a. 28 USC § 1331 – the district courts shall have original jurisdiction of all civil actions arising under the constitution, laws or treaties of the US

        i. Fed Courts are Limited Jurisdiction authorized by Art. III § 2

    b. *Louisville & Nashville R.R. v. Motley* – P claimed D breached an agreement to give P free RR passes for life for not suing the RR. Fed Stat. Prohibits passes retroactively

        i. **Well Pleaded Complaint Rule – P's complaint must clearly contain the federal question as an integral part – may not anticipate D's answer to raise a Fed Question (i.e. D claims he is protected by the 1st amendment)**

        ii. *Rule 12(h)(3)* – Rule 12(b)(1) is not waivable – D or the court can sua sponte move to dismiss the case for lack of subject matter jurisdiction at any time – subject matter jurisdiction is structural not a right

    c. Challenging Fed Question Jurisdiction – district court will:

        i. Carefully identify the P's claim – does it arise from state constitution, C/L, state statutes, etc.

        ii. Ask what the Federal Question(s) is - Identify carefully the Art. III arising under question to make sure to identify all of them

        iii. Write down the elements of the state law claim (i.e. negligence = duty, breach, causation, damages) – this establishes the prima facie case

        iv. Ask does the Fed Question give rise to the state law claims

        v. Is there nonetheless a power state interest in federalizing the case?

    d. **Declaratory Judgment Act 28 USC § 2201-2202** – empowers fed. dist. court to hear certain cases in which potential D seeks not a coercive remedy but a declaration of rights as long as the case arises under fed law or fed question

  e. **Losing Federalism** – if P loses in fed court on a 12(b)(1) for lack of subject matter jurisdiction he can file in state court, if he loses in fed court on a 12(b)(2) – personal jurisdiction- cannot refile b/c Fed court's ruling is biding is state court.

  f. **Collateral attack-** only allowed by special circumstances

       i. D appears challenges subject matter and loses – bound by judgment, may not thereafter challenge in a second action

       ii.   **D appears fails to challenge subject matter jurisdiction and loses on merits-** parties who have appeared but failed to challenged subject matter jurisdiction may generally not thereafter attack it's judgment in another court

       iii.   **D defaults-** if objecting to personal jurisdiction entitled to collateral attack

II. Diversity Jurisdiction

  a. 28 USC § 1332 – civil actions between citizens of different states, US citizens and foreign citizens or foreign states against US citizens. Must exceed 75k

       i. 1332(a) citizen of a state requires (1) US citizenship (2) domiciliary of the state

       ii.   1332(c) corporations are citizens of the state (1) in **place of incorporation** and (2) where it has its **principle place of business**

       iii.   **Test for Principle Place of Business – nerve center and muscle test – courts must look at both**

           1. Nerve center – location of CEO's and other administrators

           2. Muscle – location of everyday business activities, manufacturing plants, etc.

  b. *Redner v. Sanders* – P sues D in NY while living in France. Claims he's a CA resident. Court says not sufficient evidence to prove CA domicile despite P's law offices and law license in CA

       i. *Citizenship determined by domicile* – can only have one domicile, to change you must physically take up residence in a different domicile with the intention to remain there

       ii.   **Strawbridge rule – requires complete diversity. Even in a case with multiple diverse parties, the existence of one party of the same state or citizenship as a party on the other side will eliminate diversity – does not apply to 3rd party impleader**

  c. **Saadeh v. Farouki** – citizen of Greece suing an alien Jordanian living in MD

       i. §1332(a)- an alien admitted to the US for permanent residence shall be deemed a citizen of the state in which such alien is domiciled

           1. Not allowed for suits between alien in a state v a citizen of that state

       ii.   **RULE: under §1332(a) a least one of the parties in a dispute must be a citizen of the state in order for the federal courts to have diversity jurisdiction**

III. Supplemental Jurisdiction 28 USC § 1367

  a. Allows Fed court to take jurisdiction over claims which don't have independent grounds for jurisdiction (not diversity or fed. question) because they are sufficiently related to other claims permissive in fed. ct.

b. Supplemental claim must be of the same case or controversy as the fed claim.

c. Question is whether supplemental claim can be brought in fed court. Primary claim must be either fed question or diversity.

   i. 1367(a) (c) (e) applies when fed question or diversity

   ii. 1367(b) only applies when primary claim is diversity

d. **1367(a)** Claim must arise out of the "**same transaction or occurrence**"

e. **Gibbs Test: the state and federal claims must derive from a common nucleus of operative fact.** Established when courts have **power** to join related state claims to a federal question claim and that they have **discretion** on whether to allow such supplemental jurisdiction

f. **1367(b) – If original claim based solely on diversity jurisdiction**, then no supplemental jurisdiction for *claims brought by plaintiffs* under (disfavored rules):

   i. Rule 14 (impleader)

   ii. Rule 19 (necessary party)

   iii. Rule 20 (permissive joinder of parties) – only disfavored when it violates the Strawbridge Rule

   iv. Rule 24 (intervention)

      1. **does cover claims under these rules *brought by D's*** (i.e. a D2 intervenes under R24 or a D2 who was impleaded claims against P)

      2. Does not cover claims brought under Fed Question jurisdiction

   v. Rules 13, 18, 23 are **favored rules**

      1. **Rule 13 (Counter Claim or Cross Claim)**

      2. **Rule 18(Joinder of Claims)**

      3. **Rule 23 (Class Action Suits)**

   vi. **The disfavored rules are only disfavored if exercising supplemental jurisdiction would be inconsistent with requirements of 1332 (i.e. violating complete diversity)**

   vii. **Disfavored rules only apply to diversity claims not fed. question**

g. **1367(c) when court may decline supplemental jurisdiction under subsection (a)**

   i. the claim raises a novel or complex issue of state law

   ii. state law claim substantially predominates over the federal claim

   iii. the district court has dismissed all claims over which it had original jurisdiction

   iv. in exceptional circumstances, other compelling reasons to decline jurisdiction

IV. **Removal**

   a. If P brings a case in state court that could be brought in fed. court D has the option of having it removed to federal court.

      i. So long as venue is proper in state court, do not need to worry if venue is proper in federal court

   b. **28 USC § 1441**

      i. **1441(a) only D can remove, must remove to the district court in which the state court is located (i.e. KC court = western district fed. court)**

      ii. **1441(b) Fed Question (1331) is always removable, if under Diversity D cannot remove if sued in the state of his domicile**

      iii. **1441(c) an otherwise non-removable separate and independent claim is removable when joined with a Federal Question 1331 claim – must not violate Art III of the constitution**

      iv. **1441(f) federal court is not precluded from hearing and determining**

10

claims because the state court did not have jurisdiction over that claim – if it is pertinent to the case and the pendant federal claim

   <u>c.</u> 28 USC §1446 removal procedure – if removed and D not served or properly served, P may serve process as if the fed. dist. ct. were the first proceeding.

   <u>d.</u> § 1447 challenging removal – must give written notice of removal. 30 days to move to remand for lack of subject matter jurisdiction , order remanding to state court is not reviewable however refusals to remand are removable

   <u>e.</u> *Caterpillar, Inc. v. Lewis*

      <u>i.</u> *Narrow exception to Groupo v. Atlas*

      <u>ii.</u> ISSUE: whether absence of complete diversity at time of removal is fatal to fed. ct. adjudication

      <u>iii.</u> HOLDING: district court's error in failing to remand a case improperly removed is not fatal to the ensuing adjudication if federal jurisdictional requirements are met at the time judgment is entered

      <u>iv.</u> **RULE: whenever it appears by suggestion of the parties or otherwise that the court lacks jurisdiction on the subject matter, the court shall dismiss the action (Rule 12(h)(3))**

         <u>1.</u> If a jurisdictional defect remains uncured at the end of a case, the judgment must be vacated

         <u>2.</u> No jurisdictional defect lingered through judgment in the District Court

      <u>v.</u> REASONING: "once a diversity case has been tired in federal court with rule of decisions supplied by state law under the regime of Erie R. Co. v. Tompkins considerations of finality, efficiency and economy become overwhelming"

      <u>vi.</u> **Easy to sue corporations simply look for place of incorporation and principle place of business**

   <u>f.</u> *Groupo Dataflux v. Atlas Global Group, L.P.* - Limited partnerships, like general partnerships require that the domicile of each partner is considered; Atlas is one entity with 4 partners…it simultaneously has 3 domiciles (TX, DE, Mex.); Grupo is from Mexico and so is one of the Atlas partners = no diversity; From the moment the case was filed in DC, there was no diversity

      <u>i.</u> As soon as D lost they moved under 12(b)(1) to dismiss for lack of diversity jurisdiction

         <u>1.</u> if they had won at trial they would not have moved to dismiss

      <u>ii.</u> **Time-of Filing Rule** – with jurisdiction of the court much depends on the state of things at the time the action was brought - Moment of filing, is when notice of removal under 1441 is filed with the federal district court clerk

THE ERIE DOCTRINE

I. The Erie Problem- State Law in Federal Courts

  a. *Erie Railroad v. Tompkins*

     i. ISSUE: must a fed. dist. ct. presiding over a diversity suit apply state C/L in resolving the dispute

     ii. *Swift v. Tyson* - previous precedent overruled by Erie

       1. Fed. ct exercising jurisdiction on the ground of diversity of citizenship need not apply the unwritten law of the state as declared by the its highest court. They are free to exercise independent judgment as to what the common law of the state is or should be

11

        2. **This doctrine is an unconstitutional assumption of powers by the courts**

        3. Reasons Court overrules *Swift*

           a. Swift ruling made equal protection under the laws impossible

           b. Erie decision will prevent "forum shopping"

           c. Violation of Federalism…Constitution does NOT allow Federal Courts to apply federal common law to matters of state law

           d. It is difficult to draw the line between local and general law…leads to a question of substantive vs. procedural issues of law

    iii. HOLIDNG: Yes, there is no fed. C/L. Federal law applies only when a specific federal statute governs the matter or where a federal question is before the court

b. **The Erie Doctrine**

    i. **Fed court sitting in diversity applies state substantive law as well as state choice of law (Klaxon) but applies Federal procedure rules (FRCPs)**

        1. Fed court must look to the state court in its jurisdiction and how that state court would apply the law – "straight down no right angles"

        2. i.e. Fed. Dis. Court of NY NY State Court NY State Choice (Application of PENN Law)

    ii. Nearly every state had a choice of law rule called lex (law) loci (location) delicti (wrongdoing); so every state would look to the law, location, and wrongdoing;

    iii. *Erie* decision sent us to NY…the choice of law/conflicts of law/lex loci delicti sent us to PA law; these are TWO distinct matters

    iv. **KLAXON held that the choice of law rules of the state where the fed. ct. sits should be applied** in terms of substantive law but federal rules apply not state rules of procedure

c. *Guaranty Trust Co. v. York*

    i. *Substance/procedure distinction* – Erie provides that all Fed courts must apply state substantive rules of law and federal procedural law

        1. *Court must determine where it is dealing with a substantive or procedural matter*

        2. *Substantive matters include matters that have substantial state interests i.e. torts, contracts, property*

    ii. ISSUE: must the federal court allow the state statute of limitations, thereby treating the matter as substantive, when the federal rule would lead to a different outcome in the case

    iii. HOLDING: Yes. Matter is procedural but is it substantive w/in the Erie doctrine if it has substantial effect upon the eventual outcome of the case. Statute of limitations substantially affected the outcome of the lawsuit, since it had run out before the action was commenced.

    iv. Fed Court in equity would apply latches, fed court sitting at law would apply Erie doctrine and state substantive law

        1. Law of latches – if P has waited too long, such that evidence has been lost

court would say you've sat on your rights too long and claim cannot be brought. Not date certain.

  2. Statute of limitations is substantive for the purposes of Erie

 v. **OUTCOME DETERMINATIVE TEST- if applying state law over federal law would change the outcome of the suit, then the law is substantive for Erie purposes – and thus the state law should be applied**

d. *Byrd v. Blue Ridge Rural Electric Cooperative*

 i. ISSUE: conflicting Fed and State rules in workers compensation matter. State rule gives determination of rule to judge, federal rule gives determination to a jury. Should issue be decided by judge or jury? Does Erie treat this SC law as a matter of substance or procedure?

 ii. HOLDING: this rule was not an integral part of the special relationship created by the statute

 iii. <u>**Erie problem occurs when state and fed law are in conflict, if they are not in conflict follow them both – if you can harmonize then do so**</u>

 iv. **Byrd Test**

  1. Is the state practice **"bound up with the definition of rights and obligations of the parties"?**

  2. Is the state rule an integral part of the state law claim or is the rule **merely a form and mode of enforcing the claim**

  3. Are there **affirmative countervailing federal policies?**

   a. i.e. In Byrd, D argued that the 7th amendment specifies the essential function of the jury – federal policy favors jury decisions

 v. **Outcome-determinative test**

  1. it is a strong consideration, but is not the only consideration

  2. **must be a <u>substantial likelihood</u>** that applying the federal rule over the state rule will cause a different outcome to occur

  3. **substantially is a higher bar than significant**

  4. i.e. in Byrd, the likelihood of a different outcome was not strong enough to justify using the state rule over the federal rule must be certainty it will be outcome-determinative

e. **Procedural** Law for Erie Purposes **(apply federal over state)**

 i. decision making power of jury over judge (Byrd)

 ii. comment on the weight of the evidence

 iii. comment on credibility of witnesses

 iv. discretion to grant a new trial if verdict appears to be against weight of evidence

 v. power to direct a verdict on issue of contributory negligence

f. **Substantive** for Erie Purposes **(apply state over federal)**

 i. choice of law (Klaxon)

 ii. statute of limitations (Guaranty)

 iii. burden of raising defense of contributory negligence (Sampson)

 iv. burden of proof of showing that P was/was not cont. negligent

    v.   commencing of suit for tolling of statute of limitations (Ragan)

    vi.   posting of bond to cover expense of D shareholder der. (Cohen)

    vii.   enforceability of arbitration clauses (Bernhardt)

    viii.   closing courts' doors to unlicensed out-of-state corp.'s (Woods)

g. ***Sibbich v. Wilson*** – held FRCP 35 trumped a state statute

h. ***Federal Rules***

    i. 28 USC §1652 – state laws as rules of decision – state laws, as long as they don't conflict with Acts of Congress or the Constitution, are rules of decision in civil actions

    ii.   28 USC §2071 – rule-making power generally

    iii.   28 USC §2072 – Rules Enabling Act – supreme court shall have power to prescribe general rules of practice and procedure and rules of evidence

    iv.   28 USC § 2074 –rules of procedure and evidence must be submitted to congress by supreme court by Dec 1 of each year

    v.   FRE 302 – in civil actions and proceedings, a defense where state law supplies the rule of decision is determined in accordance with state law

    vi.   FRE 501 – the privilege of a whines, person, government, state or political subdivision thereof shall be determined in accordance with state law

i. ***Hanna v. Plumer***

    i. Two lines of cases

       1. Hannah Line - Federal rule or statute on point in conflict with state law

          a. If procedural follow fed law, if substantive follow Erie/state law

       2. Relatively Unguided Erie: Federal practice on point in conflict with state law no fed statute on point exists – Byrd v. Blue Ridge

    ii.   ISSUE: Whether in diversity action service of process is made under Rule 4 of FRCP or by manner prescribed by state law

    iii.   **HANNA TEST: When situation is covered by FRCP test is twofold:**

       1. **Whether the applicable rule is w/in the scope of the Rules Enabling Act 28 USC § 2072 (relates to the practice and procedure of the dist courts – Sibbach)**

       2. **Whether such rule transgresses constitutional bounds**

          a. **If it falls under the Rules Enabling Act and is Constitutional Follow the Federal Rule**

    iv.   **Constitutional Test – though falling into the uncertain area between substance and procedure, if the rule is rationally capable of classification as either procedural or substantive, then it is constitutional**

    v.   HOLDING: Rule 4(d)(1) Satisfies the test – service of process at the usual place of abode, D was served at his home when service of process was given to his wife

    vi.   The broad command of Erie is the same as the Enabling Act: federal courts are to apply state substantive law and federal procedural law

    vii.   The court has never failed the Hanna test

    viii.   **Relatively Unguided Erie Test:**

1. **Is the state law bound up in the federal law?**
2. **Is there an affirmative federal countervailing consideration?**
3. **Is the difference btwn state law and federal practice worth substantially violating the twin aims of Erie?**
   a. **Discouragement of forum-shopping**
   b. **Avoidance of inequitable administration of the laws**

j. Statute of limitations
   i. When claim actually arises
   ii. Tolling – from time to time the statute will stop running
   iii. Duration
   iv. Commencement of claim – have you started or commenced your action in 3 years? Or is it time barred? (3ys 1 day)

k. *McKenna v. Ortho Pharmaceutical Corp* - Embolism burst in McKenna's brain as a result of a blood clot from taking birth control pills produced by Ortho
   i. P had forum shopping choice – could bring claim in PA state court and they cannot remove, or in Fed Dist Ct. in WD of PA (§1332) – attorney chose Fed. Ct.
   ii. Fed Dist judge looked to OH stat. of limitations to decide when the action commenced
   iii. **Under Erie always look straight down, once in PA state law, use Klaxon to apply the choice of law of the state where the Fed Court is sitting.**
   iv. If McKenna had filed in Fed Dist Ct. in OH, court would have applied OH law, OH stat of limitations - State law unclear

l. Rules for Fed Judge to Determine State Law
   i. Fed judge asks himself has the state supreme court recently ruled on this very issue? (has to be a very recent decision)
   ii. Is there a state statute that answers the issue? (doesn't matter how old as long as it's on the books it is to be obeyed, if the legislature doesn't change it follow)
   iii. Fed just tries to predict as best as possible what the state would say if asked, what the law of the state is on that question to prevent reverse forum shopping (judge won't follow old case law cause it will lead to reverse forum shopping)
   iv. Look at rulings of court of appeals in that state and cases that aren't on point but suggestive of how courts would rule generally about these kinds of issues, look to restatements and law review articles as well.
   v. Certification law
      1. You can certify the question – fed judge frames the issue and asks the supreme court in that state how it would answer the question and then follow the state supreme court's answer
      2. Can slow down the process, have to wait until state supreme court gets to it

m. Reverse Erie
   i. Most federal questions can be brought in state court

    ii.   Federal questions come up as a defense (freedom of speech, press, etc.)

    iii.   State judges rule on federal criminal law on the state level all the time

    iv.   What if you have a federal question claim in state court?

        1. You have to apply the federal law to a state claim

        2. States follow state rules of procedure, as matters of substance follow federal law

REMEDIES

I. Remedies

  a. Monetary damages are from courts at law

  b. Injunctive relief is equitable (75% of the cases)

     i. Both can offer specific or Substitutionary relief

  c. Types of Equitable Relief:

     i. constructive trust – declared over funds a D has wrongfully diverted

     ii.   rescission or cancellation – of a contract

     iii.   reforming of a contract

     iv.   an accounting – court determines what D owes in complex financial matters

     v.   quiet title or remove clouds from the title – property remedies

  d. Types of Legal Specific Remedies: (not all specific remedies are *equitable*)

     i. replevin – to recover personal property

     ii.   ejectment – to recover possession of land

     iii.   writ of mandamus – court orders a lower ct. or public official to perform an act required by law

     iv.   habeas corpus (a civil writ most commonly used in criminal cases)

  e. Rule 1 – merges equity and law

  f. Rule 9(g) – must specifically state special damages

     i. i.e. permanent disability as a result of an injury, medical damages, etc.

  g. Rule 10(b) - a party must state claims or defenses in numbered paragraphs separately if they do not arise from the same occurrence or transaction (common nucleus of operative fact)

  h. Rule 54(c) – default judgment must not differ from what is demanded. Every other final judgment other than a default judgment should provide entitled relief even if the relief is not demanded for in the pleadings

     i. Rule of Grace – if you make a mistake in your 8(a)(3) motion and after discovery and trial you deserve not what you claimed but simply damages judge will give you damages even though it was in your pleading

  i. Amendment VII – right to trial by jury, and no reexamining of facts tried by a jury

     i. Remedy in law = jury trial

     ii.   Remedy in equity = bench trial

  j. Rule 38 – tells how to demand right to a jury trial

     i. 38(a) – right to a jury only if preserved by 7th amendment (only if remedy in law, if equitable there is no jury trial)

  k. OLD RULE - 1616 King James I – Equity court defers to law court, in order to be entitled to an equitable remedy the P has to show that their legal remedy was inadequate

i. Equitable jurisdiction lies only where there is no adequate remedy at law

ii. Does not exist all that much anymore

l. Federal Injunctions

i. injunctions are the most prevalent form of equitable relief – enforced by *contempt* proceedings

ii. Federal judges are hesitant to enter an injunction because in theory an injunction goes forever - Injunctions are very time consuming for the judge to oversee and enforce so deny injunctive relief and simply award damages

m. Stereotype of the Courts

i. Courts of Equity were flexible – adjusted to the needs to the parties

ii. Courts of Law were rigid and full of technicalities

II. Provisional Remedies

a. 64(a) Preliminary Injunctions -Only issued on notice to the adverse party

i. 4 part test to grant Preliminary Injunction (Majority)

1. P will suffer irreparable injury w/o injunctive relief
2. P will probably prevail on merits
3. Balancing equities – D's will not be harmed more than P is helped by the injunction
4. Granting the injunction is in the public interest

ii. *William Inglis & Sons. Baking Co. v. ITT Continental Baking Co.*

1. Alternative Test – one moving for preliminary injunction must prove:
   a. Combination of probably success and possibility of irreparable injury
   b. Or serious questions raised and the balance of hardships tips sharply in his favor
   c. <u>It isn't necessary for P be reasonably certain to succeed on the merits. If the harm that may occur to the P is sufficiently serious it is only necessary that there's a fair chance of success on the merits</u>

b. Rule 64(b) Temporary Restraining orders

i. granted for short period not to exceed 10 days, can be extended but no longer than 10 days.

ii. Granted w/o notice or hearing to the other side ex parte (fundamental due process denial)

iii. Cannot be appealed

iv. Granted only if:

1. it clearly appears that there will be **immediate and irreparable injury**
2. filing party certifies the **efforts made to give adverse party notice and why notice should not be required**

c. Rule 64(c) Posting a Security

i. Party must post a security as the court deems necessary

ii. to cover damages incurred by any party wrongfully enjoined/restrained

iii. no security must be posted by US or an officer or agency thereof

PLEADINGS

I. Pleading
- a. Common law pleading – writs
    - i. Rule 2 – abolished writs – there is only one type of action, civil action –
        1. this is really a lie b/c P can fail to state a claim (12b6) by not meeting all of the elements of the old writ
        2. it is a useful lie because it eliminated the highly technical nature of common law writ pleading.
    - ii. Writs were formula based on commonly recurring fact patterns – we differentiate and distinguish different civil actions – writs now comprised of causes of action/elements of the claim/claims/ legal theories/ etc.
- b. Code Pleading
    - i. cause of action – "field codes" – facts and causes of action replace writs and forms of action
    - ii. Missouri is a code pleading jurisdiction
    - iii. Problems – courts interpret "cause of action" to refer to substantive law (tort, contracts, property , etc.) and treat each cause of action as mutually exclusive
    - iv. code pleading encourages senseless battles over form – such as whether the pleading was too specific by pleading "evidence" or too general by pleading "conclusions"- handled by discovery
- c. Notice Pleading
    - i. Claims pleading by FRCP – don't have to plead every cause of action
    - ii. **Rule 8 - General Rules of Pleadings**
        1. **8(a) claims for relief must contain:**
            - a. **8(a)(1) – grounds for court's jurisdiction**
            - b. **8(a)(2) – short statement showing pleader is entitled to relief**
            - c. **8(a)(3) – must tell judge which remedy you seek, may include relief in the alternative or different types of relief**
        2. ***Bell Atlantic Corp v. Twombly*** – new pleading standard allegations of P's complaint when taken as true must show not merely that it is possible P is entitled to relief that that it is plausible that P is entitled to relief
        3. **<u>Ashcroft v. Iqbal – applies Twombly in all civil actions, overrules Conley v. Gibson which never applies – pleading standard is PLAUSABILITY</u>**
            - a. **<u>Plead enough facts so that if the facts are taken as true it is plausible that you will win – no conclusory or evidentiary claims – mere notice will not do</u>**
            - b. **<u>Grounds that you will win must meet plausibility standard</u>**
    - iii. Pleading is simply notice not fact revelation, for that there is discovery
    - iv. Discovery – where the facts are uncovered that supposedly back up the claim
    - v. Responses to Pleas (p345)
        1. **Dilatory pleas** – not on the merits
            - a. "not here" - challenges **jurisdiction** of the court -12(b)(1), (12(b)(2), 12(b)(3)
            - b. "not now" - **pleas in suspension** – capacity to sue – 9(c) – can't sue now until conditions precedent are fixed capacity, 17(b) capacity to joinder
            - c. "not like this" – **plea in abatement** – defect in the pleading, i.e.

failure to name an absent party – 12(b)(4), 12(b)(5), 12(b)(7)

    2. **peremptory pleas** – on the merits

        a. "so what" - **demurrer** – failure to state a claim on which relief could be granted, concedes truth of facts but challenges legal sufficiency – 12(c) judgment on the pleadings 12(b)(6) failure to state a claim

        b. "didn't happen or I didn't do it" - **traverse** – concedes legal sufficiency but **Special Pleading Rules**

II. Special Pleading Rules

  a. ***Stradford v. Zurich Insurance Co.***

    i. Doctor had his own office building, building floods, insurance company won't pay. Doctor sues for non-payment of property damage insurance policy

    ii. Insurance company counterclaims that Doctor attempted to defraud them, insurance company is not specific in their claim of what the fraud is – violates Rule 9(b) – primary purpose of Rule 9(b) is to afford a litigant accused of fraud fair notice of the claim and the factual ground upon which it is based

      1. **Rule 9(b) in alleging fraud or mistake, a party must state with particularity the circumstances constituting the fraud or mistake but malice, intent, knowledge and other conditions of the mind may be alleged generally**

      2. **Rule 9(f) date, time and place is material when testing sufficiency of a pleading**

    iii. Here the court granted leave to amend counterclaims by insurance company, D move for summary judgment- granted

  b. Affirmative Defenses

    i. D must prove affirmative defenses

    ii. Rule 8(c) lists some of the affirmative defenses – confession and avoidance

      1. If you have affirmative defense and you don't plead it you've lost it

    iii. P must prove prima facie case

    iv. If ___ and if ____ and if ____ then P wins; unless___ or ____ then D wins

      1. Burden of producing evidence

      2. Burden of persuasion – reasonable doubt or preponderance of evidence

      3. Burden of pleading

  c. ***Walker v. Norwest Corp.***

    i. RULE: a district court necessarily abuses its discretion if it bases its ruling on an erroneous view of the law – no abuse here Rule 11 sanctions were appropriate

  d. **RULE 11-** Requires all papers to be signed by the attorney (if party is represented). It also provides for sanctions against the attorney or client for harassment, frivolous arguments, or a lack of factual investigation. The purpose of sanctions is deterrent, not punitive

    i. **11(a)** – Signature - pleadings must be signed by attorney or by unrepresented party themselves and give address and phone number – unsigned papers are stricken unless corrected once omission is pointed out

      a. Applies to: Pleading, **written** motion (includes digital), or other paper

    ii. **11(b)** Representations to the Court

      1. By presenting a pleading, written motion or other paper – whether by signing, filing, submitting or later advocating it. An attorney certifies that to the best of their knowledge they did not violate Rule 11

    iii. <u>**Rule 11(b) Violations**</u>

1. Legal
   a. 11(b)(1) - presented for an **improper purpose**, such as to harass or to cause unnecessary delay or needless increase in cost of litigation
   b. 11(b)(2) - the claims, defenses, and other legal contentions are **not warranted by existing law or are frivolous** (represented party may not be sanctioned for a b2 violation)
2. Factual
   a. 11(b)(3) - the allegations and other factual contentions **lack evidentiary support** or are **unlikely to have evidentiary support after reasonable discovery**
   b. 11(b)(4) - **denials of factual contentions are not warranted on the evidence** or **denials are not reasonably based on a lack of information or belief**

iv. 11(c)(1)(A) - **by motion of a party**
   1. Safe Harbor provision – 11(c)(1)(A) – notice of the claimed Rule 11 violation shall be served upon alleged violating party pursuant to Rule 5 and alleged violating party has **21 days** to rescind it or correct it before the court will allow the Rule 11 motion
   2. Safe Harbor doesn't apply to Rule 11 motions against **complaints** – it would be useless since D must file answer within 20 days of filing of complaint – required by Rule 12(a)(1)(A)

v. 11(c)(1)(B) – by court, **sua sponte**
   1. court must enter an order describing the conduct in violation and direct the party to show cause why it has not violated Rule 11
   2. 11(c)(2) motion for sanction must be made separately from any other motion and must describe the specific conduct that violates 11(b). Motions must be served under Rule 5. Not presented to the court if the 11(b) violation is withdrawn or corrected within 21 days after service
   3. 11(c)(3) sua sponte- on the court's own initiative it may order an attorney, law firm, or party to show cause why conduct specifically described in the order has not violated Rule 11(b)

e. ***Christian v. Mattell, Inc.***
   i. **HOLDING:** vacate the district court's Rule 11 orders, b/c do don't know if they were b/c of the frivolous complain or lawyer's extrinsic misconduct
   ii. **RULE: Rule11(a) does not authorize sanctions for discovery abuses or misstatements made to the court during an oral presentation**
   iii. Oral motions included under 28 USC § 1927 – requires bad faith
      1. subject to §1927 – attorneys may be liable for excessive costs caused by their unreasonable and vexatious multiplication of proceedings
      2. attorney will have to pay cost of wasting cts. time, where unreasonable and vexatious
      3. this covers oral motions whereas Rule 11 does not

f. Sanctions
   i. If there is 11(b) violation court has discretion on whether to impose sanctions or not
   ii. May be imposed on attorneys, parties/clients, law firms
   iii. Law firms are jointly responsible for violations of their partners, associates or employees
   iv. Limitations:
      1. no monetary sanctions against a **represented** party for an 11(b)(2)

violation

        2. no monetary sections when Rule 11 raised **sua sponte** unless court issues order to show cause (show violation) before the violating party dismisses voluntarily or settles

        3. must be **what is sufficient to deter repetition of such conduct or comparable conduct**

   v. court shall (1) describe conduct in violation and (2) explain basis for sanctions

   vi. types of sanctions allowed

        1. nonmonetary directives

        2. order to pay a penalty into court (**fine**)

        3. order directing payment to the moving party of some or all attorney's fees and other expenses incurred as direct result of violation

  g. Motions excluded from Rule 11

   i. disclosures and discovery requests

   ii. Rule 26-37 motions, or responses or objections thereto

   iii. 8(b) denial - denies facts – "not true"

   iv. 8(c) affirmative defenses - "yes but" **plea of confession & avoidance** – conceded truth of facts & legal sufficiency but raised additional facts which will cause dismissal in your favor

III. **Responding to the Complaint**

  a. **Default** – a D who fails to respond to the complaint can have a default judgment entered against him

   i. Rule 54(c) - a default judgment must not differ from demand. If default judgment only relief can be equal to what was plead

  b. **Pre-Answer Motion**

   i. **Rule 12(a)** – gives D 20 days to answer the complaint or file a pre-answer motion, can be extended to 60 days if the D waives service of process.

        1. If you need additional time

            a. Request from P's counsel additional 30 days by making an appearance to file motion pursuant to Rule 12

            b. If counsel won't give additional time request it from the judge

   ii. Rule 12(b) – defenses infra

        1. Rule12(b)(1)-(5) are waivable defenses

        2. **Waiver of 12b defenses**

            a. 12(h) – 12(b)(2), (3), (4), and (5) are waived if not brought as a motion (i.e. pre-answer motion) under this rule nor included in a responsive pleading (answer) or an amendment permitted by Rule 15(a)

                i. those are: lack of personal jurisdiction, improper venue, insufficiency of process, and insufficiency of service of process – **if they aren't plead at all, they are waived**

                ii. 12b defenses cannot be raised on appeal (except lack of subject matter jurisdiction

                iii. can be raised in **pre-answer motion, answer**, or **amendment if allowed under Rule 15**

   iii. **Rule 12(c) – Motion for Judgment on the Pleadings**

        1. After pleadings closed, but early enough not to delay trial, a party may move for judgment on the pleadings

   iv. **Rule 12(e) - Motion for a More Definite Statement**

1. Lets D require P to give "a more definite statement of a pleading which is so vague or ambiguous that they cannot reasonably respond"
2. Rarely successful – courts refer to discovery
3. Will probably be more common under Iqbal's plausibility standard

    v. **Rule 12(f) - Motion to Strike**
1. Allows party to challenge a pleading that fails under the substantive law even though the rest of the pleading states a claim or defense
    a. Used to remove irrelevant and prejudicial allegations in a pleading

c. **Answer**
    i. Rule 8(b) Denials
1. party shall admit or deny the averments of the claim
2. a denial can be based on
    a. information and belief, OR
    b. if party is without knowledge, party may so state and this **will serve as a denial**
3. **"denials shall fairly meet the substance of the averments denied"**
    ii. **General denial** – denies each and every allegation of the complaint –party may do so but it may be subject to Rule 11 sanctions if not reasonable to file just a general denial
1. cannot be done in 99% of the cases
2. must deny everything from personal jurisdiction to subject matter jurisdiction.
    iii. **Specific Denial – may deny designated portions of P's complaint**
1. **Only way to assert a denial in federal court**
2. **Must make clear what is admitted and what is denied so as to adequately inform P**
    iv. **Rule 8(d) Failure to Deny**
1. if a responsive pleading is required to an averment in a pleading, the averment is admitted when not denied (except averments as to amounts of damage)

d. **Equitable Estoppel** – D may be prevented from later denying an averment which it should have denied if this would be prejudicial to the P
    i. *Zielinski v. Philadelphia Piers Co.*
1. FACTS: D failed to make adequate denial which would have alerted P that they had sued the wrong party. D's failure to deny prejudiced P since the statute of limitations had run, barring them from suing the true D
2. HOLDING: court made the wrong D stay as the D (didn't matter too much though since their insurer was the same insurance company for the true D (Carload Inc.))
    ii. **Rule 15(c)(3)** passed since this case fixes it, **allows amendment to *relate back* if the wrong party was named**
1. **there was no proof of bad faith on the part of either party**
2. P was maybe partly to blame since they didn't specifically allege agency of the D (which might have made D more aware that they needed to specifically deny agency)
    iii. unless P reasonably caused D's mistake in failing to deny, their failure to deny is an admission

e. Affirmative Defenses
    i. **D must plead affirmative defense or risk waiving them**
    ii. **What is an Affirmative Defense?**

1. **Rule 8(c)** gives an explicit list defining the affirmative defenses, but
2. **Rule 8(c)** also requires **"any other matter constituting an avoidance or an affirmative defense"** be pleaded as an affirmative defense

iii. *Layman v. SW Bell* - D did not produce the evidence proving easement until the trial and they failed to plead the affirmative defense of easement
1. documentation of an easement claiming a privilege to trespass is an affirmative defense which must be pleaded even though easement is not explicitly listed as affirmative defense, it is "any other matter constituting an **avoidance"**
2. HOLDING: D. may not now claim the affirmative defense – it was waived (modern litigation probably would have granted leave to amend)

iv. **the rule is <u>avoidance</u>, the rule is not "surprise"**

v. <u>**burden of production is on the D therefore the burden of pleading is on the D**</u>

f. Reply
i. **Very rare, listed in Rule 7(a) but must have permission of the court**
ii. **Courts would rather use discovery than pleadings**

g. **Amendments**

i. Rule 15(a) – party may amend its pleading once:
1. Before being served w/ a responsive pleading
2. w/in 20 days after serving the pleading – window of opportunity to unilaterally change your answer do not ask courts permission just do it!

ii. Rule 15(b) – in all other motions party may amend with other party's consent and by filing a motion with the court asking for the court's leave

iii. Rule 15(c) – relation back

iv. *Beeck v. Aquaslide*- D slide maker was misled by 3 insurance companies who had inspected slide – when D finally inspected slide itself (some considerable time later), D determined it was not their slide. D was granted leave to amend and severance to have a separate trial to determine who made slide
1. Beecks could have sued Kimberly Village - allow Rule 14(a) to bring additional claims against other parties. P should either sue the end of the chain (Kimberly village – they would have impled the other D's) or sue the entire chain. stupid just to sue aquaslide
2. HOLDING: app. ct. upheld because it could not find **an abuse of discretion** since there was not sufficient proof that prejudice would result nor that D had acted in bad faith. **also said trial ct. did not abuse discretion in applying <u>Rule 42 to sever</u> to have a separate trial to determine who made the slide**
3. there was no prejudice against P because to find prejudice **you would have to assume that D would prevail on the merits** there was no bad faith on part of Aquaslide but they were stupid not to check the slide for themselves P was also culpable since they didn't check the slide either

v. Appellate Review of decisions granting or denying leave to amend only for **abuse of discretion**

vi. **Rule 15(b)** – amendments to conform to evidence - court may allow amendment right away if evidence is brought at trial that is outside of the issue of the pleadings and the adverse party *has burden of showing that allowing such amendment would be* prejudicial

vii. **Relation Back – Rule 15(c)**
1. Amendment is allowed to **relate back** to the original filing "**whenever the**

23

claim or defense asserted in the amended pleading arose out of the conduct, transaction, or occurrence set forth or attempted to be set forth in the original pleading" (Rule 15c2)

  a. OR if allowed by the law creating the statute of limitations (15c1)

  b. OR if the amendment changes the party of the naming of the party (15c3)

2. *Moore v. Baker* – relation back not permitted in a medical malpractice claim when Pl. had pleaded informed consent claim (arising *before* the treatment) and sought to later amend to add a negligence in surgical procedure claim (arising *during* the treatment)

  a. **the complaint did not give Def. notice of the new claim now being asserted (in the attempted amendment)**

  b. the new claim did not arise out of the **same conduct, transaction, or occurrence** as the claims in the original complaint

  c. so, the new claims are barred by the statute of limitations

3. *Bonerb v. Caron Foundation* - P slipped and fell on poorly maintained basketball courts while participating in mandatory exercise program at D's Rehab. center

  a. HOLDING: relation back was allowed because the new alleged theory of counseling malpractice **relied on the same set of *operational facts*** as the original claim of negligently maintained basketball courts

4. **To reconcile *Moore* and *Bonerb***

  a. **notice of litigation** – statutes of limitations are designed to preserve this

  b. In Moore, D had no notice of new complaint whatsoever – different facts needed for each claim

  c. In Bonerb, even though P was relying on a new legal theory, it was based on the same set of facts that had already been alleged in the original complaint

5. **Reasons for having statutes of limitations**

  a. memories dim with time

  b. documentary storage and other demonstrative evidence gets lost

  c. allows business planning and life planning

  d. society needs peace

JOINDER

I. Joinder Overview

  a. 18(a) , 13(b) Liberal joinder rules

   i. Serve two purposes

    1. Legal efficiency – get large disputes settled all at once

    2. Jury verdicts could come out differently on two trials on same set of facts – inconsistent results on identical facts and that strikes us as wrong even if we can explain it away

  b. 20(a), 23, 24(b) Must have at least one issue in commonality

  c. 13(g), 13(a), Must be of the same transaction or occurrence

  d. 14(a)(1) Impleader - only when contribution or indemnity

  e. Historically there was plaintiff's autonomy, could choose if to sue when to sue and whom to sue, couldn't always choose where to sue (personal jurisdiction)

II. Joinder of Claims

a. **RULE 18 – most liberal joinder rule, P can join as many claims as he wishes whether related or unrelated as long as there is jurisdiction**
   i. **Applies to claims, counter-claims, cross-claims and/or 3rd party claims**
   ii. **P sues D in claim 1 and claim 2 both can be joined by Rule 18**
   iii. **Permits joinder but does not compel it**
b. **RULE 13(a)- Compulsory Counter Claims – does it arise out of the same transaction or occurrence and does not require the joinder of another party.**
   i. **Exceptions – don't need to claim if**
      1. **Pending in another action when action commenced**
      2. **If primary claim does not establish personal jurisdiction (i.e. attachment) it is in rem**
   ii. **Mandatory Claim - Omitting a counterclaim that is later held to be compulsory carries a penalty of losing the ability to bring it later.**
   iii. **Certain rules apply:**
      1. **if claim is brought supplemental jurisdiction attaches under 1367**
      2. **Must be brought of the D waives the ability to counterclaim**
      3. **If a judge rules that it is permissive you have not lost the counterclaim**
c. **RULE 13(b) – permissive counter-claims – if it is a claim against any party NOT arising out of the same transaction or occurrence that is the subject matter of the opposing parties claim it is permissive**
d. **Rule 13(g) – cross-claim against a coparty – must arise out of the same transaction or occurance, or there is subject matter jurisdiction over the claim or property in the claim**
e. **RULE 42(b) - separate trials** - only uses separate trials to determine particular issues and claims – the suit comes back together at the end – separate claims for separation of trials
   i. for convenience; to avoid prejudice; for expedition and economy
   ii. may be used on: claim, cross-claim, counterclaim, 3rd party claim, or of any separate issue or multiples of these
f. Rule 42a - consolidation - does not make it one law suit (still have 2 separate docket #'s) – but it assures equality in the outcomes of similar lawsuits

III. Joinder of Parties
   a. <u>**RULE 20 – Permissive Joinder of Parties**</u>
      i. **Requirements** (mild) – may join parties if:
         1. Arising out of the same transaction or occurrence or series of and
         2. At least one question of law or fact common to all these parties
      ii. Appeal – denial of joinder is only reviewable for **abuse of discretion**
      iii. *Mosley v. GM*
         1. FACTS: a group of P employees alleged they were discriminated against on basis of color and race. D corp. tried to claim the joint actions were unmanageable and that they only shared one common problem
         2. HOLDING: joinder should have been allowed since the parties need share **only ONE question of fact or law common to all the parties** – the fact that they were all injured by the same general policy of discrimination
            a. Blacks and women were granted release time on the same terms as white males
         3. Most likely a wrong decision, there was no common question of law
      iv. In joinder you have to worry about personal and subject matter jurisdiction
      v. **Res Judicata** – thing adjudicated – claim preclusion applies if:
         1. In second action same parties

25

2. Second action same claim
3. First action on the merits
   a. If those three are met then the second claim cannot be made
   b. Even though the rules of joinder have only one rule that says compulsory joinder of claims (13a) you can still lose your claim because of the doctrine of Res Judicata

b. **Misjoinder and Severance RULE 21** – once misjoinder is discovered the judge can clean it up and the lawsuit just keeps going
   i. Parties need to be added or dismissed they are done so by the judge
   ii. Severance - Court may also sever claims against a party – separate trials

c. <u>**RULE 14 Impleader**</u>
   i. **14(a) for a D to implead a 3rd party it must be**
      1. **A situation of INDEMNITY (contracts)**
         a. **Means I deny all liability but if I am found liable, 3rd party is liable to me for every dollar I have to pay – dollar for dollar reimbursement**
      2. **A situation of CONTRIBUTION (between tortfeasors)**
         a. **If there are joint tortfeasors they are both equally liable and fault is allocated between defendant and impled 3rd party**
   ii. **Prevents the D from claiming "it was him, not me"**
   iii. once there is one valid 3rd party claim made under 14(a), any other 3rd party claims can be added on by RULE 18(a) –third party claim , whether they are related or not
   iv. *Price v. CTB, Inc.*
      1. Facts: CTB puts equipment in poultry houses, becomes irrelevant to claim. Co defendant Latco is being sued for the quality of their workmanship – Latco impleads ITW (a nail maker) for implied indemnity
      2. ISSUE: is that indemnity action permitted under Rule 14(a) when Alabama has never adopted contribution
         a. Can't apply contribution because they are a federal court sitting in diversity applying Alabama law per ERIE
         b. Fed judge applies indemnity to the claim
      3. HOLDING: the court decided that ITW properly impleaded in this action.
      4. RULE: under 14(a) a D may assert a claim against anyone not a party to the original action if that 3rd party's liability is in someway dependent upon the outcome of the original action
   v. Exercising Supplemental Jurisdiction 3 part test:
      1. If it is a claim by a plaintiff
      2. There is a disfavored rule
      3. when exercising supplemental jurisdiction would be inconsistent with the Gibbs test "common nucleus of facts"
         a. 1367(b) – when a 3rd party D is implead it is permissive
   vi. Kroger v. Omaha Public Power District – Kroger is widowed b/c husband is electrocuted, brings a federal claim under diversity § 1332 suing OPPD (IA resident v. NE company) who no longer owns the decedents employer – cannot sue Paxton b/c of the workers compensation law (cannot sue your employer under workers' comp.)
      1. Summary Judgment for OPPD – they owed no duty to Kroger
      2. Kroger then brings a direct claim under 14(a)(3) against Owen Equipment
   vii. *Owen Equipment v. Kroger* - P sued OPPD power company for her

husband's death, but OPPD impleaded Owen, the crane owner. Pleadings and responsive pleading all said Owen was NE citizen, but it turned out they were IA citizen, so they were not diverse from P – P had used 14(a), sentence 7 to file additional claim against Owen, then OPPD settled out.

1. SCOTUS Rules
   a. To avoid P from suing a company in diversity in the hopes that they implead a 3rd party that they wanted to sue but couldn't b/c they are a non-diverse party
   b. The claim is dependant on diversity, removing the diverse party become a new and independent claim
   c. "If you don't like our rules don't bring the case to our court" P choose to bring suit upon state-law claim in fed court where federal rules apply
2. HOLDING: Suit dismissed against Owen for lack of complete diversity. **In a diversity suit, there is no supplemental jurisdiction over 14(a)-sentence 7 claims by original P against the 3rd party D if those claims do not have <u>independent basis</u> for diversity jurisdiction under 1332**
3. **Once a court has supplemental jurisdiction if they do they retain it even though diversity may be lost at some point along the line (i.e. summary judgment of OPPD)**
   a. this decision was codified into §1367, Supplemental Jurisdiction
4. Congress could pass a statute modifying 1332 and do away with complete diversity because Strawbridge is simply an interpretation of Art. III however Article III requires SOME diversity, even if minimal
5. Dissent: Justice White – requires complete diversity only between the P and the partys he actually brings into the suit not those that are impled under Rule 14 also 28 USC 1359 – prohibits collusion to dummy up fed subject matter jurisdiction where it doesn't exist

d. **<u>RULE 19 – COMPULSORY JOINDER</u>**
   i. **raised by: (rule doesn't specify)**
      1. **the court (in only a few circumstances)**
      2. **one of the parties, typically the D. will raise the objection**
   ii. **Necessary party** – the party must be joined if possible
      1. the party **shall be joined** if they are deemed to be **necessary**
      2. must meet either:
         a. 19(a)(1) – in the person's absence, complete relief cannot be accorded among those already parties, or
         b. 19(a)(2) – the person claims an interest relating to the subject of the action and is so situated that the disposition of the action in the person's absence may
            i. (i) as a practical matter **impair or impede the person's ability to protect that interest**, or
            ii. (ii) leave any of the persons already parties subject to a **substantial risk of incurring double, multiple, or otherwise inconsistent obligations**
      3. if the necessary party objects to venue, and joinder of the party would render the venue improper, that party shall be dismissed from the action
   iii. **Indispensible party** – the suit should be dismissed if the party cannot be joined and is indispensable
      1. the necessary party cannot be joined for some defect (no jurisdiction, etc.)

or the party will not join voluntarily

2. the action should be dismissed if the non-joinable necessary party is deemed indispensable

3. factors to consider:

    a. to what extent a judgment rendered in the person's absence might be **prejudicial** to the *person* or *those already parties*

    b. the extent to which, by protective provisions in the judgment, by the shaping of relief, or other measures, the **prejudice can be lessened or avoided**

    c. whether a **judgment rendered** in the person's absence **will be adequate**

    d. **whether the plaintiff will have an adequate remedy** if the action is dismissed for nonjoinder

iv.   *Temple v. Synthes Corp.* - D files a Rule 12(b)(7) motion to dismiss for failure to join a party found to be necessary and indispensible when Temple failed to join the Dr. and Hospital

1. Synthes must make the argument that the hospital and doctor are indispensible and necessary parties unless joining those parties would destroy jurisdiction

2. HOLDING: as potential joint tortfeasors with Synthes, Dr. Larocca and the hospital were merely permissive parties – not required under Rule 19

3. Synthes could have impled both of those parties but they were not required parties

v.   **Pleading reasons for nonjoinder**

1. If pleader is aware of a necessary party (who meets 19(a)(1) or (a)(2)) who they are not joining, they must plead why they have not joined them

2. If you know your D is going to raise a **12(b)(7)** failure to join an indispensable party, then you need to explain why you are not joining the party and how you think they are not indispensable

vi.   19(a) most likely occurs when:

1. There is a promissory note or a loan w/ a co-signer

2. Joint-owners of property and only one is suing

3. Trust or Will with multiple beneficiaries/legetiees

4. Insurance proceeds or litigation over the corpus of a trust and you need interpleader

5. Often the solution for rule 19 is interpleader

vii.   **Rule 19(b) When Joinder is not feasible**

1. **19(b)(1) – judge must dismiss if there is prejudice towards a P or the existing parties**

2. **19(b)(2) court considers prejudice could be lessened or avoided by**

    a. **Protective provision in the judgment**

    b. **Shaping the relief**

    c. **Or other measures**

3. **19(b)(3) – whether judgments in the persons absence would be adequate**

4. **19(b)(4) P would have an adequate remedy if the action were dismissed for non joinder**

viii.   *Helzberg Diamond Shops. v. Valley West Des Moines Shopping Center* – Lords must be joined but Missouri has no jurisdiction over them. Rule 19(a)(1)(B)(i) – Lords must be joined b/c it would impair or impede Helzbergs ability to protect their interest

  1. 19(b) required the court to look to the extend in which preduc

  2. HOLDING: Lords is not an indispensable party, and satisfies all of rule 19(b)

e. **<u>RULE 24 INTERVENTION</u>**

 i. In for a penny in for a pound – it is sometimes better to file an amicus curia brief instead of putting your two cents in and getting stuck with the troubles of a trial

 ii. Appearing Amicus Curia you are not subject to discovery or cross-examination but you still get to brief the case and make your points to the court

 iii. Intervention of Right 24(a) court must allow intervention when

  1. 24(a)(1) if given the right by federal statute

  2. 24(a)(2) three qualifications for intervention

   a. Claims an interest to the property or interest of the transaction

   b. Disposing of the action impedes movants ability to protect its interests

   c. Unless the parties adequately protect their interests

 iv. ***NRDC v. US Nuclear Regulatory Commission*** – Kerr-McGee tried to intervene in the matter and is turned away by the district court, on appeal they are allowed to intervene

  1. because they are distinguished in that:

   a. They are the largest producer of uranium in NM

   b. They have a license application renewal pending

  2. <u>Does Res Judicata apply?</u> No because there are not identical parties involved

  3. <u>Stare Decisis?</u> When a case of first impression then the next case is duty bound to follow the first decision, a case of first impression the court thororoughly looked through the relevant facts so when decision is made it probably is a decision that ought to be followed unless there is a very very good reason not to follow it

  4. So How is Kerr-McGee different from US Nuclear?

  5. if you seek intervention under 24(a) and it is denied it is immediately appealable and the lawsuit is frozen in place in the district court but if under 24(b) it is not immediately appealable

 v. if you think 24(a) is allowed you can move for a 24(b) so you can become a party and then it become non-appealable

 vi. Permissive Intervention 24(b) court **may** permit party to intervene when:

  1. when statute of the US confers a conditional right to intervene,   OR

  2. when an applicant's claim or defense and the main action have a question of law or fact in common.

  3. **Other considerations**

   a. In exercising its **discretion**, court shall consider whether the intervention will *unduly delay* or *prejudice* the adjudication of the rights of the <u>original parties</u>

 vii. Procedure for Intervention – 24(c)

  1. Application – motion to intervene must be served on the parties as provided in Rule 5; shall state the grounds for intervention; and must be accompanied by a pleading setting forth the claim or defense

  2. Participation – party comes in as a full party unless it is a conditional permissive intervention and the court imposes restrictions

  3. see 2403 if constitutionality of a state statute or act of congress is in

question

viii. **§ 2403 – Intervention by US or a State - constitutional question**

1. **(a)** U.S. attorney general <u>**shall**</u> be permitted to intervene on behalf of the US if the **constitutionality** of an act of congress affecting the public interest is drawn into question

2. **(b)** State attorney general <u>**shall**</u> be permitted to intervene if the **constitutionality** of a state statute affecting the public interest is drawn into question

3. if 2403 doesnt apply (i.e. another state's atty. general wants to intervene since his state has similar statute), the requirements of 24 must be met (LA atty. general must try 24a or 24b – he will fail on 24a in the hypo from class, but he may be allowed to permissively intervene under 24b)

ix. **Appeal**

1. intervention of right is **immediately appealable**

2. persmissive intervention is **only appealable after trial**

x. **Effect of FAILURE TO INTERVENE**

1. **A party's decision to intervene is never mandatory – they will not be bound by the judgment even if they have notice and fail to intervene**

2. *Martin v. Wilks*

a. FACTS: The Black Firefighters won a suit against the city, which resulted in a consent decree imposing goals for hiring/promotion of black FF's. The White FF's bring suit later, claiming that they are subjects of reverse discrimination

b. HOLDING: The White FF's were not bound by the consent decree and could have their own day in court. "**a voluntary settlement in the form of a consent decree between one group of employees and their employer cannot possibly "settle" voluntarily or otherwise, the conflicting claims of another group of employees who do not join the agreement**"

3. <u>Exception</u> – a party may be bound when in *certain limited circumstances,* the party has its interests adequately represented (no conflicting interests) by someone with the same interests who is a party

4. Rule 19 should be used to join a necessary party if you want them to be bound by the judgment (Res Judicata'ed)

f. **Interpleader**

i. allows a person to avoid the risk of **multiple liability** by requiring two or more persons with actual or prospective claims against him to assert their respective **adverse** claims in a single action

ii. May be commenced as an original action or as a counterclaim

iii. Stakeholder

1. may take part - need not be "disinterested" – may himself claim the right to the entire stake

2. may choose not to take part - may deposit the stake into the court's registry or post bond and court will then discharge the stakeholder from the interpleader action (statutory interpleader requires deposit or posting of bond, but Rule 22 interpleader does not require deposit of the property nor posting of bond)

g. **Statutory Interpleader – 1335, 1397, 2361**

i. **1335 - only minimal diversity required** (removes limitations on SM J)

1. at least two diverse claimants (it's okay if the Pl. and one of the claimants

are nondiverse)

     2. money or property in possession of the stakeholder must be $500 or more

  ii.   **1397** – **venue** lies in the judicial district in which any of the claimants reside (expands venue provisions) – ***cannot be just where the property is deposited*** (but can be under Rule 22 – see below) – under stat. interpleader, venue is improper if it is not where one of the claimants resides

  iii.   **2361- permits nationwide service of process**

     1. statutory authority for injunctions in aid of interpleader

  iv.   **NOTICE and POWER**

     1. Notice comes from the nationwide service of process

     2. Power comes from the money/property (stake) deposited with the court which provides the minimum contacts out of which the claimants' claims arise

  v.   **statutory interpleader requires deposit of the property with the court or posting of bond (while Rule 22 does not)**

h. **Rule Interpleader – RULE 22**

  i. **complete diversity required** and **$75+K** (if diversity J) <u>OR</u> **Federal question** (i.e. the statutory eminent domain action in NM from class HYPO)

  ii.   **venue** – same as federal venue but also **CAN ALSO BE WHERE ONLY THE PROPERTY IS** – this differs from statutory interpleader (i.e. in Chicago, since that is where the funds are deposited) – stat. interpleader does not allow venue for only the place of property (one claimant must reside where the suit is brought for stat. interpleader)

  iii.   **notice** – service under Rule 4

  iv.   injunction – only basis is in § 2283- "where necessary in aid of jurisdiction"

  v.   **deposit with the court is *optional* under Rule 22 (but it is mandatory under statutory interpleader**

  vi.   **If stakeholder's possession has ceased (if he gave the property to one of the claimants), then it's probably too late for him to use interpleader**

  vii.   **Interpleader *inappropriate* if the stakeholder's liability to one claimant is not inconsistent with the others**(i.e. Interpleader inappropriate if wife#1's claim is that the Ins. Co. was negligent in changing the policy when it should not have; then this is different than wife#2's claim of "I get the money since the policy says I do" – this is subtle difference. company may have to pay twice in this situation)

     1. **Rule 22 says the claims of the claimants need not be identical, but should be adverse and independent of each other**

  viii.   **Dividing up the limited pie: another use of Interpleader**

  ix.   *State Farm v. Tashire* – **dividing up the pie** - truck driver collides with a bus in Calif., but truck driver's liability insurance is capped at 20,000, so the max state farm has to dole out is $20K. Passengers sue driver in various states and one sues in Canada. State Farm files interpleader in Oregon and tries to enjoin the other actions from proceeding

     1. HOLDING: Oregon could not stop the other actions (esp. the one in Canada) since this was outside the scope of injunctions allowed by 2361. Other ct.'s could proceed as they wanted but could not execute on their judgments – would have to come to Oregon to divvy up the $20K. – this prevents the first winner from running up to Oregon and grabbing all of the 20K

x. ***Cohen v. Rep. of Phillipines*** - P's use statutory interpleader (since there was only minimal diversity) to join Braemer (individual claiming a security interest) and the Phillipines (govt. claiming ownership) for proceedings to determine who owns the $5million paintings. Marcos intervenes as of right and other claimants appeal – the **statutory interpleader could not initially join Marcos because she was oversees and it only allows for *nationwide* service of process not service abroad**

    1. HOLDING: Marcos met 24(a)(2), so she was allowed to intervene as of right – her request was timely (even though she had waited 5 months to see outcome of possible settlement negotiations) and she has an adverse interest in the paintings and the existing parties are unlikely to adequately protect her interest.

    2. Timeliness determined by:

        a. how long applicant knew of his interest before making the motion

        b. prejudice to the existing parties from any such delay

        c. prejudice to applicant if the motion is denied

        d. other unusual circumstances

i. **CLASS ACTIONS – RULE 23**

    i. general aspects

        1. often huge amounts of money at stake

        2. can have huge social and economic impact

        3. can bring in huge numbers of parties

        4. common with credit card/securities fraud

    ii. <u>**Certification – 23(a)**</u> – these requirements must be met in order for a class to be certified for purposes of a class action lawsuit

        1. **(1) Numerosity** – must be so large the joinder of all the members of the party individually would be impracticable

        2. **(2) Commonality** – there must be questions of law or fact common to the class

            a. doesn't matter if some members are damaged more than others

            b. *commonality <u>is defeated if liability must be proven separately</u>* (Sprague v. GM), but it is **not defeated for differences in damages**

        3. **(3) Typicality** – the claims or defenses of the representative parties must be typical of the claims or defenses of the class

            a. doesn't matter that the members were affected differently by the same policy (i.e. the female athletes were all affected by the same general discriminatory policy, even though they were in different sports and suffered different effects of the discrimination – *Comm. for Equity v. Mich. H.S.A.A.*)

            b. based on the pleadings – i.e. the policy must *allegedly* discriminate against the female athletes (if the judge clearly wants to get rid of the class action if it is borderline frivolous then he will find a way that it doesn't meet one of the certification requirements)

        4. **(4) Adequacy of Representation** – the representative parties will fairly and adequately protect the interests of the class

            a. represented parties <u>can't have adverse interests</u> from the rest of class; but may be *different* interests

            b. this is about due process, since you neither have notice nor your day in court

    c. your champion must be vigorously representing your interests

    d. rep. parties' **law firm must be pretty good** - law firms of represented parties must have sufficient resources to carry the suit

    e. **if different remedies could bias certain parts of the class, _subclasses_ may be created (each with their own champion) to determine appropriate remedy**

iii.   <u>Type of class action – 23(b)</u> – must fall under 1 of these 3 categories – **b1, b2 ,or b3**

    1. **<u>23(b)(1)</u>** – two concerns:

        a. (A) Rock and a hard place - if separate actions may catch a D with **double liability – inconsistent judgments**

        b. (B) separate actions could harm individual members of the class - there is a **limited pie to be divided up** and would need everyone present but don't have everyone present (i.e. litigation over water rights out west)

    2. **<u>23(b)(2)</u>** – **injunctive or declaratory relief**

    3. **<u>23(b)(3)</u>** – questions of law or fact common to the whole class **<u>predominate</u>** over any questions affecting individual members; and a class action is **<u>superior</u>** to other available methods for fair and efficient adjudication of the controversy - **(money damages) – this is where the big money is – <u>4 factors determine whether the class predominates and has superiority:</u>**

        a. (A) – **the interest of members** of the class **in individually controlling** the prosecution or defense of **separate actions**

        b. (B) – the extent and nature of any **litigation** concerning the controversy **already commenced** by or against members of the class

        c. (C) – the desirability or undesirability of **concentrating the litigations of the claims in the particular forum**

        d. (D) – **difficulties** likely to be encountered **in the management** of a class action

            i. must be manageable ***compared to the alternatives***, *not compared to doing nothing at all*

            ii.   alternatives might be Rule 20, Rule 24, multiple lawsuits and then consolidating on an issue or two which is common and then again letting them proceed on their own merits

    4. b3's are the most common ($$$) but the hardest to pursue due to the requirements and the 23(c)(2) requirement of <u>notice</u>

iv.   23(c)(1) certifying the class

    1. Timely certification – after filing the court must in a timely manner decide if this is class action

    2. must define the class very specifically , the issues and the members of the class and also appoint counsel - 23(g) court will appoint the lawyer in the class action suit

    3. denial of class certification may be amended or altered before final judgment

    4. Best practicable under the circumstances – higher than due process and Mullane

v.   Must be aware of res judicata- parties of a class are bound and cannot bring a later action simply because they did not get the judgment they wanted in the class action suit – the members of the **NOTICE** – 23(c)(2) – notice only **statutorily** required for b3 – **Due Process may warrant notice of b1 and b2 classes**

1. "the **best notice practicable under the circumstances**, including <u>individual notice</u> to all members <u>who can be identified</u> through reasonable effort " – maybe certified mail, 1st class mail, by publication
   a. *Esien v. Carlisle & Jacqueline* - if certify b3 and notice required the P must pay for the notice to the members of the class – P' s law firm will most likely pay for this
2. **the party seeking notice must pay for it** – this can be big barrier to b3 class actions – firm may have to front the bill or if they can't afford, drop the action
3. **simply because 23 is silent as to notice for b1 and b2, doesn't mean notice is never required for b1 or b2**
4. <u>**Sliding Scale of whether NOTICE is required for b1 or b2**</u>
   a. range: lofty, policy suit ------- how much money am I gonna get
   b. if it is a lofty, policy based suit, notice may not be required
   c. if it is over property rights of 300 claimants, you had better give notice

vi. *Phillips Petroleum v. Shutts* – the 27,000 non-Kansas residents who received notice and did nothing had **impliedly consented to jurisdiction**

1. **Footnote 4- this case only applies to cases for predominantly money judgments and says nothing about equitable relief also says nothing about J asserted over a *D class***
2. <u>**DUE PROCESS REQUIREMENTS for class action to be binding on absentee plaintiffs:**</u>
   a. no minimum contacts needed
   b. absent P's must still be given notice which meets Mullane test
   c. must be given opportunity to be heard and participate in litigation
   d. absent P's must be provided with "opt-out" opportunity
   e. absent P's must be adequately represented at all times by the named P's
3. in Phillips, due process requirements were satisfied as to the absent plaintiffs
4. but Kansas law should not have been applied to all claims blanketly

vii. <u>**Reach of Judgment Rule 23(c)(3) who is bound by the judgment**</u>

1. **(b)(1) or (b)(2) action** – judgment, whether favorable or not to the class shall affect:
   a. Anyone found to be a member of the class by the court
2. **(b)(3) action** – judgment, whether favorable or not to the class shall affect:
   a. Those to whom the 23(c)(2) notice was directed,
   b. And those who have not requested exclusion ("opted out"),
   c. And found to be a member of the class by the court

viii. <u>**If a party to a class action suit brings a separate claim later they are subject to Res Judicata**</u>

j. <u>SUBJECT MATTER CONSIDERATIONS</u>

i. Supreme Tribe of Ben-Hur v. Cauble – you don't need complete diversity of all members of the class action suit only complete diversity from the D

ii. Snyder – the party's entire claim must exceed 75+k

iii.   Zahn v. Int'l Paper - there is no aggregation under 1332 when the claims are dissimilar so court doesn't allow it under Rule 23 either – only P with the 80k claim stays all the P's of the Class Action were thrown out for having claims under 75K

iv.   Exxon Mobile v. Allapattah – gets around Zahn – Rule 23 is not disfavored rule under 1367 – supplemental jurisdiction will allow all the smaller claims that could not be aggregated b/c they arose out of common nucleus of operative fact and Rule 23 is not disfavored – so long as there is an original claim over 75k

v.   **CLASS ACTION FAIRNESS ACT (CAFA)**

  1. **ONLY APPLIES TO DIVERSITY NOT FEDERAL QUESTIONS**

  2. **§1332(d) (2)**

      a. **If claim is not 75+k will allow aggregation of smaller claims so long as they exceed $5 million dollars**

      b. **minimal diversity required – you can have a citizens of the same state as the D on the claim so long as ONE P is diverse from the D**

  3. **§1332(d)(3) – federal judge has discretion to dismiss the claim if 1/3 - 2/3 of the P's are from the forum state and the Primary D is from the forum state. Court considers:**

      a. National and international interest

  4. **§1332(d)(4) – FEDERAL COURT MUST THROW OUT IF – more than 2/3 of P from the forum state and the primary D is from the forum state**

      a. State interest here – the class action is tied to the interest of the state because there is so little diversity

  5. **§1453 – special removal statute just for CAFA claims** (works like 1441)

  6. **§1711 – 1715 (apply to all class actions not just those under CAFA)**

      a. **Notification must be given to federal and state agencies -** state attorney general is the default if no state agency

      b. This is mandatory

      c. Problem – what is the state agency? It is not always clear who is to be notified

  7. A single D can remove and not all D's have to join in the removal

vi.   23(e) – procedures for settlement, voluntary dismissal or compromise

  1. must give notice to all members of the class – must be able to prove the notice

  2. if binding court will review for fairness

  3. settling for Res Judicata

      a. must be able to prove there was notice if settling

vii.   Amchem Products, Inc. v. Windsor

  1. Members of the party are "present P's" and have been exposed to asbestos but there are a group of "future Ps" who have yet to discover they have been affected by the asbestos

  2. Proposal of settlement is worked out before the lawsuit even arises

  3. They are looking for the judge to settle so they can claim Res Judicata

  4. Conflict of interest exists – cannot represent current P's and settle and then later represent future P's b/c of Res Judicata - so there is a requirement that a separate law firm experienced in class actions will represent the future P's –

  5. Problem - predominance requirement in Rule 23(b)(3) cannot be found

because there are all kinds of diseases that arise out of asbestos exposure and some are more serious than others

6. Another problem exists – the present class cannot be approved by Rule 23(a)(4) 's requirement that that named parties will fairly and adequately protect the interests of the class BECAUSE THE FUTURE CLASS CANNOT BE PREDOMINATELY DEFINED

    viii. **Appeal – 23(f)**
1. Within ten days of an order of class certification, a court of appeals may **in its discretion** allow an appeal of the order granting or denying certification
2. An appeal does not stay the proceedings unless directed by district or appellate court

    ix. Class Action attorney's fees
1. "Common fund" doctrine – when money damages awarded, courts will award the attorney a fee taken from the common fund
2. Other cts – start with appropriate hourly rate and adjust according to factors such as special risks and novelty issues

Pleadings Review

I. Rule 11 implications
  a. may want to make statements contingent
    i. "on or about"
    ii. "reasonably believed"

II. Plaintiff must plead
  a. all elements of prima facie claim
  b. special damages

III. D must plead affirmative defenses

IV. Use lots of paragraphing – break it up to get lots of admissions - the more you parse your claim the more admissions you will get

V. Prima Facie Claim or Affirmative Defense?
  a. Prima facie case: "If __ and __ and __ then Plaintiff wins"
  b. Aff. Def.'s: "Unless __ or __ then D wins"

VI. 3 ways to allocate whether something is prima facie claim or Aff. Def.:
  a. 1)fairness – which party is most likely to have the evidence in hand, give them the burden of pleading it
  b. 2)probability – give burden to the one alleging the stated facts which are most improbable (if you are asserting something put in mail was never received, then you must plead it)
  c. 3)policy reasons – if you are arguing against something presumed by public policy you must plead it (you must plead that the child born in that marriage was illegitimate)

VII. Negative pregnates
  a. "D beat P with stick on Green Street
    i. Don't just say: "D denies that D beat P with stick on Green Street" – this means D still beat P just not on Green Street
  b. C.Para. 14: "D drove a 1998 Ford automobile with defective brakes"
    i. Don't just say "D denies paragraph 14"
  c. courts used to treat D's response as an admission to the first part – but now courts freely grant leave to amend

VIII. Journalists – write your paragraph #1 for the journalists reading your pleading if it's a high media case

IX. **Pleadings' Impact on Discovery**
   a. Rule 26a1 – initial disclosures
   b. Rule 26b – overall scope of discovery
   c. **Pleadings help frame discovery**
      i. **plead broadly for broad discovery**
      ii. **plead narrowly for narrow discovery**

DISCOVERY

I. **Overview**
   a. "Fact Revelation and Issue Isolation"
      i. modern pleading much less important now – discovery more important
         1. Pleading FRCP's (3 pages) vs. Discovery FRCP's (30 pages)
      ii. a lot of common law pleading and code pleading activities now occur during discovery
   b. Discovery has 3 purposes:
      i. obtain admissible ev. both for and against you
      ii. pin down opposing side to a story
      iii. promote settlement
   c. Rule – 26-37
      i. 26b – scope
      (a) relevancy
         (i) look to the pleadings for matter relevant to claim or defense (4 corners of the pleadings)
         (ii) for things relevant to subject matter of claim you can go beyond pleadings
         (iii) have to understand relevant substantive law to understand relevancy
      ii. relevancy also depends on rules of evidence
         1. 401- defines relevance for purpose of trial
         2. 402- defines admissibility
         3. 403- elaborates on admissibility (relevant but excluded)
            a. lots of things are discoverable but not admissible (3 circles)
            b. things can also be irrelevant but calculated to lead to admissible evidence (outer circle pre 2000 it was the scope of discovery, narrowed in 2000)
            c. **Current scope of Discovery is now the next to largest circle, relevant and reasonably calculated to lead to evidence**
            d.
      iii. 26a – stage one mandatory disclosure (unilateral)
         1. don't wait for the other side to ask for it
         2. Parties must meet early in suit and offer the following items within 14 days
            a. Names of witnesses
            b. Descriptions of documents (that disclosing party may use to support claims and defenses)
            c. Calculations of damages
            d. Copies of insurance agreements
      iv. Five discovery instruments
         1. 30 – oral depositions
         2. 33- interrogatories
         3. 34 – production of documents and inspection of land and tangibles
         4. 35 – physical and mental exams
         5. 36 – requests for admissions

        6. 37 – sanctions (Rule 11 does not apply to discovery instruments)
- **v.** 26e-duties to supplement (ethical duty)
- **vi.** 26g- signing disclosures, discovery requests, responses and objections
- **d. Waves**
  - **i. Wave 1 – initial disclosure** (85 days after D "appears")
  - **ii.** <u>**Wave 2 – optional – use of 5 discovery instruments**</u>
    1. coordinate interrog. and doc requests (ask questions about doc's)
    2. take depo's of parties – nail them down to a story fast
    3. take depo's of non-party witnesses
    4. medical – depose physicians
    5. experts
    6. requests for admissions
  - **iii.** <u>**Wave 3 – disclosure of expert testimony – 26a2**</u> (90 days before trial)
  - **iv.** <u>**Wave 4 – pre-trial disclosure – 26a3**</u> (30 days before trial)
    1. witnesses that you will call
    2. witnesses that you may call
    3. documents, etc. that may be offered into evidence
- **e.** <u>Scheduling (sequencing and timing)</u>
  - **i.** Conference of the parties – 26f – **parties _must_ confer before starting discovery** unless parties agree, court order, or unless proceeding exempt from initial disclosure by 26a1E
  - **ii.** Wave #1 – 26a1 – initial disclosure
  - **iii.** Report of the parties of discovery plan – 26f
  - **iv.** Scheduling conference – 16b (if needed)
    1. deadline for report ("discovery plan") is 14 days after conf.
  - **v.** scheduling order – 16b

II.   Scope
- **a. Basic test of Relevance – Rule 26b1**
  - **i.** "relevant" to the _claim_ or _defense_ of any party
  - **ii.** relevant info need NOT be admissible at trial so long as the discovery **appears** <u>**reasonably calculated to lead to the discovery of admissible evidence**</u>
    1. just because something is inadmissible does NOT make it undiscoverable – could be useful info in framing party's theory
  - **iii.** very broad
  - **iv.** exceptions: privileged information
  - **v.** <u>limitations – 26b2</u> – court may choose to limit if it determines any of these:
    1. (i) – discovery sought is unreas. cumulative or duplicative or available from some other source more convenient, less burdensome, or less expensive
    2. (ii)party seeking discovery has had ample opportunity by discovery in the action to obtain the information sought already
    3. (iii)**burden or expense outweighs the likely benefit** –taking into account:
       a. needs of the case
       b. amount in controversy
       c. parties' resources
       d. importance of the issues at stake in the litigation
       e. importance of the discovery in resolving the issues
  - **vi.** Examples
    1. _Blank v. Cromwell_ – P's were allowed to discover information on advancement of femal attorneys to partners in a firm even though P's claim was based on discrimination of female attorneys in firms _hiring_

       2. *Stefan v. Cheney* – P did not have to answer interrogatory about whether he had engaged in homo. conduct in a case concerning P's *status* as a homosexual or not.

    vii. **FREvid. 401** – **"Relevant Evidence"** – evidence having any tendency to make the existence of any fact that is of consequence to the determination of the action more probable or less probable than it would be without the evidence

III. **Privileges**

  a. Fed. R. Evid 501- originally approved by Supreme Court as 501-09 but Congress has refused to codify testimonial privileges and current 501 is the comprise

  b. may be **waived** (explicitly, or implicitly by actions inconsistent with priv., - they can also be *abused*)

    i. attorney-client: client can waive

    ii. clergy-communicant: both must waive

    iii. Example – Albert sues Barbara for his injuries and also claims emotional distress – by injecting this into case, he has probably waived his privilege to not disclose discussions with his therapist

  c. privileges very from state to state, federal privileges are uniform throughout system

    i. If there is a conflict state law trumps (Congress made the Erie choice for us)

  d. **types:**

    i. every state has attorney-client priv.

      1. *Upjohn rule* – corporation's privilege extends beyond top control group of corp. to lower level employees

    ii. most have

      1. doctor-patient

      2. husband-wife

      3. psychotherapist

      4. attorney-work product

      5. atty-work product for experts

    iii. some have journalistic privilege (federal courts do not have this)

  e. 5th amendment – can be raised in depositon if would open person up to criminal prosecution based on the incriminating statements (unless person already acquitted – but remember, no double jeopardy protection between state/federal)

  f. scope of privilege

    i. Albert could still be asked if he was seeing a psychotherapist – he just can't be required to disclose what he told his psychotherapist

    ii. waiver – if Albert disclosed his discussions with therapist to his insurance company, then he has waived privilege probably

  g. when a plaintiff sues for injuries they waive their doctor-patient privilege

  h. testimonial privileges are disfavored

    i. somewhat narrowly construed depending on privilege and situation

IV. **Discovery Timeline**

  a. Starts when served or appeared in the suit

    i. Service is when served or when service has been waived

    ii. Appearance is defendant's filing of some paper or motion showing participation including 12b motions and answers

  b. R. 16b-within 90 days of appearance or 120 days after service judge shall hold a scheduling conference

    i. Discusses how discovery and other pretrial matters should proceed

  c. R. 26f- requires meeting without judge "as soon as practicable and in any event at least 21 days before a scheduling conference"

i. 26d- other forms of discovery (interrogatories, depos, etc.) can't be used until 26f meeting

ii. 26a1- parties at meeting or within 14 days after it must exchange disclosure lists

d. **Interlocking these provision requires parties to exchange required disclosures at least seven days before the scheduling conference and at the latest four months after the complaint is served.**

i. Where defendant has appeared the disclosure will occur no later than 85 days after appearance.

e. 26b1E- exemption categories to disclosure

i. Smaller claims

ii. Those where a well developed record or absence of counsel make it unnecessary or unfair

1. advisory committee notes suggest that very large cases in which close supervision will displace Rules may also be exempt

V. **INITIAL DISCLOSURE (wave 1)**

a. 26a1A – says only must disclose these things that *you* will use to support *your* claim or defense (disclosure not based upon other party's claims/defenses) unless solely for impeachment

b. If service takes **more than 30 days** you go with a 120 day rule (26b)

c. If service takes **less than 30 days** you go with a 90 day rule (16b)

i. R. 26f says go back in time 21 days then

d. 26a1- count forward 14 days (this is the final day for Wave 1 disclosures)

e. Positives to case only have to be disclosed at this point (26a1B "**may use** to support")

i. If positive is not directly related then on the face of pleadings you don't have to disclose it.

1. if pleading is amended though and it becomes relevant then it will have to disclose

f. Initial Disclosures required – 26a1A

i. A – name (address, telephone if known) of **each individual** likely to have disc. info. that disclosing party may use to support its own claims/defenses

ii. B – copy or description of: all **documents**, data compilations, and tangible things in possession, custody or control of party – that they will use to support their own claims/defenses

iii. C – **computation of any damages** claimed and make available materials on which computations based

iv. D – any **insurance agreement** (when insurance may be liable for paying part)

v. E – proceedings exempt from initial disclosure rules

g. failure to disclose – see below – Rule 37c – barred from bringing the ev. later

h. disclosure of expert testimony – 26a2 (Wave 3)

i. pretrial disclosure – 26a3 (Wave 4)

VI. **DISCOVERY INSTRUMENTS (wave 2 – optional)**

a. Don't have to be taken in order

i. If you depo before other discovery (when they get educated) you may get an unvarnished version of the truth

b. Conventional wisdom is to send out interrogatory request and document production and the same time or link them

c. **Interrogatories (Rule 33)**

i. only can be used on **parties** to the suit

1. must use rule 45 to get non-party to produce documents (you subpoena the documents)

ii. limit of 25 interrogatories (unless leave of court or written stipulation)

              1. can't ignore extra interrogatories

                    a. could move under 26c for a protective order (killing a gnat with a sledge hammer)

                    b. confer with opposing counsel and advise them of the issue so they can correct it

                    c. object b/c number of interrogatories exceeds 25

    iii. can't be done until after 26f conference (unless exempt)

    iv. party has 30 days to answer and/or object to interrogatories

    v. much cheaper than depositions (but doesn't get as much info)

    vi. answer to interrogatory is only **a piece of evidence** (which can be contradicted by other evidence) – NOT conclusively established (like an admission is)

              1. must be answered truthfully and if a party believes something might have bearing on case then they must disclose it

d. Depositions (Rules 28, 30, 31, 32)

    i. much more expensive than interrogatories (but more detailed)

    ii. first depose parties, then witnesses

    iii. Rule 30 – oral depositions

              1. w/o permission the total number of depos by one side cannot exceed 10 – R.30a2A

              2. limited to one day of 7 hours unless provided otherwise by the court

              3. When attorney can instruct client not to answer – 30d1

                    a. only when necessary to:

                          i. preserve privilege

                          ii. enforce a limitation directed by court

                          iii. present a motion under 30d4 (to stop bad faith)

              4. 30b6 – deposition of corporation – must give notice with reasonable particularity as to the matters on which examination is requested – corp. chooses someone for the depo and may designate matter on which person can testify

    iv. Rule 31- depos upon written questions

              1. in between depos and interrogatories

                    a. rarely used

                    b. lawyer writes questions, sends them to the court reporter presiding at the depo who then asks the questions and records the answers

                          i. cheaper but it yields less information

    v. if opposing counsel asks question that is beyond the scope of knowledge

              1. object

              2. ask for recess and instruct client/witness

                    a. make sure they understand they can say I don't know

                    b. can also say who they should ask the questions of

    vi. if a question is believed to be an area covered by a privilege

              1. objection must be specific enough to explain why its privilege

                    a. if they persist with that line then you can instruct witness not to answer (26b5)

                          i. if info is not privileged or privilege has been waived move to compel under R. 37

    vii. for documents/testimony form non witnesses you get a subpoena under R. 45

              1. subpoena duces taca (for documents only)

              2. depo would be taken in conjunction with the subpoena (R. 30 along w/ R. 45)

              3. they can ignore initial depo request

a. file for regular subpoena (for person) and if they ignore they're in contempt/arrest, etc.

   viii. Rule 32 – use of depos in court proceedings

     1. 32a1 – may use depo to impeach witness when testimony in trial doesn't match the depo

     2. 32a2 can offer opposing party's depo at trial for any purpose (exception to hearsay rule)

     3. 32a3 – either side can use depo of anyone if court finds a,b,c,d,or e (i.e. witness dead, unable to attend due to age illness imprisoned, etc.)

e. <u>**Rule 34 - Production of Documents and Things and Entry upon Land for inspection or other purposes**</u>

   i. produce and permit inspection and copying

   ii. must be within scope of 26b

   iii. must be **in possession, custody, or control of a party upon whom request served**

   iv. documents may have to be disclosed during Initial Discloser – see 26a

   v. document = "any medium for recording data or information" (photographs included)

   vi. failure to disclose or produce documents – may result in not being able to admit it at trial (see 26g)

   vii. **does not cover non-parties (must use Rule 45)** - documents from non-parties - use Rule 45 – but probably should just ask first (surprising what you can get voluntarily by just asking)

   viii. **Procedure**

     1. request must set forth individual item or category

     2. describe each with **reasonable particularity**

     3. producing party is to produce documents/things **as they are kept in the usual course of business OR shall label them to correspond with categories in the request**

f. <u>**Rule 35 - Mental/Physical exams**</u>

   i. limited to 2 types of people: a **party** or **a person in custody of or under legal control of a party**

   ii. mental or physical condition must be **in controversy** (must be some basis in the facts for raising the issue of person's mental/physical health)

   iii. have privacy to physical or mental injuries but it is waived in part

   iv. need <u>**"good cause shown" in addition**</u> to 26b scope of discovery requirement in order to get exam

     1. if P suing for damages from injury, then there is good cause to have him examined

     2. reciprocity – each entitled to each other's reports of the exams

       a. P is entitled to see D's doctor's report

       b. D is entitled to copies of P's own doctor's report

   v. exams of non-parties (i.e. eye exam of a witness) – **generally, not allowed** (unless party voluntarily agrees to of course)

     1. unless **under custody or legal control of a party** (i.e. employee of a party, or child of a party)

     2. being an employee of a defendant doesn't open you up to R. 35 examination

       a. not a party

       b. need to show more (person is lying—his vision is impaired so he couldn't have seen without his glasses)

g. <u>**Rule 36 – Request for Admissions**</u>

    i. doesn't uncover evidence as much as it makes evidence irrelevant by taking an issue out of controversy

        1. use to eliminate essentially undisputed issues (D is a corp. in Washington) – notice pleading makes Rule 36 useful

            a. R. 36a –you can ask questions about application of law to fact

    ii. If party thinks the request is <u>on an issue which should go to trial</u>, party may not object to the request merely on that ground – **party may deny the matter in good faith** (subject to 37c provisions) – or set forth reasons why party can't deny or admit

        1. R. 37c—the party failing to admit had reasonable grounds to believe that they might prevail on the matter (can deny w/o getting hurt for it later, unless grossly unreasonable)

    iii. **If time lapses** – if read literally, rule 36 says the matter is **admitted**

        1. some courts have said its not admitted

    iv. 36b – **effect of admission** – any matter admitted is **conclusively established** unless court on motion permits withdrawal or amending of the admission

        1. interrogatory answer is only evidence which can be refuted

        2. admission is *conclusively established*

    v. **sufficiency of answer** – court may order matter admitted or request amended answer

    vi. **lack of knowledge not sufficient reason for failure to admit/deny** – party has a **duty to make reasonable inquiry** – if after that still not sufficient knowledge, then party may say they can neither admit or deny

    vii. **ADMISSION ONLY APPLIES TO *THIS* PROCEEDING – CAN'T BE USED IN ANY OTHER PROCEEDING (i.e. can't be used as Collateral Estoppel in later suit)**

    viii. <u>**Admission vs. Interrogatory asking same thing**</u>

        1. admission = conclusively established – can get a jury instruction stating that "four other scouts tripped over this wire"

        2. interrogatory = only a piece of evidence – may not be submissible to jury under hearsay rule (can use them for impeachment)

h. **All of the above rules require cooperation by lawyers, a timetable, mechanisms for enforcing discovery and disclosure obligations**

i. Broader discovery into the "subject matter involved in the action" if "good cause" is shown

VII. <u>**Enforcement Mechanisms (37 and 26g)**</u>

a. **37a2 - Motion to Compel Disclosure or Discovery** (both require good faith effort to confer first)

    i. Compel disclosure – 37a2A

    ii. Compel answer to deposition question or interrogatory – 37a2B

    iii. **must make good faith effort to confer first** - moving party must certify that they have in good faith conferred or attempted to confer with the other party not making the disclosure in an effort to secure disclosure w/o court action

    iv. **evasive and incomplete disclosures, answers, and responses = failure to disclose, answer or respond**

b. sanctions immediately available (w/o motion to compel)

    i. 37d – **"total failure"** - court may take any actions "as are just" for failure to answer or object to interrogatory (33) or for failure to respond to request for inspection (34)

    ii. 37g – failure to attend or participate in good faith in a 26f conference

c. 37b – sanctions not available until after court orders a party to comply

    d.

e. **Rule 37c – Failure to Disclose** (during wave 1 - initial disclosure)

i. **barred from using as evidence** - party not allowed to use as evidence **any witness or info** not disclosed that was required by 26a or not amended as required by 26e2

f. **Rule 26g** (similar to Rule 11)

i. requires parties to sign and certify disclosures, discovery requests, and objections – certification that to the best of attorney's knowledge, info, and belief, formed after a reasonable inquiry that the request, response, or objection is:

1. **consistent with these rules** and **warranted by existing law or good faith argument for extension thereof**
2. **not for any improper purpose**
3. **not unreasonable or unduly burdensome or expensive**

ii. punishes parties for unjustified requests and refusals even when parties' behavior does not violate a court order

iii. punishment (unlike Rule 11) is suggested by the Rule as only attorneys' fees

VIII. **Protective Orders – Rule 26c**

a. may **totally prohibit** certain discovery or just **limit scope** of the discovery

b. moving party has burden of showing **"good cause"**

c. objector raising privilege must **detail what is privileged and why privileged** (not original rule – was amended to this)

d. to protect a **party or person** from **annoyance, embarrassment, oppression, or undue burden or expense**

e. contains list of orders judge may use (26c1-8)

IX. **Discovery and Privacy Concerns**

a. **26c – protective order** - *Stalnaker v. K-Mart* – normally P wants privacy protection but it's D who wants it in this case – D tries to exclude discovery of non-party witness on the *voluntary* sexual relations between the employees – asking for protection from **embarrassment** – court denies in part and grants in part – court limits the discovery as to only the activities with Mr. Graves to extent they show any conduct on his part to encourgage, solicit, or influence any employee

b. **35 – special limits on use of discovery to compel physical/mental exams**

i. strong interest in privacy for mental and physical exams (esp. for mental)

ii. requires **good cause** and **at controversy**

iii. applies to **any party in the action** (need not be adverse to movant for exam and can be the Def.)

iv. *Schlagenhauf* – bus driver (laundry list of exams) – he would have to submit but movant's failed to show **good cause** and failed to show medical/physical condition of driver was **at controversy** (dissents said it certainly was at cont.)

X. **Attorney Work Product Privilege**

a. *****resist the inclination to view this privilege as broader than it really is*****

b. **Attorney Work Product (26b3)**

i. the law of this comes from *Hickman v. Taylor* and **26b3** which has replaced Hickman in part

ii. **RULE 26b3: documents and intangibles prepared in *anticipation* of litigation can only be obtained in discovery if party demonstrates:**

1. **substantial need** AND
2. party is **unable w/o undue hardship to obtain the substantial equivalent** of the materials by other means
3. 26b3 applies to categories 1-2. Category 4 never discoverable
4. category 3 is uncertain (Hickman v. Taylor is it) – suggests that we don't want to put attorney in place of having to defend the accuracy of his memory in

writing down the earlier conversations

   iii. <u>4 categories:</u>
1. you interview witness, write it down, have witness sign as to accuracy
2. you interview witness and write down notes, but no approval
3. hadn't written down before, but you write it down when other side asks you to record your conversation with the witness from your memory
4. your mental impressions (i.e. "this person is hostile" or "they have great memory", etc.)

   iv. Category 4 (opinion work product) always protected from disclosure – **mental impressions always protected**

   v. Category 1-3 still privileged, but can be overcome

   vi. **burden rests on the moving party (who wants to invade privacy) to show substantial need and undue hardship**

   vii. 26b3 – 2nd paragraph (an **exception** to showing required for obtaining cat. 1 documents)
1. cat. 1 signed by party: other side can get just by asking with no showing required
2. cat. 1 signed by non-party witness: non-party witness may ask for the writing of their statement (cat. 1) and the witness can get it just by asking with no showing required
3. tapes included in cat. 1 (see definition of "statement previously made" – A and B)

   viii. this privilege not limited to attorney – can be materials prepared by the representative of a party

   ix. *searching factual interrogatories* – must be answered – i.e. they can ask if you spoke with a certain witness – everything factual must be disgorged

   x. "you can probably get everything you want if you ask for it in the right way"

   xi. Is this privilege waivable? law not clear

   xii. again, **don't overstate this privilege**

c. <u>AWP for Experts (26b4) – (Wave 3 – experts)</u>

   i. Testifying Experts – 26b4A
1. may be deposed
2. identity must be disclosed in disclosure of experts (Wave 3) – 26a2A
3. written report required if employed for expert testimony (26a2B)

   ii. Non-testifying experts – 26b4B
1. facts known or opinions held by them cannot be discovered by deposition of interrogatory unless provided by 35(b) (report of examiner in mental/physical exam) OR
2. upon a showing of "**exceptional circumstances under which it is impracticable for party seeking discovery to obtain facts or opinions on the same subject by other means**"
3.

   iii. What's an "Expert"?
1. FREvid 701
2. FREvid 702

d. Raising the Work Product privilege – 26b5

   i. shall make claim *expressly* and shale describe the *nature of [the things not produced]* in a manner that will enable other parties to assess the applicability of the privilege

   ii. **even if person is a non-testifying expert, can get some info on them by making them raise the privilege – 26b5**

e. *Thompson v. TheHaskell Co.* – protective order denied b/c of ***exceptional circumstances*** – therapist had examined P 5 days after alleged harassment occurred – this was unique change to know exactly what P's mental state was at that point – so expert wasn't protected by "AWP for experts"

f. *Chiquita* – marine surveyor, a non-testifying expert, had studied vessel's loading rigs and viewed documents – D was not allowed to compel discovery since expert was non-testifying – **he did have to turn over the documents though** (they don't become privileged simply by giving them to the expert)

      i. the distinction is not facts vs. opinions – both are covered by 26b4B

XI. **Sanctions under Rule 37**

    a. 26g – shall impose sanction

    b. 37 – may impose sanctions

    c. district courts have substantial discretion in imposing sanctions under Rule 37 and are reviewed only for *abuse of discretion*

    d. *Chadusama v. Mazda* – app. ct. found that dist. ct. had abused discretion in issuing order to compel against Mazda and imposing sanctions resulting in default judgment against Mazda – P had made a HUGE list of discovery requests (tried to get every doc Mazda had really) and Mazda tried to give them nothing – Mazda made a "near herculaen effort following compel order and was then dealt default judgment. Dist. ct. had severely mismanaged discovery by failing to rule to settle many disc. disputes. Default judgment was too severe.

SUMMARY JUDGMENT

I. <u>**Rule 56**</u>

    <u>**a.**</u> <u>**Two Main Requirements for SJ:**</u>

        <u>**i.**</u> there must be **no genuine issue of material fact**

        <u>**ii.**</u> party seeking SJ must be **entitled to judgment as a matter of law**

    <u>**b.**</u> <u>**Procedural Req.'s of Rule 56:**</u>

        <u>**i.**</u> Time

            <u>**1.**</u> 56(a) for **claimant (Plaintiff)** (claim, counterclaim, cross-claim)

                <u>**a.**</u> generally, <u>**20 days**</u> after **commencement of the action OR** (rule 3 says action commenced on filing of complaint)

                <u>**b.**</u> after **service of a motion for SJ by the adverse party** (if other party has moved for SJ)

            <u>**2.**</u> 56(b) for **defending party (Defendant)** (against a claim, counterclaim, cross-claim)

                <u>**a.**</u> <u>**any time**</u>

    <u>**c.**</u> can be on **one issue OR on all issues** in the case (i.e. SJ on main issues, trial on the damages)

        <u>**i.**</u> 56(d) – when case not fully adjudicated on motion – **some issues remain for trial**

            <u>**1.**</u> court will specify what facts are **uncontroverted** – these facts are **deemed established** – trial shall proceed accordingly

            <u>**2.**</u> court will also specify **what facts are actually and in good faith controverted**

    <u>**d.**</u> Supporting documents

        <u>**i.**</u> **affidavits, depositions, answers to interrogatories, admissions, and admissible documents** (56c, e)

        <u>**ii.**</u> pleadings are <u>not</u> admissible evidence (they are only assertions) – but of course judge looks at them to see what parties are trying to prove

    <u>**e.**</u> **Evidence supporting SJ - Affidavits** – may move for SJ with or without supporting affidavits

  i. form (56e) – evidence required:
    1. shall be made on **personal knowledge** – NOT hearsay – statements must set forth such <u>facts</u> as would be ***admissible in evidence*** (hearsay is inadmissible)
      a. it is true that inferences are included in "personal knowledge" but "inferences and opinions must be grounded in observation or other firsthand experience. They must not be flights of fancy, speculations, hunches, intuitions, or rumors" – *Visser v. Packer Engr. Assoc.*
    2. **When a SJ motion Is correctly made, opposing party cannot rely on a denial of that proof – Opposing party**
  ii. 56f - when unavailable to nonmovant – **nonmovant may say that there has not been sufficient discovery**
    1. court may deny SJ motion OR
    2. grant continuance on the motion
  iii. 56g - affidavits filed in bad faith – court may order party pay other party's attorney's fees incurred b/c of the affidavits
f. sufficient discovery must have been performed before SJ can be granted – the discovery must show that there is no genuine dispute as to the material facts
g. <u>Burdens of proof</u>
  i. the party that will have the burden of proof at trail has the equivalent burden at summary judgment
  ii. this means that the standard for summary judgment will apply differently depending on which party is moving for summary judgment
  iii. Plaintiff must show enough evidence to let a rational trier of fact find in its favor
  iv. **Example**
    1. P trying to collect on unpaid note that D is denying having signed – P must prove that D signed the note. P could have audiotape of deposition of D admitting he signed it along with 26 disinterested witnesses who say they saw him sign it – <u>all D must do is submit affidavit denying that he signed a note</u>
    2. this creates a material issue of fact – there is a need for trial to determine D's credibility in denying signing the note (now D might want to worry if he is blatantly lying, but nonetheless no SJ)
h. *Celotex* – P could not prove that D company supplied asbestos to husband's work site so SJ is granted – D did not have to prove that they did not supply materials – D must simply show that P cannot win
i. Nonmovant's response to SJ:
  i. must show that there is genuine issue of material fact
  ii. or, if facts undisputed, that movant is not entitled to judgment as matter of law
j. **Nonmovant *does not* have to show that they [the nonmovant] will win at trial!**

JURIES

I. **7th amendment** – when can you get a trial by jury?
 a. right to a trial by jury **7th Amendment does not apply to state courts!**
  i. "preserve" right to trial by jury – this means 1791 not chancery (**no right to trial by jury in courts of equity**
  ii. Equitable Jurisdiction:
    1. wanted injunctive relief or other relief only available at equity
    2. wanted to use a more flexible procedural device only available at equity
    3. had a claim that could only be brought at equity (a trust, incompetence/guardianship)
 b. don't confuse with 6th amendment (deals w/ criminal juries which are much different)

   c. used to be easy distinction – P files at law jury;   P files at equity no jury

   d. Now, we must ask: **Is there equity jurisdiction over the claim?**

   e. Size of Juries
- **i.** Rule 48 – Fed. Juries: 6-12 juries

   f. **LIST OF EQUITY (NO JURY)   AND LAW (JURY)**
- **i.** At Law
    1. money damages – law (jury)
    2. trover, replevin – law (jury)
    3. rent – law (jury)
    4. ejectment – law (jury)
- **ii.** At Equity
    1. Injunction – equity (no jury)
    2. specific performance – equity
    3. contract reformation – equity

   g. many federal civil juries now only have 6 jurors – more efficient

II. **Requesting a trial by jury - Timeliness**

   a. 10 day rule – Rule 38(b) – party must request jury for an issue **no later than 10 days after service of the last pleading directed to such issue**

   b. party may specifies issues for which requesting jury trial – otherwise, presumed that party has requested *all issues* be tried by jury

   c. 10 + 10 rule – Rule 38(c) – party has 10 days after being served for request of jury to request jury on additional issues not already requested

III. **Choosing a Jury – Voir Dire – Rule 47**

   a. **Challenging for cause** – may strike potential jurors during voir dire
- **i.** standard – "cause" is:
    1. **probability of bias or prejudice**
- **ii.** Rule 47 – Selection of Jurors
- **iii.** if **juror conceals or lies** on voir dire
    1. to get new trial, party must prove
        a. juror failed to answer honestly
        b. a material question
        c. a correct response would have provided a valid basis for challenging cause
- **iv.** general rule – once relatives and employees of the parties have been dismissed, courts are reluctant to dismiss for cause
- **v.** no limit on challenges for cause

   b. Peremptory challenges
- **i.** 28 USC §1870 – gives each side 3 peremptory challenges + additional challenges if alternate jurors are selected
- **ii.** may strike a juror for **any reason or for no reason at all (Exception: Batson Rule)**
    1. lets lawyers dismiss jurors they have a "hunch" about but not sufficient cause
- **iii.** **Batson Rule – held that systematic striking of black jurors *without a justification* based on nonracial factors violated D's right to equal protection**
    1. first developed in criminal jury trial (Batson)
    2. now extended to civil jurires - Edmondson v. Leesville Concrete
    3. Requirements
        a. opposing counsel must establish a **pattern**
        b. then may require counsel to provide a **race-neutral justification** for their peremptory strike

48

iv.   most courts have said race is the only basis for which peremptory challenges may not be used

v.   *Purkett* – court said it was okay to use peremptory challenge b/c "juror 22 had long curly hair, beard, and looked unkept"

TRIALS

I.   **What is a Trial?**

a.   Step 1 – jury selection

b.   Step 2 – impanel jury, administer oath

c.   Step 3 – Opening **Statement** – it is NOT argument (otherwise other side will object)

d.   Step 4 – Plaintiff's Case in Chief

e.   Step 5 – Defendant's Case in Chief (this is not the real beginning of D's case – they have started it already in cross-examination)

f.   Step 6 – Plaintiff's Rebuttal evidence (must not be new arg. – must respond to D)

g.   Step 7 – Closing Arguments / Summation

h.   Step 8 – Jury Instructions

i.   Step 9 – submittal – jury begins deliberations

j.   Attorneys should put all objections to instructions on record **otherwise they are <u>waived!</u>** – rarely will judge change instructions – jurors will then be told to being deliberations

k.   Step 10 – Verdict – counsel may ask to poll verdict

l.   Step 11 – Jury Discharged

m.   Step 12 – Post-verdict Motions (j.nov, remitittur, additur)

n.   Step 13 – Entry of Judgment

o.   Step 14 – Appeal – notice of appeal is filed with district court, not ct. of appeals

II.   **Burden of Production**

a.   P must provide enough evidence where **reasonable-fair minded people may reach different results**

b.   P must get past "x" into region where jury is

c.   Direct verdicts for D if P can't get past "x"

d.   Direct verdicts for P if P goes all the way past "y"

e.   *Reid v. San Pedro RR* – **the dead heifer case**

     i. D RR had duty to keep fence repaired

     ii.   D RR did not have duty to keep gate shut

     iii.   heifer wanders onto tracks and is killed

     iv.   no direct evidence of whether heifer went through broken fence or an open gate

     v.   Judge should have directed verdict for D since evidence said it was equally likely for heifer to go through the open gate as it was to go through the broken fence – P did not carry his burden of producing evidence

     vi.   reasonable fair minded people would not know how the cow got on the tracks

     vii.   **don't be confused by court's (and Yeazell's language) – not "more likely than not" – this is burden of persuasion language**

III.   **Burden of Persuasion**

a.   most civil trials: "**preponderance of the evidence**"

     i. or "more probable than not"

     ii.   51/49 - if jury is **"totally at sea"** (ev. is split 50/50) then they find for Defendant

b.   some civil trials: "clear and convincing evidence" (where claims are disfavored by the law) – it lies somewhere between preponderance and beyond reasonable doubt (criminal standard)

IV.   **Presumptions (FREvid. 301 and 302)**

a.   examples

     i. children born to married couple presumed legitimate

        ii. when you mail something in appropriate envelope – presumed to get there in due time

  b. presumptions are rebuttable

  c. **FREvid 301 – bursting bubble rule**

        i. Patent example - presumption puts bouncy ball in D's court, past the y

        ii. D's evidence then pushes ball back between x and y

        iii. **bursting bubble** – P still has burden of persuasion – so if jury is at sea they find for D

        iv. some states are **"non-bursting bubble" J's**

            1. jury must find for P in situation above since

  d. **FREvid 302** – Fed. judge sitting in diversity in a non-bursting bubble state, then judge follows the state law (makes the Erie choice for you)

  e. remember, **judges enter judgments, juries render verdicts**

V. **Directed Verdict (or Judgment as a Matter of Law – Rule 50)**

  a. May be filed at any time during jury trial after other party has been entirely heard on an issue – directed verdict must be <u>at the close of all the evidence</u> in order for it to be reserved and renewed as a JMOL

  b. Some cases go to jury even when facts are entirely undisputed (i.e. negligence)

        i. the jury is the "undoubted arbiter of credibility"

        ii. also give to juries questions that require them to apply general, open-ended standards to the facts of the case – jury must then apply the open texture of the law to those facts (i.e. negligence)

            1. "forseeability", "good faith", "negligent" are *ultimate factual questions* – reasonable people can differ as to the conclusion even though they don't differ as to the facts of the case

        iii. *RR Co. V. Stout* – facts were entirely uncontested

  c. Rule 51 – Jury Instructions

        i. get your objections to jury instructions on record or you forever waive your ability to claim they are error on appeal

        ii. jurors instructed that it must be unanimous decision (usually – 6 out of 6 in federal) – maybe 10 out of 12 or 8 out of 9 in some J's

  d. *REDMAN* - "THE REDMAN FICTION"

        i. court said as of 1791 a verdict could be directed, but no JMOL's (judgment notwithstanding the verdict) b/c of 7th amendment **ReExamination Clause**

        ii. but, **judge could reserve ruling on a directed verdict motion until after jury renders verdict and then rule – this becomes a JMOL – judgment notwithstanding the verdict (This is "The Redman Fiction")**

        iii. RULE 50(b) – JMOL – "Renewing Motion for Judgment After Trial"

VI. **New Trial – "Which Flavor?" – legal error OR factual (verdict contra)**

  a. **Rule 59 and Rule 61 – New Trials**

        i. deal with New Trials

  b. **reasons for new trial based on case law**

        i. 2 REASONS:

            1. **flawed procedures** – process leading up to verdict has been flawed (gives a judge a chance to correct herself)

            2. **flawed verdicts** – most common = verdict is against the weight of the evidence

        ii. **Rule 59** – New Trials where **verdict is contrary to the weight** of the evidence

            1. must follow a verdict (duh)

            2. may be on **judge's own initiative OR**

<u>3.</u> on **a party's motion**

iii. <u>Rule 61</u> – New Trials due to **legal error**

<u>1.</u> need not follow a verdict

<u>2.</u> same as a *mistrial*

<u>c.</u> <u>THE LIND FACTORS</u> – Help judge determine if verdict is Contrary to Weight

<u>i.</u> Judge can't grant new trial for verdict contrary to the weight where:

<u>1.</u> 1) SWEARING MATCH - the disputed facts turn on the credibility of the witnesses

<u>2.</u> 2) SIMPLE CASE - the case is relatively straightforward, even simple

<u>3.</u> the *Lind v. Schenley Decision <u>IS</u>* the federal law on this issue even though not a US Sup Ct decision

<u>4.</u> "judge should not set the verdict aside as contrary to the weight of the evidence and order a new trial simply because he would have come to a different conclusion if he were the trier of the facts"

<u>5.</u> Moore: the judge's duty is essentially to see that there is no **"miscarriage of justice"**

<u>d.</u> Errors of Fact

<u>i.</u> Directed Verdict – Rule 50

<u>ii.</u> JMOL – (which is really a reserved ruling on a directed verdict per the Redman Fiction) – Rule 50

<u>iii.</u> New Trial – verdict contrary to the weight of the evidence - Rule 59(a) – (Moore's "miscarriage of justice")

<u>e.</u> Errors of Law

<u>i.</u> Mistrial – Rule 61

<u>ii.</u> New Trial – only if the legal error is inconsistent with substantial justice – Rule 61 (there is a lot of harmless legal error that is not inconsistent with substantial justice) – ruling reviewed de novo

<u>f.</u> Cannot appeal a grant of new trial NOT a final judgment

VII. <u>Conditional New Trials (Rule 50(c))</u>

<u>a.</u> New trial limited to damages

<u>i.</u> judge must be convinced that whatever influences led the jury astray on damages did not **infect** the judgment on liability as well

<u>b.</u> Remittitur and Additur

<u>i.</u> remittitur – judge orders a new trial unless the plaintiff agrees to accept reduced damages

<u>ii.</u> **additur** – analogous to remittitur except judge increases damages (**NO ADDITUR IN FEDERAL COURTS** – Many states still allow it)

<u>1.</u> Sup. Ct. said remittitur was just modifying a decision already made by jury while additur was making an award no jury ever made

<u>iii.</u> Is this Consitutional?

<u>1.</u> Sup. Ct. says P must have choice between lower damages and new trial

<u>iv.</u> When should judge grant?

<u>1.</u> "shock the conscience" test OR "passion, bias, or prejudice" test

<u>2.</u> but if the verdict is so excessive how does judge know this didn't affect jury's decision on liability as well?

<u>v.</u> How to calculate the new damages?

<u>1.</u> 3 approaches:

<u>a.</u> highest amount a jury could award

<u>b.</u> a reasonable amount

<u>c.</u> the lowest reasonable amount

vi. <u>**P cannot appeal after accepting remitittur – part of accepting remittitur is giving up the appeal**</u>

VIII. <u>**Notes and Problems on JMOL and New Trial (see handout)**</u>

a. **1) Motion for Directed Verdict must be made <u>at the close of all the evidence</u> in order for the Redman Fiction to work and for the JMOL to be available as a reserved directed verdict motion**

    i. usually, directed verdict motions may be at any time after party has been fully heard on an issue at trial

b. 2) motion for verdict to be set aside as "contrary to the law and evidence" – this is malpractice – sounds both like a motion for new trial for legal error and either a motion for new trial for verdict contra to the weight or a JMOL (which is about *fact)*

c. **3) Rule 50(b) – JMOL must be filed (the directed verdict motion must be renewed) no later than <u>10 days after entry of JUDGMENT (not verdict)</u>**

d. 4 Possibilities

    i. GRANT JMOL   GRANT New Trial

    ii.   GRANT JMOL   DENY New Trial

    iii.   DENY JMOL   GRANT New Trial

    iv.   DENY JMOL   DENY New Trial   (most common)

e. **4) GRANT JMOL   GRANT New Trial**

    i. court granted JMOL – they also ruled on motion for new trial in case the JMOL is reversed on appeal

    ii.   Trial Judge's Dilemma: If D claims numerous errors in evidence and instructions and trial court has granted conditional new trial – then Trial court has ruled JMOL but also admitted that there were errors in the trial sufficient to justify new trial

    iii.   If trial ct. grants JMOL, it does <u>not</u> automatically grant new trial for verdict contrary to the weight (standard for new trial verdict contra – may be abuse of discretion to also grant new trial b/c Lind factors present and 7th amendment)

    iv.   **50c1 – if appellate court reverses JMOL, the new trial proceeds *unless appellate court orders otherwise***

    v.   Isn't there strong possibility that trial judge's ruling on JMOL also "infected" his ruling on granting the new trial for verdict contrary to the weight?

f. **5) GRANT JMOL   DENY New Trial**

    i. Plaintiff should bring own motion for new trial *for legal error* (instead of verdict contrary to the weight since the P likes the verdict -50c2) – if denied, P should appeal the JMOL

    ii.   On appeal, **Defendant as appellee, may question the trial court's denial of its motion for new trial (50c1) – "appellee may assert error in the denial [of the motion for new trial]"**

g. **6) DENY JMOL   GRANT New Trial   The "MUDD" Line**

    i. The Mudd line - The bouncy ball in trial judge's mind was juuuust past "x" (outside of JMOL land) but not very far into land between x and y

    ii.   **a) P <u>cannot</u> immediately appeal the grant of new trial – It is NOT a final judgment**

    iii.   **b) D cannot appeal the JMOL yet either since it's NOT a final judgment yet (exception: can always try for an interlocutory appeal which is discretionary) [not correct read question carefully]**

    iv.   c) If D wins 2nd trial, now final judgment so P can appeal the earlier ruling granting new trial – chances probably won't be good – we've had two trials now – but depends on reason for new trial

        1. if for legal error, must have been some good reason for trial judge to grant new trial (since most legal error harmless) – so app. ct. probably won't overturn

    2. if for verdict contrary to the weight, and the case was swearing match and relatively simple (lind factors) – then good chance app. ct. will overturn – they take the 7th amendment seriously, folks

  v. d) If P wins the 2nd trial, court probably will not grant a new trial to have a 3rd trial - b/c now P has won twice at trial – but if there is massive legal error, then judge may say we're gonna do this until we get it right

  vi. e) If P wins the 2nd trial, NOW D can appeal the denial of the JMOL at the end of the first trial

  vii. f) If D had only moved for JMOL and not for new trial, trial court can still grant new trial **sua sponte** (59d)—D may not have moved for new trial b/c even though verdict was against them a new trial would almost certainly return a larger verdict

 h. 7) **DENY JMOL   DENY New Trial**

  i. a) if app. ct. affirms denial of JMOL, it can still review the denial of motion for new trial – but rule 50 does not say they *must* review it – D must appeal it (app. ct. won't just review it on their own – must be asked to review it)

  ii. b) Say trial ct. denied both motions on grounds that P did not have to prove res ipsa but the court of appeals finds P was required to prove it – then this is serious legal error – ct. of app. would respond by reversing trial judge's denial of motion for new trial on basis of serious legal error—can enter JMOL for D

  iii. **c) If App. ct. decides to reverse the denial of JMOL (and GRANT JMOL), can P in some way make a new trial motion? Rule 50(d) – Yes, P may assert grounds for new trial and app. ct. may grant new trial or remand to trial ct. to determine if new trial should be granted (trial ct. had ruled on D's motion for new trial – not P's yet) – and this would have to be new trial for legal error (can't be verdict contrary since P won the verdict). This irritates the panel you should file a motion for a contingent new trial with the trial judge during the 30 day window D is using to file appeal (say judge and jury were excellent but for good cause I believe that D counsel will appeal your judgment and bring this motion conditionally)**

    1. Plaintiff's argument: (motion to reconsider)R. 61

    2. **point 1** – P says don't reverse denial of JMOL

    3. **point 2** – P says don't reverse denial of new trial motion

    4. **point 3** – if JMOL denial is reversed (JMOL granted) then P moves for new trial due to legal error ("look at me – I had all this legal error against me and I still won the trial!")

IX. **The Sanctity of the Jury**

 a. **FREvid 606**

  i. 606(a) – jurors may not testify as a witness before that jury

  ii. 606(b) - in an inquiry as to the validity of the verdict, **jurors may not testify** about matters during deliberations or about anything that effected their mind or emotions in assenting or dissenting to the verdict

  iii. **exception** – juror may testify on question of:

    1. **extraneous prejudicial information was improperly brought to jury's attention OR**

      a. (ex. – juror who conducted experiments with flammability of aluminum wire at home and reported results to rest of the jury)

    2. **any outside influence was improperly brought to bear on any juror**

  iv. *Peterson v. Wilson* – judge had met with jurors and determined that they completely disregarded his instructions so he granted new trial

<ol start="1" type="1">
<li>5th cir. thought this was for error of fact and applied Lind Factors and found abuse of discretion by trial ct. in granting new trial (swearing match and simple case) – it was really for legal error in that the judge disobeyed FREvid. 606 by meeting with the jurors – so the 5th Cir. landed on their feet for the wrong reason</li>
</ol>

<ol start="22" type="i">
<li>v. policy – to protect sanctity of verdict; once jurors who have been sequestered are back out in public and their friends give them trouble, they would want to change their verdicts</li>
<li>vi. Rule 60(b) – may allow judgment to be set aside under vary narrow circumstances – for fraud (bribery of judge or jurors) – this is not an appeal</li>
</ol>

b. Rule 49 – Special Verdicts and Special Interrogatories
- **i.** judges don't like to use this rule
- **ii.** If **case is complex**, trial judges may be asked to use it
- **iii.** **Special Verdicts**
  1. court asks juror's factual questions that step by step lead them to the verdict
  2. if there are inconsistencies, judge may send jurors back to reconsiderm otherwise mistrial (new trial for legal error) – this is why judges like general verdicts – they cover up the inconsistencies
- **iv.** General verdict accompanied by **special interrogatories**
  1. hopefully the jurors answers will be consistent with the verdict
  2. if answers are internally consistent but not with the general verdict, judge can just change the general verdict w/o sending jurors back

X. Bench Trials – Rule 52
- **a.** the "x" line does not exist in a bench trial
- **b.** **Rule 52(c)** - judge should enter verdict for D if P has never got the ball to the right of the burden of persuasion line – all D's ev. would do is push the ball farther left
- **c.** If court of appeals is to reverse the trial judge's findings of fact, then in their mind **the bouncy ball is not just to the right of the burden of persuasion line, it is a lot farther to the right – standard is "clearly erroneous"**

APPEALS

I. Overview
- **a.** no constitutional right to an appeal – constitution does not require it anywhere
- **b.** 3 types of error can be raised on appeal:
  - **i. Procedural error** – trial ct. made an error in applying a rule of procedure or evidence
  - **ii. Substantive error** – court improperly instructed the jury as to what statute required or as to what the common law was
  - **iii. Factual error** – judge or jury found the facts incorrectly
- **c.** Why have appellate system?
  - **i.** fairness to litigants – places check on trial court
  - **ii.** protects integrity of judicial process
  - **iii.** engenders confidence in the system
  - **iv.** avoids piecemeal law - risk of getting lots of different law at the bottom – as go higher, get to more coherent law
- **d.** Purpose of appeals rules:
  - **i.** limit the persons who can seek review of trial court decisions
  - **ii.** limit when trial court decisions can be appeal
  - **iii.** limit depth of scrutiny an appellate court may exercise over an appealable trial court decision
- **e. Balance** – fairness to the litigants vs. "correctness" of the result

II. **Requirements for an appeal**
   a. **Overview – Requirements to Appeal**
      i. Must be **Timely**
      ii. Must be **Adverse**
      iii. party must not have **Waived** their right to appeal by not objecting at trial court level
         1. unless under an exception to waiver rule
      iv. Must be **a Final Judgment** (or an exception thereto)
         1. unless under an exception to Final Judgment Rule
   b. **Timeliness**
      i. FRAP 4(a)(1) – within **30 days** of judgment or order entered that party is appealing from (60 days for appeal involving the U.S.)
         1. file notice with clerk of the *district court*
      ii. Filed too late – FRAP 4a5 and 4a6 cite to 2107 which may allow party to appeal late
      iii. Filed too early – not a final judgment yet – FRAP 4a4 may allow notice of appeal to still be valid
   c. **Adversity** – judgment must be adverse to a party in order for them to be able to appeal it – **a judgment granting relief different from what one requested**
      i. adversity is <u>result-oriented</u> – did the party get the relief they requested?
      ii. in some special cases, a decision may still be adverse – i.e. because of the collateral effect a finding of some issue may have (issue preclusion) even though the award would be the same regardless of the finding on that issue
      iii. *Aetna Casualty v. Cunningham* – P sues for compensatory damages on breach of K and fraud claim – P wins all damages requested under breach of K claim but loses fraud claim – P was allowed to appeal b/c losing the fraud claim was adverse – D was about to go bankrupt – and fraud judgments have more weight in bankruptcy proceedings
      iv. <u>Damage examples</u>
         1. P sues for $100K in damages – jury finds for P and awards $50K – this is adverse to both parties
         2. P sues for $100K on 3 theories – jury finds for P and awards $100K for P but only on 1 of 3 theories – not adverse to P since he got full damages even though 2 of his 3 theories were rejected
      v. <u>Injunction Examples</u>
         1. P sues for injunction to stop picketing
         2. If injunction granted, only adverse to D
         3. If partial injunction granted (picket only during morning) – then adverse to both parties
      vi. *Doctrine of Mootness* – one may not appeal from a judgment when circumstances have changed in such a way that relief is no longer possible
         1. **exceptions:**
            a. question raised by the claim is likely to recur (as for other plaintiffs)
               i. P appeals decision of trial court upholding Iowa's 1 year residency requirement for obtaining divorce, but 1 year has passed so P no longer needs remedy – but app. court heard the appeal since other P's who have not met 1 year requirement will be affected
         2. mootness can result from **settlement** – party who has settled can't appeal a decision of a lower court

55

   d. Waiver – issue must be raised in trial court as a predicate to appeal

      i. can't raise claim for first time on appeal

      ii. a claim must be **preserved for review** in the trial court or can't bring it on appeal – **you had better raise the issue at the trial court level**

         1. this encourages *well-informed trial court decisions* – makes everybody bring their arguments at trial court so they can make good decision

      iii. get your objection on record with the trial court – otherwise parties would not object and would build error into the record at the trial level so they have reason reserved for an appeal

      iv. fosters efficiency

      v. unique position of the appellate courts

         1. trial court is only once removed from the accident – appellate court is twice removed

         2. appellate court not in position to hear evidence for first time or to decide on new issues

      vi. The "exception"

         1. at common law, party had not only to raise the argument in trial court but also make a formal **"exception"** to the trial court ruling in order to preserve the issue for appeal

         2. <u>Rule 46</u> - **did away with exceptions – but did not do away with waiver doctrine**

            a. Rule 46 – requires party "make know to the court the action which the party desires the court to take…"

            b. if party has no opportunity to object, then they are not prejudiced for not objecting

      vii. <u>Denial of 12b6</u> - D's 12(b)6 is denied – D should still renew with objections to evidence and instructions in order to preserve the issue for appeal (to be on the safe side)

      viii. Exceptions to Waiver Rule

         1. <u>Cross-Appeals</u>: If appellee lost on a defense or claim below and wants to preserve the objection in case the case is reversed, he must **cross-appeal**

            a. <u>exception</u>: appellee may make new arguments *in support* of the judgment without cross-appealing (even though attacking lower court's reasoning or insisting on a matter ignored or overlooked by lower court) – p.758, Yeazell

            b. cross-appealling party can only raise those arguments made at trial

         2. <u>change in law</u> during appeal – generally, appellant is out of luck and cannot raise the issue on appeal – but if its very fundamental change, court may consider it

         3. <u>"plain error" rule</u> – where the error has seriously affected the fairness, integrity, or public reputation of judicial proceedings – appellant need not have raised issue at trial court to still be able to appeal

         4. <u>subject matter jurisdiction</u> – parties or the court sua sponte may raise for first time on appeal

  e. <u>Are limits on appeals constitutional? Yes</u>

      i. no constitutional right to appeal

      ii. some burden on appeals is constitutional

         1. *Lindsey v. Normet* – court struck down statute requiring tenants to post double bond to appeal a summary eviction judgment (arguably since only applied to tenants)

2. *Bankers Life v. Crenshaw* – court upheld a statute imposing a 15% penalty on unsuccessful appeals
3. states have interest in discouraging frivolous appeals and conserving judicial resources
   iii. FRAP 38 – allows ct. of app. to award just damages and single or double costs to appellee if they determine that an appeal is frivolous

f. **Final Judgment Rule** – can only appeal from a final judgment – with certain statutory exceptions (**28 USC §1291**) – this rule is statutory, not constitutional

   i. <u>Final Judgment</u>- "one which ends the litigation on the merits and leaves nothing for the court to do but execute the judgment"

   ii. <u>Which of these are final judgments?</u>
      1. grant of 12b6 motion to dismiss for failure to state a claim? Yes
      2. denial of 12b6? No (case continues so not final)
      3. order granting motion to strike scandalous matter from pleading? No
      4. order denying motion to strike scandalous matter from pleading? No
      5. order granting motion to amend? No
      6. order denying motion to amend? No
      7. grant of summary judgment on all issues? Yes
         a. grant of summary judgment on less than all issues? May not be final
      8. denial of summary judgment? No
      9. order for directed verdict / judgment as a matter of law? Yes
      10. Denial of directed verdict /jml? No

   iii. FJR does not deny you the right to assert various types of error on appeal

   iv. **Rule 54(b)** – applies to multiple claim actions where "one or more but fewer than all the claims or parties" have been finally decided and are found to be otherwise ready for appeal – **judge may certify the appeal to allow the "done" parties to appeal and not have to wait for everyone else**
      1. judge will have to weigh the efficiency considerations
      2. **generally, an order is not final until court rules on all requests for relief**
      3. 54(b) is an exception – **judgment can be final even though all relief requests not disposed of**
         a. encourages joinder of parties and claims – lets the parties who are "done" appeal and move on

   v. *Liberty Mutual v. Wetzel* – both parties though that the judge's order was a "final judgment" but Supreme Court says No. Dist. ct. essentially made a partial summary judgment finding D liable (for having employment practices violated Title VII) but not resolving issue of damages or injunctive relief – D tried to appeal, but Sup. Ct. said no final judgment
      1. Rule 54b did not apply to this case - even though P asked for different forms of relief – P's case still based on only one claim – that the employment practices violated Title VII
      2. 1292 also did not apply in Wetzel – the district court had not ruled on the injunction (nor any of the other requests for relief) – even if this was a denial of an injunction, D could not appeal that denial (**he had not requested it! duh**) – P who requested it was not the one appealing

g. **Courts may raise the question of "appealability" on their own, <u>even if</u> both parties are seeking appellate review** (compare to subject matter J – may always be raised sua sponte)

h. **Exceptions to Final Judgment Rule:**
   i. Rule 54(b) when multiple claims/parties (see above)
   ii. **Interlocutory decisions – 28 USC §1292(a)(1)**

1. interlocutory order = order rendered by a judge prior to a final decision - such an order relates to an intermediate issue and as such does not dispose of the case on the merits (**they are "Not-Final" judgments which may be appealed immediately**)
2. **1292 (a)(1) - Injunctions**
   a. **applies only to preliminary injunctions NOT TRO's** (which have a short duration – 10 days under Rule 65)
   b. a denial of SJ in favor of one seeking permanent injunction does NOT give rise to immediate appeal
   c. "an order granting, refusing, dissolving, or modifying the injunction" is immediately appealable
   d. party may immediately appeal grant/denial of preliminary injunction
   e. this is due to special nature of injunctions and their potential for harm
3. **1292 (b) – Certification of Interlocutory Appeals (trial judge thinks he is likely to be wrong)**
   a. If Dist. judge finds:
      i. controlling question of law
         1. can't be issue of fact
      ii. substantial ground for difference of opinion on
         1. usually means no binding precedent and lower courts handle inconsistently
         2. there can't be substantial disagreement in a case of first impression
      iii. immediate appeal may *materially advance the ultimate termination of the litigation*
   b. then Dist. judge **may** decide to send case immediately to Court of Appeals
   c. Court of appeals **may** then allow such an appeal [**both dist. court and Court of Appeals must approve**] if application is made to it **within 10 days** of the district judge's order
   d. rarely used and granted (100 out of 40,000 fed. appeals)
   e. the district court proceedings are not stayed while interlocutory appeal is considered unless the Court of App. orders the proceedings be stayed
iii. **Practical Finality – 3 pronged test**
   1. **"Collateral Order Doctrine"** ("The *Cohen* Exception")
   2. **Requirements – an order must:**
      a. **conclusively determine** the disputed question
      b. resolve an **important** issue **completely separate from the merits** of the action
         i. (importance of the right asserted) + (separable)
      c. be **effectively unreviewable** on appeal from a final judgment
   3. "effectively unreviewable" = only where the order at issue involves an **asserted right** the **legal and practical value** of which **would be destroyed** if it were not vindicated at trial
   4. Does NOT depend upon the likelihood of eventual success on the merits
   5. *Lauro Lines v. Chasser*
      a. D trying to immediately appeal a denial of his motion to dismiss suit in a US court when P passengers had signed a forum selection clause requiring suits be brought in Italy
      b. court said this denial of motion to dismiss was NOT immediately

appealable
- c. it did NOT fall under the Collateral Order Doctrine since it was not an important enough right asserted
- d. not sufficiently important to overcome policies militating against allowing interlocutory appeals – court has said so for rights from jurisdictional limitations set by Congress – same rule applies for limits made by private agreement

6. **Practically final - and thus immediately appealable** based on Cause Of Death
   - a. denial of motion to dismiss based on **absolute or qualified immunity**
      - i. "right not to stand trial" is only vindicated if immediate appeals lies from a trial court order (erroneously) denying such a right
   - b. an order requiring disclosure of materials claimed to be protected by attorney-client privilege and work-product privilege
   - c. death knell –practically out of court
   - d. LIST ON PG. 641 NOTE 5

7. **Not practically final – and thus not immediately appealable:**
   - a. denial of motion to dismiss for lack of jurisdiction (not immediately appealable)
   - b. denial of motion to dismiss due to a forum selection clause (Chasser)
   - c. orders refusing to certify class actions (Coopers)
   - d. LIST ON P.642 YEAZELL

i. Rationale of interlocutory appeals – balance the costs
   - i. costs of allowing interlocutory appeals
      1. costs of an unnecessary extra appeal if trial judge turns out to be correct
   - ii. costs of denying interlocutory appeals
      1. costs of an unnecessary or unnecessarily long trial if trial judge turns out to be wrong

j. **Mandamus**, an extraordinary writ
   - i. statutory basis comes from the **All Writs Act** – 28 USC §1651
   - ii. **orders a public official to perform an act required by law** – may be a judge of a lower court
   - iii. is NOT to be used as a way around the final judgment rule or away to avoid the rules limiting interlocutory appeals
   - iv. only exceptional circumstances amounting to a **judicial usurpation of power** will justify the invocation of this extraordinary remedy
   - v. examples where applied
      1. trial judge denies jury trial
      2. to question propriety of a 1404 transfer by Dist. Ct. out of a circuit and into another (justified by 1651 – writs "in aid of their respective jurisdiction")
   - vi. higher court may deny the writ of mandamus but in its opinion come very close to granting it – by strongly suggesting that the trial judge do what the mandamus would have required
      1. *Kerr v. US Dist. Ct.* – affirmed Ct. of App.'s denial of writ of mandamus requiring in camera (judge in chambers) review of documents to determine whether privileged – but strongly suggested that the Dist. Ct. review docs in camera

PRECLUSION

I. <u>**RES JUDICATA** – **Claim Preclusion**</u>

   <u>**a.**</u> **Elements**

      <u>**i.**</u> **Same Claim**

      <u>**ii.**</u>   **Same Parties**

      <u>**iii.**</u>   **Resolved on the Merits**

   <u>**b.**</u> Purpose of RJ

      <u>**i.**</u> **judicial economy** - encourages parties to bring claims in efficient large packages

      <u>**ii.**</u>   **integrity of judgments** - prevents inconsistency in successive judgments

   <u>**c.**</u> <u>**Same Claim**</u>

      <u>**i.**</u> 3 tests

        <u>**1.**</u> "same writ" or "same legal theory" test (old CL view)

          <u>**a.**</u> very narrow

          <u>**b.**</u> i.e. No RJ if first suit on ordinary negligence and second suit is based on strict liability

        <u>**2.**</u> "same evidence" test

          <u>**a.**</u> even if you have 2 separate legal theories, but they rely on the same evidence, then they are precluded

        <u>**3.**</u> **"same transaction or occurrence" test**

          <u>**a.**</u> Federal Rule

          <u>**b.**</u> most common

      <u>**ii.**</u>   NO RJ if party was prohibited from bringing the claim in the first suit - can't be blamed for not raising an issue in first suit if you were prohibited from raising it

        <u>**1.**</u> *Frier v. City of Vandalia*

          <u>**a.**</u> Frier was not prohibited from raising the due process claim in the earlier state suits, so he is now barred by RJ since he did not bring the claim then – broad "same transaction or occurrence" test used

      <u>**iii.**</u>   judgment entered by state court which is later being considered for RJ effect in federal court – federal judge should give FF&C and look back to state court to determine the RJ effect they would give it

      <u>**iv.**</u>   Rule **13a** – compulsory counterclaim (similar to RJ)

        <u>**1.**</u> 13a is only triggered to preclude party if they filed a pleading in the first suit (did not trigger in Martino since they had not filed answer in first suit)

        <u>**2.**</u> 13a applies <u>only</u> to "same party" – **does not include "parties in privity"** whom are usually included under RJ

      <u>**v.**</u> *Martino v. McDonald's*

        <u>**1.**</u> same parties is met – McD of Ottumwa and Martino are parties in privity, so it's okay that McD of Ottumwa was not in first suit

        <u>**2.**</u> resolved on the merits is met - a consent decree **is** a judgment on the merits (the judge memorializes the settlement – judge adopts the findings of fact and conclusions of law of the parties in a consent decree)

        <u>**3.**</u> same claim? was the claim a compulsory counter-claim that should have been brought in F-1? Yes, a victorious judgment for P's in F-2 would be **inconsistent with and undermine** the other parties' judgment in F-1

      <u>**vi.**</u>   outside of 13a – there is **a narrow set of CL compulsory counterclaims**

        <u>**1.**</u> based on **inconsistent judgments**

      <u>**vii.**</u>   **Inconsistent Judgments – must determine whether inconsistent or not**

        <u>**1.**</u> HYPO – AgChem supplies farmer with herbicides and he never pays. AgChem sues for breach of K and farmer argues that price was not agreed

upon – jury verdict for AgChem.

    2. Farmer then sues AgChem claiming their product killed his crops – AgChem argues RJ – Was Farmer's claim a "narrow CL" compulsory counterclaim in suit 1? No – judgments would not be inconsistent so this does not fall under the CL comp. counterclaim rule (RJ)

d. Same Parties

    i. don't have to have identical parties

    ii. can have **parties in privity**

    iii. *Searle Brothers v. Searle*

        1. Partnership (Searle Bros.) sues Edlean after she had won divorce judgment against Woodey Searle (father of the two Searle brothers) which awarded Edlean the "Slaugh House" property – Partnership claims it owns half interest in the house.

        2. Edlean argues that Searle Bros. is party in privity with Woodey

        3. Edlean argues 5 points:

            a. Woodey represented interest of sons?

                i. no, he represented his own interest in a divorce

            b. Sons failed to intervene?

                i. not barred just b/c they failed to intervene (white firefighters and black firefighters case from last semester) – brothers never actually became a party

            c. Sons testified as witnesses – they argued that they had ½ interest and obviously were not believed since Edlean got the house?

                i. as a witness, they had no attorney, can't choose issues to argue (this is NOT due process in the slightest)

            d. Edlean argued family relationship was privity?

                i. family relationship can be privity (i.e. husband and wife own car together – wife is bound when husband loses suit; father sues in property dispute and loses – he dies and property goes to son who tries to sue – barred by RJ) – **otherwise, family relationship is NOT privity**

            e. Woodey was agent of partnership? (best arg)

                i. Woodey was not representing partnership – he was in the suit in capacity as himself not in capacity as an agent

        4. capacity of party – determine what capacity the party is in when they are in the first suit (may not be in privity in that capacity)

            a. HYPO – Acme pharm. gives Mrs. Smith, a salesperson, a company car – Mr. Smith wins the car in a divorce settlement even though she claims it's not hers. Is Acme barred by RJ? No – they are not in privity when Mrs. Smith is in suit in her capacity as wife and not employee/agent

            b. HYPO – P sues D who injured him in auto accident – sues for car damage, broken leg, head injuries and wins $150K verdict – D appeals and then P dies during appeal. P's administrator now sues for wrongful death and claims no RJ since suing for a death and not for injuries – this is still same claim: the death is the same thing as the possible early death of P recovered for in P's firt suit (head injuries) – Admin. is party in privity.

            c. Effect of Appeal in First Suit - Can D still use S-1 since still on appeal? Yes **RJ applies to earlier appeals also – Rule 60b will allow**

judgment to be reopened if it is based upon an earlier judgment that was overturned.

e. **Resolved on the Merits**

    i. *Semtek v. Lockheed Martin*

        1. YIKES! – see Notes

        2. **RJ effect of a Federal diversity judgment** – give it the RJ effect that the State in which the Fed. Ct.'s would give it – apply state preclusion law

            a. **unless conflicting federal interest!** (see last page of Semtek) apply Hanna

        3. **RJ effect of a Federal question judgment** – give it the RJ effect of federal preclusion law

    ii. 6 types of dispositions at CL that were "on the merits":

        1. disposed of on jurisdictional grounds (SMJ or PJ) – **never on merits**

        2. lack of venue – **never on the merits**

        3. insuff. of service of process or insuff. of process – **never on merits**

        4. other procedural dispositions (nonjoinder of indispensable parties, resistance to discovery, failure to prosecute) – **never on the merits**

        5. substantive law (if disposition was failure to state a claim upon which relief can be granted – demurrers at CL; or disp. was on P's motion – a nonsuit; or summary judgment or judgment on the pleadings) – such disposition **may or may not be on the merits**

        6. factual basis (demurrer, SJ, judgment on pleadings) – **may or may not be on the merits at CL**

            a. SJ on contributory negligence – on the merits

            b. SJ on statute of limitations – not on merits; could go to another state, like in Semtek

            c. **at common law, needed more info to determine whether a factual dismissal was on the merits**

    iii. **Rules of Thumb – 5 of them – for determining whether on the merits**

        1. if it was directed verdict, JMOL, or entry of judgment on the verdict – **always on the merits**

        2. where no jury present, after P's case in chief or close of all evidence, if judge made ruling, **it was on the merits**

            a. Rule 52 bench trial does this in federal court

            b. can move after close of P's case in chief for judgment as a matter of law (directed verdict) – **this is on the merits**

        3. default judgments under Rule 55 – **on the merits for RJ purposes**

        4. demurrers at CL (just like 12b6) – may be factually based or legally based

            a. if P comes back with substantially the same lawsuit then the demurrer will be RJ'ed - if P has new facts or new questions of law then no RJ

            b. judge in second suit must look at the pleading and compare to first suit to determine if RJ

        5. Rule 41a and 41b

            a. 41b pretty much worthless for RJ (Semtek)

            b. 41a is voluntary dismissal (at CL, courts dealt with this nonsuit same as demurrer) – judge will compare complaints like he did under #4 and determine if RJ'ed – see 41a below

    iv. Statute now requires judges to put in all matters of disposition

        1. must include magic words: either "with prejudice" or "without prejudice" – **but don't rely on this**

<u>**2.**</u> if judge says nothing, **presume "without prejudice"** – but it's a rebuttable presumption

<u>**v.**</u> 41b covers involuntary dismissals (12b6's, 12c's – judgment on pleadings, SJ's) – but:

<u>**vi.**</u> **41b no longer controls RJ, so go back to the CL rules**

<u>**vii.**</u> "dismissal without prejudice" – primary meaning is that P may return to same court with the same claim (normally when w/o prejudice – no RJ in the next court) – but, **if you get a 41b, there may be RJ based on CL saying it is with prejudice**

<u>**viii.**</u> HYPO – F-1 judge issues 41b dismissal "with prejudice" b/c court lacks SMJ

<u>**1.**</u> file in F-2, judge looks at RJ effect F-1 judge would give it – all "with prejudice" says is can't go back to same court – F-2 is *different court* now so No RJ

<u>**ix.**</u> **Every Rule 52 – bench trial judgment – is ON THE MERITS even though it says "without prejudice"** (brought to you by Antonin Scalia)

<u>**x.**</u> **RJ effect of voluntary dismissal under Rule 41a – usually, not on the merits unless P has vol. dismissed twice** – normally, at CL was without prejudice, but has been altered by statute: (1) if before close of P's case in chief without prejudice; (2) if after close of P's case in chief with prejudice

<u>**1.**</u> **41(a)(1)** – P acts unilaterally and dismisses suit before answer or before D moves for SJ – then automatic and **without prejudice**

<u>**2.**</u> **41(a)(2)** – if D has filed SJ motion, then P must get judge's permission for voluntary dismissal – judge may dismiss upon such terms and conditions as he deems proper – 41a2 **presumed without prejudice unless judge says otherwise**

<u>**3.**</u> P who voluntarily dismisses twice – **41a says this is on the merits** – P is barred from filing 3rd suit

<u>**xi.**</u> *Gargallo v. Merill Lynch*

<u>**1.**</u> court determines that OH claim preclusion law would bar Gargallo's suit – based on Ohio 'emodies the same cause of action" test

<u>**2.**</u> however, the judgment was rendered by a state court that lacked subject matter jurisdiction on the claim (which was exclusively within federal jurisdiction)

<u>**3.**</u> so, OH court would not preclude Gargallo's claim, thus the gederal court will not preclude it either – **OH law says judgment rendered by court lacking SMJ should not be given preclusive effect (this is the Restatement view)**

<u>**xii.**</u> **Federal Rule says give claim preclusive effect even if rendered without SMJ**

<u>**1.**</u> HYPO – F-1(OH) who did not have SMJ renders judgment. P files in F-2(CA) and F-2 judge looks over to F-1 judge in Ohio and does what he would do, which would be to give FULL RJ EFFECT – honor our judgment until the judgment is set aside (by 60b4)

<u>**II.**</u> **<u>COLLATERAL ESTOPPEL – Issue Preclusion</u>**

<u>**a.**</u> **Elements**

<u>**i.**</u> **Same Issue**

<u>**ii.**</u> Issue **actually litigated**

<u>**iii.**</u> Issue **actually decided**

<u>**iv.**</u> Issue **was necessary to be decided** (essential to the judgment) – not obiter dicta

<u>**b.**</u> **The Same Issue**

<u>**i.**</u> Civil vs. Criminal burdens of proof

<u>**1.**</u> criminal burden is much higher: "beyond a reasonable doubt"

<u>**2.**</u> civil burden is lower: "preponderance of the evidence"

        <u>3.</u> <u>Ex. 1</u> – D is acquitted in crimal trial; then Govt. sues D in civil trial – no issue preclusion, because we don't know where the bouncy ball was in criminal trial (all we know is it was less than reas. doubt – don't know if more than preponderance)

        <u>4.</u> <u>Ex. 2</u> – reverse – Govt. wins in civil action – then in criminal trial no issue preclusion since burden is much higher – don't know if bouncy ball was far enough

        <u>5.</u> <u>Ex. 3</u> – If found guilty in criminal trial, then burden is easily met for civil trial

<u>c.</u> **Actually Litigated and Determined**

    <u>i.</u> *Illinois Central RR v. Parks*

        <u>1.</u> RR was not able to use issue preclusion against Jessie since the jury did not necessarily find him contrib. negligent in first suit (may have found he didn't sufficiently prove damages) – it was a general verdict – **"opacity of the general verdict"**

        <u>2.</u> to prevent this, RR could have submitted special interrogatory to jury under rule 49

        <u>3.</u> The jury did find RR negligent so Jessie could now offensively use this finding to collaterally estop RR from arguing it was not negligent

<u>d.</u> **Essential to the Judgment**

    <u>i.</u> <u>Judgment in the alternative</u> – i.e. dismisses on **two issues** (or rules based on 2 alternative reasons) – (Rest. Judgments §27)

        <u>1.</u> i.e. P files in F-1 and D's moition to dismiss is granted for no PJ 12b2 and no SMJ 12b1, then D refiles in state court S-2 and D claims collateral estoppel

            <u>a.</u> if F-1 judge dismissed for no SMJ, S-2 judge does not care; but if F-1 judge dismissed for no PJ then this applies in S-2 also (assuming F-1 and S-2 in same state)

            <u>b.</u> **Rest. 2d – says <u>neither</u> issue should be given claim preclusive effect in this situation – WHY?**

                <u>i.</u> judge may not have given adequate consideration for both since he had two options

                <u>ii.</u> P also may not have appealed if 2 dispositive issues were staring him in the eye

    <u>ii.</u> <u>Appeal of judgment in the alternative</u>

        <u>1.</u> if appellate court affirms both issues and either would be sufficient alone to support the result, then give issue preclusive effect to **both issues**

        <u>2.</u> if app. ct. affirms on one but not the other, give issue preclusive effect **only to the first determination**

        <u>3.</u> if app. ct. affirms on one but does not consider the other, give issue preclusive effect **only to the first determination**

<u>e.</u> **Mutuality of Parties**

    <u>i.</u> Old rule required mutuality of parties – had to have the same parties in A-1 as in A-2 (P1 and D1)

        <u>1.</u> no good reason to require mutuality – why should a party who is not bound by the RJ effect of a judgment not be able to assert collateral estoppel against a party who is bound by its RJ effect?

        <u>2.</u> **mutuality requirement has been abandoned – F&FO is our test for due process**

    <u>ii.</u> In a mutuality jurisdiction, parties could not claim collateral estoppel in examples below, *unless you could show privity to satisfy mutuality requirement*

    <u>iii.</u> Defensive nonmutual collateral estoppel developed first – P1 could foresee such a

situation
- **iv.** <u>Defensive Nonmutual Collateral Estoppel</u>
    1. <u>A-1:</u> P1 v. D1 (P1 loses)
    2. <u>A-2:</u> P1 v. D2
    3. D2 uses def. nonmutual col. estoppel ("throws up a shield")
- **v.** <u>Offensive Nonmutual Collateral Estoppel</u>
    1. <u>A-1:</u> P1 v. D1 (P1 wins)
    2. <u>A-2:</u> P2 v. D1
    3. P2 uses off. nonmutual col. estoppel ("throws up a sword")
- **vi.** **Federal courts allow both kinds of nonmutual collateral estoppel** (they adopted offensive nonmutual in *Parklane Hosiery*)
    1. some jurisdictions don't allow it
- **vii.** **Why do some courts not allow offensive nonmutual collateral estoppel? (why do they "stop at defensive nonmutual collateral estoppel?)**
    1. it does not promote judicial economy in the same manner as defensive does
        a. def. col. estop. gives P strong incentive to join all potential D's
        b. off. col. estop. creates the opposite incentive – a wait and see attitude to see if another P's outcome is favorable (and then choose to rely on it – if they lose then you can still bring your own suit since you're a stranger)
    2. it may be unfair to Defendant – D may not have had F & FO to litigate the issue in the first suit
- **viii.** *Parklane Hosiery*
    1. D Parklane claims P should not be able to use off. non. col. estoppel because first suit was for injunction (so no jury available) and this suit was for damages (7th amendment right to jury trial) – court says: 7th amendment? Heck with that.
    2. P was allowed to use off. nonmutual col. estop. against Parklane – P was not being rewarded for not joining the first suit since P could not have joined first suit – it was action by the SEC
    3. there was also no unfairness to D's – it's foreseeable that private suits will follow a successful government suit
    4. the judgment in the first suit was not inconsistent with any prior judgment
    5. D will not have any procedural opportunities available that weren't available in the First suit
    6. **HYPO** – change facts of parklane – first judgment was in state court, S-1 who finds against Parklane
        a. In F-2, judge must give FF&C to S-1 and must do what the S-1 judge would do – if state of S-1 would not allow offensive nonmutual collateral estoppel, then F-2 cannot allow it
        b. but, if parties were same in S-1 and F-2, then we have mutuality and offensive *mutual* collateral estoppel would work
- **f.** **"The Victim" of Issue Preclusion – F & FO**
    - **i.** In order to use nonmutual collateral estoppel against a party, they must have had a **full and fair opportunity to litigate the issue in the first action (F&FO)**
    - **ii.** **F&FO – <u>Full and Fair Opportunity</u> – Rest. §29 Judgments – consider whether: (8 factors to consider)**
        1. treating issue as conclusively determined would be **incompatible** with an applicable scheme of administering remedies in the actions involved
        2. the **forum** in the 2nd action affords the party against whom preclusion is

asserted **procedural opportunities** in the presentation and determination of the issue that were **not available in the first action** and that could **likely result in issue being determined differently**

    3. the person seeking to invoke favorable preclusion, or to avoid unfavorable preclusion, **could have effected joinder in the first action between himself and his present adversary**

    4. the determination relied on as preclusive was itself **inconsistent with another determination of the same issue**

    5. prior determination may have been **affected by relationships among the parties** to the first action that are **not present in the subsequent** action, or apparently was based on a **compromise verdict or finding**

    6. treating the issue as conclusively determined may **complicate determination of issues** in the subsequent action or **prejudice the interests of any party** thereto

    7. the **issue is one of law** and treating it as conclusively determined would **inappropriately foreclose opportunity for obtaining reconsideration of the legal rule** upon which it was based

    8. **other compelling circumstances** make it appropriate that the party be permitted to re-litigate the issue

  iii. *Teitelbaum Furs, Inc.*

    1. S-1: govt. convicts teitelbaum in criminal case for stealing his own furs and trying to collect insurance for theft – Teitelbaum took the 5th amendment

    2. S-2: Teitelbaum v. Insurance Co. – he sues his insurance co. to try to recover value of furs – Teitelbaum says no nonmutual collateral estoppel against him since he took the 5th in first case – court said sorry, **that was just your strategy** – you still had F&FO in first case, so you are issue precluded

g. Cannot use issue preclusion **against a stranger** – he/she never had his/her **day in court**

  i. (D cannot use defensive nonmutual issue preclusion against a new P)

h. **Issue Preclusion and Contributory/Comparative Negligence**

  i. Contributory Negligence

    1. HYPO – A-1: L v. N for negligence – N claims contrib. but L wins

      a. if L won, then jury necessarily found N negligent and L contrib.

      b. A-2: R v. L for negligence – can L assert his victory as a shield? No, R **is a stranger** to A1 (he never had his day in court)

    2. HYPO – A-1: B v. R for negligence – B wins

      a. if B won, then R was negligent and B was not contrib.

      b. A-2: R v. H for neg. – can H throw up a shield? Yes, this is defensive nonmutual CE

      c. Instead, A-2: H v. R – can H throw a sword? depends on the J – this is offensive nonmutual col. estoppel – did R have F&FO? If so, then yes

  ii. Comparative Negligence

    1. HYPO – S-1: Driver A (found 70% negligent) v. Diver B (30%)

      a. S-2: Passenger v. Drvs. A & B –can Passenger throw a sword? Yes, in general, that is allowed (if state allows nonmutual)

      b. Can Passenger sue only A and throw a sword? Yes, and most J's say can get 100% of his injuries by joint and several liability (A can then sue B and throw a sword – its mutual now too)

    2. HYPO – S-2 state has modified rule on joint and several saying she can only recover from each driver in proportion with their fault

      a. S-2: Passenger v. Driver A – passenger **is a stranger** to first action so may choose not to accept S-1's determination of A's liability and relitigate (A can't throw up a shield to stop Passenger for going for 100%)

    b. but, passenger may not accept the finding of liability without accepting the limitation on its amount – **MUST TAKE THE BITTER WITH THE SWEET**

    c. <u>S-2:</u> Instead, Passenger v. Driver A – passenger throws a sword at Driver A to get $70K from him based on S-1

    d. <u>then in S-3:</u> Pass. v. Drv. B – now pass. does not want to be bound by S-1 and get more than $30K from B – NOPE – **GOTTA TAKE THE BITTER WITH THE SWEET**

3. HYPO – **phantom defendant situation** (party who could have been sued in first suit but was not) – collateral estoppel may not be possible if the addition of the phantom defendant would change the percentages of comparative negligence

    a. seems sensible to throw preclusion out in this situation

    b. in more aggressive J's, a D who was found comparatively negligent in first action may be estopped from denying that he had at least *some* negligence (how much is that? 1%?)

i. **Lots of Subsequent Plaintiffs (Prior Inconsistent Judgments)**

    i. *State Farm*

      1. S-1: P1 v. D (D wins)

      2. S-1': on remand for trial, D wins

      3. S-2: P2 v. D (D wins)

      4. S-3: P3 v. D (P3 wins)

      5. S-4: P4 – P25 now want to use offensive nonmutual collateral estoppel (ONCE) against D – can all the subsequent P's throw a sword? No

      6. **No Off. Nonmut. Col. Estop. when the prior judgments are <u>inconsistent</u> – court says there was no F&FO**

      7. **-But, a number of subsequent determinations to the contrary may allow off. nonmut. col. estop. to later be used by subsequent P's**

      8. if prior verdict was product of **jury compromise**, then loser should also not be precluded by the judgment (how can D attack the verdict if the jury not allowed to testify to impeach their own verdict)

<u>Reopening Judgments (or Setting Aside Judgments) – Rule 60b</u>

I.   **<u>Rule 60</u>**

    a. Rule 60a – clerical mistakes

    b. **RULE 60b**

      i. Motion - on motion and upon such terms are just, court *__may__* grant party relief from an earlier judgment: (entirely discretionary)

        1. (1) mistake, inadvertence, surprise, or excusable neglect

        2. (2) newly discovered evidence which by due diligence could not have been discovered in time to move for a new trial under Rule 59(b) – 10 days

        3. (3) fraud (extrinsic or intrinsic), misrepresentation, or other misconduct **of an adverse party**

          a. extrinsic – "fraud on the court" – more serious – bribery, threats, etc.

          b. intrinsic – only between parties, i.e. one party perjured herself

        4. (4) judgment is void (i.e. no SMJ, etc.)

        5. (5) the judgment has been satisfied, released, or discharged, or a prior judgment upon which it is based has been reversed or otherwise vacated, or it is no longer equitable that the judgment should have prospective application

      6. (6) any other reason justifying relief from the operation of the judgment (the "catch all" last resort – this is **slim pickings**)

    ii. Timeliness

      1. (1-3) must be **within a reasonable time** <u>and</u> within 1 year (may still be untimely if within 1 year)

      2. (4-6) may still be timely within a year but have to be **within a reasonable time**

      3. severe time limits b/c 60b motions are disfavored

    iii. Does it matter what *type* of judgment it is? (not in the rule)

      1. court may give less weight to a default judgment

      2. may give more weight to judgments that have gone through full appeals process

    iv. Remedy – court has discretion – will do whatever logically makes sense at that point

  c. Do NOT overstate its practical availability – post-trial motions and appeals are the primary mechanisms for correcting errors

  d. **relief under 60(b) is NOT a substitute for appeal – YOU ALWAYS WANT TO APPEAL AND NOT HAVE TO RELY ON 60b**

  e. *US v. Beggerly* – land dispute

    i. the "independent action" survives despite Rule 60(b), though it did abolish the old CL writs (coram nobis, coram vobis, audita querela, bills of review, and nature of review)

    ii. Beggerly trying to bring independent action since 1 year limit had passed for his possible 60b2 or 60b3 claim (newly discovered evidence that couldn't have been discovered with due diligenge; fraud or misrepresentation of an adverse party)

      1. these probably would have failed anyway – he now discovered the documents easily so prob. no due diligence and not clear that govt. had tried to hide them

    iii. no independent action since no grave miscarriage of justice – didn't even come close

  f. **Independent Action** – an extremely narrow channel of obtaining relief from a judgment (a.k.a. "original action") that is *outside the relief provided by 60b* – (Beggerly was trying for one since he couldn't bring 60b)

    i. Requirements:

      1. **grave miscarriage of justice**

        a. ex. a forged document – might qualify as new evidence of fraud on the court

      2. **would change the outcome of the original action**

        a. probably don't need "absolute certainty", but the standard on this is unclear

        b. i.e. if the documents had been admitted, there was no absolute certainty that Beggerly would have won in the first suit

Miscellaneous

I. **Rule 65 – TRO's and Preliminary Injunctions**

  a. TRO's

    i. chronologically, start with 65b – Temporary Restraining Orders (TRO's)

    ii. TRO's granted w/o notice to other side – last 10 days, renewable up to 10 days – not a final judgment

  b. Preliminary Injunction

    i. common – esp. in const. or civil rights cases

      1. What's $$ value of being able to speak freely or not be discriminated against?

       ii. immediately appealable (as an exception to final judgment rule) whether or not granted or denied

       iii. **may be a way of getting expedited trial**

          1. judges don't want to have two trials

          2. **consolidation** – can have trial on merits at same time as determination of injunction (if wins, becomes permanent injunction)

             a. many of these cases are on pure law and not facts

II. **Rule 62a-d – Stay of Proceedings to Enforce a Judgment**

   a. **12 days to file a motion for <u>JMOL</u> or in the alternative for <u>new trial</u>**

   b. judge can collect on the judgment 10 days after judgment

   c. so, may have pending JMOL while other side is trying to collect

   d. **Monetary judgments**

       i. under 62, **A Party may stay the collection on the judgment pending the JMOL/new trial motion**

          1. court will require party to post a **supersedeas bond (62d)** to cover costs

   e. **Equitable judgments (injunctions)**

       i. the judgment loser must comply while pending *unless the court of appeals will stay it*

Themes for Civil Procedure

1. **Notice** – timely served and content fairly apprises what's at stake

2. **Hearing** – your day in court – reasonable opportunity to put your best foot forward with your chosen champion to fight your battles

3. **Power** – legitimacy of the court sitting in judgment over you (reciprocity, inconvenience, etc.)

4. **Efficiency** – come on strong in recent times – liberal joinder, discovery – expanding RJ and col. estop., expanding comp. counterclaims, etc. – under docket pressures (cost-benefit analysis)

5. **Self-Critical** – appeals – we know and assume mistakes will be made (2 sorts of mistakes – 1)innocent or unintentional mistakes and then 2)non-innocent mistakes of prejudice, parochialisms, passion, malice, etc.)

6. **Finality** – full, faith, and credit, SOL, juries can't impeach own verdict, narrowness of 60b setting aside, RJ, col. estop. – all this directed at peace – at some point need for peace supercedes need to fight for resolution

7. **Consistency** – preclusion (RJ and col. estop.), Erie, choice of law rules, narrow 60b

8. **Impartiality** – jury (Batson rules for race discrim.), disqualification of a judge

9. **Self-Interest** – it's fairly unforgiving system (your lawyer messes up – you're stuck), full of rules some highly complex must think of everything all the time even though hard – it's all put on self-responsibility – your lawyer better be reliable – don't raise an objection at trial, it's lost

10. **Balance** – Justice / Mercy – hard choices are not between good and evil but between good and good. – mercy is to say I will take each case on its special facts – justice is not ad hoc it's the unforgiving, albeit even handed, in a way that does not ameliorate the result in a specific case –

we see some judges that have more nature of justice and some of mercy

11.

CONTRACTS

Intro & Assent

I. Fundamentals of Contracts
   a. Voluntary exchange creates wealth
      i. Pareto efficient – someone better off, none worse off
      ii. Kalder-Hicks efficient – total wealth enhanced, but someone worse off, potentially Pareto efficient if winner compensates loser
   b. Necessary to force performance when facts chance
      i. Between the promise and the actual performance
   c. Ultimate goals- create wealth via Efficiency or ethical means
   d. Enforce the parties expectations
   e. RST 1 – contract is a promise for which the law provides a remedy
   f. Economic Remedies
      i. C/L must pay damages if breach
      ii. *Naval v. Charter* -Efficient Breach Hypothesis – promisor will exercise option to breach and pay expectation damages instead of performing when in promisor's best interest
      iii. Pareto-improving- transaction that makes no one worse off while making someone better off

II. Assent – intent to do something and manifestation of intent w/ words or actions
   a. Offer and acceptance, determined by an objective test
   b. Must have control to have assent, must have capacity to contract (RST 14 &15)
   c. If there are different meanings there is no mutual assent
   d. Specific Performance – ruling requiring party to fulfill duties of contract
      i. RULE: an agreement or mutual assent is essential to a valid contract (***Lucy v. Zehmer***)
      ii. **TEST: has the promisor done something to make promisee (or reasonable person) believe that the promisor intends to be bound**

OFFER

Pen ultimate step in contracting is the offer

I. What Constitutes an Offer
   a. RST 24 – offer is the manifestation of willingness to enter into a bargain, so made as to justify another person in understanding that his assent to that bargain is invited and will conclude it
      i. Would a reasonable person in the position of the offeree feel they have the power to close the deal by saying yes?

II. **Requirements for a Valid Offer**
   a. **Manifestation of present contractual intent**
   b. **Certainty and definiteness of terms**
   c. **Communication to the offeree** – must be communication to offeree, in no other way will it create power of acceptance – i.e. if A prepares an offer for B intending to mail it but never does no contract
   d. **TEST – Would a reasonable person in the position of the offeree feel that if he accepted the proposal a contract would be complete**

III. Price Quotes and Advertisements
   a. Price Quotation – a simple quotation of price usually construed merely as an invitation to the buyer to make an offer (***Owen v. Tunnison***)
   b. "For Immediate Acceptance" – D's quotation of prices for immediate acceptance is more than

a quotation and constituted an offer (***Fairmount Glass Works v. Crunden-Marten Woodenware Co.***)

    c. Advertisements – generally deemed invitations to deal b/c (1) are usually indefinite as to quantity and other terms (2) sellers ought to be able to choose with whom they deal and (3) gives the seller another say and protects them from oversubscription

        i. Exception to Ad Rule – advertisements addressed to the public are considered binding if the facts show that some performance is definitely promised for something requested (***Lefkowitz v. Great Minneapolis Surplus Store***)

        ii.   Bait and Switch Ads – Uniform Deceptive Practice Act prevents these

ACCEPTANCE

I.   **Acceptance** – a voluntary act of the offeree whereby he exercises the power of the offer

    a. Default Rules

        i. **RST § 30** – acceptance can be by any means reasonable in the circumstances when they are unclear

        ii.   **RST § 32** – acceptance either by promising to perform what the offer requests or by rendering the performance as the offeree chooses

        iii.   **RST § 50** – manifestation of assent though the manner invited or required

    b. Offer may only be accepted by the person to whom it is made

    c. Acceptance must be unequivocal and unqualified

II.   **Requirements for valid Acceptance**

    a. Acceptance by Promise - **Bilateral contracts** – acceptance requires the offeree to give some type of return promise

        i. All that is required is the counter promise based on reasonable person standard

        ii.   **Acceptance by Promise - RST§ 56 - unless otherwise specified, the offeree must notify the offeror of his acceptance by promise seasonably and with reasonable diligence**(***Int. Nat'l Filter v Conroe***)

        iii.   Can also be **Acceptance by Performance RST § 62 – when offeree has to choose** btwn acceptance by promise and acceptance by performance **a beginning of performance is an acceptance** – such an acceptance **operates as a promise to complete performance**

    b. Acceptance by Performance **Unilateral Contracts** – offeree specifies contract occurs only on completion of performance

        i. **RST § 54 – when offer invites acceptance though performance, notice is not required unless specified, if offeror has not means of learning of the performance contractual duties are discharged unless**

            1. Offeree exercises reasonable diligence to notify

            2. Offeror learns of the performance in a reasonable time

            3. The offer indicated that notification was not required

        ii.   Notice is not required. Kx upon commencement or completion (***White v. Corlies and Tift, Carbolic Smokeball,***)

        iii.   Very rare – only way to accept is to complete 100% of performance – for the most part unilateral Kx's are limited to offers for rewards

        iv.   When the offeree doesn't clearly specify whether acceptance had to be by promise or performance, the mode chosen by the offeree has to indicate to the offeror that he has accepted

            1. Action must be reasonably calculated to put the offeror on notice

            2. The beginning of performance constitutes a promise to complete performance

    c. Notice of Acceptance – if not specified default rules apply

        i. Attempted acceptance by promise – RST § 56 governs

  ii. Attempted acceptance by performance – RST § 54 governs
    1. Offeror Discharges his duty if there is no adequate means of learning of performance, offeree fails to use reasonable diligence to inform, offeror doesn't learn of acceptance and offer doesn't indicated that notice is not required *(Bishop v. Eaton)*

 d. Shipment of goods is an acceptance
   i. UCC 2-206 – order or offer to buy goods for prompt or current shipment invites acceptance by
    1. Prompt promise to ship
    2. Prompt shipment of conforming or non-conforming goods
     a. If shipment is non-conforming goods and buyer is seasonably notified that the shipment was a mere accommodation then no acceptance, that shipment is a counter-offer and a rejection of the original offer and not an acceptance *(Corinthian Pharmaceutical v. Lederle)*

 e. Silence not ordinarily acceptance
   i. RST § 69 –silence and inaction only operate as acceptance when
    1. the offeree (1) takes benefit of offered services (2) with reasonable opportunity to reject then and (3) with reason to know that they were offered with expectation of compensation
    2. Offeror stated or given reason to understand that silence or inaction is acceptance and the offeree, in remaining silent, intends to accept the offer – intent is key to acceptance
    3. Due to previous dealings it is reasonable that the offeree should notify the offeror if he does not intend to accept
     a. Ongoing relationship where parties understand that silence is acceptance *(Hobbs. V Massasoit Whip)*

III. **Terminating the Power of Acceptance**
 a. **Lapse of the offer (RST § 41)- after some period of time an offer lapses – if no time specified it lapses after a reasonable time:**
   i. reasonable time necessary to conduct due diligence *(Ever-tite v. Green)*
   ii. value volatility – rapid price fluctuations can cause a lapse *(Ever-tite v. Green)*
   iii. face to face conversation – offer ends with the conversation
   iv. offer for a reward must be notorious if it excites vigilance
   v. lapse cannot be waived by the offeror, if offeree accepts after the lapse it is a counter offer that original offeror can accept but not by silence (RST § 69)

 b. **Offeror's Death or Legal Incapacity (RST § 48) – acceptance terminated by offeror's death or supervening incapacity even if offeree doesn't know of offeror's death**
   i. Offer terminates on death of offeror, debt does not terminate on death of offeror
   ii. Death or incapacity does not terminate power of acceptance under option contract
   iii. Death of a party after contract formation may affect obligations of the contract

 c. **Revocation by the Offeror (RST § 42) – an offer can be terminated any time before acceptance**
   i. General Rule – offer is freely revocable, power of acceptance is terminated when offeree receives from the offeror a manifestation of an intention not to enter into the contract
   ii. **Firm Offers – UCC 2-205 – a merchant's signed promise to keep an offer open will be enforceable regardless of consideration - stays open for 3 months if:**
    1. Must agree on terms supplied by/on the form
    2. Offeror must be a merchant
    3. Offer must be signed

4. If form supplied by offeree, offeror must separately sign the form to keep it open

iii. **Option Contract – promise made that effectively limits the offeror's power to revoke. Usually option expressed directly or indirectly for a fixed period in which the offeree must "pick up" option**

1. Must clothe the promise – offeree must give something in return for the promise (***Dickenson v Dodds***)
2. RST § 25 - The option – a promise which meets the requirements for the formation of a contract and limits the promisor's power to revoke an offer

iv. Direct or indirect communication of revocation

1. RST § 43 – revocation indirectly – power of acceptance is terminated when the offeror takes an action inconsistent with intention to ender K and offeree receives reliable information to that effect – info must be from reliable source and true
2. General Offers – RST § 46 – notice of termination of offer must be given publicly in a manner equal to that given to the offer when no better means of notification available

   a. Constructive notice – doesn't matter if person who saw original offer saw the revocation (i.e. newspaper revocation)
   b. Revocation must be on the same terms as the offer in the same medium to same audience

d. Offeree's Rejection – power of acceptance terminates when you make initial rejection, later acceptance is considered a counter-offer

i. **Mirror Image Rule – acceptance must be on the terms proposed by the offer without the slightest variation (*Minneapolis and STL RR Co v. Columbus*)**

ii. **Battle of the Forms – purchase order from has legal type to benefit the offeror, the offeree's acceptance/order form has legal type beneficial to the offeree – when terms differ who's terms do we use?**

1. **Last Shot Rule – the terms are those included on the last form that was exchanged between the parties prior to mutual performance**

iii. These Rules do not apply to the sale of goods per UCC 2-207

e. Mailbox Rule – involve communications about acceptance, rejection and revocation

i. Acceptance occurs when offeree sends the message
ii. Revocation by the offeror occurs when the offeree actually gets the message
iii. Rejection by the offeror occurs only when the offeror actually gets the message
iv. **Acceptance on answer rejection and revocation on receipt**
v. Default Rules for Mailbox Rule

1. RST § 40 – when offeree has already sent counteroffer or rejection and later sends acceptance, acceptance only valid when offeror receives it before counteroffer/rejection
2. RST § 42 – ability to accept terminated when offeror manifests intention not to enter Kx
3. RST § 43 – offeree's power to accept terminated when offeror actions in a manner that is inconsistent with the acceptance
4. RST § 46 – when an advertisement or general offer is made offeree can no longer accept if a public termination is given in the same manner
5. RST § 58 – acceptance must comply with the terms of the offer
6. RST § 60 – if an offer state time, place, etc. of acceptance they must be followed. If not specific you do not have to strictly follow them
7. RST § 61 – acceptance that requests a change or addition to the offer is not

invalidated unless assent to those terms is required
8. RST §63(b) – acceptation of an option Kx is not operative until received by the offeror

IV. **UCC 2-207 Additional Terms in acceptance or confirmation – varying acceptances**
  a. **Alters mirror image rule and last shot rule in regards to merchants and the sale of goods**
  b. **2-207(1) – tells us when we have a contract on the basis of writings. Alters mirror image rule by allowing additional or different terms than those offered or agreed upon unless acceptance is made conditional on assent to the different or additional terms**
    i. **If acceptance is definite and seasonable then there is acceptance even if there are different or additional terms**
    ii. **No acceptance if the written acceptance says contract is binding if only assent to additional terms**
  c. **2-207(2) – tells what additional terms apply if there is a valid acceptance –**
    i. **applies if there is a contract based on (1) provided:**
      1. **Both parties are merchants**
        a. UCC 2-104 – a merchant is a person who deals in goods, holds himself out as having knowledge about the goods or who has agents that hold themselves out as having particular knowledge of the goods
      2. **Offer does not expressly limit the terms of the offer**
      3. **Additional terms do not materially alter the deal**
        a. UCC 2-207 Material Alteration
          i. Alter – those that negate warranties, those requiring higher guaranty than is industry standard, those that allow a seller to cancel upon buyer's failure to meet invoice when due, and those that require complaints to be made in unreasonable or uncustomary time, arbitration clauses
          ii. Don't Alter – dealing with exemption due to supervening causes, those fixing reasonable time for complaints and those limiting rejection for defects within customary trade tolerances
          iii. **What constitutes a material alteration? – the alteration must be surprising and a hardship (must result in a surprising hardship)**
            1. Surprising & Hardship = material alteration
            2. Surprising but not Hardship = material alteration
            3. Not Surprising but Hardship = no material alteration
              a. The Key is if there is an UNREASONABLY SURPRISNG HARDSHIP
              b. AN ALTERATION IS MATERIAL IF CONSENT TO IT CANNOT BE PRESUMED
      4. **Notification of the additional terms is given in a seasonable or timely manner**
    ii. When Terms Differ but there is a valid contract
      1. Knockout rule – apply 2-207(3) use like terms and UCC gap fillers for different terms (Majority)
      2. Use the offeror's terms (Leading Minority Rule)
      3. Treat the different terms the same way 2-207(2) treats additional terms (Minority View)
    iii. Additional terms are only construed as proposals for additions
  d. **2-207(3) – if no contract on the basis of writings but both parties perform that is sufficient to establish a contract for the sale. Terms of contract not governed by Last**

Shot Rule.
    i. **Terms of the deal are all the terms where writings agree**
    ii.   **Any disagreement is eliminated and replaced w/ default terms of the UCC**
    iii.   Conflict in **Shrinkwrap/Clickwrap licenses**
        1. **Written confirmation (Step-Saver v. Wise)** – when product arrives after ordering and has additional terms they are considered written confirmation and 2-207(2) analysis applies
        2. **Rolling K analysis** – since most people expect additional terms inside the box, acceptance does not occur until consumer has a chance to read over the terms and 30 days has elapsed
        3. **New Rolling K Analysis – since a reasonable person expects terms inside the box, notice is not important, only need the right to return the product and if a reasonable person would expect terms to be inside the box (ProCD v. Zeidenberg)**

CONSIDERATION

I.   **Consideration**
    a. **RST § 71** - either (1) performance or (2) a return promise
        i. Must be bargained for
        ii.   Performance may consist of
            1. An act other than a promise
            2. A forbearance – waiver of any legal right at the request of another
                a. Must be (1) absolute or (2) for a definite or reasonable time
            3. The creation, modification or destruction of a legal relation
        iii.   Past performance is not valid for consideration
        iv.   Some promises are enforceable w/o consideration
            1. RST § 83 – reiteration of a promise to pay a debt discharged by bankruptcy
            2. Minor- an infant (under 18) enters into a contract and after 18 reiterates his promise, subsequent promise is enforceable despite not being supported by consideration
            3. RST § 82 – Statute of Limitations on a collection action (borrowed money) – original borrower agrees to pay after the statute runs out is enforceable

II.   **BARGAINED FOR EXCHANGE TEST** – RST § 79
    a. A performance or a return promise msut be bargained for
    b. Bargained for if it is sought by the promisor in echange for his promise and is given by the promisee in exchange for his promise
    c. LAMBERT TEST
        i. DID IT INDUCE THE PROMISE? MUST INDUCE THE PROMISE
        ii.   WAS IT INDUCED BY THE PROMISE? MUST BE INDUCED BY THE PROMISE
            1. If the answer to both of these is yes then there is consideration
            2. Must have a reciprocal inducement
        iii.   Once the test is met there is no additional requirement of
            1. Benefit/detriment
            2. Equivalence in the values exchanged
            3. Mutuality of obligation

III.   Promises Not Supported by Consideration
    a. Moral Obligation
        i. No moral consideration BUT moral obligation + promise to pay = legally enforceable
        ii.   If the promisor has a moral obligation and the moral obligation is based on the

receipt of a benefit then enforceable
1. Cannot be gratuitous
2. Promisor cannot be unjustly enriched
3. Promise is enforceable only to the amount of the benefit
4. Only done to the extent necessary to prevent injustice
   b. Sufficiency/Peppercorns
   i. Peppercorn- the clear appearance that the parties are attempting to evade the gratuitous promise rule by adding a small exchange – not supported by consideration
1. Is the promisee masking a gift? No consideration
2. Have to be able to do the action or else it is a peppercorn – narrow proviso
   c. Gratuitous promise
   i. Gratuitous promise – the court will not enforce promise to give a gift with no benefit
1. Nominal consideration doesn't work – if you're simply naming that you've given consideration or you're making a gratuitous promise there is no consideration
   ii. Non enforceable
   iii. **Fundamental Consideration Rule – a promise to make a give is not legally enforceable**
   d. Rewards
   i. Thing that is given must have been induced by that promise
   ii. If did not know of reward but performed anyway - no contract
1. RST § 51 – an acceptance by completing the requested performance w/o knowledge of the offer is okay unless the offeror manifests a contrary intention
   iii. Knowledge of reward BUT performance for an ulterior motive – contract
1. RST § 81(2) – the fact that the promisee does not induce a performance or return promise does not prevent the performance or return promise from being consideration
2. Would a reasonable person in the position of the promisee deem the promise a plus factor that would cause him to be more likely to perform even if there is a subjective reason for performance?
   e. Illusory promises – looks like a promise but has no teeth and is impossible to break
   i. A statement which appears to be promising something but which in fact does not commit the promisor to do anything
   ii. Not supported by consideration if return promise does not bind the maker
   iii. A promise is illusory if a party's performance of that promise is entirely at the option of that party
IV. Promises as Consideration
   a. Employment agreements – covenants not to compete
   i. RULE: employment agreements are at will – employee is free to quit at any moment for any reason and employer is free to fire employee at any moment for any reason
   ii. There is consideration in employment agreements if
1. If employee makes a promise in order to get hired
2. If employee has been working for a while employer asks for a return promse but nothing additional is given to the employee
3. Promise for continued at will employment (MO & OH VIEW)
4. Promise for continued at will employment PLUS actual at will employment for some reasonable period of time after employee signs covenant (TN Supp. Ct. View)
   a. MN VIEW - Promise of continued at will employment is not consideration

b. Satisfaction clauses

    i. Not illusory promises

    ii. Objective Standard - Reasonable person standard – if a reasonable person would find satisfaction or deem satisfaction received

        1. Often there will be a satisfaction issue where reasonable minds will not differ – i.e. waiting on an engineering report before buying a building

    iii. Subjective Standard – Good Faith Standard – satisfaction is determined by promisor's determination that he is not satisfied when made in good faith, based on his own judgment, fancy or taste

        1. Satisfaction conditions can have reasonable minds differing sometimes – matters of taste

    iv. In order for promise to be non-illusory it must bind the promisor

    v. Courts prefer to impose reasonable person standard

V. UCC 2-306 Requirement, Output and Exclusive Licensing Contracts

    a. Exclusive Licensing/Dealing K's – "I give you the rights or I will deal only with you"

        i. UCC 2-306(2) requires reasonable effort, anytime exclusive agency, unless otherwise specified

        ii. Wood v Lucy – anytime someone accepts an exclusive agency and licensor's only compensation is from profits on the sale implied duty to undertake reasonable efforts to market goods

        iii. Contracts for exclusive licensing are not illusory

            1. If exclusive licensee does nothing with the rights they were promised he is not breaking any promises BUT

            2. There is an implied promise that an exclusive licensee will use a **good faith effort** to sell the product/name/object otherwise licensor wouldn't have agreeged

        iv. UCC 2-306 – if the licensor is silent assume that the licensee must use best efforts

        v. Majoritarian Default Rule - if judges know upfront that most parties are going to bargain for a term they will read that term into the background of the law and use a good faith effort to assume it's there

        vi. TEST - look for terms that imply that the promise is conditional then look to see if the promise is illusory in that the person has complete control over the condition

    b. Requriements K's – "I will purchase from you all that I require"

        i. UCC 2-306(2) – I promise to buy all that I in good faith require and if there is a dramatic change in demand I cannot force you to fill those needs

        ii. This promise is based on good faith standard

    c. Output K's – " I will sell you all that I produce"

        i. UCC 2-306 – I promise to sell you all that I in good faith produce and if there is adramatic change in production I cannot force you to buy them.

        ii. Promise is based on good faith standard

    d. Good Faith Standard – it must run its business in a usual manner, buying or selling as they normally would

        i. These K's often occur in a business to business transaction where one company offers a requirement and another offers an output in the same deal to guarantee supply and demand

PROMISSORY ESTOPPEL

I. Traditional View

    a. RST § 90 Promissory Estoppel Exists When:

   i. There is a promise

   ii. Promisee relies on that promise

   iii. Reasonable person in the postion of the promisor would expect reliance (promise induces reliance)

   iv. Justice requires enforcement (necessary to prevent injustice)

  b. If these elements were satisfied the promisor was not allowed to assert lack of consideration

  c. **P/E estops promisor from saying that lack of consideration makes the promise not enforceable if promisor has made a promise that has induced the promisee's reliance**

II. Modern Approach

  a. There is a promise

  b. Promisee or a 3rd party relies on the promise

  c. There is a remedy that justice requires – an amount of money lost by breach of the promise

   i. **Reliance interest** – goal of P/E damages is to put the promisee in the position as if the promise had not been made - **where would the victim have been if the promise had not been made – give that amount of money which was the loss to her reliance on the promise**

    1. **Most common P/E remedy**

   ii. **Expecancy interest -** goal of K law is to put the promisee in a position as if promise had been kept – promisee gets put in the postion they would have been if the promise had been kept and performance of the contract had occurred

  d. Reliance need not be of a definite and substantial character

   i. Makes it much easier to assert P/E because small reliance gives way to damages, but they will be small damages

III. Charitable subscription

  a. a promise to make a charitable gift to an institution or something of the like is enforceable

   i. Reliance not necessary by the promisee

   ii. Has not altered the practice of P/E

RESTITUTION

I. Restitution

  a. A perons will not be allowed to enrich himself unjustly at the expense of another

   i. If unjust enrichment – restitution pays back amount of the unjust enrichment

  b. RST § 371 – restitution is measured as justice requires, by either

   i. The reasonable value to the other party of what he received in terms of what it would have cost him to obtain it from a person in claimant's position

   ii. Or the extent to which the other party's property has been increased in value or his interests advanced

  c. If you are unjustly enriched you are legally obligated to pay back the remedy you received

   i. Restitution is an equitable remedy - may only be used if all legal remedies have been exhausted

II. Implied in Law Promises

  a. 3 types of promises generally

   i. **Express promises** – actually state the promise in the K (orally or in writing)

   ii. **Implied-in-Fact** – because of the dealings between the parties, we know that this is what they intended to do – there was is an actual promise but it is not expressed)

   iii. **Implied-In-Law** – the promise is totally made up based on the court's sense of justice – it's the right thing to do

1. One who is enriched at the expense of another has made an implied in law promise to pay back the amount of his enrichment
2. Express and implied in fact are both actual promises – enforceable by law
3. Court must be convinced to enforce implied in law – P is only entitled to restitution damages

b. No Restitution if Promise is:

   i. **Gratuitous** – if the enrichment is a gift the benefit provider can't sue to recover – NO implied in law promise
      1. CAVEAT – services provide by a professional who usually provides such services for a fee or the provision of services is tremendiously burdensome then restitution
         a. D desn't have to know P is a professional
   ii. **Officious** - unjustified intermeddling with the person or property of another – NO implied in law promise
      1. CAVEAT: honest mistake on the part of benefit provider and recipient is wholly innocent then no restitution HOWEVER if the recipient is in a position to stop the negligent conferment of a benefit the provider CAN sue for restitution
   iii. **Legal Remedy Available** – if the benefit provider has a legal remedy available – NO implied in law promise
      1. Includes breach of contract action- if benefit provider can bring a breach of contract he must do
      2. Actions seeking money damages are actions in law
      3. Specific performance is an action in equity – only available if no action in law available

III. **Carving out Restitution**
   a. **Court looks at all enrichment by a 3rd party action**
   b. **Then cuts out all cases in which enrichment was a gift**
   c. **Then cuts out all cases in which 3rd party was acting officiously**
   d. **Then cuts out all cases of enrichment where the 3rd party has a legal remedy**
   e. **Remainder is the possibility of Restitution**

IV. **Common Instances of Restitution**
   a. **Emergency services by medical professionals**
   b. **Benefit provider mistakenly provides the benefit to the wrhong person and the person benefited is aware of the mistake**
   c. **When the benefit provider has begun the action and the deal falls apart they are allowed restitution for the performance rendered**

LIABILITY PRIOR TO CONTRACT FORMATION

I. Irrevocable Option K's
   a. Unilateral K – once offeree has accepted the K is not complete until performance is rendered – there is no contract liability for the offeror he is free to revoke the offer
   b. Firm Offer – is an offer that the offeror promises he will not revoke for some period of time
   c. **RST § 45 - when offeree invites acceptance by performance and not promise an option K is created when offeree tenders or begins performance**
      i. Offeror's duty of performance under any option K created this way is conditional on the completion of the invited performance in accordance with the terms of the offer

d. Offer to enter into unilateral K is read legally as 2 promises
  i. I offer to pay you a reward for your performance – express promise
  ii. I offer to keep the first offer open for a reasonable time for you to complete performance IF you begin performance – Option k
    1. If you begin performance you accept the option and the promise is broken if there is revocation – implicit offer to enter option k

II. **Subcontractor Bids**

a. ***Drennan v. Star Paving Co.*** - D never makes promise only makes offer, no consideration for the promise but reliance by P on subcontractor's bid so P/E applies
  i. MASH UP of the RST in this case (leads to RST § 87)
    1. RST § 45 – implies option k which would constitute a promise (creates a promise here)
    2. This allows court to use RST § 90 – Promissory Estoppel
      a. Implied promise to keep the offer open – offer to enter unilateral k
      b. All other elements of P/E met
      c. Promise relied on by the contractor
  ii. **RST § 87 – option contract**
    1. **Offer is binding as an option K if**
      a. **In writing and signed by offeror**
      b. **Recites a purported consideration**
      c. **Proposes fair exchange w/in a reasonable time**
      d. **Is made irrevocable by statute**
    2. **Offer which the offeror should reasonably expect to induce action or forbearance by offeree before acceptance and inuces such action IS BINDING AS AN OPTION K**

III. Failed Negotiations

a. Misrepresentations
  i. Occurs when person says they are going to deal but doesn't really intend to
  ii. Very difficult to recover – D can say " I meant it at the time I made the deal but I retracted my promise later" and not commit misrepresentation
b. Good Faith/Fair Dealings
  i. UCC 1-203 impose duty of good faith and fair dealing in contract BUT
  ii. Can do anything you want during negotiations b/c no duty exists until execution/performance
  iii. Different in International Law – UNIDROIT Art. 2.15 – creates liability for entering into a K in bad faith – requires duty of niceness in negotiations
c. Restitution
  i. One party gives to the other some kind of down payment and the deal falls apart, one party has been unjustly enriched
d. Promissory Estoppel
  i. Hoffman v. Red Owl Stores – promisor promises that they are going through with the deal and promisee detrimentally relies on that promise
    1. Does not have to be as definite as a breach of contract action
  ii. Courts are reluctant to employ P/E b/c it will become more reasonable for people to rely on assurances made in negotiations
    1. Negotiations are non binding so P/E only applies when
      a. There was a very specific promise made up front
      b. There was a pattern of stringing one party along

STATUTE OF FRAUDS

I. Statute of Frauds
   a. You do not have to have a writing to make a contract enforceable – certain contracts are not enforceable because they do not satisfy the statute of frauds
   b. Oral contracts are totally enforceable, statute of frauds defines rules on which particular contracts do have to be in writing in order to be enforceable

II. **Is the contract w/in the statute of frauds? (CMYLEGS)**
   a. Types of contracts that fall under the statute of frauds
      i. **C**redit – offer to extend credit to another
      ii. **M**arriage – promise to marry
      iii. **Y**ear – if it cannot be completed within a year of making the contract
      iv. **L**and - sale or transfer of land
      v. **E**xecutorship promise – executor of an estate uses his own money to do something
      vi. **G**oods- contract for sale of goods in excess of $500
      vii. **S**uretyship – when you promise you will answer for another's debt if they fail to pay the debt
   b. Entire effect of statute of frauds is prevent the enforcement of contracts that come within the statute but don't comply with the statute (are not in writing and not signed by party to be charged)
      i. The party charged- the party that is the D in the breach of contract action
   c. Goes to the enforcement of a contract not the validity of a contract
   d. Most Common Types
      i. One Year Clause
         1. Not concerned how long it will take but rather how long in the future performance must be – performance must be w/in one year of EXECUTION of K
         2. If a K is not **logically possible** to be finished in a year it is NOT w/in SOF – **if it is logically impossible it will fall w/in the Statute of Frauds**
         3. **Applies only if the contemplated performance could not logically be done w/in one year**
         4. if K involves promise of something for a lifetime (i.e. I promise to give you a place to stay if you promise to care for me for my lifetime), it is still logically possible for performance to be completed within a year (you could die)- *not within one year rule*
         5. HOWEVER, if K involves promise of something for a specified time or date (i.e. you promise to live here for five years, I promise to care for you during that time), it is not logically possible for performance to be completed within a year, even if you die
            a. Termination of K may occur within a year
            b. But statute of frauds does not apply unless completion of performance can occur in less than a year
         6. UNILATERAL CONTRACTS – be careful with these
            a. Offer to enter unilateral K that last longer than a year does not fall within the statute of frauds (i.e. you forebear from something for 2 years and I will pay you $100 – the execution of the K is the end result of completing performance)
            b. the relevant time period is one year from the moment of contract execution (which does not occur until K is accepted)
            c. acceptance only occurs upon complete performance and execution begins after that

        d. option K that is created by RST § 45 is an implied in law K – since it is a creation of the law the SOF is not applied to those types of K's

        e. one year rule will most likely not apply

  ii.   Suretyship

    1. Contract to answer for the debt of another (*Strong v. Sheffield*)

    2. Defining Characteristics: :

        a. **There must be two parties that could be D's in a collection action by the creditor**

        b. **Cannot be novation – where one debtor substitutes for another – one party to a contract is substituted for another party to the contract**

    3. Guaranty can be a type of suretyship – guarantor cannot be acting solely in his own benefit

    4. The potential for fraud is significant so the policy aim is to prevent debtors from trying to opt out of the debt by having the K in writing

    5. Cautionary – if you need to have a promise for exchange you will be cautious about making promises. Here

    6. EXCEPTION: if a surety promises to pay the debt of another and the surety's main purpose is not to help the debtor but instead to secure some benefit for himself then the surety is enforceable even though it does not comply with the statute of frauds

III. **Is the Statute of Frauds satisfied?**

  a. K for services (anything other than K for goods) **RST § 131**

    i. **Full expression of the terms of the deal**

      1. Reasonably identify subject matter of the K

      2. Evinces that a K has been made

      3. State w/ reasonable certainty the terms of the unperformed promises

        a. Multiple documents strung out and connected w/ parol evidence

          i. Oral evidence and testimony

    ii.   **Signed by the charged party**

      1. Letterhead can count as a signature

      2. Includes electronic documentation (i.e. electronic signature in email)

      3. If the marking that identifies is **automatically produced it is <u>NOT</u> a signature**

      4. For SOF all that needs to be shown is that a writing COULD HAVE BEEN produced or did exist at some point

  b. **K for the Sale of Goods > $500 <u>UCC 2-201</u>**

    i. (1) alteration of full expression requirement - only 3 requirements in the writing (easier)

      1. Must evidence a K for the sale of goods

      2. Signed by the party to be charged

      3. Must specify a quantity

        a. Other terms are not necessary

        b. Can enforce the contract up to a half dozen

        c. Can string together multiple writings to evince a single written K

        d. Written offer and oral acceptance the offeree cannot enforce

    ii.   **(2) merchant's exception – provides a way when there is an oral sales agreement by sending a written confirmation. 6 part test:**

      1. **K between merchants**

           2. **One party sends a written confirmation to the other**

           3. **w/in a reasonable**

           4. **written confirmation is sufficient to satisfy SOF against the sender**

           5. **the recipient of the confirmation has reason to know its contents – if it came to your mailbox and it's not in an envelope that looks like junk mail you ought to know what the contents of the envelope is**

           6. **doesn't object to it w/in 10 days – that acts as if she herself had signed it as well**

      iii.   (3) other exceptions

           1. Custom goods – seller on reliance from an oral contract by the buyer and the buyer revokes the offer – enforceable

           2. Judicial admission – admission in a judicial proceeding (some sort of court filing) that a contract existed there will be an enforceable K even if paragraph 1 is not satisfied - enforceable

           3. Partial performance – if there is partial performance for a K for the sale of goods where either side has done SOME of its performance then K is enforceable up to the amount of the partial performance - if possible to apportion the court will do so

Restatements

- S. 1: Contract Defined.
  - o A contract is a promise or set of promises for which the law provides remedy for breach or recognizes duty for performance.
- S. 14: Infants.
  - o Contracts voidable for those under 18, unless statute provides otherwise.
- S. 15: Mental Illness or Defect.
  - o (1) Contract voidable for mental illness or defect if a) cannot reasonably understand the nature and consequences of the transaction, or b) cannot reasonably act in relation to the transaction, and the other party has reason to know of this condition.
  - o (2) Power of avoidance terminates the entire or partial contract when made on fair terms and the other party is without knowledge of the mental illness or defect, unless such avoidance would be unjust. Court may grant relief.
- S. 17: Requirements of a Bargain.
  - o (1) Contract requires a bargain of manifested mutual assent.
  - o (2) Contract formed regardless of bargain in s. 82-94.
- S. 20: Effect of Misunderstanding.
  - o (1) Mutual assent not manifested when parties attach materially different meanings and a) neither party knows or has reason to know of the other meaning attached or b) both parties know of have reason to know of the other meaning attached.
  - o (2) Manifestations operative, with meaning attached by a party, if a) that party does not know of any different meaning attached, but the other party knows or b) has reason to know the different meaning.
- S. 24: Offer Defined.
  - o Manifestation of willingness to enter a bargain, so another person is justified in believing that assent is invited and will conclude the bargain.
- S. 26: Preliminary Negotiations.
  - o Not an offer if the other person knows or has reason to know that they cannot conclude the bargain without a further manifestation of assent from the offeror.
- S. 27: Existence of Contract Where Written Memorial Is Contemplated.
  - o Manifestations of assent that are sufficient to create a contract are not prevented from

operation simply because the parties want a written record. However, the circumstances may show the agreements to be preliminary negotiations.

- ☐ S. 30: Form of Acceptance Invited.
  - o (1) Offer may require acceptance in words, performance, refraining from performance or leave the choice to the offeree.
  - o (2) If not specified, acceptance in and by any reasonable manner and medium.
- ☐ S. 32: Invitation of Promise or Performance.
  - o If there is doubt about acceptance between promise or performance, offeree chooses.
- ☐ S. 33: Certainty.
  - o (1) Offer cannot be accepted to form contract unless terms are reasonably certain.
  - o (2) Terms are reasonably certain if they provide a basis for determining breach and appropriate remedy.
  - o (3) One or more open or uncertain terms may show not an offer or acceptance.
- ☐ S. 36: Methods of Termination of the Power of Acceptance.
  - o (1) Can terminate offeree's power by
    - ☐ (a) Rejection or counter-offer.
    - ☐ (b) Lapse of time.
    - ☐ (c) Revocation by the offeror.
    - ☐ (d) Death or incapacity of the offeror or offeree.
  - o (2) Terminated by non-occurrence of any condition of acceptance in offer.
- ☐ S. 37: Termination of Power of Acceptance Under Option Contract.
  - o Notwithstanding s. 38-49, power under option contracts not terminated by rejection or counter-offer, revocation, or death or incapacity, unless requirements met for discharge of contractual duty.
- ☐ S. 38: Rejection.
  - o (1) Power terminated by rejection of offer, unless offeror has manifested contrary intention.
  - o (2) Manifestation of intention not accept an offer is a rejection unless offeree manifests an intention to take it under further advisement.
- ☐ S. 39. Counter-Offers.
  - o (1) Offer from the offeree to the offeror on the same matter, but different terms.
  - o (2) Offeree's power terminated by counter-offer, unless the offeror has manifested a contrary intention or unless the counter-offer manifests a contrary intention of the offeree.
- ☐ S. 40. Time When Rejection or Counter-Offer Terminates the Power of Acceptance.
  - o No termination by rejection or counter-offer until received. If both acceptance and rejection mailed before either is received, the first to arrive rules.
- ☐ S. 42. Revocation by Communication From Offeror Received by Offeree.
  - o Power of acceptance terminated when offeree receives from offeror a manifestation of intent not to enter proposed contract.
- ☐ S. 43. Indirect Communication of Revocation.
  - o Power of acceptance terminated when offeror takes definite action inconsistent with intent to enter contract and the offeree acquires reliable information to that effect.
- ☐ S. 45. Option Contract Created by Part Performance or Tender.
  - o (1) If offer invites acceptance by performance and not promise, option contract created when the offeree tenders or begins or tenders a beginning of the invited performance.
  - o (2) Offeror's duty conditional upon completion or tender of invited performance in accordance with the offer.
    - ☐ Com. E. Offeree not bound to complete, but offeror bound if completed.
- ☐ S. 46. Revocation of General Offer.
  - o When offer made by advertisement in newspaper or other publication or to a number of

unknown persons, power terminated when notice of termination given publicly by equal advertisement and no better means of notification reasonably available.

- ☐ S. 48. Death of Incapacity of Offeror or Offeree.
  - o Power terminated when offeree or offeror dies or incapacitated.
- ☐ S. 50. Acceptance of Offer Defined; Acceptance by Performance; Acceptance by Promise.
  - o (1) Acceptance of an offer is the offeree's manifestation of assent to the terms and in a manner invited or required by the offeror.
  - o (2) Acceptance by performance requires at least partial performance or tendering and includes acceptance by a performance which operates as a return promise.
  - o (3) Acceptance by promise requires the completion by the offeree of every act essential to the promise.
- ☐ S. 51. Effect of Part Performance Without Knowledge of Offer.
  - o An offeree who has already rendered partial performance requested by an offer by learning of it may accept by completing the requested performance, unless the offeror manifests a contrary intention.
- ☐ S. 52. Who May Accept an Offer.
  - o Acceptance only by person who is invited to furnish consideration.
- ☐ S. 53. Acceptance by Performance; Manifestation of Intention Not to Accept.
  - o (1) Can be accepted by performance only if the offer invites such an acceptance.
  - o (2) Except as stated in s. 69, rendering of a performance not an acceptance as long as offeree exercises reasonable diligence to notify the offeror of non-acceptance within a reasonable time.
  - o (3) When acceptance by performance and not promise, not acceptance if the offeree manifests an intention not to accept before the offeror performs his promise.
- ☐ S. 54. Acceptance by Performance; Necessity of Notification to Offeror.
  - o (1) When acceptance by performance, no notification necessary unless requested by offer.
  - o (2) If offeree has reason to know that the offeror has no adequate means of learning of the performance with reasonable promptness and certainty, contractual duty discharged unless
    - ☐ (a) Offeree exercises reasonable diligence to notify the offeror of acceptance.
    - ☐ (b) Offeror learns of the performance within a reasonable time.
    - ☐ (c) Offer indicates that notification of acceptance is not required.
- ☐ S. 56. Acceptance by Promise; Necessity of Notification to Offeror.
  - o Except as stated in s. 60 or when offer manifests a contrary intention, essential to acceptance by promise that offeree exercise reasonable diligence to notify the offeror of acceptance or that the offeror receive the acceptance seasonably.
- ☐ S. 58. Necessity of Acceptance Complying With Terms of Offer.
  - o Acceptance by promise or performance must comply with the requirements of the offer.
- ☐ S. 59. Purported Acceptance Which Adds Qualifications.
  - o Attempted acceptance that is conditional on offeror's assent to additional or different terms from the offer is a counter-offer.
- ☐ S. 60. Acceptance of Offer Which States Place, Time or Manner of Acceptance.
  - o If place, time or manner of acceptance are specified, must be complied with. If simply suggestions, another method of acceptance is possible.
- ☐ S. 61. Acceptance Which Requests Change of Terms.
  - o An acceptance that requests a change or addition of the offer's terms is not invalidated unless the acceptance depends on the changes or additions.
- ☐ S. 62. Effect of Performance by Offeree Where Offer Invites Either Performance or Promise.
  - o (1) When offeree given choice to accept by promise or performance, the tender, beginning, or tender of a beginning of the invited performance is an acceptance.
  - o (2) Such an acceptance operates as a promise to render complete performance.

☐ S. 63. Time When Acceptance Takes Effect.
- o Unless the offer provides otherwise,
- o (a) Acceptance in and by a manner and medium invited by an offer is operative and completes the manifestation of mutual assent as soon as out of the offeree's possession, regardless of whether it reaches the offeror; but
- o (b) Acceptance under an option contract is not operative until received by the offeror.

☐ S. 69. Acceptance by Silence or Exercise of Dominion.
- o (1) Silence operates as acceptance only when:
  - ☐ (a) An offeree takes the benefit of offered services with reasonable opportunity to reject and reason to know that they were offered with the expectation of compensation.
  - ☐ (b) The offeror has stated or given offeree reason to understand that the offeree can assent by silence or inaction, and the offeree does so.
  - ☐ (c) Previous dealings make it reasonable that the offeree should notify if he does not want to accept.
- o (2) An inconsistent act with the offeror's ownership of offered property binds the offeree with the offered terms unless they are manifestly unreasonable. If the act is wrongful against the offeror it is an acceptance only if ratified by him.

Defenses to Contract Enforcement (the K is formed, but is it enforceable?)
I. Why do we care?
- a. The point of contracting is to create wealth through VOLUNTARY, Pareto efficient exchange (transactions)
- b. We look to *status of the parties, behavior of the parties, and substance of the resulting bargain*

Status of the Parties
II. Seeking relief from the promise by disqualifying certain classes of persons from committing themselves to K and a promise of a person w/o capacity is voidable

III. **Minors (Infancy)**
- a. *GENERAL RULE:* **A "…K of a minor, other than necessaries, is either void of voidable at his option…"**
- b. **The minor may void the K (disaffirm) while still a minor or w/i a *reasonable amount of time from when the minor reached the age of majority*** – some states regulate through statutes
  - i. RATIONALE? To protect the immature minors from entering into K that are detrimental to them
  - ii. **What is "reasonable"**? – there is no 'hard and fast' rule
- c. "Necessaries" – that which is necessary to sustain a living.
  - i. Food, water, shelter, legal services, health care, education/car (depending on situation)
  - ii. The dissent argues that the car was a necessity to support the family – not convincing argument.
  - iii. ***Kiefer v. Fred Howe Motors, Inc.*** P bought a car representing himself as 21 (age of majority). P attempted to return car due to troubles after reaching 21 years of age and D refused. P sued for purchase price. HELD:: for P; K was voidable at his option – better to bring the case up to the legislature
- d. **REMEDIES for DISAFFIRMANCE (getting out of K):**

i. Minor gets out the K and can get restitution for payments already made to the seller but must return the goods to the seller
    1. Notice that this does not take into account the depreciation of the car for the 2 years P had it.
ii.   Some states allow full restitution by the minor to the seller is he misrepresented his age
iii.   If the K was for the sale of services, the minor gets restitution and the seller gets nothing back as punishment for contracting w/minors.

e. *Reformation of Infancy Rule*
    i. Standard form Ks by sellers alleviate this problem w/a signature by buyer stating they are not below the age of majority. Then if minor attempts to get out of K, seller can claim deceit.
    ii.   NY/CA – Ks would be brought b4 the court and signed to affirm the child was of adult competence
    iii.   Rebuttable Presumption Approach – there is the ability to rebut the idea that a person under 21 was not an adult (can show they were mature enough to K)
    iv.   Statutory procedure to remove the mark of "minor" from the person so that he can freely enter Ks whenever
        1. All open up the possibility of more litigation

IV. Mental Incapacity

a. *GENERAL RULE*: **RST § 15** --- A person incurs only voidable contractual duties by entering into a transaction if by **reason of mental illness or defect**...he is **unable to act in a reasonable manner** in relation to the transaction and the **other party has reason to know of his condition**...
    1. *KEY QUESTION*: was the person mentally incompetent at the time of mutual assent?
    ii.   "reason of mental illness or defect" – less serious than medically classified psychosis should suffice
        1. Court sets this standard high – need to protect the integrity of contracting so that someone doesn't use this if they just don't like how the K turned out
        2. **Must be serious - psychosis**
    iii.   "unable to act in a reasonable manner" – unwise and foolhardy (rational is a way to describe this)
        1. Not simply "not thought out" but actually irrational
    iv.   "other party has reason to know" – based on past evidence or currently knowledge
b. *Orterlere v. Teachers' Retirement Board* school teacher on leave for mental illness changed her retirement plan and upon death, left husband and children with nothing. HELD:: system was aware of woman's "mental illness" (she was on leave) and should not have allowed the change in the first place
    i. This condition impairs her volition – the court expanded the definition of mental incompetence to include a volitional defect
    ii.   If she was insured through a private corporation, the change may have been enforceable b/c part of the test is whether the company had reason to know of her incompetence (school board did but not a private insurer)
c. *Cundick v. Broadbent* P sold crop to D for a much lower price than FMV. P's family sued to void the K for reason of mental incompetence. HELD:: no evidence as to

impaired mental condition of P at the time of mutual assent. Parties renegotiated deal showing affirmation of mutual assent; K stands.

V. **Intoxication**
   a. RST § 16: You can void a K on the basis that you were intoxicated if you were so intoxicated that you were <u>not in control of your actions</u> ***AND*** the <u>other party knew</u> that you were intoxicated.

Behavior of the Parties
VI. **Duress (Improper Coercion)**
   i. *Two ways of dealing w/duress: focusing on "duress" (*Austin*) and using "consideration" (*Alaska Packers*)*
   b. The defense of duress is available if the D can show that he was *unfairly coerced* into entering into the K or into modifying it
   c. **RST § 175:** *"any wrongful act or threat which <u>overcomes the free will</u> of the party"* (i.e. improper threat – see § 176).
      i. A **subjective standard** is used to determine whether the party's free will has been overcome – depends on that person (so if D can show he was unusually timid, he may be able to assert duress)
         1. But a "person of ordinary firmness" standard is evidentiary to determine whether the defense of duress can be used
   d. Ways of committing duress:
      i. Violence or threats
      ii.   Imprisonment or threats of it
      iii.   Wrongful taking or keeping of a party's property or threats to do so
      iv.   Threats to breach a contract or to commit other wrongful acts (oppress one's legal rights)
         1. If a party threatens another party, it is *irrelevant* that the party has a legal right to follow through
            a. Ex. P works for D as an *at-will* employee. D threatens of fire P unless he agrees to sell shares of stock to D. P is probably under duress and if he does sell, a court would probably void the transaction (even though he is an at-will employee and D probably could terminate him for this – still duress)
   e. **RST § 176**: Threat is improper if:
      i. It is a tort or a crime
      ii.   Criminal prosecution is threatened
      iii.   Law suit w/o good faith basis
      iv.   Breach of duty of good faith and fair dealing
      v.   Resulting exchange isn't fair AND
         1. The threatened act would harm the recipient and would not benefit the person making the threat
         2. The effectives increased by prior unfair dealing by person making the threat
         3. What is threatened is otherwise a use of power for illegitimate ends
      vi.   ***Most common = threat to breach the contract unless it is modified or a new one is drawn up – this <u>will be duress IF the threat, if carried out, would result in irreparable injury that could not be avoided by a lawsuit or other means AND the threat is made in the "breach of good faith and fair dealing</u>***
   f. HYPO: Man goes to buy hurricane supplies for impending storm and the price is jacked up. This is the NOT the type of duress that should invalidate a K – K stands.

g. **Example:** *Austin Instrument, Inc. v. Loral Corporation* D had a K w/the govt. and a sub-K w/P. Sub-K threatened to stop delivery unless D signed additional provisions. D conceded b/c it had no other choice and sued to recover additional funds paid. HELD:: P obtained D's K under duress and it was voidable.

    i. <u>**TWO COMPONENTS OF DURESS:**</u>

    ii.   **An improper threat**

        1. In this case, the threat was improper b/c there was no rationale for price increase in new K AND P was using leverage against D (bad faith)

    iii.   **No reasonable alternatives**

        1. Attempted to look at other sub-K but would all have made original K late (not an option)

    iv.   Therefore, the choice was either to concede to Austin's demands or fail to meet the deadline of the govt. K this constitutes duress

h. <u>**REMEDY?**</u> Usually restitution – the party claiming duress is allowed to recover an amount sufficient to undo the unjust enrichment that the other party has obtained

VII.   **Undue Influence**

    a. Different than duress – "persuasion which overcomes the will w/o convincing the judgment" – the influence is so oppressive as to call into question the validity of the K

        i. Basically taking advantage of a weakened state and exerting dominance over another party.

    b. *Odorizzi v. Bloomfield School District* P was accused of homosexual activities at school, board members came to his house and told him to resign or they would make the allegations public. HELD:: K was voided for reason of undue influence.

        i. There was no "duress" here b/c there was nothing "improper" although there was a threat w/no reasonable alternatives – still not rising to the level of duress

    c. **Factors of Undue Influence:**

        i. Discussion of the transaction at an unusual or inappropriate location

        ii.   Consummation of the transaction in an unusual place

        iii.   Insistent demand that the business is finished at once

        iv.   Extreme emphasis on untoward consequences of delay

        v.   The use of multiple persuaders by the dominant side against an single servient party

        vi.   The absence of third-party advisers to the servient party

        vii.   Statements that there is no time to consult financial advisors or attorneys

          1. Undue influence requires both **subjective** and **objective** showings

            a. "reasonable person standard" (OBJ)

            b. "own self" (SUBJ)

               i. To avoid the problem of oversensitivity

    d. **RST § 177:** When undue influence makes a K voidable:

        i. Party under domination or by virtue of relationship

          1. Clear subordinate to board members (P was teacher)

        ii.   Unfair persuasion/coercive bargaining

          1. Went to P's house (2 v. 1) right after the allegations were stated – not a good time (clearly unfair)

    e. If a party's manifestation of assent is induced by one who is not a party to the transaction, the K is voidable by the victim unless the other party, in good faith and w/o reason to know of the undue influence, either gives value or relies materially on the transaction

VIII.   **Pre-Existing Duty** (similar to duress in *Austin*)

a. **RST § 73:** Performance of a Legal Duty – requires consideration
b. <u>Modification of a K</u> (this ***still requires consideration*** to be valid):
   i. **RST § 89:** a promise modifying a duty under a K not fully performed on either side is binding
      1. If the modification is fair and equitable in view of circumstances not anticipated by the parties when the K was made; or
      2. To the extent provided by statute
      3. To the extent that justice requires enforcement in view of material change of the position in reliance on the promise
c. ***UCC § 2-209**: modification w/o consideration but ONLY FOR SALE OF GOODS!!*
   i. UCC abolished the pre-existing duty rule by § 2-209
   ii. Must still be in good faith dealing
d. ***Alaska Packers' Ass'n v. Domenico*** Ps agreed to perform certain duties on fishing boat. In the middle of the season, Ps refused to perform unless D paid more. D agreed but upon returning, only paid amount under K. HELD:: K modification was void – D only owed original amount to Ps b/c change under those conditions would be duress.
   i. **Any modifications to a pre-existing K must come w/additional duties. Otherwise, the pre-existing duty rule comes into play and there is no consideration (not enforceable)**
      1. **But the *slightest additional duties will suffice***
         a. Ex. Contractor threatens to walk off unless owner pays more for home. Owner agrees and Contractor agrees to put in new window fittings (even though it will actually <u>save</u> the contractor money) – this is enough to have consideration
e. **Remember that CONSIDERATION is a "bargained for exchange" – <u>required to have an enforceable K</u>** (RST § 71)
   i. Construction contracts – contractor started but then realizes its going to cost more than he thought; he threatens to walk out unless owner pays more; owner pays more – most courts would say that since contractor was already legally obligated to complete the house, the contract modification might be under duress and even if it's not, there was no consideration for the increase in price b/c contractor had a pre-existing duty to complete the house
   ii. Rewards/bonuses – if the promisee is already under obligation to do the act, then no consideration for the modification
   iii. Debts – sometimes a creditor's allowance of letting a debtor pay less than the full amount he owes is NOT binding b/c the debtor was already obligated to pay the whole debt – neither is allowing debtor more time to pay (same reason)

IX. **Concealment/Misrepresentation**
   a. ***Misrepresentation can be used either as a defense against enforcement by the <u>mis-representing party</u> or as grounds for recession or damages by the <u>mis-represented- to party</u> suing as P***
   b. A person has a duty to disclose to another w/whom he deal facts that "in equity or good conscience" should be disclosed
      i. This suggests: (1) honesty and (2) good faith
   c. **RST § 164:** if a party's manifestation of assent is induced by either a ***fraudulent or a material misrepresentation*** by the other party upon which the recipient is ***justified in relying***, the K is voidable by the recipient at her option
   d. **RST 162: Fraudulent and Material**
      i. A misrepresentation is <u>fraudulent</u> if the maker intends his assertion to induce a

party to manifest his assent and the maker
   1. Knows or believes that the assertion is not in accord w/the facts OR
   2. Does not have the confidence that he states or implies in the truth of the assertion OR
   knows that he does have the basis that he states or implies for the assertion
ii.   A misrepresentation is <u>material</u> if it would likely induce a reasonable person to manifest his assent, or if the maker knows that it would be likely to induce the recipient to do so.

e. **<u>Elements of Proof</u>**
   i. **Other party's state of mind** – does not have to be intentional (negligent or innocent misrepresentation works)
   ii.   **Justifiable reliance**: recipient of the misstatement must *in fact rely* and must have *been justified in believing* the misstatement
      1. Sometimes, if the liar knows he is misrepresenting a fact, a gullible person (i.e. someone who doesn't check it for themselves) may be protected b/c D knew he was lying (intentional)
   iii.   **Misrepresentation of a _FACT_** (rather than opinion): § 168(1):
      1. Difference b/t saying "we inspected the house and there are no termites" (MR) and "as far as we know, there are no problems" (probably not)
      2. If the lying party holds themselves out to be **experts** or there is a **fiduciary relationship** b/t them, then this may give more grounds for MR
   iv.   **Concealment** and **non-disclosure**
      1. Usually MR is an affirmative statement but courts may enforce MR when there was an omission or half truth
         a. But there is <u>no liability for "bare non-disclosure"</u>
            i. So just not saying anything about the termites in the house is a "bare non-disclosure" but if D had said something like "oh there are no insects – we just had the house fumigated" this <u>would</u> be a misprepresentation
      2. There is *no general duty to disclose **EXCEPT for:***
         a. *Half truths*
         b. *Taking positive action to conceal the truth*
         c. *Failure to correct a past statement*
         d. *Fiduciary relationship*
         e. *Failure to correct a mistaken statement by other party*
            i. Ex. Jeweler knows Customer thinks the jewel is an emerald but really it's fake
   v.   *Court may not allow for damages but may rescind (void) the K*
      1. *But __a contract entered into under duress is only voidable by the WRONGED party – NOT the WRONGDOER__*
   vi.   Best defense against a claim of misrepresentation? Not an affirmative statement but this will not usually work b/c the court now allows for non-disclosures to count as misrepresentation if there is a special relationship

f. *Casefile #23* Jenkins pretends he is a minister who sells Bibles but he actually goes to people's houses looking for antiques. He went to a woman's house and bartered for some fly fishing equipment worth thousands. She didn't know it at the time but later found out. Jenkins sold the equipment for over $30,000. *We want to know whether we have to tell her how much it was worth or whether he can just settle w/her for $5,000?*
   i. **In general, there is no duty to disclose unless there is a special relationship OR a situation where something is said to create ambiguity or uncertainty to**

remedy this ambiguity created by prior false statements

    ii.   Concealment (termites) concealment occurs when a party takes actions intended or known to prevent another from learning a fact about the transaction

        1. § 160: active concealment = misrepresentation

        2. § 161: non-disclosure is equivalent to misrepresentation when it is a half-truth (not acting in good faith when one party knows the other is relying on him)

    iii.   *Answer: there is no special relationship b/t Jenkins and the woman nor were there any false statements. Thus, Jenkins probably did not have a duty to disclose*

Substance of the resulting bargain

  X. **Unfairness Presented by <u>Standardized Contracts</u>** (Ks of Adhesion)

    i. A court will usually hold a party to the terms of the K; but in some cases, the terms are so *grossly unfair* that the court will not enforce the contract

  b. **STANDARDIZED CONTRACTS**

    i. Consist of non-negotiated, pre-drafted terms put together by one party, w/room for negotiation on few, if any, terms ("take it or leave it" stuff)

      1. This usually results when there is *grossly less bargaining power* on one of the parties (the 'big guys' towering over the 'little guys')

  c. Pros to Standardized Contracts

    i. Easy (reduces transaction costs)

    ii.   Economies of scale in legal expertise

    iii.   Reducing risk (setting precedent) and facilitating commerce

  d. Cons to Standardized Contracts

    i. One party has little control

    ii.   Can result in unfair bargaining power/result (take it or leave it)

      1. Still, it would be bad policy to ban adhesion Ks

  XI. *To avoid enforcement of a K, the party must show:*

    i. *It was a K of adhesion AND*

    ii.   *Terms violate his <u>reasonable expectations</u> or is <u>unconscionable</u>*

  b. **Reasonable Expectations:**

    i. Determination is based upon *whether a reasonable person in P's position would have expected that the clause in question was present in the K*

      1. So an <u>unusual or burdensome</u> clause in the <u>fine print</u> may fail the reasonable expectations test and give rise to rescinding contract

  c. <u>**UNCONSCIONABILITY**</u>

    i. What is "unconscionability"?

      a. *So <u>shockingly unfair</u> that it should not be enforced*

    2. Lack of meaningful terms

    3. Unequal bargaining terms

    4. Terms unreasonably favorable to one side

    5. Inability to understand terms

      a. Think "Cheerios" – grocery store has the upper hand

      b. Think parking ticket stub – you may not even realize you are entering into a K and if that has all sorts of fine print, and you just think it's a receipt, then the court may not enforce the terms

    ii.   Essentially an absence of meaningful choice on the part of one of the parties together w/contract terms that are unreasonably favorable to the other party

1. Usually arises when the party <u>realizes he is entering a K</u> but *sometimes may also be enforced where the party does NOT realize he's entering a K*
   a. Like the parking lot example above

iii. **RST § 178: When a Terms is Unenforceable on Grounds of Public Policy**
   1. A promise or other term of an agreement is unenforceable on grounds of public policy if legislation provides that it is unenforceable or the interest in its enforcement is clearly outweighed in the circumstances by a public policy against the enforcement of such terms:
   2. In weighing the interest in the enforcement of a term, account is taken of:
      a. The parties' justified expectations
      b. Any forfeiture that would result if enforcement were denied
      c. Any special public interest in the enforcement of the particular term
   3. In weighing the public policy against enforcement of a term, account in taken of:
      a. The strength of that policy as manifested by legislation or judicial decisions
      b. The likelihood that a refusal to enforce the term will further that policy
      c. The seriousness of any misconduct involved and the extent to which it was deliberate
      d. The directness of the connect b/t the misconduct and the term

iv. **RST § 208**: Dealing w/Unconscionable Terms: court can (1) refuse to enforce K; (2) enforce K w/o unconscionable term; or (3) limit the application of unconscionable term to avoid injustice.
   1. Many cases in recent history are for the sale of goods – so we look to the Code and it is usually the same even at common law or RST

v. **UCC § 2-302(1)**: Unconscionable Contract of Clause
   1. Basic test = **whether, in light of the general commercial background and the commercial needs of the particular trade or case, the clauses involved are so *one-sided* as to be unconscionable under the circumstances existing at the time of the making of the contract….*prevention of oppression and unfair surprise*…and not of disturbance of allocation of risks because of superior bargaining power**
      a. *The K must be judged as of the <u>facts existing at the time of K signing</u>*
   2. This is usually used by <u>consumers</u>
      a. The court assumes that contracts b/t two business people should not receive this benefit b/c they are presumed to have similar bargaining power and expertise
   3. If the court finds the contract unconscionable as a matter of law, what is the legal significance?
      a. The court can:
         i. Refuse to enforce the contract
         ii. Enforce the remainder of K w/o the unconscionable term
         iii. Limit the application of the unconscionable term so as to avoid any unconscionable result
   4. Whether it is unconscionable or not is a **question as a matter of law, a**

question for the judge, rather than the jury (concern for playing on jury sentiment).

d. There are two types of Unconscionability – Procedural and Substantive
    i. Procedural Concerns
        1. One party was induced to enter the K w/o having any *meaningful choice* – "boilerplate" language and "adhesion contracts"
            a. Clues as to Procedural Unconscionability:
                i. Belief by the stronger party that there is no reasonable probability that the weaker party will fully perform the K;
                ii. Knowledge that the weaker party is unable to receive benefits from K;
                iii. Knowledge that weaker party is unable reasonably to protect his interests, etc.
    ii. Substantive concerns
        1. The contract is unduly unfair and one-sided
            a. Usually involve excessive price (usually 2x or 3x more), or an unfair modification of either the seller's or buyer's remedies (liquidated damages, reducing seller's liability for non-conforming goods, limitation on seller's warranty liability, etc.)
        2. UCC § 2-718: a term fixing unreasonably large liquidated damages is VOID as a penalty
            a. A liquidated damages clause setting an unreasonably *low* amount might also be held to be unconscionable
        3. UCC § 2-719: limitation of damages for breach of warranty is unconscionable for consumer purchases but <u>not for commercial purposes</u>
    iii. Sometimes arbitration clauses are found unconscionable
e. **REMEDIES:**
    i. May excise the unconscionable clause (get rid of it)
    ii. May "reform" the contract by modifying the term
    iii. May refuse to allow P to recover at all on the contract
f. ***Casefile #24*** Mary was injured while taking scuba lessons. She signed a K including an exculpatory clause (i.e. scuba co not liable for injuries). Now Mary wants to sue and says the exculpatory clause is unfair (***unconscionable***).
    i. ***TEST: whether the terms are so extreme as to appear unconscionable according to the mores and business practices of the time and place***
    ii. ***Absent meaningful choice + K terms reasonably one-sided***
        a. Absence of meaningful choice = required **procedural unconscionability** (fraud or duress)
        b. K terms unreasonably one-sided = required **substantive unconscionability**
            i. NOTE: to the extent that one is really strong, the other can be weak and still find unconscionability
        2. *If unconscionability existed at the time of K execution, the K is NOT enforceable*
    iii. ***ANSWER: Mary cannot claim that the provision was unconscionable. This is necessary for business purposes.***
g. ***O'Callaghan v. Waller*** P, tenant in D's building, injured herself on courtyard due to D's alleged negligence. K had an exculpatory clause, relieving D of liability for injuries on the property due to negligence. HELD:: exculpatory clauses are generally enforceable unless (1) it would be against settled public policy or (2) there is something in the social

95

relationship of the parties militating against enforcement

    i. In this case, exculpatory clause was enforced b/c of:

        1. Lessor-lessee relationship has been considered a matter of private, not public, concern

        2. Exculpatory clauses for landlords benefit tenants as well

        3. Landlord/tenant relationship is not possessed of the monopolistic characteristics that have held EC invalid

        4. The subject is appropriate for legislative rather than judicial action

    ii. Parties can always renegotiate these terms at renewal and tenants benefit from lower rents.

h. ***Graham v. Scissor-Tail*** Ks stated that any disputes would be arbitrated. P asserted arbitration provision was unenforceable. HELD:: K of adhesion was unconscionable.

i. ***Carnival Cruise Lines v. Shute*** D argued that forum selection clause was part of K of adhesion; should not be enforced. HELD:: forum selection clause was enforceable b/c P (1) has special interest in limiting forum; (2) avoids confusion; and (3) savings are passed on to consumers through lower ticket prices

    i. **RST § 211:** the party must sign and <u>manifest assent</u> and must have reason to believe that writings like this one are used to manifest assent in situations such as the present one.

XII. **The Duty of Good Faith Performance**

a. What is "good faith performance"?

    i. Promise not to act in an arbitrary or irrational manner

    ii. Refrain from doing "anything which will have the effect of destroying or injuring the right of the other party to receive the fruits of the K

    iii. Honest in fact

    iv. Following reasonable commercial standards

    v. Avoiding opportunistic behavior

    vi. Using "best efforts"

b. ***Dalton v. ETS*** P took SAT twice, 2nd time score went up a lot, D investigated and refused to report 2nd score b/c expert said it was a different person. P supplied additional evidence regarding sickness and firsthand accounts he was there but D refused to examine. HELD:: P was entitled to specific performance = D must examine the additional proof in good faith and make a determination.

    i. By not looking at P's proof, D did not act in good faith

c. **Good Faith Bargaining b/t Merchants**

d. ***Eastern Air Lines v. Gulf Oil*** P and D had a requirements K. D thought P was acting in bad faith by fluctuating amount of jet fuel bought. HELD:: P did not act in bad faith. Fuel demands fluctuate and it is widely known in this industry. Both parties knew this and took this into account when making prices/amounts for first K.

    i. Between ***merchants***, "good faith" means "***honest in fact and the observance of reasonable commercial standards of fair dealing in the trade***" (UCC § 1-201).

    ii. Other UCC provisions dealing w/"good faith"

        1. 2-306 – imposes a duty of good faith in requirements K

        2. 1-201 – good faith means honesty

        3. 2-103(a-b) – involves merchants

            a. #2 and #3 are proposed to be combined into § 1-201(b)(20)

        4. 2-208 – deals w/commercial standards

        5. 1-205(1) – deals w/commercial standards

            a. (a) behavior of the parties in earlier transactions

b. (b) industry practices and behavior

e. ***Market Street Associates v. Frey*** P had K w/D which allowed P to buy back property at very low price if negotiations broke down b/t P and D. They did break down and P sought to impose provision allowing for buy back but did not disclose this provision to D. HELD:: Court allowed the case to go to trial instead of issuing summary judgment for D.

  i. "good faith" is the **duty not to act "opportunistically"**

f. ***Bloor v. Falstaff Brewering Corp.*** P and D had a K in which D was to use his "best efforts" to promote and maintain a *high* volume of sales, and the K contained a liquidated damages provision for failure to do so. D lost a substantial amount of money attempting to promote P but after a new owner came in and turned P's company around, P sued D for failure to use "best efforts." HELD:: D was liable for breach of K and awarded lost profits but not liquidated damages.

  i. A "best efforts" clause imposes an obligation to act w/good faith in light of one's own capabilities.

  ii.   Court cites *Wood v. Lucy (Lady Duff)* – analogy is best efforts is to be implied in the K b/c D's profits were derived from sales on P's products

RESOLVING DISPUTES OVER K TERMS – WHAT PERFORMANCE IS REQUIRED?

XIII. **Parol Evidence Rule**

 a. *Essentially, many people enter into preliminary negotiations, either orally or written, prior to coming to a full contract*

  i. They do not intend for these communications to be contracts but at the very end, their contract usually contains all of these elements

  ii.   But sometimes it doesn't – what if you agreed to something orally but never actually put it in the contract?

    1. Usually the PER will not allow you to contradict the contract with this term if you agreed to it <u>before the final contract</u> and you <u>failed to include the term in the later contract</u>

 b. The PER says that *a writing intended to be a <u>full and final</u> expression (Total Integration) of their agreement may <u>not</u> be <u>supplemented or contracted</u> by any written or oral agreements <u>made prior to the writing</u>*

  i. Essentially this PER protects the sanctity of written agreements, even at the expense of fulfilling the parties' actual intentions

    1. Now remember, if this is only a partial integration (final but not full), the PER does not apply and that evidence re: prior oral agreements may readily be admitted ***if they are consistent (not if they contradict terms)***

  ii.   Ex. P and D enter into oral negotiations whereby P wants to buy hotel from D. D agrees to include all the furniture and give P one year to pay. They employ a lawyer to draft up the contract and both sign it. The contract is silent on furniture and says P only have 6 months to pay.

    1. If D can convince court that this is a <u>full and final</u> integration, P cannot prove that the furniture was part of the deal or that D originally agreed to give him one year instead of 6 months to pay.

    2. But in considering whether this is <u>full and final</u>, the *judge may consider all evidence* (so though the outcome is harsh, it is somewhat mitigated by the fact that judge can conclude it is not full and final)

 c. ***Remember that PER covers oral and written agreements made <u>prior</u> to the contract***

  i. What if the agreement is made at the same time?

    1. Some courts treat this as a "prior" agreement

    2. Corbin says to treat this as evidence that contract is not a total integration

(not full and final) and thus allow evidence in

d. **The PER does not bar admission of evidence of *oral* agreements made <u>after</u> the writing – *can always supplement AFTER K***
   i. Unless there is a "no oral modification (NOM) clause
      1. Then the agreement would have to be signed in writing by both parties
         a. Remember that NOM clause can be waived if one party induces the other to accept reliance on their oral statements that some provisions of the contract will not be relied upon or enforced
         b. Ex. D constructs home for P. Construction contracts often have NOM clauses. P asks D to add some length to the porch. D says we have to put it in writing. P says, I don't want to be bothered, I'll be sure you're paid. P later refuses to pay. NOM clause was probably waived by P's statement of assurance of pay.
   ii. Under UCC § 2-209(2) a NOM will usually be effective
e. The PER does not bar admission of evidence about the <u>meaning of terms</u> to the K
f. **Rules of Interpretation**
   i. Generally, an **ambiguous term** is construed **against the drafter**
   ii. Evidence of 'custom' may be admitted to show the parties intended for a K term to have a particular meaning (course of performance, course of dealing, or trade usage)
g. The court may **supply a reasonable term** in a situation where the **K is silent** (courts routinely supply duty to act in good faith)

XIV. Typical Course of Dealing
   a. Contract dispute arises and case goes to court
   b. Parol evidence is offered to contradict written agreement
   c. Other party object
      i. Judge decides whether contract is full and final (? of integration)
      ii. If agreement is full and final, PE is not admissible
      iii. If agreement is not full and final, consistent PE will be admitted

XV. **UCC PAROL EVIDENCE RULE**
   i. § 2-202 Terms…set forth in a writing intended by the parties as a *final expression…may not be contradicted* by evidence of *any prior agreement or of a contemporaneous oral agreement* but may be *explained or supplemented…by* <u>course of performance</u>…or <u>consistent</u> additional terms unless the court finds that this was a complete and exclusive statement of the agreement."
   b. **When does PER NOT APPLY?**
      i. Illegality, fraud, misrepresentation, duress, mistake, lack of consideration or any other fact that would make the contract void or voidable
         1. PER never prevents evidence that would show no contract exists or that the contract is void
         2. So if you enter into an agreement and prior to it, the Seller told you that the property was really profitable, this WOULD be admissible b/c it would go to the Seller's misrepresentation or fraud and may invalidate the contract
      ii. Conditions – if the parties orally agree to a condition but the contract does not specify the condition, almost all courts will allow evidence of the condition to come in despite the PER
         1. Why? The very existence of a condition shows that the writing was not a total integration and the condition does not contradict, only supplements the writing
   c. *Casefile #28* H wants to collect his employment bonus which was due at the end of the

first year. He only worked there for 5 months. He thought the bonus was pro-rated so he wants the bonus for 5 months based on what the lady in the office told him before he signed the contract. The actual contract says nothing about pro-rated and company refuses to give him the bonus.

      i. *ANSWER: the PER should be invoked here. The attorney is trying to get a prior oral agreement to contradict the terms of the contract. The law firm would probably prevail here. The statement about prorated bonus was made prior to the written contract and b/c it is an important term, we would expect that it would be included in the actual contract. Bad attorney!*

XVI. **Principles of K Interpretation**

  a. *Casefile #30* Internet agreement; John signed a K w/Maroon Net for "unrestricted internet access". Maroon Net has a "fair use" policy – the more you use it, the slower it gets. John never received any "agreement" from MN; he just received a form explaining how to get and use an email account. John filed class action against MN for breach of contract in failing to provide unlimited access. So what does "unrestricted internet access" mean?

      i. *ANSWER: we don't have the actual agreement. The advertisement seems clear and unambiguous. But MN wants to bring in extrinsic evidence to show that other providers do the same thing*

          1. *The answer hinges on whether the court will allow in additional information (extrinsic evidence)*

          2. *Using the Chicken case, we can say that maybe trade usage should be entered – if the term is ambiguous (which is probably is since the dispute arose) we can look to extrinsic evidence*

            a. *What evidence? Depends on the tests below*

     ii. Common Fact Pattern:

          1. Parties enter K

          2. Dispute arises regarding one of the terms of K

          3. Parties offer different interpretations of disputed term

            a. Similar to PER – but different b/c in PER, one party is trying to introduce something not in the writing. Here, the ? is not the terms. The term is clearly there, we are disputing the meaning of the term

    iii. So how to decide these cases?

          1. Step One: clear or ambiguous terms?

            a. In deciding ambiguity, court could look to <u>K itself</u> or could look <u>at everything else</u>

          2. Step Two: *if disputed language is ambiguous, use extrinsic evidence to interpret it*

            a. Can look to dictionary definition, negotiations b/t parties, trade usage of the term (even despite PER)

            b. This extrinsic evidence CAN be evaluated by the jury, not the judge

          3. Step Three: *if disputed language is unambiguous, the judge will give it meaning*

    iv. *How does the judge decide whether it is ambiguous or not?*

          1. **Four Corners**

            a. No extrinsic evidence whatsoever, only w/i 4 corners of the K

          2. **Plain Meaning Rule**

            a. Will not hear evidence about parties' preliminary negotiations but they can hear about the "context" of the agreement (circumstances that existed prior to contract formation)

3. **Liberal Rule**

   a. Evidence of prior negotiations *is* admissible for the limited purpose of enabling the trial judge to determine whether the language in dispute lacked clarity

   v. Course of performance, course of dealing, and trade usage can also show some evidence of term interpretation

   1. Course of performance wins out over the other two (if there is a conflict)

   vi. Parties can avoid potential uncertainties of PER by using a <u>merger or integration clause</u> when writing K (writing includes EVERYTHING parties agreed to) – most contracts include something like this

XVII. **Too Much Ambiguity - <u>MISUNDERSTANDING</u>**

a. Courts are comfortable w/some ambiguity in contracts – however, at some point, the courts may hesitate to enforce the K due to too much ambiguity

   i. *The parties may think they have a K but they may have different interpretations of key terms in the K –* **this might result in not having a "meeting of the minds" and we might not even have a contract in the first place**

b. If the misunderstanding is sufficiently major, it may prevent a K from existing at all

   i. RST § 20 - ***<u>If the misunderstanding concerns a material term and neither party knows or has reason to know of the misunderstanding, then no K</u>***

   ii. The objective theory of contracting (reasonable person) does not apply here – it is about the *<u>subjective intent</u>* of the parties – they have to have the same subjective understanding and is not, then it may not be a K

c. **Gely's Questions (we went through each case w/these questions)**

   i. **What was the disputed term?**

   ii. **Was the disputed term objectively clear?**

   iii. **Was there a subjective agreement? Did the parties share a meaning?**

   iv. **Did the other party know or have reason to know of the meaning attached by the other side?**

   v. **Contract or No K?** *(usually if the answer to ANY of these is "yes", then there would be a K but if the answer is "no" to all of these, then there wasn't a K)*

   1. Like in *Raffles*, the answers were all no – so no K
   2. Like in *Oswald*, the answers were all no – so no K
   3. Like in *Colfax*, the answers were no to the first two but yes to the last one – there WAS a K in this case

d. ***Raffles v. Wichelhaus*** A offers to sell B goods off a ship called *Peerless*. There are two ships. A subjectively intends one ship while B intends another. HELD:: There is no K b/c A and B were in subjective disagreement as to the meaning of the term –*Peerless*. Neither had reason to know of the discrepancy – this was **an ambiguous term**

e. ***Oswald v. Allen*** D owned 2 coin collections. She thought she was selling one to the foreigner but he thought she was selling all. The term "swiss coin" was ambiguous. HELD:: There was no K b/c the term was ambivalent.

f. ***Colfax Envelope Corp. v. Local No. 458-3M*** dispute over staffing requirements for printing machine. HELD:: Court ENFORCES the K b/c P should have known that there was a typo and union meant something different based on trade practices. Since P didn't inquire prior to signing, court upholds K.

   i. **If a term in the offer or acceptance is ambiguous and one party *knows or should know* that she has a different understanding as to the meaning than does the other party, a K will be formed *on the term as understood by the other*** *(unknowing) party*

1. So in *Colfax*, P should have known that there was a typo and didn't inquire, thus, court construes in favor of union and enforces K.
2. If one party is at fault (i.e. knew or should know) then they bear the burden of the K – if there is no fault (neither party knew or should have known) then there is usually no K (equal fault)
   a. ***This is the lesser cost avoider – whoever was more "at fault" will be bound to the contract on the <u>other party's terms</u>***
   ii. *There is no UCC provision dealing w/misunderstanding – left to case law*

g. If the misunderstanding involves only a **minor term** the court will usually enforce the K and use the more reasonable or fair meaning of the disputed terms
   i. RST § 201 – if there is a case as in *Peerless* where the material misunderstanding prevented a K from being formed, **one party <u>may</u> waive** the misunderstanding in favor of other party's interpretation
      1. EX. Buyer intended first ship while Seller intended second ship. Buyer learns of Seller's contrary understanding and waits for second ship and accepts goods then. If Seller later learns that Buyer intended the goods to arrive on the first ship, Seller can't claim misunderstanding and demand goods back.
      2. EX. Buyer intended first ship and Seller intended second ship. Buyer learns of Seller's contrary understanding prior to second ship arriving, waits for it to arrive, and then objects. Most courts would say that Buyer has "waived" right to claim misunderstanding by failing to seasonably object when he learned of the discrepancy

XVIII. **Supplying the Missing K Terms – Warranties**
   a. A warranty is a kind of guaranty or promise by a seller of goods that they will have certain characteristics
      i. UCC recognizes:
         1. Express warranty
         2. Implied warranty of merchantability
         3. Implied warranty of fitness for a particular purpose
         4. Warranty of title and against infringement
   b. **TO PROVE BREACH OF WARRANTY, PLAINTIFF MUST PROVE:**
      i. **D made a warranty, express or implied, under one of UCC provisions;**
      ii. **Goods were defective <u>*at the time of sale*</u> (i.e. that they did not comply w/the warranty);**
      iii. **Buyer's loss or injury was <u>*proximately*</u> and <u>*actually*</u> caused by the defect (and not by buyer's negligence or inappropriate use of goods);**
      iv. **No affirmative defense, including disclaimer, SOL, lack of privity, lack of notice and assumption of risk, applies.**
   c. **Express Warranty (UCC § 2-313)**
      i. ELEMENTS
         1. An affirmation of ***<u>fact</u>*** or ***<u>promise</u>*** (NOT OPINION or PUFFING)
         2. That ***<u>relates</u>*** to the goods <u>AND</u>
         3. Becomes part of the ***<u>basis of the bargain</u>*** b/t the parties (meaning that buyer must ***<u>rely</u>*** on seller's warranty)
      ii. EXAMPLES
         1. The car has never been in an accident = express warranty (FACT)
         2. The car runs smoothly = no express warranty (OPINION)

3. Fine print in sales contract will almost always be found to form the "basis of the bargain" whether buyer reads it or not
   a. If buyer doesn't rely on the warranty, then no breach
   b. Ex. Seller tells buyer car goes up to 150mph. Buyer says I'll never take it above 50mph. Buyer probably can't claim breach of warranty if the car won't go past 70 mph.
   iii. Sometimes a P can recover for a breach of warranty based on a "middleman's" statement – i.e. not the actual manufacturer but a 3rd party
   iv. Sometimes the seller will make a statement *after money has changed hands*
       1. The courts are split as to whether this is actually the "basis of the bargain" – might better serve as a modification to the original agreement
   v. A description of goods (7/8" nails) is an express warranty
   vi. A sample or floor model will also be held to be an express warranty (w/i reason – no two TVs are exactly the same but they have same general features)

d. **Implied Warranty of Merchantability (UCC § 2-314)**
   i. *Most important warranty*
   ii. A warranty is implied that the goods are merchantable for sale if the seller is a merchant who deals in goods of the kind
       1. **This only applies when the seller is a *MERCHANT*!!!** (§2-201)
       2. This does NOT mean that the goods are perfect – it means that the goods are *fit for the ordinary purposes for which such goods are used*
   iii. What is "merchantable"? (UCC § 2-314)
       1. Goods must pass w/o objection in the trade under the K description
       2. Goods must be **"fit for the ordinary purposes for which such goods are used"**
       3. Goods must run w/i variations permitted by the agreement
       4. Goods must be adequately contained, packaged and labeled
       5. Goods must conform to the promises or affirmations of fact listed on container or label, if any.
   iv. To prove **breach** of merchantability:
       1. The merchant sold the goods
       2. Which were defective at time of sale
       3. Causing injury to the ultimate consumer
       4. The proximate cause of which was the defective nature of goods
       5. The seller received notice of injury

e. *Casefile 33.1* Pettit contracts w/MegaByte to develop password protection software. Software took more than 1 year to produce and cost $58K. Now we find out that the software can only support a limited number of passwords at a time. To fix it, it will cost over $15K.
   i. Is this for a "good"? If so, was there an express warranty? An implied warranty? Assuming there was a warranty, was it breached?
   ii. *ANSWER: yes, probably a good. Deals more w/goods and parts than w/services (so the bulk is a good)*
       1. *Seller could argue: program performed capably for the current needs. We didn't promise that it would have future increased capacity*
       2. *Buyer could argue: the warranty of merchantability should include some notion of future capacity, that you are buying a good today but that it will also continue to meet future needs (w/i reason)*

f. **Implied Warranty of Fitness for a Particular Purpose (UCC § 2-315)**
   i. UCC provision does not require seller to make any sort of statement (that is why

its different than an express warranty)

  ii.   Seller does NOT have to be a merchant

  iii.   TO PROVE **BREACH** OF WFPP:

    1. Seller must have reason to know of buyer's purpose *at the time of contracting*

    2. Seller had reason to know that the *buyer was relying on seller's skill and judgment* to furnish suitable goods

    3. *Buyer did in fact rely* on seller's skill and judgment

      a. Ex. Buyer goes into Seller's print store. Buyer tells Seller what type of printer she needs. Seller recommends one but doesn't make any express statements. Buyer can probably recover for breach of implied WFPP if the machine does not perform.

  iv.   If *buyer insists upon a particular brand* of goods, then he is not relying on seller's skill/judgment, thus, no WFPP

  v.   ***Lewis v. Mobil Oil Corp.*** P wanted to convert sawmill to hydraulic equipment. Mobil offered a particular oil to use w/equipment but the machine failed. P had to buy new machine and new oil. HELD:: there was a warranty of FPP b/c Mobil knew of the specific purpose for which P was using oil and P relied on P's recommendation.

    1. A 'particular purpose' differs from an 'ordinary' purpose in that it envisages a specific use by the buyer which is peculiar to the nature of his business whereas the ordinary purposes for which goods are used are those envisaged in the concept of merchantability.

g. **DISCLAIMERS (avoiding implied warranties)**

  i. *ALWAYS EVALUTE WHETHER THERE WAS AN EFFECTIVE DISCLAIMER*

  ii.   Seller will often attempt to escape warranty liability which he might otherwise incur, by disclaiming it

    1. Particularly like w/IWMerchantabiltiy b/c he can't really control it

  iii.   *Express Warranty* § 2-316(1): when disclaimer and warranty conflict, warranty should be construed narrowly to avoid conflicting w/disclaimer. However, if there is no way to make the two consistent, the disclaimer is ineffective.

    1. Description: if you describe something as a specific way, you cannot later disclaim that warranty and get out of it

    2. Oral warranty and written disclaimer: same rule as above (if you can't resolve the conflict, then disclaimer is ineffective) but remember PER – if seller can show that written disclaimer was a total integration, no evidence of prior oral warranty is admissible

  iv.   *Merchantability* § 2-316(2): the disclaimer *must mention the word "merchantability"* and *must be "conspicuous"* (but not in writing)

    1. Conspicuous --- §1-201; the person must be AWARE – it must somehow stand out (underline, set apart, all caps, different color), NOT in the fine print of the document

  v.   *Fitness for a Particular Purpose* § 2-316(2): must be _in writing_ and be _conspicuous_ but *need not use particular words*

    1. "there are no warranties which extend beyond the description on the face hereof"

  vi.   § 2-316(3)(a): seller can avoid these hassles of disclaiming ***implied*** warranties by simply stating good is sold "as is" "with all faults" or other language which reasonable signals to buyer that there is no express or implied warranty

    1. However, if seller makes any comments about goods' merchantability or FPP, then these are <u>express</u> warranties b/c seller actually said them and they are effective (not waived)

vii.   Sometimes the course of dealing will indicate that buyer has "waived" right to implied warranties

    1. Ex. Cattle farmer buys lot of cattle. Gets rid of the ones he doesn't want. Court may say that cattle farmer has waived right to warranties for the ones he does take – no recourse if they are defective

viii.   If a seller wants an effective disclaimer, usually must be done PRIOR to signing of the sales contract – ***most courts hold that the post-contract disclaimer is <u>NOT effective</u>***

    1. In a few cases a seller may be able to get a buyer to agree to a modification of the contract but the buyer must not only agree but must also sign the disclaimer if K is over $500 – hard to do!

ix.   The point is that while warranties may be implied, they are relatively easy to avoid – if the seller is careless, he will be punished!

x.   **REMEDIES:**

    1. Sometimes disclaimers are effective even if they limit the buyer's remedies. But there are some times when disclaimer is NOT effective in limiting the remedies:

      a. If the good ***fails to perform its essential purpose***, the disclaimer may be ineffective and buyer may recover under this act

        i. Ex. Buyer buys car. Contract limits Buyer's remedies to fixing defective parts. Buyer finds over 14 defective parts. Court may invalidate disclaimer and allow Buyer to recover by either money or getting <u>new</u> car

      b. Unconscionability to limit buyer's remedies

        i. Limitations on personal injury is unconscionable on its face (presumption of unconscionability) but limitation in the commercial setting is not (buyer bears burden)

xi.   ***S.C. Electric and Gas Co. v. Combustion Engineering*** P got boiler unit from D. In K, there was a disclaimer saying 'there are no other warranties, whether express or implied, other than title.' P argues that disclaimer was invalid b/c it wasn't conspicuous. HELD:: warranty was valid. The correspondence prior to contract should have alerted P that there was no other warranty besides title (§ 2-315(3)).

XIX. **Performance, Breach, and Discharge of Contractual Duties**

  a. <u>**CONDITIONS**</u>

    i. An event which must occur to require a particular performance

    ii. **Condition Precedent**

      1. Any event, other than a lapse of time, which must occur <u>before</u> performance under the K is due

      2. Uncertain event that must occur b4 the duty comes into being – marks the beginning of an obligation

      3. Promisee has burden of proof

      4. "Associate must pass the bar for employment to become effective"

    iii. **Condition Subsequent**

      1. Any event which operates by agreement of the parties to discharge a duty

of performance <u>after</u> it has become absolute

    2. Uncertain event that if occurs, discharges duty to perform – extinguishes an obligation already created

        a. True CS are rare – sometimes they show up in insurance contracts stating that a suit must be brought w/i a certain time or the claim is discharged

    3. Promisor has burden of proof

    4. "Hired associate. Employed is discontinued if applicant fails to pass the bar"

  iv. There is <u>no substantive difference</u> b/t CP and CS – the non-occurrence of CP or occurrence of CS both discharge contractual duties

b. **Three Types of Covenants**

  i. <u>Mutual and independent</u> – either party may recover damages from the other for the injury he may have received by breach of the covenants in his favor, and where it is no excuse for D to allege breach of covenants on the part of P

  ii. <u>Conditions and dependent</u> – the performance of one depends on the prior performance of another, and therefore, till this prior condition (CP) is performed, the other party is not liable to an action on his covenant

  iii. <u>Mutual conditions to be performed</u> – if one party was ready and offered to perform his part, and the other neglected or refused to perform his, he who was ready and offered has fulfilled his engagement, and may maintain and action for the default of the other – though it is no certain that either is obliged to do the first act

c. **Express Condition** --- applies to any condition on which the parties agree, whether their agreement is stated explicitly, or merely implied from conduct – may be "implied in fact" (RST § 226)

  i. Example: K says O will pay C $5000 w/i 10 days of satisfactory completion of the work. Satisfactory completion is an express condition to O's duty to pay (though not explicitly stated).

  ii. Usually courts require *strict compliance w/express conditions* (they are <u>strictly enforced against the party subject to them</u>)

  iii. The court does not want forfeiture (that is, where one party prepares or takes substantial steps towards completing their performance but interpretation as a condition may relieve the other party of performance – not fair)

    1. Court may hold that the contract has been "substantially performed"

  iv. Sometimes courts will "excuse" the condition as long as it was not materially part of the agreed exchange

    1. Ex. D carries cargo belonging to P under K that says it is express condition of D's liability that P give written notice of damage w/i 10 days of realizing it. P waits 6 months and then notifies D of claim. This is too late and D does not have a duty to pay P – the condition of requiring 10 days notice was NOT excused – P failed to comply.

  v. Satisfaction as a Condition

    1. RST § 228: satisfaction is determined by a **reasonable person of the obligor would be satisfied**

        a. This means "good faith" = "subjective honesty"

        b. You must perform if you are subjectively satisfied in good faith

d. *Casefile #31* employment contract provided for an annual bonus calculated at a certain % of company profits for the prior year. The agreement was able to be terminated by either party as long as they give 30 days notice. Forsight was notified of his termination 10 days prior to end of fiscal year. Thus, he was late in giving his notice of election as to when he wanted his annual bonus. *Was the 14 day notice an ESSENTIAL TERM of the contract?*

    i. **Burden of proof is on the promisor – employer here – they have the burden of showing that a certain condition would let them off the hook. If employer can show that Forsight failed to comply w/an essential term, they do not have to pay him the bonus.**

    ii. *ANSWER: the court will look to the intention of the parties to see if the condition was <u>expressly necessary for the promise</u>. If the condition goes to the essence of the contract, then it will be held to be a necessary term*

        1. *If it was a promise, then the other side can sue for damages but not breach the K*

        2. *If it was a condition, then the other side can breach the K.*

e. **Constructive Condition** --- one not agreed on by the parties (even by implication) but which the court imposes as a matter of law, in order to ensure fairness

    1. Usually used in bilateral contracts (where each party makes condition)

    ii. Example: A promises to perform services for $1000. Nothing is said as to when payment is due (b4 or after A completes work). A tells B, A wants payment up front and a court would probably hold that A's performance is a constructive condition of B's duty to pay and thus, B doesn't have to pay until work is done

        1. Usually courts require *substantial compliance w/constructive conditions*

        2. This is where each party's substantial performance is conditional on the other. B's performance of paying A is conditional on A performing and A performing is conditional on assurance of being paid

    iii. ***Kingston v. Preston*** P apprenticed for D and agreed that D would eventually retire. P made payments to take over business and had to provide "good and sufficient security" approved by D "at or before the sealing and delivery of deed" to get business. D refused to give P business. HELD:: D clearly wanted to approve of P prior to giving him business and since P didn't meet the CP, judgment was for D (duty to perform did not arise b/c P failed CP b/c the two promises were <u>dependent</u>)

    iv. ***Stewart v. Newbury*** conflict arose b/c one party refused to pay in intervals and wanted to pay lump sum at end of performance. Is D's obligation to pay conditioned on P's action/completion of performance? HELD:: the obligation to pay is <u>dependent</u> on the P's completion of substantial performance of K

f. Remember that ideally, performance will be concurrent

    i. If you can't get concurrent performance, doing precedes giving – meaning that if the party doesn't tender the goods, the other party's duty to pay doesn't even begin yet.

    ii. **Independent v. Dependent**

        1. If conditions are dependent, failure to satisfy one condition allows other party to suspend performance

        2. If conditions are independent, failure to satisfy one condition does not allow other party to suspend performance

            a. Usually insurance policies and real estate dues

g. **Difference b/t Condition and Promise**

    i. Failure to satisfy <u>promise (duty)</u> allows innocent party to sue for damages but NOT to suspend or terminate performance

    ii. Failure to satisfy <u>condition</u> allows innocent party to suspend or terminate performance

        1. So it is important to distinguish

iii.   How to Tell:

1. Intent is more important than words: things like "provided that", "unless", "if", "on the condition that" etc.
2. **There is a slight preference for resolving ambiguous phrases as promises rather than conditions b/c it mitigates the effect on the K**

iv.   Think about *Jacob & Young* again – if the court interpreted the "Reading pipes" as a condition, it would be extremely unfair to the Contractor b/c it meant that the owner could not pay and discharge his duty to perform. If it was a promise, then all the owner could get is damages but he still had to pay.

XX.   <u>**PERFORMANCE**</u>

a. **Substantial Performance at Common Law**

i. ***The performance does not have to perfect but it does have to be consistent w/the purpose of the K***

1. Remember that <u>*substantial performance is the OPPOSITE of material breach*</u>
2. If the party has materially breached, then they have not substantially performed and vice versa

ii.   If a party fails to substantially perform but the performance could easily be cured, then the other party can suspend and **party failing to substantially perform has a chance to CURE**

1. If they cure, then party must pay
2. If they fail to cure, then the party is discharged of duty to perform

iii.   If the party fails to substantially perform but the failure is a gross deviation from K, then other party is discharged of duty to perform their end of the bargain

iv.   **TEST FOR SUBSTANTIAL PERFORMANCE:**

1. **Did the injured party get what he wanted (in general)? (Yes = SP)**
2. **Is compensation available by an offset for damages? (No = SP)**
   a. **Can the damages be ascertained? (No = no SP, MB)**
3. **Greater part performance, more likely SP, less likely MB**
4. **If the breaching party is likely to cure, more likely SP**
5. **Was the breach a willful breach? If no, more likely SP**

v.   **A <u>delay in performance</u> is usually <u>not a material breach</u> <u>*unless it significantly deprives the other party of the benefit of the contract*</u>**

1. **A delay in performance suspends the other party's duty under the contract – even if the party cures, he will have to pay damages**
2. **If a delay is likely to hinder the non-breaching party in making substitute arrangements, it's more likely to be material**
   a. A contracts w/B to perform for 3 weeks. B gets sick before performance and A gets a sub. A's substitute was reasonable and B's breach is probably material. Wouldn't have to pay B anything unless she did perform (quasi-contract; unjust enrichment)

vi.   ***Jacob & Young v. Kent*** P built home for D, K called for certain pipe, P used a *substantially the same* pipe. D sued for breach after he found out. HELD:: P had satisfied the obligation under the K (i.e. he *substantially performed* the K).

b. **Perfect Tender Rule**

i. **There is no substantial performance under the UCC (sale of goods), MUST BE PERFECT**

ii.   <u>*UCC RULE*</u>*: If the seller fails, in any respect, to conform to the contract, the buyer may renege*

1. *But the courts usually interpret this similar to substantial performance*

          a. Look to these factors:
- i. Trade usage; course of dealing; course of performance
- ii.   Seller generally has a right to cure

   iii.   UCC § 2-601: "if the goods or tender of delivery fail in any respect to conform to the K, buyer may: (1) reject the whole; (2) accept the whole; (3) accept any commercial unit or units and reject the rest.
1. This means absolutely perfect. <u>Any</u> deviation of <u>any</u> kind justifies the buyer getting out of the K.
2. The effect can be pretty harsh under the UCC Perfect Tender Rule so courts attempt to mitigate the harshness w/limitations…

   iv.   <u>Limitations to 601 (PTR):</u>
1. UCC § 2-602: rejection of goods must be w/i a reasonable time
2. UCC § 2-606: allows buyer who has already accepted goods to revoke that acceptance if non-conformity substantially impairs their value to him
    - a. Acceptance means "after reasonable opportunity to inspect" or "doing something inconsistent w/seller's rights"
3. UCC § 2-608(1): buyer may revoke when:
    - a. Accepted goods w/reasonable assumption their nonconformity would be cured but it wasn't seasonably cured OR
    - b. Accepted w/o discovering the defect when it was reasonable to do so (i.e. had some indication they should be conforming)
        - i. Must be w/i *a reasonable time*
4. UCC § 2-612: allows a buyer under a K for delivery of goods in installments to **reject** an installment only if a non-conformity as to the goods **substantially impairs the value** of that installment, and only claim breach where the substantial impairment of the value of the whole K.
5. UCC § 2-508: gives seller power to cure a defective tender if the ***time for that performance has not yet expired***
    - a. Sometimes, the buyer may even have a right to cure *after* the time for performance has expired
    - b. To the extent that the seller fixes the problem, then buyer no longer has the ability to reject the goods
        - i. If buyer refuses to accept the cure, then buyer breached

   v.   Essentially these limitations say "we give the buyer an opportunity to inspect and if buyer fails to do so or does something inconsistent w/seller's ownership of goods – buyer can't go back on PTR"

   vi.   Once the buyer has validly rejected the goods, buyer **must hold them in reasonably safety for seller to pick up**
1. To the extent that buyer fails to do so, buyer may be liable for damages

  c. OTHER REMEDIES:
- i. Cover: buyer may purchase conforming goods from a 3rd party and recover the difference b/t cover and contract price from the breaching seller
- ii.   Contract/market difference: if buyer doesn't cover, he may recover difference b/t contract and market price at time of breach
- iii.   May recover incidental and consequential damages (see *Hadley* case below)

XXI. **BREACH OF CONTRACT**
  a. Repudiation should be shown an announcement of an intention not to perform
- i. Should be positive and unequivocal

ii.　　Party's language must be sufficiently positive to be reasonably interpreted to mean that party cannot or will not perform
1. Need not be only in words

b. **Material Breach**
i. Breaking a condition of the K is a material breach
ii.　　Breaking a promise is NOT a material breach
1. May still be able to get damages but you cannot suspend performance or breach the K yourself in this case (like you could for a material breach)
iii.　　**Factors for Material Breach (same test as substantial performance)**
1. **Degree to which the V got what she bargained for**
2. **Compensation in damages would make the victim whole**
3. **Possible forfeiture by possible breacher**
4. **Willfulness of the breach**
   a. **To recover, the party must show 2 things:**
      i. **There WAS a material breach AND**
      ii.　　**That party gave other reasonable time to CURE and they didn't cure**
iv.　　If we have a material breach the other party can suspend his own performance –
1. That party can't terminate unless she gives the other party opportunity to cure
2. If breaching party fails to cure, then innocent party is released from obligation and can bring suit for any damages incurred as a result of the other party's failure to perform
v.　　Cure: general rule – opportunity has to be reasonable in light of circumstances
1. Much more important in contract for the sale of goods (UCC)
2. Remember, if the time for performance has not yet expired, the seller has at least until the time of performance to cure (sometimes longer) (UCC § 2-508)
vi.　　***Walker & Co. v. Harrison*** D stopped payment on lease b/c P failed to clean the sign of tomato residue. HELD:: though failure to clean was failure to perform an obligation under K, it was NOT a material breach. Thus, D failing to pay rent was the breach and instead, P was entitled to damages.
1. Teaches us that it is tricky b/c if you think the K was breached and it wasn't actually a material breach, then failure to pay will be a material breach and that party is screwed (damages to other party)

c. <u>**ANTICIPATORY REPUDIATION**</u>
i. Here, the performance has not begun yet but there is a breach (that is the difference, above the performance had already started)
1. A party's indication that he would like to perform but will be unable to has NOT committed an anticipatory repudiation but the other party can STILL suspend performance
ii.　　**ELEMENTS: RST § 250**
1. A statement by the obligor to the oblige indicating that the obligator will not or cannot perform his contractual duty
2. A voluntary affirmative act which renders the obligor unable or apparently unable to perform w/o such breach

a. Can be a
   i. Statement,
       1. Vague doubts are NOT enough
          a. "I don't think I can do this" – not good enough
       2. But if other party requests assurances in hearing these doubts, if the party fails to assure that they will perform, this might be enough for AR.
       3. The statement must be <u>made to promisee</u>
       4. If the party <u>requests more favorable terms,</u> this is a case by case analysis but…
          a. If the request indicates an <u>intention not to perform unless the new conditions are met,</u> this is probably enough for AR
   ii. Action making performance impossible or
       1. Act must make the performance <u>impossible</u> AND the act must be <u>voluntary</u>
       2. Sometimes a delegation of a duty to perform personal services may constitute an AR
   iii. Indication that he will be unable to perform
       1. Promisee may <u>suspend performance</u> for sure
       2. Js are split on whether suit may be brought immediately if the reason for inability is outside of promisor's control (most say still can bring suit)

3. *Essentially an indication that the party cannot or will not perform their duty under the K*
   a. *Bankruptcy is often seen as an AR. But a party's* apparent *insolvency is NOT an AR*
      i. *But if they appear insolvent, you should suspend your performance and ask for assurances*
4. *Remember that even if the above factors are met, if the breach being threatened via AR would be <u>material</u>; if it's not material, this is not enough for an AR – must be MATERIAL*
5. *Also, a party who ARed does have a right to retract (see below for when it's not okay to retract AR)*

   iii. When the party anticipatorily breaches, the other party has options
1. Can terminate performance immediately and sometimes sue then too
   a. You risk that court will not find anticipatory repudiation. You might be then be deemed breacher if the other party's actions do not constitute an anticipatory repudiation.
2. Give them a change to repent and take it back
   a. If you keep going and pile up damages, court may find you failed to mitigate and now allow you to recover damages
3. Suspend and demand assurance
   a. We see this option when people aren't sure they will be paid
   b. If the oblige doesn't receive assurance, she can treat failure as a repudiation and demand damages
   c. But we need to be sure that there are (1) reasonable grounds to believe that the other party might breach and (2) the assurance demanded is not excessive

iv. **Courts refuse to allow for AR where the repudiator owes no further performance – you MUST wait until the time for performance occurs to sue**

1. **Usually this is in the case of payment of money (unilateral K)**

    a. This is why we have acceleration clauses – so the creditor doesn't have to wait around – you would want to sue immediately

v. ***Hochster v. De La Tour*** D employed P. Prior to start date, D repudiated on contract. HELD:: After D repudiated, P considered himself available for other employment. P may sue immediately or wait until time for performance has passed.

1. There is an implied covenant b/t the parties that in the waiting time prior to start of K, neither will do anything to the prejudice of the other inconsistent w/their future relation

2. Failure to live up to this gives rise for suit and damages – in considering damages, jury may look to all that happened and was likely to happen

3. ***If a party anticipatorily repudiates, most courts (using this case) say that you CAN bring a suit immediately, even before the time for performance has arrived***

    a. ***Court likes to dispose of the matter promptly***

    b. ***The aggrieved party needs certainty so they can move on***

vi. ***McCloskey v. Minweld*** D worked w/P on subcontract. D wrote a letter to P, advising P of the difficulty of procuring the materials. HELD:: D was not saying "I intend not to perform"

1. To give rise to a renunciation of K, there must be an **absolute and unequivocal** refusal to perform or a distinct and positive statement of an inability to do so.

vii. Retraction of Repudiation

1. A party who makes a repudiation can retract it until…

    a. The other party sues

    b. The other party gives notice that it accepted repudiation

    c. The other party relies on your repudiation to their detriment

2. ***U.S. v. Seacoast Gas Co.*** Seacoast anticipatorily repudiated the contract, then they said they retracted this but P had already signed another K to fulfill P's obligation. HELD:: a party can retract its repudiation BUT it has to give notice and it has to be before the other party relies on repudiation to their detriment

viii. ***Ultimately, AR just gets you in to court earlier. If you think the other party breached, you can still sue but you just have to wait until the time for performance has passed. AR lets you sue before time for performance.***

ix. REMEDIES

1. Difference b/t market price when party learned of AR and the contract price plus an incidental or consequential damages

d. **Assurance of Due Performance**

i. ***Casefile #42*** Training facility contracted for some equipment. There were doubts over the terms of the contract and we were not sure they were going to deliver. Facility ends up securing performance from another supplier.

1. ***RULE: when reasonable grounds for insecurity arise, the other party may demand assurance <u>in writing</u> and until he receives such assurance, he may suspend his performance.***

2. ***ANSWER: reasonable grounds for insecurity? Probably, based on the email and only performing pursuant to phone call. In writing? Yep, the***

email on April 5th.

        3. *Who breached? Probably the company who purported to sell them the equipment – they demanded assurance and didn't get it.*

  ii. *In class, I said I think the seller is trying to change the contract.* The original K said that seller would <u>install</u> the machines. But now they are saying that they will just drop them off.

  iii. But the counter is that the buyer agreed to have a "level and open" space, per the K

        1. We should look to industry practice – what does this usually mean?

        2. Are there any other provisions in the K that suggest who's responsibility this was? (the cement contractor and the leveling of the floor)

  iv. *So who is at fault depends on who was in breach. This is where you argue!*

XXII. **<u>EXCUSED PERFORMANCE</u>**
  a. **Mistake**

  i. A belief not in accord w/the facts (RST § 151)

  ii. Most courts require that the mistake be <u>mutual</u> (unilateral mistakes will not get you out of a contract).

  iii. *The mistake must have existed just prior to the contract (not future)*

  iv. *ELEMENTS of Mistake (RST § 152)*

        1. *Mutual mistake of <u>fact</u>*

        2. *Made as to the <u>basic assumption</u> on which K was made*

        3. *Which has a <u>material effect</u> on the agreed exchange of performances*

        4. *Mistake is not one for which the adversely affected party <u>bears the risk</u>*

  v. **(1) Both parties** had to make the same mistake **of fact**

        1. Not an opinion, hope, or forecast

        2. Not a mistake as to the law either

        3. HYPO: Suppose the parties entered K on belief that land will produce more plants than it actually produced. *This is NOT a mistake of fact – it is a projection or forecast!*

  vi. **(2) Basic assumption** means the mistake must be related to a central component of the contract (parties' agreement)

        1. Is there an unbargained for or unexpected gain or loss here?

          a. Where the A thinks the violins are brand X and B thinks they are brand Y, this goes to the basic assumption of the contract

          b. Market conditions and financial ability mistakes will usually NOT go to the basic assumption of the K

          c. Thus you cannot use mistake doctrine to avoid contract liability

        2. The existence of the SM of K. In *Renner*, the K was for the sale of land for farming– clearly the existence of water was important to the sale of land

          a. Look out for real estate contracts where promised acreage cannot be conveyed – if it is large, probably basic; if not, probably not.

          b. Look out for purchase of unique work of art where parties are mistaken as to origin or creator – probably basic

  vii. **(3) Material effect** on the agreed exchange

        1. Parties must show a severe imbalance of the outcome of the bargain if the court enforces the K

          a. If the court enforces the K, the mistake will greatly prejudice one party and other will essentially get a windfall

        2. In *Renner*, the K was for sale of land so if there is no water, you get

nothing and the seller gets your $ for no exchange! Bad!
3. But where there are other remedies besides terminate of the K based on mistake, the court is less likely to allow use of avoidance via mistake
   a. Could reform the contract or provide restitution
viii. **(4) Adversely affected party bears the risk**
1. Did the party who wants out of the K in some way assume the risk that the mistake would occur?
2. RST § 154: Three ways to assume the risk
   a. By agreement
      i. Expressly agreed – no way out
   b. Limited knowledge (conscious ignorance)
      i. Party enters K knowing that he has limited knowledge; court may say that you signed the K anyway so we're not going to let you out of it
   c. Allocated by the court
      i. Court allocates risk to a party if it is reasonable under the circumstances surrounding contract
         1. Ex. if Seller sells land for lower price b/c it's only good for farming but right before or at the time of sale, Seller/Buyer find oil and minerals, the Seller CANNOT avoid the contract b/c Seller is better allocated to find out that risk on her land
         2. Ex. if Builder agrees to build building and both parties think soil is fine but really it makes building much harder, Builder CANNOT avoid contract b/c the risk was reasonably allocated to him to know condition of land (he's in the business)
ix. ***Stees v. Leonard*** D agreed to complete building on P's lot. D stopped performance after building collapsed twice due to soil problems. P brings action to recover payments and value of lost lot. HELD:: D's obligation was to build the building regardless of what it took. PER prevented D from introducing evidence re: the proposed oral agreement D and P entered into in terms of draining the soil (which P didn't do and it was not in K)
x. ***Renner v. Kehl*** P bought land to use for farming and told D this expressly. After buying land, P found out D knew there wasn't sufficient water on the land to farm. HELD:: this was a mistake, it was material and P didn't assume the risk so D bore the burden. P could cancel K.

b. **Relief?**
   i. Permitted to rescind the contract and undo the deal if there truly was a mistake that meets the above requirements
      1. Everyone gets restitution (makes the how they were prior to K)
      2. If restitution is not sufficient, parties may get reliance damages
   ii. Cannot use mistake if you acted in bad faith
   iii. Cannot use mistake if you failed to read the contract
   iv. Sometimes court may "reform" the contract is a little tweaking would fix the problem but not if the mistake had a "material effect" on the agreed performance

XXIII. **IMPOSSIBILITY AND IMPRACTICABILITY**

a. Events occur <u>after the execution of the contract</u>, events <u>greatly alter the value</u> of the deal

    i. *Remember that impossibility, impracticability, and frustration of purpose are <u>gap fillers</u> (that is, parties are free to contract around these rules and the court will enforce them – but these are <u>defaults</u> in absence of any express provisions in relation to unexpected events)*

b. ****IMPOSSIBILITY****

c. ***If performance by a party has been made literally <u>impossible</u> by the occurrence of unexpected events, then the contract may be discharged.***

    i. Common situations:

        1. Destruction or unavailability of the subject matter of K

        2. Death or incapacitating illness of a party

        3. Supervening illegality (where a K is legal when it is entered into but subsequent change in law renders its performance illegal)

    ii. *Basic idea: if performance by one side is impossible or impracticable, then the party should be excused from performance*

        1. If it's just a general thing, you probably can't get out of it

        2. But if the <u>impossible part is specific</u>, you probably can get out of it

    iii. **IMPOSSIBILITY RST § 261: ELEMENTS**

        1. **Event occurred <u>after</u> the contract was made**

        2. **Non-occurrence of hardship was basic assumption upon which K was made**

        3. **Party seeking avoidance is not at fault**

        4. **Agreed performance is literally impossible (NO ALTERNATIVES) and did not state whether duty is discharged (b/c it wasn't contemplated)**

            a. **The duty to render the performance is <u>discharged</u> unless the language or the circumstances indicate to the contrary**

        5. One way to protect against having the burden fall on you…you can write into you K "act of god" clause: in the event of some overpowering supervening event, my duty is discharged…

        6. Must be careful when drafting these clauses – if you list out types of supervening causes and leave something out you might not be covered. We interpret the general terms (hardship) to be of the same kind as the specific term. A court may say hardship does not equal labor events

    iv. ***Remember that impossibility deals w/events AFTER the creation of the contract***

        1. ***If it happens at or before the contract, it is usually mistake or fraud***

    v. There IS a difference b/t:

        1. "The thing cannot be done" (objective – this is okay) and

        2. "I cannot do it" (subjective – this is not okay)

            a. Insolvency – if the party is insolvent, he probably CANNOT use impossibility b/c it is his own doing

            b. Strike – if the parties employees go on strike, usually CANNOT use the impossibility defense

            c. Sickness/death – if the contract was for <u>personal services</u> (i.e. cannot be delegated) this IS usually enough to use impossibility

            d. Supervening illegality (legal at the time of K but subsequently declared illegal) – you CAN use impossibility

    vi. **Basic Assumptions (which if violated, may constitute impossibility):**

1. Government intervention won't directly prevent performance of contract (government ban – YES; government regulation – NO)
2. Person necessary to the performance will not die or become incapacitated
   a. Learned Hand formula: B>P*L
   b. Dead b/c of his own fault (suicide)? Doesn't matter. If you OD on drugs, you are still liable.
   c. Dead but contract was assignable? Then you must assign – cannot claim impossibility if contract was not for personal services
   d. Dead/sick but not your fault? Then both parties may be excused
vii. ***Taylor v. Caldwell*** P agreed to rent D's music hall. Hall burned down. P sued for breach claiming damages b/c he incurred preparation $ but never got to get it back b/c hall was destroyed. HELD:: D was not liable for breach but each party was entitled to restitution.
   1. The K was for rental of a ***particular*** building that ***no longer existed*** (this makes it ***literally impossible to perform***)
   2. However, if the K had said "a building to perform" – then D could NOT have used impossibility b/c all it said was a building, not a specific one so even if he planned on using the one that burned down, he could have found another one
      a. **Temporary impossibility?** RST § 269 – it simply *suspends* performance until the temporary condition changes – then you evaluate it after that point
viii. If contractor agreed to "build a building from scratch" and when he is almost done it burns down, this is NOT impossibility!
   1. Some courts are leaning towards making this impossibility but you might be able to argue for "impracticability" below…
ix. If contractor agrees to "renovate an existing building" and it burns down, this IS impossibility b/c he agreed to renovate a *particular* building
x. **Impossibility due to 3rd Party**
   1. What if the middleman fails to come through?
      a. If the source of the goods was not specified in the second contract, usually the seller is out of luck
      b. If the contract is specific and the 1st seller fails to perform, the seller for the 2nd contract cannot use impossibility b/c *that seller impliedly bore the risk that she would be unable to make the necessary contract to procure the goods*
   2. The real question is ***how did the parties allocate the risk?*** If they didn't, then ask ***how would the parties have allocated the risk had they thought about it?***
      a. If the original seller is excused from 1st contract by impossibility, then usually 2nd seller will also be discharged via impossibility
xi. ***Selland Pontiac v. King*** P contracts to buy 4 buses from King. They also made separate contract w/GMC for the chassis for the busses. King gets buses from Superior. Superior goes out of business before King can deliver buses. P has to sell chassis at lower price (b/c w/o buses they are useless). P sues D HELD:: for D. Neither party had any reason to anticipate Superior would go out and it was specifically stated in the contract that Superior was King's supplier. Thus, King could not be said to have *assumed the risk of Superior's insolvency* and King is not liable for breach (impossible to perform!)

d. ** IMPRACTICABILITY**

    i. *If performance by a party has been made highly <u>impractical</u> by the occurrence of unexpected events, then the K may be discharged*

        1. *Similar to Impossibility but less stringent (easier to get out of K)*

    ii. *Was it foreseeable?*

    iii. *Were there alternatives?*

    iv. **RST § 261**---- requires the following:

        1. Where <u>after</u> the K is made,

            a. *Distinguishes impracticability from mistake*

            b. *Mistake = before or at time of K*

            c. *Impracticability = after K was made*

        2. A party's performance is made <u>impracticable</u>

            a. *Court seems to suggest this means "increased and unreasonable costs"*

        3. <u>Without his fault</u>

        4. By the occurrence of an event, the non-occurrence of which was made a <u>basic assumption</u> on which the K was made

            a. *Has to be central to the transaction that a particular condition was or was not going to be presenta*

        5. His duty is discharged (excused)

        6. Unless <u>the language or circumstances indicate otherwise</u>

            a. *How is the risk allocated?*

                i. *Who is better able to bear the risk? (buy insurance, diversify risk, etc.)*

e. *Is an increase in cost enough to render something impracticable?*

    i. *Depends on degree of cost increase (very significant in light of overall cost)*

        1. *AND*

    ii. *Nature and reason for cost increase (must be extreme – not just market fluctuation)*

f. **Costs must be extreme**

    i. **Depends on foreseeability - the more foreseeable, the less likely the parties intended that the buyer would bear the risk of such a large cost increase**

        1. If the parties agree on a fixed price, the risk of a rise in the market price is *foreseeable* so the court will usually hold that the parties *implicitly allocated the risk of the price rise on the party <u>agreeing to supply the good or service for the fixed price</u>.*

        2. Ex. ***Gulf Oil*** Gulf Oil agreed to supply fuel to Eastern Airlines. Gulf finds itself in a position where they are supplying for $5 when market price is $11 so they stop performance. HELD:: for Eastern – though this is a hardship for Gulf, they implicitly assumed the risk b/c the Mid East was in a situation where this was a foreseeable result. Should have put a clause in the K.

    ii. HYPO: Suppose that a shipping company is going to ship something from US to Iran. Ship sunk in Suez Canal, now its impassable the way they planned to navigate. Impracticable? HELD:: 1st prong is not satisfied – no impracticability (there were alternatives)

    iii. HYPO: Jan 2000, K to purchase new condo. Price is $1 million. You planned on making payments w/your stocks which are now worthless. HELD: NO impracticability – not a defense in this case

g. **Relief?**

i. **RST § 272: Relief Including Restitution:** [Impracticability and Frustration of Purpose]: (1) ….either party may have a claim for relief including **restitution** under the rules 240 [Part Performance as Agreed Equivalents] and 377 [Restitution in Cases of **Impracticability**, Frustration, Non-Occurrence of Condition or Disclaimer by Beneficiary] (2) ….if those rules together…will not avoid injustice, **the court may grant relief on such terms as justice requires**, including protection of the parties' reliance interests

ii. **Courts also allow reliance damages in some cases (quasi-contract)**

h. *Mineral Park Land v. Howard* D agreed to remove dirt from P's property. D removed a lot of dirt but then didn't finish. P now sued for money he paid for total removal minus the work that D did do. HELD:: *impossibility is not a defense here – it was <u>possible</u> to finish the work, albeit at a higher rate HOWEVER, <u>court expands the definition of this defense to IMPRACTICABILITY now</u>*

   i. *Impracticability = if completion can only be done at an excessive and unreasonable cost*

   ii. Courts now have to draw a line b/t "impossible" and "impracticable"

   iii. We need to constrain this definition a bit

      1. *UCC § 2-615* incorporates the similar principle for sale of goods

XXIV. <u>FRUSTRATION OF PURPOSE</u>

a. *When unexpected events, occurring <u>after the K is made</u>, completely or almost completely destroy a party's purpose in entering into the K, the parties may be excused from performing*

   i. *Coronation case*: D books apt to see King's coronation and pays a premium to get a good view. Coronation cancelled. D refuses to pay. HELD:: for D – D's essential purpose for entering K was frustrated. The parties acknowledged that purpose of rental of apt was to see coronation. If K was completed now, D would derive no benefit from sitting in the apt at the stated time for two days – no coronation was happening. D is excused from performance w/o breach of K.

b. **RST § 265: Frustration of Purpose**

   i. Where, **after** a contract is made,

   ii. A party's **principal purpose** is

   iii. **Substantially frustrated** *w/o his fault*

   iv. By the occurrence of an event the **non-occurrence** of which was a **basic assumption** on which K was made

   v. His **remaining duties** to render performance are **discharged**

   vi. **Unless** the language or the circumstances indicate the contrary

c. **Factors to Consider:**

   i. **Foreseeability** (foreseeable, then probably no frustration)

   ii. **Allocation of risk** (implicit allocation, then prob not frustrated)

   iii. **Degree of frustration** (all {frustrated} or partial {prob no frustration})

   iv. **Fault of parties** (if there is fault, probably not frustrated)

      1. HYPO: P enters K w/D to operate car dealership. Restriction on dealership laws and D allows P to use premises for other purposes. HELD:: P cannot use frustration of purpose defense (it was foreseeable and his purpose was not ALL frustrated – he had options)

   v. If it was foreseeable, then the parties probably allocated the risk. If the parties allocated the risk, then it was probably foreseeable (go hand in hand)

d. UCC view: the UCC does not *expressly* grant the frustration of purpose defense to seller or buyers. But both sides may be able to use the doctrine

        i. It's *more likely that a <u>buyer</u>* of goods *would use this*

           1. Common law fills the UCC gaps – under § 1-103(b), the common law applies unless displaced by the particular provisions of this act

        ii.   It's rare that a seller will use it but they could if they had a case where they could use the § 2-615(a)'s general impracticability languge to support a frustration defense – that is, the seller might be able to avoid the contract if performance has become impracticable "by the occurrence of a contingency the non-occurrence of which was a basic assumption upon which the K was made."

e. ***Casefile #40*** S booked bonefish fishing vacation w/guide. Nearby accident resulted in spill which made water murky (no chance it will be okay for trip). S cancelled trip and company still wants him to pay. Does he have to? Or was the purpose of the trip frustrated?

        i. Impracticability involves an impediment to performance

        ii.   Frustration of purpose involves a situation where change in circumstances makes worthless the value of other party's performance

           1. It's not that I can't perform or that it is impossible but rather its just not worth my time. What you were going to give me no longer has value to me.

               a. Man, we thought impracticability was easy – this is even easier to get out of K – you no value the performance! CAREFUL W/USING THIS

        iii.   **Application**

           1. Do we have frustration of purpose?

               a. After the K is made, no one could fix it (i.e. substantially frustrated), w/o customer's fault, maybe it was foreseeable (this is where you argue!)

           2. Depends on whether you take the narrow (spill) or broad (murky water) view – if you define it narrowly, then it probably wasn't foreseeable. But if you define it broadly, then maybe it was foreseeable.

f. **REMEDIES FOR IMPOSSIBILITY, IMPRACTICABILTIY AND FRUSTRATION OF PURPOSE**

        i. If the party's duty is discharged, he may sometimes be able to recover restitution damages or even reliance damages for the work he did in anticipation of performance

        ii.   Restitution:

           1. If a party has made a **down-payment** – usually can recover restitution

           2. If a party has conferred a **benefit** – usually can recover restitution

               a. Remember **cheaper cost avoider** – whoever is the cheaper cost avoider will bear the burden

           3. If the party has a **pro-rate contract** (to be paid in installments) – usually limited to the pro-rate contract price for recovery

               a. But if reasonable value is **less** than pro-rata, can only recover reasonable value of work

                    i. Ex. Plumber installs pipe for $1000, payable in two installments. Before he can finish, building is destroyed.

                        1. Market value = $600, can only recover $500 (pro-rata share of contract price)

                        2. Market value = $400, can only recover $400 (market value is less than pro-rata share)

           4. If the party is to **pay upon completion** – usually get restitution for market

price

    a. Halfway through performance, building is destroyed. Builder spend $12,000 on supplies; market price of improvements is $18,000. Can recover $18,000 b/c it was market price right before the destruction.

  iii. Reliance:

    1. Theoretically, 2nd RST allows for reliance damages but court will rarely give them

ENFORCING THE CONTRACT – REMEDIES?!?!

Remember to distinguish b/t "on the contract" and "quasi-contract"

"on the contract" – when there is a legally enforceable contract and the D has breached. The damages will be based on the terms of the contract

"quasi-contract" – when the contract is not enforceable for some reason (unenforceably vague, illegal, discharged (impossibility/frustration of purpose), when P materially breaches). The damages will be based upon the actual value of performance rendered, irrespective of any price set out in the contract (usually restitution)

XXV. **EQUITABLE REMEDIES – Injunction or Specific Performance**

 a. ***Specific relief*** – making the party actually perform the contract

   i. Court is reluctant to use this b/c it is administratively messy

   ii. *Should only be used when monetary damages are extraordinary*

 b. Reasons why a court might grant SP

   i. Incommensurability (the value of some things cannot be measured in money)

   ii. Uncertainty (value too speculative) or value of performance difficult to calculate

 c. When might a court grants SP/Injunctions (specific relief)?

   i. Land transfers – usually YES b/c each tract of land is unique and there really is no other way to compensate the person

   ii. Employment/non-compete – sometimes YES (using an injunction; not using specific performance)

   iii. Forbearance (non-competes) – usually YES

   iv. Sale of business – usually YES

   v. Patents and copyrights – usually YES

   vi. Personal services – usually NOT b/c it appears like involuntary servitude

   vii. Sale of goods – usually NOT

 d. ***Campbell Soup v. Wentz*** C contracted w/D to deliver all the carrots they were going to grow during the season. Market price increased and W refused to perform. C wanted SP HELD:: SP was used in this case b/c ***carrots were special – money damages were inadequate b/c C couldn't get the carrots from anywhere else***

 e. ***Klein v. PepsiCo*** P contracted to buy corporate jet by Pepsi. Pepsi refused to deliver after inspection showed crack in engine blades. K sued for SP. HELD:: No SP here b/c the ***jet was NOT unique*** – K said that there were other ways of obtaining the jet (clearly there were damages, just money damages, not SP)

   i. UCC § 2-716: SP is appropriate where goods are unique OR "in other proper circumstances

    1. Where the goods are NOT unique (as in jet (there were 3 others)) then the UCC will not enforce the K using SP (but will give other remedies – see below)

2. UCC will give SP when the buyer "cannot cover" – that is cannot procure substitute goods w/i a reasonable time

f. ***Laclede Gas v. Amoco Oil*** D agreed to supply propane for P. Due to market price increase, D reduced supply, increased price, and then terminated K. HELD:: Granted SP b/c of the long-term relationship b/t the parties.

    i. The buyer was buying gas AND buying an expectation of long term supply of propane gas w/o interruption – can't use money to put the buyer in the position he would have been had the K been performed

    ii. ***So we are compensating not only the gas here, but the expectation of supply w/o interruption – remember that this is something that money can't buy – that's when we use SP***

g. ***In summary, money damages are preferred to SP***

h. ***SP will be granted where money damages are inadequate***

i. ***Money damages will be inadequate when: (1) it is difficult to calculate damages, (2) the value of performance is hard to measure, (3) the performance is unique, (4) if MD will not fulfill the expected bargain***

LEGAL REMEDIES – MONEY DAMAGES

XXVI. EXPECTATION DAMAGES

a. Main goal/interest of contract law remedies: to enforce the bargain by putting the innocent party in as good a position was they were had the contract been performed (this is the ***expectation interest***)

    i. We don't want to put the party in a <u>better</u> position than they would had been in had the K been performed; just the <u>same</u>

    ii. ***These are the <u>usual damages</u> awarded for breach of contract***

        1. **Normally this means the P is awarded the <u>profit</u> which she would have made had the K been performed**

    iii. Ex. P contracts w/D to buy home for $500,000. D reneges b/c market price went up and later sells for $700,000. P is entitled to recover the additional $200,000 from D b/c she would have been in possession of the house that was worth that at the time if D had not reneged the bargain

    iv. Ex. P contracts w/D to fix his hairy hand. D fails to do so. P can recover *the difference b/t a perfect hand (what he was promised) and the value of a scarred and hairy hand (what he has)*

        1. Difference b/t what he would have had had the contract been performed and what he has now.

b. **RST § 347**: *expectation damages = loss in value + other losses – cost or loss avoided*

        1. You can think about this as if the P was getting the "profit" which she would have made had the K been performed

        2. You are giving the P "the benefit of the bargain"

    ii. **Loss in value**: the value of the performance promised to the innocent party minus the value of performance actually received

    iii. **Other losses**:

        1. Incidental damages – costs and expenses incurred by the injured party in attempting to deal w/the breach and in taking action to seek a substitute performance or reduce losses

            a. So assume Gely sells me his car. I breach and don't show up. Now he has to spend another $50 to run another ad in a newspaper to find a new buyer. Gely would not have incurred this expense had I not breached.

2. Consequential damages – losses suffered by the injured party beyond the mere loss in value of the promised performance and resulting from the impact of the breach on other transactions dependent on the K
   a. Suppose I make a K w/A and then make a separate K w/B to sell B what I was supposed to get from A. Now when A doesn't perform, I loses the transaction w/B. This is consequential damages – results from A's breach

iv. **Costs or loss avoided**:
1. Costs avoided - savings accrued to injured party resulting from the breach
2. Loss avoided – other beneficial effects to the injured party resulting from salvaging or reallocating some resources that would have otherwise been sued in performing the breached K
   a. *This does NOT include overhead (Vitex Manufacturing)*
      i. *This benefits P* (b/c P doesn't have to deduct this from the damages)
      ii. The reasoning? The costs would have been incurred no matter whether P and D contracted so it should not be a 'cost saved' – it isn't in reality.
3. ***If the party cannot determine how much it would have cost them to complete the rest of performance, they cannot recover (must show damages w/reasonable certainty)***

v. To the extent that any of these three categories exist, they will affect the amount of expectation damages the innocent party may receive

c. Emanuels says: *expectation damages = value of D's promised performance (usually contract price) – whatever benefit, if any, P received from not having to complete his own performance*
   i. Benefits: expenditures which P would have had to make but didn't have to b/c P did not have to complete his performance
      1. Ex. O contracts w/C to build home. K provides that half way through, O is to pay C $150,000. C completes half the work and demands payment. O refuses. At this point, it would have cost C $100,000 to complete the performance.
         a. Expectation damages = $300,000 - $100,000 = $200,000
   ii. HYPO: Landscape co. agrees to do some work for homeowner. Cost $2,000 in materials and $1500 in labor. In exchange. H agrees to pay $5,000 for work.
      1. MG (Landscaper) performs all work, H refuses to pay. Expectation damages are: $5000 (loss in value) + $0 (no other losses) - $0 (no cost or loss avoided) = $5000 total expectation damages
   iii. HYPO: MG performs all work. H pays $1000 down payment but refuses to pay rest.
      1. $4000 (loss in value) + $0 - $0 = $4000 (b/c the $1000 down payment was already paid)
   iv. HYPO: MG purchased all materials. Owner cancels day b4 work supposed to start. MG has to rent storage $500/week for 3 weeks. MG can resell some materials for $1000. H refuses to pay full $5000.
      1. $5000 (loss in value) + $1500 (incidental damages – no consequential damages) - $2500 (cost or loss avoided for reselling other materials for $1000 and not paying for labor at $1500) = $4000 total expectation damages

    d. **Cost of completion v. Diminution in value**

        i. *Only the diminution in value should be awarded, especially in situations where the P receiving the economic benefit for full performance is <u>greatly disproportionate</u> to the cost of performing the work*

          1. This is "economic waste"

        ii.   RST § 348: the court should not grant the cost of remedying defects "if the cost is...*clearly disproportionate* to the probable loss in value" to the P

          1. Ex. $300 diminution in value is grossly disproportionate to the $29,000 cost of performing the work

          2. Ex. $20,000 diminution in value is not grossly disproportionate to the $30,000 cost of performing the work

        iii.   Think ***Jacob & Youngs v. Kent*** the cost of tearing out all of the pipes and putting in "Reading manufactured" pipes in would have been economically inefficient since the total "market value" was substantially the same.

          1. Criticism the P specifically contracted for the "Reading" pipes so by allowing this result, we are allowing contractors (Ds) to behave immorally and not give P what the K says

            a. Solution? If D's breach is <u>*willful*</u>, then the court will probably punish D – then they are more likely to award the cost of completion rather than diminution in value

    e. **RST § 352**: ***<u>the P can only recover damages that he can establish with "reasonable certainty"</u>*** – P must show the amount of his losses w/*reasonable certainty*

        i. Major application – when P says that he could have "made profits" – P must show those "profits" w/reasonable certainty

          1. This is particularly important when the P claimed profits on a business not yet in operation

        ii.   If there is uncertainty, the court will usually resolve it in favor of the P and against the D.

        iii.   Courts are especially unlikely to find that lost profits are sufficiently demonstrated when the venture depends on the <u>public whim</u> (like in entertainment and sports contracts)

        iv.   Non-compete agreements – courts are also speculative of applying lost profits made the D as an example of 'reasonable certainty' b/c usually, P could not have made the same profits, absent competition, as the D made by competing

          1. *If you cannot show reasonable certainty, you cannot recover*

    f. **Seller's Remedy**

        i. COVER under UCC § 2-716 = ***Contract Price – Cover Price + Incidental Damages***

          1. Problem: after many years in the restaurant business, John decides to close operations and retire. He enters into a K to sell the furniture and kitchen equipment to Ben for $12,000. Ben breaches the contract. Assume John tries to find another buyer by advertising in the appropriate outlets and calling potential buyers. John spends $150 in ads and another $50 in phone calls. Ultimately John is able to resell to Mara for $8,000. What are John's damages? (depends on the option seller chooses)

            a. COVER – under § 2-706, Contract Price – Cover Price + Incidental Damages (12,000-8,000+200 = 4200)

          2. Assume John decides to keep the goods. Assume also that at the time of breach, the same type of equipment had a market value of $10,000. What are his damages?

        a. Under § 2-708(1), John's damages are Contract Price – Market Price - $2000. (12,000-10,000 = 2000)

        b. Similar under buyer's remedy under 2-713

   3. Assume that John was not a retired restaurateur but John manufactures and sells restaurant equipment. Assume that Ben breaches $12K K. John is able to resell to Mara for $12K. Has John suffered any damages?

        a. At first look, it seems as though John has not suffered any damages – he hasn't lost any money

        b. But looking at 2-708(2) (on chart), this allows John to make the argument that he lost profits

        c. Had the K been performed seller would have been able to make two sales (one to Ben and one to Mara). Thus, seller should be allowed to recover the lost profit of that lost sale

   4. He essentially lost the profits related to 2nd sale

        a. i.e. Mara needed this too so if Ben would have kept his K and performed, John would have gotten $12K from Ben and then another $12K from Mara for her separate transaction

        b. But now he only has one sale so he essentially is worse off and only made $12K once, not twice

  ii. ***R.E. Davis v. Diasonics*** Seller agreed to sell medical equipment to someone, he breached, then seller resold for same price. Lost profits? HELD:: how do we know the 2nd sale would have been made? He could have just gotten lucky! We get a "LOST VOLUME SELLER"

   1. This is where the seller is asking to be compensated for a hypothetical sale that may not have happened

   2. ***Lost volume seller – one that has a predictable and finite number of customers and that has the capacity either to sell to all new buyers or to make the one additional sale… (see pg. 622)***

        a. ***If there hadn't had been a breach, you would have solicited and sold to the ultimate buyer and the sale would have been profitable for you (as well as the original sale)***

   3. § 2-708 allows a seller to bring <u>*action for the price*</u>, where buyer has accepted the goods, or where seller is unable to resell the goods

        a. This is a type of specific performance – requiring the buyer to do what he should have done – but don't overthink this! It's pretty straightforward

   4. TEST: would the 2-708(1) measure adequately compensate the seller? If not (the los seller test met) then the profit measure is appropriate even if the seller engaged in reselling

 g. If lost profits are too speculative, the court will usually adopt an ***alternative*** in ***reliance damages***.

XXVII. **Damages under the UCC**

 a. ***Casefile #56*** UCC has almost the same remedies as case law. Contract was for the sale of 50,000 blue plastic footballs for $35K. The intended retail price was $2 but since they are so crappy, the University isn't even sure that they can get anything for them.

  i. ***ANSWER: we look to <u>buyer's remedies</u> under the UCC. Under UCC, performance has to be PERFECT (perfect tender rule). Buyer can:***

   1. ***Reject the goods***

   2. ***Reject the goods and seek alternate performance (cover)***

   3. ***Accept the goods***

        a. ***Amount of remedy depends upon which option buyer takes***
    4. ***University could take any of these remedies***

XXVIII. **RELIANCE DAMAGES**

    a. To put the innocent party in the position she was before the contract was formed, by compensating her for any expenses she has incurred or suffered as a result of the contract (this is the ***reliance interest***) (RST § 349)

    b. Sometimes expectation damages are not sufficient. So the court will award reliance damages like in:

        i. P cannot show **lost profits** w/certainty but can nonetheless show items of expenditure

            1. Can't recover lost profits w/o certainty but may be able to recover expenditures incurred in anticipation of performance or part performance

        ii. P is a vendee under a land contract who sues the vendor for refusal to convey property to him and **J doesn't award expectation** for this

            1. Or where **expectation damages are too speculative**

        iii. No legally enforceable K but P is entitled to come protection (**promissory estoppel**)

        iv. Where there is a **losing contract** (i.e. non-breaching party would have lost money anyway – still can recover something)

    c. *Remember that reliance damages are a <u>component</u> of expectation damages – they are normally hidden in there*

        i. *Think about it*

        ii. *Cost to P of work already performed + total profit P would have made on the contract*

            1. *Cost to P of work already performed = reliance damages*

            2. Ex. Contractor expends $300 in supplies and should be paid $4/sq. ft. of roofing. After he put up 100 sq ft. owner repudiates on K. At trial, P can show that (1) he spent $300, (2) $4 is the standard, (3) based on prior work, he makes 25% profit. HELD:: he will be able to recover $800, ***$300 of which is the reliance damages that he spent on the supplies***

    d. Sometimes reliance damages are given in cases like *Hawkins v. McGee* where the doctor promised a result and did not achieve it

    e. **Limitations on Reliance Damages**

        i. When the D's **only obligation** under the K is to **pay money**, the reliance damage amount will usually be **limited to the contract price**

        ii. **RST § 349:** most courts refuse to allow reliance damages to exceed expectation damages, but place the burden of proof on the D to show what the P's losses would be

            1. P is not required to rebut D's allegation that the P would have lost money on the K, unless the D comes forth w/actual satisfactory evidence of this allegation

        iii. But if D is able to <u>*prove*</u> that P would have suffered a <u>*net loss*</u>, the P's *reliance recovery* is <u>*limited*</u> to what his <u>*expectation damages*</u> would have been

        iv. Most modern courts allow recovery of **both essential and incidental reliance damages** so long as the incidental damages are foreseeable

            1. But some courts do distinguish and in those jurisdictions, courts deny recovery for incidental damages

            2. ***Essential damages:*** those made in preparing to perform the K , or in actually performing it

3. *Incidental damages:* those made by P b/c he anticipated that the K would be performed, but which do not relate directly to performance

    a. Remember that P *usually cannot recover expenses from before the K was signed* b/c those are not "in reliance"

f. ***When reliance damages are calculated, they are usually done so according to the <u>cost of the P</u> rather than value to the D***

    i. Even if P's expenditures were all incurred in preliminary preparations to perform, the D breached b4 P even began actual performance so P will be able to recover his cost of preparation

        1. *This contrasts w/restitution which is measured in regards to value to D (benefit to D)*

g. UCC § 2-715(1) – allows an aggrieved buyer to recover "incidental damages"

XXIX. RESTITUTION DAMAGES

a. To put the parties in the position they were before the contract was formed by asking D to return any benefits she has received during the course of performance (this is the ***restitution interest***)

    i. ***Determined in regards to <u>value to D</u> (benefit to D) rather than in cost to P***

        1. This is NOT the subjective value to D – it is <u>the market value</u>

b. Usually used where D's expectation damages is not calculable to a sufficient certainty to be recovered (see below)

c. Restitution *is not limited to contract price* – completely different from the reliance equation above

    i. Rationale? to permit the D to use his breached contract to limit recovery would pay him a premium for his own wrong

    ii. Also price might change depending on how much work was to be done (i.e. discount for more work performed when the lower amount was actually done)

d. *Restitution is NOT available where the P has <u>fully</u> performed the K – most courts <u>do not allow P to recover restitution in this case!</u>*

e. ***When do we give restitution?***

    i. ***Losing contracts***

    ii. ***Where party seeking restitution is the party who breached***

    iii. ***Promissory estoppel*** (we won't be tested on PE)

        1. How do we get restitution? **Quasi contract**

            a. This is a cause of action, not a remedy

            b. Use this when there are no other remedies available (court focuses on unjust enrichment – benefit received by D)

        2. Use this for interests not protected by contract law

            a. **Sentimental value** (most of the time P cannot recover this b/c it is hard to prove w/certainty)

            b. **Emotional distress** (problem w/quantifying)

            c. **Punishment to the party in breach**

f. ***US v. Algernon Blair*** P contracted to perform sub-contractor work for D. Only part of the work was done and P terminated work. D showed that if P had fully performed, P would have sustained a loss. HELD:: for P. though the normal expectation damages would produce no recovery, P is entitled to ***quantum meruit***. P's measure of recovery will be the "reasonable value of performance"

    i. The idea of "quantum meruit" is to allow a promisee to recover the value of services he gave the D irrespective of whether he would have lost money on the K or been unable to recover

    ii.   How is this value measured?

        1. **RST § 371: amount for which P's services could have been purchased** – the extent to which the other party's property has been increased in value

g. ***Britton v. Turner*** P agreed to work for D for one year but left after 9 months. HELD:: P could recover in *quantum meruit* for the services he gave D over those 9 months.

    i. ***RULE: if a "party actually receives labor or material and thereby derives a benefit and advantage, over and above the damage which has resulted from the breach of K, the law, raises a promise to pay to the extent reasonable worth of such excess***

h. ***Kirkland v. Archbold*** the builder whose breach of K is merely negligent can recover the value of his work but one who has <u>willfully</u> breached the K cannot recover. P is entitled to restitution for any benefit conferred to D at this point

i. If the P breaches the K, he may be entitled to recover the amount by which D has been enriched but the defaulting P's suit must be brought in quasi-contract.

XXX. THREE LIMITATIONS ON DAMAGES
a. **AVOIDABILITY – DUTY TO MITIGATE**

    i. **RST § 350:** *An aggrieved promisee is not allowed to recover loss that it could reasonably have avoided*

        1. ***Essentially, you have to take reasonable steps to mitigate your damages and failure to do so may result in you not being able to recover those damages***

        2. The injured party incurs no liability to the party in breach for a failure to mitigate but the damages will be reduced if mitigation was required and failed to be done

    ii.   Duty to mitigate requires P to make *reasonable efforts* to mitigate damages

        1. P is not required to: enter dubious contracts, incur considerable expense or inconvenience, disorganize his business, damage his reputation or honor, break any other contracts, etc. to mitigate

    iii. **Personal services contracts – does not require P to accept any position that is substantially different from or inferior to the one contracted for**

    iv. ***Rockingham County v. Luten Bridge*** P decided not to build bridge they contracted w/D to build. After notifying D, D continued to build and sought to recover full amount. HELD:: P breached and D was entitled to expenditures up to that point BUT the *American Rule requires the non-breaching party mitigate their damages* after the K was broken. Thus, D's failure to stop building was <u>avoidable</u> and thus, not recoverable

        1. **American Rule** – after an absolute repudiation or refusal to perform by one party to a K, the other party cannot continue to perform and recover damages based on full performance

           a. The D must, so far as he can w/o loss to himself, mitigate the damages caused by P's wrongful act

    v. ***Parker v. 20th Century Fox*** P contracted to do a movie. D breached but offered another movie to P. P refused. D argues P did not mitigate. HELD:: in general, there is a duty to mitigate but here, P was entitled to full compensation b/c *there was enough difference b/t the two roles that the court found them not equal* – thus, no duty to take it (no available mitigation)

        1. RST § 350: if the alternative K that you could have entered into is different in important ways, then you do not have to take it

        2. An offer of reemployment by an employer will not diminish the

employee's recovery if the offer is not accepted if circumstances are such as to render further association b/t the parties offensive or degrading to the employee.

vi. ***Jacob & Young v. Kent*** case about the "Reading" pipes – where the difference in value is nominal or nothing, the court will usually not give damages b/c it would be economically wasteful *unless the party breaches the K willfully*

1. **DEFAULT RULE:** Generally, damages will be cost of completion – we want to give party the money to fix the defective performance
2. **MINORITY RULE:** If this amount is grossly and unfairly out of proportion, then the damages will be difference in value
   a. ***Groves v. John Wunder*** where the Ker willfully and fraudulently varies the terms of a K, he cannot sue thereon and have the benefit of equitable relief
3. In some cases, such as where the property is held solely for investment, the court may conclude as a matter of law that the damage award cannot exceed the diminution in value.
4. Where the property has special significance to the owner and repair seems likely, the cost of repair may be appropriate even if it exceeds the diminution in value

vii. ***The key is figuring out what the K was really about – then we decide how to compensate the innocent party***

1. Jacob & Young – no evidence the K was about the pipes – it was really about the house (so no recovery)
2. But if a guy in their family had stock in "Reading pipes" then maybe we would have made them tear them out and put new ones in b/c that goes to the essence of the K (***Peevyhouse v. Garland Coal***)

viii. **Sale of Goods (UCC)**

1. BUYER:
   a. Usually parties must attempt to *"cover"* for the goods – this means he ***must attempt to purchase goods from another supplier***
      i. Essentially, the UCC says the buyer <u>must</u> mitigate if he can and if he doesn't he won't be able to recover those lost profits
   b. If buyer covers, ***Damages = Cover Price – Contract Price***
   c. If you decide not to cover, then your damages are calculated per **UCC § 2-713, *Damages = Market Price – Contract Price***
      i. If the market price is less than the cover, you only get the market price if the buyer decides not to cover
2. SELLER:
   a. Duty to mitigate applies to a seller as well
   b. Seller may choose:
      i. To resell – seller can then recover difference b/t resale and contract price (2-706)
      ii. To not resell – difference b/t contract price and market price (at the time and place of tender) (2-708)
      iii. Can't resell – if the goods are so highly customized that the seller cannot resell, then the seller may be able to

recover the contract price (2-709)

    c. If none of these will work to put the seller is as good a position as he was had the contract been performed, then the seller may recover lost profits from the transaction

        i. These include profits from the transaction plus any incidentals minus reasonable costs

  3. If a party attempts to mitigate and incurs additional costs, they may be able to recover those costs whether or not the attempts to mitigate are successful.

ix. ***Tongish v. Thomas*** D's argument – damages should be measured by (market price – contract price) – under UCC § 2-713 (buyer's remedy). P's argument – damages should be measured by loss of expected profits. P says that using buyer's remedy would put D in a better position than he would have been in had the K been performed (would essentially punish the seller). But the court finds for buyer's remedy anyway.

  1. **MAJORITY: award market damages even though in excess of P's loss**. MINORITY: reduce market damages to the P's loss w/o regard to whether this creates a windfall for D

  2.

b. **FORESEEABILITY**

  i. Normally, courts will only allow recovery for **foreseeable damages**, otherwise, it might be unfair to the D!

  ii. So what is **foreseeable?**

    1. *Hadley v. Baxendale* 2 rules. Damages that…

      a. *(1) Arise naturally, i.e. according to the <u>usual course of things</u> from the breach of K itself*

      b. *(2) Arise from the <u>special circumstances</u> under which the K was actually made if an only if these special circumstances <u>were communicated by the P to the D</u>*

    2. So essentially..

      a. *(1) The court will "impute" foreseeability to the D as to those damages which <u>any reasonable person should have foreseen</u> whether or not the D actually saw them AND*

        i. *These are <u>direct or general damages</u>*

      b. *(2) The court will award damages as to <u>remote or unusual consequences</u> but only if the D had <u>actual notice</u> as to the possibility of those consequences*

        i. *These are <u>special or consequential damages</u>*

  iii. **RST § 351:** basically codifies the *Hadley* ruling which is universally followed

    1. **The rule of *Hadley* is almost <u>universally followed in American courts</u>**

  iv. Remember that the *parties are free to allocate the risks themselves* and the court will enforce this agreement (the other rules we are learning are just default rules if the parties do not contract around them)

    1. One way to do this is for the P to give notice to D of special circumstances of the K (thereby meeting #2 above)

      a. Ex. Telegraph Co makes every sender of a telegram sign a K which provides that any remedy for a mis-sent telegram is limited to the price of the telegram. This allocation of risk will probably be enforced by the court even though the actual damages might be much higher.

2. The D must have "knowledge" of the special circumstances
   a. If cases of borrowing money, money is presumed to be an "available commodity" and thus, available from other sources. Often the borrower will only be able to recover the difference b/t the market rate of interest and the rate called for in the K (if lower) but if the borrower can show that the lender KNEW he would have a hard time getting other funding, the borrower may be able to recover more money

3. 3rd party? if the 3rd party liability was *foreseeable* then the party may be able to recover this liability.
   a. If a seller of goods knows that the buyer has a K to resell the goods, then seller will be liable for damages which the buyer is forced to pay to his own purchaser in cases of breach

v. **Remember: *foreseeability is determined <u>at the time the contract was made</u> – you must determine whether the possibility of damages was sufficiently likely when the K was executed*** (*subsequent knowledge after K is formed but before breach is irrelevant!*) *– RST § 351*

1. **On the other hand: *certainty relates to how clear it is <u>at the time of the suit</u> that the alleged losses in fact occurred, and that were caused by D's breach***

vi. **<u>UCC</u>** - § 2-715(2) is pretty liberal in terms of foreseeability

1. Allows a buyer to recover "consequential damages resulting from seller's breach" – defined to include *"any loss resulting from general or particular requirements and needs of which the seller <u>at the time of contracting</u> had reason to know and which could not reasonably be prevented by cover or otherwise as well as injury to person or property proximately resulting from any breach of warranty"*
   a. The buyer who 'covers' (procures substitute goods – makes another transaction) may recover the amount by which the cost of cover exceeds the contract price, plus any costs of arranging the covering transaction (these are costs in the 'ordinary course')

2. Problems of foreseeability arise when buyer can't cover – when buyer is…
   a. **Middleman** – if buyer is unable to cover (assuming this was foreseeable), the seller will be held to have foreseen this possibility of lost profits and *seller is liable for them*
      i. But seller is not liable if they are extremely large
   b. **Manufacturer** – buyer must first show that his inability to cover was foreseeable to the seller and must show that *seller had reason to know that the buyer would be using the item to produce goods and services*
      i. But again, seller is not liable for extreme damages

3. **Breach of warranty** – any injury to person or property may be recovered for as long as it was "proximately caused" by the breach of warranty
   a. Many courts allow for lost profits due to defective goods (Casefile w/the defective footballs)

4. UCC § 2-719(3): parties are given substantial latitude to modify their liability for consequential damages – may be limited or excluded unless it is unconscionable to do so

vii. **Receivership**

1. Used to denote a situation in which an institution or enterprise is being held by a receiver. In law, a receiver is a person "placed in the custodial responsibility for the property of others, including tangible and intangible assets and rights. Types of receivership
   a. A receiver appointed by a government regulator pursuant to a statute
   b. A privately appointed receiver and
   c. A court appointed receiver. The receiver's powers "flow from the document(s) underlying his appointment – a statute, financing agreement, or court order

viii. *Casefile #53* Tage Rods sells fishing rods. Leapord (client) contracted with them and never got his rods. He needed them for a fishing expedition and had to go to great lengths to get them (go around to stores (more $), overnight delivery, and a plane to get them to the fishing location. Tage agrees they breached the contract but claim that damages are excessive.

1. *ANSWER:* The price difference from the fishing rods is probably foreseeable (meets #1 of *Hadley*) so yes, recoverable
2. The cost of the plane? This is not foreseeable (fails #1 of *Hadley*) nor was it "mutually contemplated by the parties" (fails #2 of *Hadley*) so nope, no recovery of this

c. **ASCERTAINABILITY**

i. RST § 352: damages must be measured w/a reasonable degree of certainty

1. Can do this using past sale (Red October case)
2. Looking backwards (seeing how much of something someone bought to resell – they clearly thought they could sell that)
3. Artistic creations – this is more difficult
   a. But when P is entitled to recover and the only uncertainty is the amount, P will not recover nothing – he will get something
4. New business – courts are reluctant to grant "lost profits" for a new business w/no basis
   a. But if you are a continuing business, they might be more likely to let you use past profits
5. Lost profits in entertainment and sports are also too uncertain many times to allow for recovery
   a. If lost profits are too uncertain, courts may allow for reliance damages

ii. *Casefile # 52* Top Cream is a cover band who hired a guitarist when their original one injured his hand. The guy recovered and Top Cream no longer needed the new guitarist. He sues and wants $1 million b/c he says that he would have been widely in demand from other groups had he been able to tour w/Top Cream. Is this certain enough to be recoverable?

1. *ANSWER: no real answer from class – you would probably argue that these are too speculate and too uncertain to be recoverable b/c there is nothing to base this off of – the market changes and its not like he was in business prior to this and we can use those numbers*

d. PUTTING IT ALL TOGETHER: Clark supposed to give Lois Superman comic (valued at $15) – Lois to give Clark notes + $10.

i. L pays $10 and copies K notes. C refuses to deliver
1. L did what she had to do – we give her $15 for market value of book to put her in the position she would have been in **expectation interest**
2. What if she asked for **reliance damages**? Then it will be $13. We think of how much money she has spent (in this case it is $10 + $3 to copy notes) – this doesn't make sense – she wouldn't ask for this b/c she can get more w/expectation damages
3. What about **restitution damages**? Then it will be $11 - $10 plus the $1 of the market value of the notes – benefit C received and what he has to give back (the notes could be worth a different value but the idea is to figure out the market value of the notes and that is the value that is required in restitution)

ii. L gave notes to C but did not pay $10. C refuses to deliver the book.
1. **E:** $5 – she would have gotten something worth $15 but she hasn't yet spent the $10 so we have to deduct that – otherwise we would be overcompensating her.
2. **Reliance:** $3 (assuming cost of copying is still $3) then this is what she spent (put her in the position she was in prior to K being performed) – reliance = compensate her for expenses occurred in performing the K
3. **Restitution:** $1 (assuming the market value is $1) this is the only benefit C has received – all he has is notes w/a market value of $1.

iii. L did nothing. C refuses to perform.
1. **Expectancy** - $15-$13 – expected minus cost avoided so $2 is the total she gets
2. **Reliance**: $0 – she did nothing, she didn't do anything, spend anything
3. **Restitution**: $0 – she transferred no benefits to Clark

iv. L pays $10, gives notes ($4 market value). C refuses to deliver comic.
1. **Expectancy**: $15.
2. **Reliance:** notes still cost $3 to copy - $13
3. **Restitution:** $14 – she paid $10 and the notes are worth $4 so $14 is the benefit that was transferred to C

v. L pays $10, gives C notes. C refuses to deliver (market value of $9)
1. **E:** $9 – this was a bad deal for her
2. **Rel:** $13 – spent $10 plus $3 to copy notes
3. **Rest:** $11 – transferred $11 worth of benefit to C (notes worth $1)

XXXI. **Liquidated Damages**
a. *__Liquidated damages__* – the sum a party to a K agrees to pay if he breaks some promise, and which, having been arrived at by a good faith effort to estimate in advance the actual damages that will probably ensue from the breach, is legally recoverable as agreed damages if the breach occurs
i. Ex. Parties agree that if seller fails to deliver (breach), seller shall pay buyer $100 and if buyer fails to pay, seller may repossess goods and keep whatever payments buyer has already made. (these are liquidated damages)
b. Rationale?
i. Avoid litigation or make the question of damages easier to resolve
ii. Makes parties more committed to the K b/c if you are tempted to breach you know the consequences of your actions

c. *But we want to make sure the parties don't "sneak in" punitive damages – that is not what K law is all about! The court **will enforce liquidated damages provisions except when they cross the line into punitive damages***

   i. *We must look at whether the provision can be justified (i.e. whether it was difficult or impossible <u>at the time K was made</u> to calculate damages)*

d. To enforce or not to enforce?

   i. Court must look to **TEST**: RST § 356

   1. **Reasonableness of liquidated damages provision**

      a. **Traditional view:** *look at "reasonableness" of the liquidated damages provision <u>at the time of contracting</u>*

         i. So if the damages looked unreasonable, regardless of the actual damages, the LD provision will NOT be enforced

      b. **Modern view:** *look at "reasonableness" of the liquidated damages provision <u>at the time of contracting</u> OR <u>actual damages when the vest</u>*

         i. LD will be enforced if it looks reasonable but the ultimate actual damages are much less (same as in traditional view)

         ii. LD will be enforced even if they look unreasonable at the time of King but turn out to be reasonable based on actual damages incurred

   2. **Extent to which potential damages were uncertain or difficult to calculate**

e. If your <u>actual damages</u> are less than the liquidated damages, you can probably still get the liquidated damages amount if it satisfies the two part test above

   i. If the actual damages are significantly less than the liquidated damages, then the court will probably only give actual damages *if the clause is for a lump sum*

      1. *Courts are skeptical of LD that don't take gravity of breach into account*

      2. *This is called a "blunderbluss" and will be struck down if the actual loss is significantly less than liquidated amount*

   ii. If the actual damages are significantly less than the liquidated damages and *the clause is a per day liquidated damages*, then court will probably give the liquidated damages <u>b/c they are PER DAY</u>

f. Suppose you have a situation where LD were included when K was made b/c of uncertainty (seemed reasonable, parties didn't have all the info). But now, actual damages did occur and they are a lot less than LD in K.

   i. Court will first look to reasonableness of LD provision and then if there is a HUGE difference, they may or may not enforce the damages

   ii. So <u>argue both sides</u>

      1. Traditional and modern rules would enforce liquidated damages regardless of whether P suffered actual damages

      2. The 2nd RST would say that P cannot recover liquidated damages if P doesn't actually suffer any losses

g. What if there were no actual damages? Still enforce LD provision?

   i. Yes, according to traditional view as long as they were reasonable at the time of making the K – some courts are moving towards RST view that they are not enforceable, but this is a split of authority

h. **Sometimes LD provisions will benefit D by limiting his liability**

i. *<u>Penalties</u>* – the sum a party agrees to pay in the event of a breach, but which is fixed, not as a pre-estimate of probable actual damages, but as a punishment, the threat of which is designed to prevent the breach. Parties to a K may not fix a penalty for its breach

   i. *We want to AVOID penalties – these are punitive damages that the court will RARELY enforce (maybe only if the breach was willful or intentionally defrauded or something but RARELY given)*

  j. ***Wassermans v. Township of Middletown*** D leased storefront to P and said if D cancelled lease, D would pay P a pro-rata reimbursement for any improvements P had made to store and 25% of lessee's average gross receipts for one year. D cancelled lease and refused to pay. HELD:: lease is enforceable and D is bound by most terms.

   i. Reimbursement provision: required payment equal to (total value of all improvements made) x (number of years left in lease term) / (total number of years left in lease)

    1. They are trying to protect the value of their improvements

   ii. 25% of gross receipts: this was not enforced b/c there was no rationale. Where did 25% come from? There was no foundation or relationship to the contract. But the first provision was reasonable so that was enforced

   iii. ***Where the LD are based on "gross profits" or "gross revenues" (i.e. not actually tied to "lost profits") the court usually will not enforce b/c it is a <u>poor estimate of actual losses</u>***

    1. ***This will be unenforceable if it materially deviates from actual losses***

  k. UCC – 2-718 – allows the P to have 2 chances for liquidated damages

   i. Reasonableness at the time the K was made

   ii. Reasonableness of amount after the breach

    1. Goes more along w/the 2nd RST and makes LD easier to get

    2. Remember to check if this is unconscionable (under that section) – sometimes if it significantly lessens buyer's remedy it might be

 l. *Ultimately…*

   i. *Court will enforce liquidate damages unless they appear punitive*

   ii. *We look at the reasonableness of including them <u>at the time K was made</u> OR <u>actual damages</u> (depending upon which view the court takes)*

THIRD PARTIES: RIGHTS AND RESPONSBILITIES

 XXXII. **Third Party Beneficiaries**

  a. Sometimes parties can contract for a contract where they are not the beneficiaries but the ultimate point of the contract is to benefit a third party

   i. In case of breach, of course the two parties can sue but the **real question is: whether the third party can sue?**

    1. Some types of third party beneficiaries can sue while other cannot

  b. *RULE: third party can sue if and only if:*

   i. *The contract showed an intent to benefit the third party and (or)*

   ii. *The promisee owed the third party a duty that the promisor was discharging*

  c. RST(1) says that creditors and donees as beneficiaries can sue, incidental beneficiaries cannot sue

  d. RST(2) says that intended beneficiaries can sue, incidental beneficiaries cannot sue

   i. So ultimately, incidental beneficiaries cannot sue

   ii. RST § 302: intended beneficiary is one that can show that recognition of a right to performance in the beneficiary is appropriate to effectuate the intention of the parties

  e. *We need to find out if the two parties to the contract intended to create a benefit in the third party*

        i. **FACTORS:**

           1. **Wording of the K**

              a. **Is the third party mentioned in K?**

              b. **Does the contract list any rights to the 3rd party?**

           2. **Surrounding circumstances**

              a. **Is the performance to be made directly to the third party?**

              b. **What is the relationship b/t promisee and third party?**

        ii.   Subcontractors cannot sue as 3rd party beneficiaries

        iii.   Lien holders can sue as 3rd party beneficiaries

f. **Creditor beneficiary (may sue)**

    i. The third party is a "creditor" of the promisee

       1. We allow this b/c we don't want multiple lawsuits – just let the creditor sue the promisor directly

       2. Ex. X owes $300 to P. X then loans $300 to D in return for D's promise to pay X's debt to P the next day. D fails to pay and P sues him.

          a. P wins. P may recover as a third party beneficiary of X

g. **Donee beneficiary (may sue)**

    i. The purpose of the contract is to confer a gift to the third party.

       1. We allow this b/c if donee can't sue, no one really can – even promisee would only get nominal damages

       2. Ex. X (dying) wants to leave house to P. X's present will leaves house to husband. B/c X will probably not live long enough to get a new will, H promises her that if she keeps the will the same, he will leave enough money to P to make up for not getting the house. H fails to keep his promise; P sues

          a. P may recover as a donee beneficiary

h. **Intended Beneficiary (may sue)**

    i. Giving this person the right to sue fits w/parties' intentions AND

       1. Either the performance will satisfy an obligation to pay money OR

       2. Either the circumstances indicate the promisee intends to give the beneficiary the benefit of the promised performance.

    ii.   *Factors:*

       1. Reasonable reliance on promise

       2. Performance runs directly from promisor to 3rd party

       3. Part of parties' overall object is to benefit 3rd party

i. **Incidental beneficiary (may not sue)**

    i. Ex. B contracts w/A to erect an expensive building on A's land which happens to be next to Cs. C is an *incidental beneficiary*

    ii.   Ex. B contracts w/A to buy a new car manufactured by C. C is an incidental beneficiary

j. ***Common Situations:***

    i. Public contracts: member of the public injured by govt. contract <u>cannot</u> sue

       1. Unless expressly provided or govt. has a duty of its own to provide the services

    ii.   Brokerage commissions: if broker is unable to collect fee from the seller, sometimes he can go after the buyer as a 3rd party beneficiary

    iii.   Life insurance: usually you can change the beneficiary at will and it is enforceable

    iv.   Clause allowing for modification or recession of the K: if this clause is here, the 3rd party cannot sue whether or not they detrimentally relies on the K

1. But if there is no clause and they otherwise would have a right to sue (intended beneficiary) they may if they:
   a. Materially change their position in justifiable reliance on the K
   b. Brings suit on it
   c. Manifests his assent to the contract at the request of one of the parties

k. ***Casefile #60*** General Construction breached the K and there are 2 subcontractors that are now suing National Insurance. We represent National insurance. We want to know why these two subcontractors are suing us? We don't have a contract w/them
   i. But we do represent GC and these subcontractors are beneficiaries to our insurance agreement with GC so they say they are intended to benefit from our contract w/GC as an intended beneficiary
      1. The subcontractors can go after National Insurance (our client) or the school but it depends
         a. NI: whether the subcontractors have other options
         b. School: terms of original contract; public/private
      2. If they go after us, we look to the factors to see if they can recover as third party beneficiaries.
         a. Were they intended beneficiaries? Did the contract explicitly state their names/did they rely to the detriment on the contract (here's where you could make an argument).

XXXIII. **Delegation of Duties**
   a. ***Delegation occurs when a party wants to have someone else <u>perform his duties</u> under the K***
   b. Typical delegation situation

Al (obligee) -------------- Bob (obligor/delegator)
                                              |
Charles now performs |
For Al   Charles (delegatee)

   o We have Al (oblige) and Bob (obligor, delegator). Bob will perform accounting work for Al. At some point later on, Bob delegates duty to Charles (delegee)
   o This is probably a good thing – we want to encourage this but there are limits.

   c. So what type of duties <u>cannot be assigned</u>?
      i. **Personal trust and confidence**: usually involving "personal judgment or skill" (lawyer/client; doctor/patient, services, etc.)
      ii. **Reliance on a particular person**: no delegation is allowed if the other party has a substantial interest in having the original promisor perform the contract
      iii. **Proposed delegate is a competitor of the oblige**: A and B have a K. A proposes to delegate to C but C is a competitor of B. Usually invalid delegation.
   d. ***Most contractual duties CAN be delegated – in general, courts will enforce delegation except for some of the situations above***
      i. ***Parties <u>can contract around these rules</u>***
         1. So if you don't want the other party to be able to delegate the duties assigned to them, just say so in the contract!
   e. The language of the contract determines to what extent the duties are delegated
      i. You can delegate the entire contract or you could just delegate a portion of it
   f. **Delegation does NOT equal Absolutism**

    i. ***The person making the delegation continues to be responsible to the other original party***

      1. So when B delegates to C, B is still responsible to A if C fails to perform – the only way out of this is to have A consent to let B out of the K

    ii. ***But the delegate is also responsible at least to the delegator and maybe even to the 3rd party as well***

XXXIV. **Assignment of Rights**

 a. Definition: "a manifestation of the <u>assignor's intention</u> to transfer it by virtue of which the <u>assignor's right to performance by the obligor is extinguished</u> in whole or in part and the assignee acquires a right to such performance (RST § 317)

   i. ***Assignment is a transfer of a party's <u>rights</u> under the K***

   ii. ***There is no consideration required***

 b. What is the controlling consideration? ***Has to be clear that the assignor was giving up any rights that he or she had under the K.***

   i. *** this is a question in the casefile – did GSD assign its rights to the larger company after merger? ***

 c. **RULE:** rights are generally assignable, except where the assignment will materially change the duty of the obligor, or materially increase the burden or risk imposed on him, or materially impair his chance of obtaining performance or materially reduces the value to him

   i. **Look to whether the assignment…**

    1. **Materially changed the duty of the obligor**

    2. **Materially increased the burden or risk imposed on him**

    3. **Materially impaired his chance of obtaining performance**

    4. **Materially reduced the value to him**

     a. **If yes to any of these, probably not assignable**

 d. **If you assign, usually you can revoke EXCEPT when…**

   i. If the assignment is put <u>in writing</u> and then <u>delivered to assignee</u> it is irrevocable

   ii. If assignee <u>relies to his detriment</u> on the assignment, this is irrevocable

   iii. If the obligor <u>gives assignee payment</u>, the assignment is irrevocable

 e. *If assignment and delegation are coupled together, they both must be valid; if one is not, neither is the other*

 f. ***Casefile #61.1*** Professor contracted to have a company make her computer program. The company she contracted with merged w/a larger company and she now thinks that she's not going to get the same service. She wants out. Can she? Is it okay for the smaller company to assign their rights to the larger company w/o Professor's consent?

   i. Probably yes. ***GSD is essentially attempting to assign getting paid. Gely says that this does not increase burden on Professor at all (she is still paying) and we always allow assignment of payments (money). But Professor could raise some of these arguments in response. Could go either way.***

   ii. Professor's argument for NO ASSIGNMENT:

    1. Professor can argue that she chose the company for a specific reason – MU grads

    2. Professor can say that GSD has more expertise than the larger mega firm (they might pay more attention to her software as opposed to the possibility it might get lost in the sea of the larger company)

   iii. GSD's argument FOR ASSIGNMENT:

    1. Might be more likely that the mega firm can do a better job

    2. They are more capable; have more people to work on; do it faster

CONSTITUTIONAL LAW

JUDICIAL REVIEW

I. **Marbury v. Madison**
   a. FACTS: Marbury – appointed justice of the peace by John Adams, appointment held over, brings law suit in SCOTUS using their original jurisdiction
      i. Can file in Supreme Court b/c of ORIGINAL JURISDICTION
      ii. Marbury sues James Madison, Secy. of State, Madison was withholding the commission of Marbury. Madison was ordered to do so by Jefferson
      iii. Marbury seeks Writ of Mandamus directed at Secy. of State to force them to give him his commission.
      iv. Problem – commission was signed by John Adams and sealed but not delivered.
      v. Obiter dictum – writing legal analysis on an issue not before the court
   b. HOLDINGS:
      i. Is Secy. of State an office to wit courts can issue a writ – YES "the writ will lie"
      ii. You can issue a writ of mandamus if the official has failed to do a ministerial act as distinct from a discretionary act – the delivery of the commission is ministerial
   c. **Judicial Review – 5 points by Marshall**
      i. The Nature of a written constitution
         1. Wherever the Constitution applies it is the superior law
         2. Judiciary has the final say – we are unique in this way
      ii. **Traditional role of the courts**
         1. **SCOTUS has the final say as to when a law is unconstitutional - It is emphatically the duty of the judicial department to say what the law is.**
         2. to give the legislature power to determine whether its own acts exceed limits set by constitution would be giving legislature a practical and real omnipotence
      iii. Judges must take an oath to uphold it
      iv. "arising under" language
         1. Supreme Court has jurisdiction over all cases arising under the Constitution, they must decide those cases by examining the Constitution
         2. This does not affect the legislature – debate constitutional questions all the time in congressional hearings
      v. Supremacy Clause
         1. Constitution is supreme law of the land
         2. conflict between state law and federal law, federal law reigns supreme
   d. **Section 13 of the Judiciary Act of 1789** – fn. b. pg 29 – SCOTUS shall have appellate jurisdiction from the circuit courts and courts of the several states in cases herein after specially provided for… [rest of the clause held to be unconstitutional] and shall have power to issue writes of prohibition to the district courts, when proceeding as courts of admiralty and maritime jurisdiction and writes of mandamus in cases warranted by the principles and usages of law, to any courts appointed or persons holding office, under the authority of the US.

II. **ART III – The Judicial Branch**
   a. **Sec 2. Cl. 2-** Court has original jurisdiction In all cases affecting ambassadors, other public ministers and consuls, and those in which a state shall be party and as to everything else SCOTUS has appellate jurisdiction
      i. Where a state is a party

138

III. **Basic Principles**
 a. **Constitution is about structure and rights**
   i. groups of people and their organizations have rights
   ii. government does not have rights – government has powers and duties
     1. residual state sovereignty
       a. states retain some sovereignty after they joined the federal government
   iii. The Frame of Government – Adams called the MA Constitution the frame of government because written constitution is the infrastructure and structure is the diffusion of power
 b. **Madisonian Vision - Structure alone, but structure in deed, is necessary to preserve our individual liberties**
   i. **Federalist 51 – I**n framing a government which is to be administered by men over men, the great difficulty lies in this: you must first enable the government to control the governed; and in the next place oblige it to control itself.
   ii. The idea of checks and balances – out of checks and balances comes liberty
   iii. Federal Gov has only enumerated or delegated powers – everything else are left to the states or the people - 10th Amendment – put in to writing to codify what was already implicit in the constitution
   iv. Men who have consented to government over then it is a qualified consent and the citizen has the right to vote to change the government
IV. Limitations on Judicial Review
 a. 5 Limitations on judicial view – checks on the court
   i. *Ex Parte McCardle* – power to strip appellate jurisdiction under the exceptions and regulations clause of Art III
     1. Art III gives unconditional power to congress as a check on the judiciary
   ii. Power of Judicial Appointment
     1. President can appoint new judges dependant on vacancy
   iii. Constitutional Amendment
     1. Some are responses to SCOTUS rulings
     2. Very difficult
   iv. Congress' power to cut budget of judiciary
     1. Art I, Sec 8, Cl. 1
     2. Can't lower existing judges' compensation directly but can cut funding
   v. Impeachment of a felonious judge
 b. Protections of the Court
   i. Art III Sec. 1 – cannot lower a judges pay
   ii. Lifetime appointment
   iii. Senate must approve all Presidential appointments
 c. *Ex Parte McCardle*
   i. Article III, Sect. 2, Cl. 2 – "in all other cases before mentioned, the Supreme Court shall have appellate jurisdiction, both as to law and fact, with such exceptions, and under such regulations as the Congress shall make." (the **exceptions and regulations clause**)
   ii. **Congress is given control over the court's appellate jurisdiction. They can limit certain areas of appellate jurisdiction**
     1. **The Constitution grants appellate jurisdiction to SCOTUS but also gives Congress the "check" on the judiciary by allowing them to strip appellate jurisdiction from the court.**
   iii. Holding - Court cannot question the motive of the legislature in exercising its

ability to limit the appellate jurisdiction of the court.

> 1. **This holding was limited to only those habeas corpus appeals arising under the 1867 act and not habeas corpus appeals under "jurisdiction which was previously exercised." (that is, under the 1789 Judiciary Act).**
> 2. Congress can only limit and regulate SCOTUS appellate jurisdiction so long as it does not alter the constitutional role the court is to play
> 3. Congress also has ability to limit jurisdiction in cases that are only under consideration but haven't been granted Certiorari

d. Refinements of McCardle

> i. *Ex Parte Yerger* – Successfully invoked original jurisdiction to grant writs of habeas corpus. Art I Sec 9 Cl. 2 – Habeas Corpus Clause – shall not be suspended unless in cases of rebellion, invasion, or public safety requires it
>> 1. **So long as one path to the court remains open, appellate jurisdiction can properly be limited**
> ii. *US v. Klein* – If Congress makes a rule of decision then it's unconstitutional – any jurisdictional limit must be neutral – Congress may not decide the merits of a case under the guise of limiting jurisdiction
>> 1. Holding – 2 holdings
>>> a. Congress cannot prescribe how a court should find an issue of fact (i.e. this fact of the case automatically exists)
>>> b. Congress cannot deny the effect of a presidential pardon – you cannot be punished for accepting a pardon
> iii. **Rule of Decision – unconstitutional to make rules in which the legislature orders the court to rule for one party or another**

e. **The Extent of Congress' power under the exceptions and regulations clause**

> i. Unclear if congress can strip the lower federal courts of appellate jurisdiction
> ii. Could we look into Congress' motives in stripping? No, McCardle said can't look at motives of Congress in doing this
> iii. What about the procedural/substantive distinction (as in removing some diversity J by raising to $100K limit)? NO , McCardle was not based on proc/subst. distinction
> iv. Congress may not use this clause to "intrude upon the core functions of the Court as an independent, coequal branch of our system of a 3 branch government"
> v. **Ambiguity is good** – Congress doesn't know how far it can go in using this weapon and Court is not sure how far it will go in striking down J-stripping statutes

V. **Supreme Court Review of State Court Decisions**

a. **SCOTUS has power to review State decisions on Federal Law**

> i. General History of Power
>> 1. in 1789, Congress exercised its power to create federal courts and did so – Initially, Congress did not give them federal question J, so they only had diversity and admiralty J
>> 2. private rights under federal law were protected by state courts applying federal law due to Supremacy Clause in Art. 4
>> 3. Under Judiciary Act, Congress limited Sup. Ct. appellate review of state courts to only cases where a US Const. of federal law claim was rejected, but not where one was granted
> ii. *Martin v. Hunter's Lease*
>> 1. Facts: Virginia Supreme Court refused to comply with SCOTUS interpretation of Treaty of Paris, which would have granted land to Martin.
>> 2. **Judiciary Act of 1789, Section 25 gives SCOTUS appellate jurisdiction over federal questions decided by the highest state court – only over those**

cases where federal right or claim was denied
  a. **Does not apply when a federal right or claim is sustained**
  b. **Art. 3, Sec 2, Cl. 1 – cases an controversies**
3. **Holding:** States are bound by Supreme Court's interpretation of Treaty of Paris
  a. 4 reasons
    i. Federal Question jurisdiction lies with SCOTUS
    ii. SCOTUS jurisdiction does not extend to courts only cases
    iii. Art I Sec 10 – Constitution does not act upon the states
    iv. To give the Constitution force it must be interpreted by SCOTUS and not individually by each state – uniformity is necessary
b. **Federal Question Review Process**
  i. writ of certiorari
    1. takes 4 justices
    2. Rule of 5 – you can get a rehearing if 5 judges vote for it
  ii. 28 USC 1257 – review is discretionary – **case must be a final decision from the highest state court possible for that case (does not mean State Supreme Court necessarily)**
c. **Limitations on Supreme Court review by state courts**
  i. **State law is not reviewable by the Supreme Court**
  ii. **Adequate and Independent state law grounds** – SCOTUS will not exercise jurisdiction if the state court judgment is based on adequate and independent state law grounds even if a federal issue is involved– if its ambiguous, the it can be appealed
    1. state courts learn to be specific – "we decided this based on the state constitution's free speech clause"
    2. **Adequacy – are the grounds fully dispositive of the case** – was the case merely decided on procedural grounds which prevented realization of the federal right?
      a. State court may be suspected of evading decision of the federal issue
      b. The procedure may be an obstacle to federal rights
    3. **Independent – decision is not based on federal case interpretations of identical federal provisions** – more deference given to state court – determination of whether the state substantive ground is independent – that is, whether no matter how the federal issue is resolved, **the state ground will be dispositive**
d. *What else is in the constitution to check the court – what other checks and balances*
  i. President nominates, Senate confirms – could be a protection or check
  ii. Can impeach a justice – for treason, bribery, high crimes or misdemeanors
    1. Serve so long as they have good behavior. Only 1 (Samuel Chase) was ever impeached but never convicted.
    2. Congress appropriates the judiciary branch, they could cut the budget of the judiciary
    3. Art V allows passage of a constitutional amendment – 2/3 House 2/3 of Senate and ¼ of all states
    4. Art 3. Sec 2. Cl 1

JUSTICIBILITY

I. Justicibility is the Court exercising self-restraint and confining its power
II. **ART III - Court only has jurisdiction over "cases and controversies"** – justiciability is

required for the purposes of jurisdiction
a. **Case and controversies**
    i. **No Political questions**
    ii.   **No collusion (no sweetheart deals)**
    iii.   **More than 2 parties**
    iv.   **The remedy for the case must be an equitable remedy or a remedy at law**
b. **Three Requirements for bring a case**
    i. **Standing**
    ii.   **mootness**
    iii.   **ripeness**
c. **Prudential Rules – non constitutional requirements**

III. **SCOTUS/Judiciary cannot render advisory opinions**
a. State courts can render advisory opinions – SCOTUS must act like a court "bring them a bloodied plaintiff"
    i. Some state courts are authorized to render advisory opinions
b. advisory opinions – an opinion of the court on a certain constitutional issue requested by a government agency (different from Declaratory Judgment)
c. Declaratory Judgment - court actually decides the rights between two parties in an actual case
d. dispute must be in personam – 2 parties raise issues that the court decides
e. Why no advisory opinions?
    i. Waste resources of the court
    ii.   Contrary to the adversarial nature of the court
    iii.   The court should not be "a roaming do-gooder, leave that to the legislature"

IV. **Why SCOTUS is so concerned with justiciability vs simply deciding on the merits.**
a. **5 reasons**
    i. Want traditional case of controversy b/c the court only acts upon real problems not hypothetical problems
        1. Only actual controversies
        2. To conserve power
    ii.   Only acts on actual controversies because of the limitations of the adversarial system
        1. P and D truly at one another's throats – clash of the titans – very best arguments and defenses
    iii.   Courts acts in personam
        1. Legislators roam the country defining ill-will etc
    iv.   The court works best when it is at least perceived to be modest in the use of its power
        1. "the least dangerous branch" – Hamilton

V. **STANDING**
a. **Constitutional Requirements for Standing**
    i. **The irreducible constitutional minimum – 3 requirements are very much related**
        1. **Injury in fact -** P must allege past or imminent injury in fact to her (i.e. harm)
        2. **Causation -** D's conduct must have caused the harm
        3. **Redressability – seeing a traditional remedy – must be a remedy in equity, remedy in law or declaratory judgment –** the court's ruling must redress the harm caused

b. **Injury in fact**
   i. Need a bloodied plaintiff – must have ACTUAL harm
   ii. Must be able to tie the actual harm to the D
   iii. each P must suffer some actual or threatened injury individually
   iv. not limited to pecuniary damages
      1. *Arlington Heights v. Metro Housing Development Corp.-* D shows they were actually harmed by arbitrary zoning, they have right to be free from arbitrary zoning

c. **Causation**
   i. P must show there is a substantial probability that the relief requested, if granted, would actually solve their problem
   ii. *Warth v. Sledin* – causation was lacking here
      1. 5 different groups sue over a zoning restriction – court find that none of the groups are directly affected by the zoning law though, just because you don't like something doesn't mean it causes you actual harm for the purposes of standing
      2. *Flast* – P must establish a nexus between the constitutional violation and actual harm
      3. *Duke Power* – harm may be the indirect cause of the statute for the purposes of standing
      4. if causation is weak court may classify the claim as a third party claim

d. **Limitations on Standing**
   i. **Rule against Third-Party Standing**
      1. **General rule** – Must assert your own rights, no 3rd party can assert your rights for you, and you cannot assert the rights of a 3rd party
      2. **Exceptions to the rule against third-party standing:**
         a. **Substantial obstacles -**may assert the rights of an absent party if there are substantial obstacles to the absent party asserting his own rights and if there is reason to believe that the advocate will effectively represent the interests of the absent party.
            i. High school health clinics notify parents before giving out contraception devices; Planned Parenthood has standing.
         b. **Mutual Interdependence -** may assert the rights of an absent party where there is a relationship of mutual interdependence between the advocate and the absent party.
            i. Pierce v. Society of Sisters (1925) (parent-school relationship);
            ii. Griswold v. Connecticut (1965) (doctor-patient relationship).
         c. **Doctrine of Substantial Overbreadth -** applicable primarily to First Amendment cases (speech and religion) and involves the "chilling" of these rights.
   ii. **Organizational standing** – organization may sue on behalf of its members even though it was not directly harmed – **3 PART TEST FOR ORGINIZATIONAL STANDING**
      1. members would otherwise have standing on their own
      2. the interests the organization seeks to protect are germane to the organization's own purposes
      3. participation of individual members of the organization are not required for the claim or the relief requested

e. Standing Cases
    i. *Sierra Club v. Morton*
        1. Held that environmental group lacked standing to challenge the construction of a recreation area in a national forest.
        2. Sierra Club did not allege that any of its members were affected by the proposed development and thus did not achieve standing
    ii.   *Allen v. Wright*
        1. Parents of black children attending public schools did not have standing to challenge IRS practices concerning denial of tax exemptions to racially discriminatory private schools.
        2. Court says it is wholly conjectural that the white parents will pull their kids out of the private school just because they have to pay more taxes
    iii.   *Craig v. Boren*
        1. Women 18+ could buy and imbibe alcohol, Male 21+ -Male between 18-20 sues tavern – owner brought suit to enjoin enforcement of a statute which allows women to buy but not males
        2. Craig turns 21 so his case becomes moot – if he could have framed as damages claim rather than injunction, would not have gone moot
        3. Tavern owner is allowed to sue to enforce rights of 3rd parties, her potential 18-20yo male customers – based on relationship between tavern owner and customer; potential contract is lost and owner is sued though owner is actually asserting the rights of the male customers
    iv.   *Massachusetts v. EPA*
        1. Federalism of the Commonwealth is trumped by the EPA pursuant to the Commerce Clause
        2. Holding: elements of standing satisfied b/c EPS's steadfast refusal to regulate greenhouse gasses present an actual and imminent risk to MA

f. **Taxpayer and Citizen Standing – Generalized Grievances**
    i. **General rule – no taxpayer standing**
        1. *Frothingham v. Mellon* – had held that federal taxpayers did not have standing to sue to challenge federal expenditures
    ii.   *Flast v. Cohen* **– upheld federal taxpayer standing in order to challenge expenditure of federal funds in violation of the establishment clause**
        1. court creates a legal fiction for structural violations
        2. the structural violation was **separation of church and state**
    iii.   <u>**Generalized grievances**</u> **–there is no standing for generalized grievances about the government – the individual must be harmed and must be separate from the general public**
        1. injury must be **personal, Identifiable and particular** to the plaintiff
        2. **Generalized grievances are not for individual rights violations – only for structural violations**
        3. **initially thought to be a prudential standing requirement but more recently has been treated as constitutional**
        4. *U.S. v. Richardson* – no standing for citizen to sue based on failure to disclose CIA expenditures – this was generalized grievance
        5. *Schlesinger v. Reservists Committee to Stop the War* – held that taxpayers have no standing to challenge membership of Members of Congress in the military reserve which was claimed to violate the prohibition of Art I Sec. 6 Cl 2 (cannot simultaneously serve in Executive and Legislature – can't serve two masters)

6. Can't allege violation of the right to a particular kind of government or the general right to have the government act according to the law – this is not injury in fact – just because you don't like it doesn't make it a violation of the constitution

iv. **Separation of Powers**
 1. Vindicating public interest is the job of the legislature not the courts
 2. The courts are there to vindicate the rights of individuals

v. *Lujan v. Defenders of Wildlife*
 1. Court finds no injury in fact to researchers who claimed that endangered animals they intended to study in the future would be injured by change in legislation
    a. Had no trip planned, funding, etc so this was not really ripe – court said no standing for lack of injury in fact
 2. ESA had "citizen suit" provision allowing citizens to sue private individual or the govt for violation of the act
    a. Court below construed this as a congressional conferral of the right of citizens to have the executive branches agency properly carry out the act through regulations – P claimed regulations not in accordance w/ the act
    b. SCOTUS rejects this saying Congress could NOT confer a right to sue based on a generalized grievance - Violated ART III case or controversy to allow congress to confer right to sue
    c. **Take Care Clause – Art 2 Sec 3 – he shall take care that the laws be faithfully executed**
    d. **Congress was not able to confer standing because the court is limited to cases and controversies – so it seems generalized grievance rule is constitutional rather than prudential – treated as both by the court**
 3. **Congress must at least identify the injury it seeks to vindicate and relate the injury to the class of persons bringing a suit** – otherwise it is authorizing suit based on a general grievance – real remedies for real victims

vi. *Raines v. Byrd* - Members on the losing side in Congress don't have standing to sue just because they lost
 1. President given line item veto to remove expenditures from legislation passed by Congress 6 members of congress sue claiming line item is unconstitutional – court does not grant standing because:
    a. They had no injury upon which to sue
    b. Votes were given full effect and were simply on the losing side
 2. *Clinton v. City of New York* - Stuck down the Line Item Veto Act

g. **Voter Standing**
 i. *FEC v. Akins* – Federal Election Campaign Act required disclosure of info to public – court finds standard per the Act not constitution
  1. HOLDING: Congress had created broad standing for voters under the act
  2. Federal voters had standing to sue FEC to obtain documents
     a. Nature of the claim makes it a generalized grievance – "I want my government to comply with the constitution" claim is nonjusticiable
     b. Generalized grievance is not a numbers game – can have millions of victims – here every US voter had standing to sue
  3. Voters had suffered concrete, particularized harm – perhaps since it was a

voting issue, which is fundamental, caused the court to confer standing

    4. Dissent argued that this was merely a suit to force government to comply with the federal election law

VI. Mootness

    a. **General rule – an actual controversy must exist at all stages of appellate review by the courts not simply when the action is initiated – mootness is a matter of timing, you acted too late, so the case is now moot.**

    b. **Exceptions**

        i. **Capable of Repetition, Yet Evading Review**

            1. **must be repetition as to the same plaintiff – 3rd party is irrelevant**

            2. Easy case – where the litigated issue will always be mooted by the passage of time

            3. Hard case – where plaintiff will not face the litigated issue again in the future but others similarly situated will

                a. Exception applies - *Roe v. Wade* – pregnancy will come to term in 9 months and render case moot unless court finds this exception (it will happen to other women, repetition and would evade review otherwise).

                b. Exception applies – *Dunn v. Blumstein* - live in jurisdiction 90 days before you can vote, new residents disenfranchised – other new resides would be subject to durational residency requirement – could move in wait 90 days, then move away, then move back and have to repeat the 90 day prohibition

        ii. **Voluntary Cessation**

            1. Question will be ruled moot as long as D stops the alleged illegal activity

            2. Once this is done D cannot go back to the old ways, has to accept new procedure for all others – gov't cannot go back to their old ways either

            3. Otherwise, D could just give up for this P to render moot but then not change its ways for future potential Ps

            4. Court will not moot the case unless the cessation by the government so that the wrong doing will not be repeated

        iii. **How to Avoid Mootness**

            1. Certify as a class action – this combined with capable of repetition yet evading review will prevent mootness (Roe and Dunn both class actions) - but if it was a class action that avoided mootness

            2. Seek damages – **damages never go moot**

            3. Seek remedy that will not become moot by passage of time

VII. Ripeness

    a. **Ripeness is also about timing (like mootness), you acted too soon so the case is not yet ripe**

    b. *UWP v. Mitchell* - under Hatch act certain classes of federal employees prohibited from participating in political campaigns; some workers sue claiming they are discoursaged from campaigning in future (not ripe) while one worker alleged that he was about to be fired for his political activities (his claim was ripe)

        i. Courts don't need to wait until you're fired – due process proceedings are taking place and once they play out you will be fired

    c. **When a Case or Controversy is Ripe**

        i. **Current prosecution underway –** *Younger v. Harris* – Harris has been indicted under federal criminal syndicalism, so his case was very ripe

        ii. **Past conduct -** no issue of ripeness arises of the constitutional question is only to determine that legal consequences of past conduct

   iii. **Suits for damages** – also relates to past conduct and doesn't lose their ripeness

 d. **Not Ripe**

   i. **Statute no longer enforced, no intent to enforce it** – if statue has not been enforced and there is no intent to enforce, the question is not ripe absent a current prosecution/enforcement

    1. *Poe v. Ullman* – ancient law prohibiting doctors from giving out contraceptives had not been enforced for years

 e. Usually **criminal prosecution must have commenced** – possible threats of prosecution are not sufficient unless you are making a facial attack

 f. <u>**Type of attack on constitutionality may matter**</u>

   i. **Facial Challenges**

    1. <u>**When a law is challenged on its face as unconstitutional**</u>

     a. **Attack on the statute as it is written**

    2. *Adler v. Board of Educ.* – P must show there is no possible application of the law which comports with the constitution - D only needs to show one application that does not offend the constitution

   ii. **As Applied Attac<u>k</u>**

    1. **the particular application of the statute is unconstitutional**

    2. **not an attack on the statute as it is written but as it is applied**

VIII. **Political Questions**

 a. Court cannot decide these issues – violates **Separation of Powers**

 b. Court will consult **6 Factors** in determining whether it's a nonjusticiable political question – sometimes only some are considered – see ***Baker v. Carr***

 c. *<u>2 major factors</u>*

   i. **Is there a textually demonstrable constitutional commitment of the issue to a coordinate political department? (attributing finality to the action of the political departments)**

    1. Court must determine whether and to what extent it is committed to other branch

   ii. **Is there a lack of judicially discoverable and manageable standards for resolving the issue? (lack of satisfactory criteria for judicial determination)**

 d. <u>**4 other factors**</u>

   i. **Is it impossible to decide the issue w/o an initial policy determination of a kind not for judicial discretion (legislative matter)**

   ii. **Is it impossible for the court to undertake independent resolution of the issue w/o showing a lack of respect for other branches?**

   iii. **Is there an unusual need for an unquestioning adherence to a political decision already made?**

   iv. **Is there a potential embarrassment due to conflicting decisions by different branches?**

 e. ***Baker v. Carr***

   i. Held that apportionment laws were not political questions and were justiciable

   ii. Created "one person one vote" standard

 f. Political questions v. Political Cases – just because a case involves a political subject does not make it a political question

   i. *Powell v. McCormack* – duly elected representative was prevented by a House resolution from taking his seat – This was a nonjusticiable political question

        a. Art I Sec 5 Cl 2 – each house may determine the rules of its proceedings, punish its members and expel w/ 2/3 vote

        b. House found that Powell met the qualifications but sought to exclude him – they did not have this power, they could punish him once seated but could not prevent him from being seated

    g. *Nixon v. US* – procedure to be used in impeachment proceedings are a political question

        i. Judge Nixon was impeached and tried by Senate – under senate rule, a senate committee could hear the evidence – Nixon sues claim that evidence had to be presented to whole Senate

        ii. Court held this was not justiciable – found **a textually demonstrable commitment of the issue to a coordinate political department -** Senate shall have the sole power to try all impeachments

        iii. Court says Senate gets to determine what "try" means in context of the law

SELECTIVE INCORPORATION

I. Natural Law Theory

    a. *Calder v. Bull (1798)*

        i. If we are to strike something down as unconstitutional we should not read natural law theory in to our constitution – it should be within the 4 corners of the constitution

II. *Contract* Clause

    a. **Art I Sec. 10 Cl. 1** – does not apply to Federal Government (5ht Amendment does this) – applies only to state a local govt.

    b. Applies only to:

        i. Existing contracts (not future contracts) and

        ii. Legislative or executive impairment of contracts; court's impairment of contracts resulting from judicial decisions and changes in the common law are not affected by this clause

    c. Standard of review – rational basis

    d. Doesn't mean much anymore but used to be a hot topic (this clause was the justification for more constitutional cases involving the validity of state laws than all of the other clauses of the Constitution together)

III. Article IV P and I

    a. **Privileges and Immunities clause – does not list all the specific P or I**

    b. **Requires that citizens of different states get treated the same as citizens of that particular state – intermediate review applies – seems similar to equal protection, not really substantive**

        i. Art IV P&I only protects citizens not corporations

        ii. State may favor its own citizens for public offices that exercise powers to govern

        iii. Does not prohibit a state from charging noncitizens higher fees for hunting licenses

        iv. Art IV P&I often overlaps with dormant commerce clause doctrine

    c. **States cannot discriminate against citizens of another state**

        i. *Corfield v. Coryell* – NJ shellfish owned by NJ so law allowing only NJ citizens to take them is constitutional and does not violate Art. IV

        ii. *Paul v. Virginia* –only citizens have rights under P&I

    d. Also often confused with durational residency requirements more properly addressed under 14th amendment equal protection clause or 14th amendment's P or I clause.

IV. Bill of Rights and Civil War Amendments

a. *Barron v. Baltimore* - **Bill of Rights does not apply directly to the states.** Only to federal government – 14th Amendment would later apply parts of the bill to the states.

b. **Civil War Amendments changed the function of the Bill of Rights as it pertains to the states, allowed SCOTUS to selectively incorporate those rights to the states**

c. **13th Amendment**

    i. **Prohibited involuntary servitude and slavery by the federal govt., states and private actors**

        1. Unique in that it reaches wholly private parties (private action covered statutorily under CRA of 64, 65, & 68)

    ii. *Slaughterhouse* – narrow interpretation; the word servitude is not so broad as to force people in to jobs, but also it does not require that people have a right to a job – see property interests under due process

d. **15th Amendment – prohibits racial discrimination in voting by Fed and State govt.**

    i. **DOES NOT COVER PRIVATE ACTORS**

V. **14th Amendment**

a. **Only covers state action – not federal or wholly private**

    i. **Added federal power over states – trumped residual state sovereignty**

b. **Substantively covers**

    i. **14th amendment P or I**

    ii. **Due process**

    iii. **Equal protection**

    iv. **US Citizenship**

        1. **Original constitution didn't define citizenship – left this to the states; this was problem when newly freed slaves were being given citizenship by Southern states – this fixed it by making it matter of federal law**

c. **Early Interpretations of 14th Amendment –** *The Slaughterhouse Cases*

    i. **14th Amendment P or I Clause** - Slaughterhouse deprives of any meaning but Saenz v. Roe gives it some in the right to travel context

    ii. *Saenz v. Roe* – equality case where CA, in budget crisis, sought to cut welfare budget for people who had just moved to the state, passed a law that said if you created domicile in CA, for the 1st year you were eligible for your prior state's TANF but not the higher CA rates.

        1. Stevens – struck down under citizenship clause, full privileges and immunities of the state as a citizen who had established domicile

            a. There are no tiers of citizenship – you either are a citizen or you're not a citizen

            b. Court later reached the same result under the Equal Protection Clause

    iii. 14th amendment Due Process Clause

        1. *Slaughterhouse* – not violated because right to a profession was not property interest – still true see due process property interest

    iv. Equal protection clause

        1. Slaughterhouse only applied it in context of freeing slaves

    v. Citizenship under the 14th amendment

        1. a citizen may not be deported nor excluded from the U.S.

        2. an alien may be deported for any of a substantial list of reasons

        3. an alien seeking entry has no constitutional right to a hearing (though a hearing is afforded by statute in most exclusion cases)

        4. but a continuously present alien or permanent resident is entitled to a fair hearing when threatened with deportation

5. U.S. citizen must intend to relinquish their U.S. citizenship; citizen has a right to do so

d. **14th Amendment P or I vs. Article IV P and I**

    i. 14th Amendment - State P or I

      1. Slaughterhouse - state privileges and immunities are not protected in the constitution

      2. State laws create the state's own privileges and immunities

      3. The court argues that this preserves federalism – Justice Fields says this does nothing that isn't already done in Art IV

    ii. Article IV - Federal P & I

      1. 14th forbids state infringement of federal P & I's

      2. Certain Privilege and Immunities listed in the Constitution – not an entirely exhaustive list

        a. right to travel to seat of govt. to assert any claims against it, conduct any business with it, to seek its protection, to share its offices, to engage in administering its functions

        b. right to free access to its seaports

        c. to demand protection of federal govt. when on the high seas or in another nation

        d. right to use the navigable waters of the U.S.

        e. privilege of writ of habeas corpus

        f. to enjoy all benefits of U.S. treaties

        g. right to become a citizen of any state in the union

        h. right to peaceably assemble and petition for redress of grievances

    iii. *McDonald - 2nd amendment issue* - Thomas would reverse Slaughterhouse

      1. Alito says P&I is so open ended that it is difficult to define and draw lines to keep a federalist republic, treating the states as subordinate counties.

      2. Thomas w/ respect to scope of P&I

        a. It's about an enumerated right that is fundamental, because it is in the first 8 amendments of the BofR – if it's listed in the first 8 Amendments it's part of the P&I of the 14th Amendment

        b. Doesn't protect aliens or corporations – reserves this issue for the future

e. **Due Process Clause of 14th amendment and Selective Incorporation – COURT ADOPTS "SELECTIVE INCORPORATION PLUS MORE"**

    i. *Twining* – holds that the right to not self-incriminate is only in B of R, which does not apply to the state and 14th Amendment does not apply B of R to states; privilege against self-incrimination was not an "immutable principle of justice – this decision was later reversed – found source of the right elsewhere

      1. *Gitlo – in dicta* – freedom of speech and press are fundamental liberties and are immutable principles of justice in unalienable possession of every citizen of government

    ii. *Palko v. Connecticut* – held that double jeopardy was not "implicit in the concept of ordered liberty" (later reversed)

      1. Cardozo rejects **absorption** – 14th amendment did not merely absorb the first 8 amendments and apply them to the states

      2. this case sets out 5 standards which **sets stage for fundamental rights analysis – the hurdles**

        a. **must be implicit in the concept of ordered liberty**

        b. **the very essence of the scheme of ordered liberty**

      c. **ranked as fundamental**

      d. **fair and enlightened system of justice impossible w/o them**

      e. **it can't be arbitrary or casual – dictated by a study and appreciation of the meaning and essential applications of liberty itself**

iii.   *Adamson v. California* – D claimed CA law that prosecution could use the fact that D didn't testify on his own behalf in their closing arguments violated the 5th Amendment

    1. HELD: 5th Amendment not applied to States here.

    2. the Fourteenth Amendment could not and was not intended to apply all of these rights to states without limitations.

iv.   *Duncan* v. Louisiana – incorporated 6th Amend. Right to jury trial to the states.

    1. **Test for Incorporation**

      a. **Is it fundamental the American scheme of justice**

         i. **Is it a fundamental right**

      b. **Is the right implicit in the concept of ordered liberty and/or deeply rooted in our nation's history and traditions**

    2. **Sources of Fundamental Rights**

      a. **History/Tradition**

         i. natural law (rejected by Iredell)

         ii.   Anglo-American Law

      b. **Constitutional Text**

      c. **Reason**

      d. **Originalism** – look at historical record for original intent

      e. **Personal preference?** (is there a bias toward upper middle class values?)

      f. Moral philosophies/utilitarianism/pragmatism

      g. States (FN14 Duncan) – Harlan calls them labs of experimentation (look at how the states are handling the issue) – this allows for law to change with the legal trends of the states

v.   Possible options for incorporation:

    1. no incorporation

    2. selective incorporation (of 1-8) and nothing more

    3. total incorporation and nothing more

    4. **selective incorporation plus more – SCOTUS Adopts this Standard**

      a. court will pick and choose from first 8 amendments but can add more if its deemed a fundamental right by the court

      b. Dissent claims this must be done with consistency and that so far it has not been done that way – Harlan and Stewart

      c. 6th amendment is unique in that it is watered down in how it is applied to the states

      d. Footnote 14 – is this procedure necessary to ordered scheme of liberty

vi.   *McDonald v. City of Chicago* – **incorporated the 2nd amendment right to keep and bear arms via the 14th Amend. Due Process**

    1. Covers the uncertainty left by *DC v. Heller* – Heller only applied to DC not to the states at large.

    2. Asked that Slaughterhouse be over turned and the P&I of the 14th Amend be extended to the states

a. Slaughter-House determined that the 14th Amendment's Privileges or Immunities Clause did not apply the Bill of Rights to the actions of states (and by extension, local governments).

b. If it had been overturned, the Selective Incorporation process may have become unnecessary, since the entire Bill of Rights, including the 2nd Amendment, would arguably be applied against the states

3. Substantive Due Process Bar to Overcome if a fundamental right is to be incorporated – fundamental to our scheme or ordered liberty or "our nation's history and tradition." – not having guns taken away by the sovereign became entrenched in the colonists' mindset

4. Liberty interest in hand gun possession for protection – liberties exist for a purpose they are not the end, but a means to an end.

5. Stevens suggest the way to happiness is to find the autonomous life

6. Breyer Dissent : Heller got the history wrong,

vii. **How the Bill of Rights Applies to the States (via Due Process of 14th Amendment – what is incorporated and what isn't?)**

1. 1st amendment – YES identically incorporated
2. 2nd amend. –incorporated via *McDonald*
3. 3rd – NO
4. 4th – YES
5. 5th – grand jury indictment NOT; double jeopardy YES
6. 6th – right to jury trial in criminal cases IS incorporated
7. 7th - right to civil jury trial NOT incorporated
8. 8th – excessive bail and fines – not decided but assumed incorporated; cruel and unusual punishment YES incorporated

SUBSTANTIVE DUE PROCESS

I. **General Rule – Due process Clause of 14th Amend prohibits states from infringing fundamental liberty interests, unless the infringement is narrowly tailored to serve a compelling state interest**

II. **Lochnerizing Era**

a. *Lochner v. State of New York –* **liberty of contract is implicit in the Due Process Clause of the 14th Amendment.** Court strikes down NY State labor law prohibiting bakers from working more than 60 hr/wk because it violates the liberty of contract between employer and employee. The purpose of the bill is unconstitutional – it is a pure labor law not a police power law

    i. Harlan's Dissent – Due Process of the 14th Amendment is subject to regulations imposed by the state police powers

    ii. **Police Power – State govt. has legislative power over regulating health, safety, general welfare and morals. Only states, Federal govt. does not have this power.**

1. **Health**
2. **Safety**
3. **General welfare**
4. **Morals**

    a. **Level 1 – when the immoral conduct directly and palpably harms another**

    b. **Level 2 – adverse impact on others is indirect**

    c. **Level 3 – most controversial – if there is no direct or indirect harm to others but nonetheless there is certain consensual** behavior that are interminable to what it is to be human – inhuman acts (i.e. bestiality, necrophilia etc.)

    iii.   **Court looks at:**
1. **The purpose of the bill (at least one of the police powers met?)**
2. **Chosen means to bring about the desired purpose**
3. **Analysis – do the means justify the ends**

b. *Nebbia v. New York* – court upholds price control legislation – change from Lochner
    i. The court is incompetent and unauthorized to deal with the regulation of the economy for the good of the people – that is up to the legislature
1. Not authorized – see Art I, court has no jurisdiction, legislature does
2. Incompetent – court structure is ill suited to do what it had been doing

c. US v. Carolene Products
    i. Facial challenge of the Filled Milk Act which prohibited milk substitutes, Court rejects the facial challenge – didn't violate 5th Amendment
    ii.   **Economic legislation gets rational basis review**
    iii.   <u>**FN 4: court will give rational basis review with 3 exceptions - the varying degree of the "presumption of constitutionality" based on:**</u>
1. **When or if the due process clause incorporates the Bill of Rights – heightened review if legislation is within scope of rights protected by the first 8 amendments**
2. **Legislative product restricts efficient function of democracy – heightened review – more than mere rational basis in these instances:**
    a. **When voting rights are restricted thus restriction democratic process**
    b. **When freedom of press, speech, association are restricted for political reasons then political process is not working- courts intervene to fix the process**
3. **Certain "discrete and insular minorities" who are oppressed by democratic processes – even when the democratic process is working well, the work product represents the majority and sometimes the majority is ugly; and this represents itself in the legislation; racial and religious and national origin minorities get punished, so in these cases Court will intervene with heightened review for the minorities**

d. *West Coast Hotel v. Parish* - switch in time – end of Lochnerization –
    i. Held that the establishment of minimum wages for women was constitutionally legitimate. The Court noted that the Constitution did not speak of the freedom of contract and that liberty was subject to the restraints of due process.
    ii.   The Court also noted that employers and employees were not equally "free" in negotiating contracts, since employees often were constrained by practical and economic realities

e. Difference between social goods and rights
    i. Rights – thought of in the negative
1. Tells govt. what they can and can't do; they counter govt's ability to restrict speech etc.
2. Restrict/confine govt.
    ii.   Goods – now it's an entitlement
1. If society is to supply those social goods then you have to stimulate and expand govt. which though taxation power can collect resources to supply these goods to citizens

III. Personal Liberties

    a. Miscellaneous Liberties

        i. *Pierce v. Society of Sisters* – OR law required children to go to public school struck down for violation of due process - parents have right to have children taught as they wish

            1. Catholic school filed suit under 3rd party standing exception b/c of relationship with parents – school was going to lose contracts

        ii. *Meyer v. Nebraska* - teacher convicted of violating law prohibiting teaching German language. Court struck down law, holding teacher and parents had liberty generally recognized by common law and protected by Due Process

            1. Liberty of teacher to teach as they wished and liberty of parents to have children taught as they want

        iii. *Skinner v. Oklahoma* – sterilization cannot be imposed as punishment for moral crimes – strict scrutiny to sterilization laws – court also mentions procreation and marriage as fundamental thus strict scrutiny

        iv. Courts says *Meyer and Pierce* are First Amendment cases – altered them to be religious discrimination cases and freedom to teach cases

IV. Right to Privacy

    a. *Griswold v. Connecticut* - Court struck down the CT law prohibited use of artificial contraception or persons assisting this use

        i. Penumbras – little zones of privacy – court calls it shadow casting – the shadow of privacy

            1. Shouldn't put them in briefs – "have become a bit of a joke"

        ii. Penumbras of privacy are cast from Bill of Rights

            1. 1st Amendment – freedom of association implies privacy – not explicitly in 1st

            2. 3rd Amendment – no quartering soldiers except in war – privacy element

            3. 4th Amendment – privacy interest in search and seizure

            4. 5th Amendment – self-incrimination – privacy in mind

            5. 9th Amendment – the enumeration of certain rights shall not be construed to deny or disparage others retained by the people

        iii. Reasoning

            1. Douglas – seems to say purpose is okay but not the means to the ends – would be okay to prohibit manufacture of contraceptives but not to ban the use of them

            2. The means are unconstitutional – invades marital privacy to have police/state search bedrooms

        iv. Black's Dissent- there is no constitutional right to privacy – accuses the court of being natural law theorists; use amendments to change Constitution; court should not do so at its own will

        v. Stewart's Dissent – we're not to determine where the law is unwise but rather whether Constitution allows it

        vi. Concurring

            1. Goldberg (famous opinion) – applies 9th Amendment – comes very close to saying 9th Amendment violated by the CT law – says 9th Amendment recognizes that there are fundamental personal rights out there that are protected from govt. but not specifically mentioned in the constitution

        vii. Counting the noses – 5 justices is the majority

    b. Personal Autonomy Cases and Family Cases

        i. *Moore v. City of E. Cleveland* - zoning laws prevented extending family (grandparents) from living in single family home with their children and grandchildren. Court says extended family should be able to live in single family dwelling despite zoning laws' definition of family – this is substantive due process

    ii.   *Zablocki v.* Redhail – state could not prohibit dead beat dads from re-marrying and obtaining new marriage license (right to marry)

    iii.   Eisnstady v. Baird – transition to privacy outside of the marital relationship

        1. The court says historically there is a right to privacy in sexual intercourse – strikes down law prohibiting sale of contraceptives to unmarried persons/couples

        2. Privacy in keeping things secret vs. privacy in making autonomous choice

            a. Girswold based on keeping things in the home secret – privacy acts in one's own home

            b. Enistadt deals with prohibition on persons right to choose to use contraception, which prohibits an autonomous choice

        3. Bridging the Gap between Griswold and Roe

            a. From privacy in secret keeping to privacy in autonomous choices – privacy in marriage to privacy in sexual intercourse

c. ABORTION

    i. *Roe v. Wade* – statute made it illegal to get an abortion except to save the life of the mother

        1. Held: autonomy of choice prevails until the line of viability, at which point the state's interest becomes sufficiently compelling enough to outweigh the choice to abort

            a. Strict scrutiny - State must have a compelling interest when liberty is fundamental

                i. fundamental rights extend to: marriage, procreation, contraception, family relationships, child rearing, and education

            b. the court determines when compelling interest exists based on three trimesters

                i. after 2nd trimester viability occurs and state has compelling interest

    ii.   **Planned Parenthood v. Casey – majority rule on abortion**

        1. Standard of Review – the law imposes an undue burden if it places a *substantial obstacle* in the path of woman seeking an abortion, if it places an undue burden it is unconstitutional

            a. a little lighter than strict scrutiny but still quite a bit higher than rational basis - downgrades standard of review slightly

        2. upholds essential holding of Roe – **"a State may not prohibit any woman from making the ultimate decision to terminate her pregnancy before viability"**

        3. court maintains viability standard – viability is the point where the state's interest is compelling

        4. Kennedy - "At the heart of liberty is the right to define one's own concept of existence, of meaning, of the universe, and of the mystery of human life. Beliefs about these matters could not define the attributes of personhood were they formed under the compulsion of the State."

        5. Rehnquist – concur in part, dissent in part – disagree with "undue burden" standard fabricated by court – at least strict scrutiny had a precedential basis

      6. Scalia's Dissent – question is not what is liberty, question is "what is liberty within the meaning of the 14th amendment"

  iii. ***Gonzalez v. Carhart** –* Partial Birth Abortions

      1. Pro-lifers aren't stopping abortions with this case, just trying to shove the reality of the situation in your face – didn't save a single fetus

         a. 0-11 weeks: vacuum aspiration – 85-90% of abortions

         b. 12-16 weeks: Dilation and Evacuation (dismember in parts and evacuate) – 10 to 14% of abortions

         c. 16+weeks - fetus head too big – use "intact D&E" if head first (can crush skull); if feet first, must use D&X – baby is 2/3 delivered (pulls fetus through cervix, crushes skull and then extracts fetus) – only 1% or less

      2. Holding: intact D&E is unlawful, D&E partial is much more common 0 Kennedy upholds the law 5-4 saying Congress had three purposes for enacting the law

         a. Prevent brutal and inhumane abortion method – looks like infanticide to the general public

         b. Protect the ethics of the medical community – health care professionals should focus on saving life not taking it

         c. The effect on the woman if they are not properly informed about the procedure

      3. Ginsburg's Dissent – responds to Kennedy's opinion:

         a. The moral concerns of the government are not tethered to any legitimate government interest

         b. The procedures deemed acceptable might put a woman's health at even greater risk

         c. Neither the intact or the partial D&E is pleasant to think about

         d. Would deprive the woman of the right to make an autonomous choice – women don't need this kind of protection

      4. Viability line survives because the act makes no distinction between doing a D&E intact before or after viability – this is a facial attack

         a. For facial attack all you need is a single instance where the act is constitutional and the attack fails – if the D&E intact is on a pre-viability fetus then it's obviously constitutional

         b. Ginsberg says this blurs the line because Congress could not recognize the viability line

      5. Court assumes that Casey is controlling in order to get Scalia and Thomas in order to circumvent Roe v. Wade

  iv. Does Equal Protection Analysis Add Anything

      1. No it does not – the equality analysis is that like things should be treated alike

      2. The issue is when are things a like – doing equal protection analysis instead or in addition to substantive due process analysis does nothing

d. Parenthood (and specific vs. general tradition)

  i. *Michael H. v. Gerald D* - CA statute conclusively presumed that a child born to a married woman is legitimate – court upheld CA's application of the is statute to deny a natural father visitation rights

      1. Scalia – PLURALITY – found no specific tradition protecting natural father's rights of a child conceived in adultery

      2. O'Connor/Kennedy concurrence – should not be limited to the most specific tradition; more generalized traditions can be used

    3. Brennan dissent – would essentially abandon tradition analysis – look to "parenthood rights" and strike down the law

e. RIGHT TO REFUSE LIFE SAVING TREATMENT (right not to die)

    i. *Cruzan v. MO Health Dept. (1990)*

        1. Facts: MO had asserted its police power and refused to take woman off feeding tube absent proof of her consent. family claimed that she had verbally told them she wouldn't want to be kept alive – guardian's decision in this case is fundamental right

            a. State may require clear and convincing evidence that individual would have made the same choice

        2. MO thinks all life is sacred – will not distinguish vegetative state as a low quality of life

        3. Competent person may refuse life-saving treatment (this right existed at C/L)

        4. Distinctions that must be made

            a. Competent v. incompetent

            b. Terminally ill v. not terminal

            c. Clear and convincing evidence

    ii. *Washington v. Gluksberg (1997*) - Washington law banned assisted suicide P says this violates his due process right to personal autonomy

        1. HOLDING: ban on physician assisted suicide did NOT violate due process

            a. rational basis review - State has interest in preservation of human life, protection of integrity of medical profession, protection of vulnerable groups (poor, elderly, disabled) and fear of slippery slope to involuntary euthanasia

            b. Court distinguishes Cruzan – **Cruzan recognized right to refuse life-saving treatment not right to die**

        2. *Vacco v. Quill* – argued at the same time

            a. Equal Protection Claim – Quill claims there is an EP gap between the Quill's of the world and the Cruzan's of the world

            b. Court says no – distinguish between PASSIVE and ACTIVE

                i. Difference between passively accepting death and actively seeing it

            c. The ban on physician assisted suicide was deemed to be reasonably related to the state's important and legitimate interests –held that the statute was not facially unconstitutional nor was it unconstitutional as applied to competent, terminally ill adults.

        3. O'Connor – is passive/active distinction really a bright line? No, given advances in palliative care – O'Connor suggests a person may have a fundamental right to die free of pain (to be given drugs which may hasten death but reduce pain) – not at issue here since WA law allowed it.

f. Same-Sex Privacy

    i. *Lawrence v. Texas* - **Supreme Court strikes down TX's same-sex sodomy law**

        1. Facts – TX statute criminalized oral and anal sex between members of the same sex, other states had laws that applied to both same sex and opposite sex, but this law was sexual orientation specific.

        2. Holding – Court strikes down statute b/c it serves no legitimate state interest which will justify intrusion into the personal and private life of the individual

    a. Court DOES NOT hold that homosexual sodomy is a fundamental right (explicitly declines to do so)

    b. For EP must show that there is a favored and disfavored group

    c. Mystery Passage - persons in a homosexual relationship may seek autonomy for these purposes:

      i. Marriage

      ii.   And institution that the law protects

    d. *Bowers v. Hardwick* is overruled

3. This holding questions all laws which are purely based on morality

    a. Depends on whether these laws are still justifiable based on their purpose and the relation the means have to the ends

4. Scalia's Dissent – no compelling govt. interest – majority is applying "unheard of form of rational basis review" – homosexual sodomy is not a fundamental right

EQUAL PROTECTION

I. Elements of Equal Protection

    a. 14th Amendment: "nor shall any State…deny to any person within its jurisdiction the equal protection of the laws."

    b. *Barbier v. Connoly* (1885) – Court expanded and brought the full range of legislative classification within the restrictions of the clause

    c. **Applies to local, state and federal govt.**

      i. 14th Amendment applies to states/local govt.

      ii.   5th Amendment applies to federal govt. – interpreted as having an equal protection mode

    d. **Three Elements of Equal Protection**

      i. **Standard of Review – three levels of review**

        1. **Rational Basis –** rational reasonable means

          a. **TEST:** is the law rationally related to a legitimate govt. purpose AND are no suspect classes and no fundamental right involved

          b. Non-suspect classes

            i. Age

            ii.   Wealth/poverty

            iii.   Disability

          c. **Rational Basis w/ Bite -** where a "quasi-suspect" class is involved and the interest involved is also strong

        2. **Intermediate Review –** important govt. interest means must be substantially related

          a. **TEST:** is the law substantially related to an important government purpose and a Quasi-suspect class is involved

          b. Quasi-suspect classes

            i. Sex/gender

            ii.   illegitimacy

        3. **Strict Scrutiny -** compelling govt. interest by the least-restrictive means

          a. **TEST:** is a suspect class and/or a fundamental right involved and is the law necessary to achieve a compelling government purpose

          b. Suspect classes

            i. Race

            ii.   National origin

        iii.   Alienage
           1. Sometimes just rational basis – Congress has power over immigration and naturalization per Art I Sec 8 Cl. 4
        ii.   **Intent - For strict or intermediate scrutiny – must prove intent by govt. to discriminate**
           1. A law that is discriminatory on its face
           2. Discriminatory application of a facially neutral law
           3. Discriminatory motive behind the law – discriminatory effect not enough, motive must be show – difficult to prove
        iii.   **Burden of Proof**
           1. Rational Basis – burden on challenger
           2. Intermediate and Strict Scrutiny – burden on government

  e. <u>**Basis for some sort of heightened review -**</u> How are federal courts to interpret the intent of the legislature or relevant government official that is being sued
      i. **Discrete & insular minority (**Carolene Products Footnote 4)
          1. Discrete – individually distinct
          2. Insular – grouped as opposed to spread out amongst population where general population can learn of falsities of stereotypes
      ii. **Immutable characteristics –** traits that cannot change
      iii. **past-prejudice and its present effects –** will it wane over time
      iv. **political powerlessness**

  f. Equal Protection v. Substantive Due Process
      i. Substantive due process – more aggressive, completely disables legislature
      ii. Equal protection just forces Congress to adjust to the "fit" of the law – doesn't disable them
      iii. Fit of the law - How well does the purpose of the classification fit the problem; and how good is the means at fixing the problem
         1. At strict scrutiny, the fit must be very good
      iv. Overinclusive/Underinclusive
         1. Overinclusive – too many people who don't have the problem are restricted
         2. Underinclusive – not everyone with the problem gets addressed; this is okay since it allows govt to attack the problem a little at a time
         3. Simultaneous over/under – some of those w/ problem are not helped and some of those w/o problem are restricted unnecessarily
      v. Overbreadth – different from Overinclusive

II. Equal Protection in Economic Regulation
  a. Pre-Lochner – equal protection used to strike down economic regulation
  b. Post-Lochner - Economic regulation gets rational basis review
  c. Purpose of the Regulation
      i. Actual Purpose – the subjective motive of the law
      ii. Apparent purpose – the object of the law
  d. *Williams v. Lee Optical of OK* – it's okay to be underinclusive; don't have to try to solve the whole problem

III. **RATIONAL BASIS**
  a. Involves non-suspect classes and no fundamental rights
      i. has been used to strike down laws that had **offensive discriminatory purpose**
  b. Rational Basis w/ Bite Cases
      i. *Romer v. Evans* – court struck down Colorado constitutional provision which prohibited state and localities from protecting homosexual conduct – homosexuals

are non-suspect and get rational basis, but court nonetheless struck down

    ii.   *City of Cleburne v. Cleburne Living Center* – struck down zoning that discriminated against mentally disabled even though only got rational basis (with bite)

IV. NON-SUSPECT CLASSES – Rational Basis Review
    a. Standard for Determining Suspect Classes
        i. Discrete – immutable characteristics
        ii.   Insular – narrow
        iii.   Past prejudice – look to history
        iv.   Minority
        v.   Political powerlessness
    b. **Disabled**
        i. *City of Cleburne v. Cleburne Living Ctr.* City's zoning regime requires special use permit for mentally disabled centers; majority claims they are applying rational basis (non-suspect class)
            1. **Rational basis review – mentally disabled are non-suspect class**
            2. Mentally Disabled
                a. Not politically powerless – have people advocating for them strongly (FN10)
                b. Legitimate distinction – these people are different in a relevant way
                c. Slippery slope – of creating more suspect classes
                d. No evidence of antipathy or prejudice against the disabled
            3. Holding – Court holds that zoning law fails rational basis review
                a. Citizens are discriminating against the disabled – and politicians can't adopt these views to act on their behalf for this improper purposes
    c. **Wealth/Poverty**
        i. **"poverty, standing alone, is not a suspect classification"**
        ii.   Classifications on account of wealth alone should not be given heightened review – apply rational basis review
        iii.   *Harris v. McRae* - upheld federal statute prohibiting funding of abortions even though burden falls on the indigent – court rejects EP challenge

V. **Quasi-Suspect Classes**
    a. **Gender – gets intermediate review**
        i. Women – get heightened review because distinct, immutable traits, and past prejudice – not really insular since spread out
            1. *GE v. Gilbert* - Pregnancy classifications are NOT gender discrimination – and thus do not get heightened review – pregnancy is an "accurate generalization" of women
                a. Get rational basis review only
                b. But it can get out Title VII federal civil rights action
                c. **Distinction between Benefits and Burdens is IRRELEVANT –** they are treated the same under EP analysis
                d. Law which classify pregnancy are not on their face gender discriminatory
                e. Pregnancy is an objectively identifiable physical condition – doesn't matter that only women get pregnant
                f. Make sure the pregnancy distinction is not a mere pretext for a gender-based discrimination
        ii.   *Wengler v. Druggists Mutual* – failed intermediate review – court found

that insurance policy discriminated against men requiring they prove they were dependant spouse, but also discriminates against women by stereotyping them as the dependant

    iii.   Gender in Education

        1.   Cannot discriminate on the basis of gender in public education

            a. ***Public schools cannot be same-sex; only private schools can be same sex***

        2. *Miss Univ. for Women v. Hogan* – male denied admission to state nursing school based on statute saying women only – court strikes it down

b. **Illegitimacy**

    i. Can't go after the innocent illegitimate child to try to discourage sexual relations outside of the marital bond – means not related to the ends

    ii.   *Nguyen v. INS* - Statute imposed different requirements for an illegitamte child born out of the US to become US citizen depending on whether citizen parent was father or mother (easier if mother)

        1.   Statute serves 2 interest

            a. Assures parent-child relationship

            b. Assures father-child relationship is more than just a legal tie

VI. SUSPECT CLASSES – STRICT SCRUTINY

a. **RACE -** if P shows there is race discrimination the burden going forward with evidence and burden of persuasion shift to the government

b. **Affirmative action may take place w/r/t (a) the terms & conditions of employment; (b) the award of government contracts; and (c) student admission & conditions of enrollment.**

    i. *Regents of the Univ. of Calif. v. Bakke* - state medical school had an affirmative action plan for admission of students. Sixteen of 100 places were reserved for Black, Chicano, Asian, and American Indian applicants. The quota plan was upheld

        1.   . The Court split 4-1-4, with Justice Lewis Powell writing the determinative solo opinion. That opinion's rationale rapidly became the law for some time.

        2.   **Powell applied "exacting scrutiny" to the racial classification, and upheld the plan on the basis of creating diversity in the student class.**

    ii.   *Metro Broadcasting, Inc. v. FCC* - held that federal affirmative action plans would be reviewed using a less rigorous standard of review than state/local affirmative action plans.

    iii.   *Adarand Constructors, Inc. v. Pena* - held that a federal affirmative action plan w/r/t minority governmental contractors would have to survive strict scrutiny. Case reversed and remanded for proceedings consistent with the opinion.

        1.   **Race gets strict scrutiny whether benign or not**

    iv.   *Gratz v. Bollinger* - held that affirmative action plan w/r/t minority undergraduate enrollment at state university was unconstitutional.

        1.   Purpose was diversity and the means of enrollment selection was by point system that assigned points merely because applicant was a minority.

    v.   *Grutter v. Bollinger* - held that affirmative action plan w/r/t minority enrollment at state law school survived strict scrutiny.

        1.   Purpose was diversity and the means of enrollment selection was a "whole file review" of applicants. The "whole file review" considered an applicant's race as one factor, but there was no quota or point system.

    vi.   *Parents Involved in Community Schools v. Seattle Sch. Dist. No. 1,* This opinion consolidates two cases (Seattle and Louisville) involving intra-district assignment of students to local school buildings within the larger school district.

1. Each school district had a different system to achieve racial balancing within each local school building, the purpose was to achieve school buildings that did not have too many or too few minorities.
2. Both systems were held to be unconstitutional.

vii. *Ricci v. DeStefano,* - City administered a written test to firefighters used to help in promotional decisions. The results of the test had a disparate effect on minorities. For reasons of diversity and the threat of a lawsuit by minority test takers, the city decided to not use the test results. Firefighters who scored high on the test sued.

1. Held that the city's action was race-based and did not survive strict scrutiny.

c. **Alienage**

i. **Federal Classification – not subject to strict scruting if they are not arbitrary and unreasonable**

ii. **State and Local Classification – subject to strict scrutiny**

1. i.e. it is unconstitutional for US citizenship to be required for welfare, civil service jobs or to become a lawyer

iii. **U.S. residency requirement – rational basis review**

iv. **state residency requirement – would get intermediate review under Art. IV P&I**

v. *Bernal v. Fainter – political function exception* – certain state and local governments can require US citizenship for employment that has a political function to it elected or not included K-12 teachers, police officers

vi. Cannot require US citizenship for notary publics or attorneys– these are not "political function" and get strict scrutiny like other alienage discrimination

vii. Undocumented Aliens – not a suspect class –subject to rational basis review

EQUAL PROTECTION – FUNDAMENTAL RIGHTS ANALYSIS

I. **Fundamental Rights Review**

a. **Court applies strict scrutiny to review subject matter that involves fundamental rights**

i. **Right to Privacy - see Substantive Due Process above**

1. Marriage/Divorce
2. Sexual Activity/Abortion/Contraceptive use
3. Family and Parental Rights – care, custody, control of children, right to live with extended family

ii. **Voting qualifications**

1. Reapportionment
2. 15th Amendment – race cannot be a qualification for voting
3. 19th Amendment – women's suffrage

iii. **Right to travel**

1. No durational residency requirements for the most part

II. **Voting Qualifications**

a. **Reapportionment**

i. *Baker v. Carr* - once got past justiciability, court created **"one person one vote" standard**

1. Court said TN had to reapportion since rural people had moved to urban areas and voting was no longer proportional

ii. 28 USC § 2284 – 3 judge panel to find facts and conclude questions of law – essentially get out a map of the state, and reapportion the state as it is appropriate

iii. *Vieth v. Jubelirer* - political gerrymandering – how much is too much because some is okay and some is inevitable – Souter says "extremity of unfairness"

1. We allow political gerrymandering, there is no discernable standard therefore it is a political question .

2. *Reynolds v. Sims* – judicially manageable standard is one person one vote, but for political party gerrymandering there is no judicially manageable and discernable standard – therefore a political question and therefore not justiciable.

   a. Traditional districting principles who's disregard can be shown straightforwardly

   b. Lines must be contiguous

   c. Can't take a district that's made up of two counties which are geographically separated and not touching

   d. Compactness

   e. Respect for political subdivisions – cities & counties not usually split in half

   f. Conformity to geographic features like rivers, mountains, and urban/rural divide

iv. **Racial Reapportionment**

1. **Shaw v. Hunt – if race is a predominant factor in reapportionment then unconstitutional**

   a. **Gerrymandering along political lines is okay – somewhat expected**

b. **Residency Requirement**

   i. Short term residency requirements are okay (50 days has been held constitutional) but long term are not (3 months is too long) because voting is a fundamental right

   ii. Apply strict scrutiny

c. Property Requirement

   i. *Hill v. Stone* – struck down requirement of property ownership before voting – restricted the right to vote and thus unconstitutional

d. Felony Conviction – convicted felons may be stripped of their right to vote – social contract

   i. We give up certain rights for others, we violate the social contract state can strip us of certain rights

e. Tabulation of Votes – because voting is fundamental, each vote is given the same effect as every other vote – not votes are given more importance or weight

   i. *Bush v. Gore* – must use uniform standards for tabulation of votes cannot just guess what the voter's intent was

      1. Florida used an "Intent of the voter" standard to determine what the voter could have and probably meant by their unclear vote – this is a violation of equal protection

III. Right to Travel

a. **Right to travel gets strict scrutiny**

b. **Four Sources of Right to Travel**

   i. **Article IV P&I** – protects against discrimination against citizens of a sister state

1. Art. IV P&I discrimination by states against citizens of sister states gets intermediate review
2. *Sup Ct. of New Hampshire v .Piper* – cannot be a member of the bar in NH unless domiciled in NH, Piper domiciled in VT.
   a. given intermediate review – no discrimination unless you can meet intermediate review
   b. practice of state to treat non-residents adversely in terms of getting fishing or hunting licenses – courts allow that as an exception
   c. **Governing Function Exception to Intermediate Review – a state, if it involves an office an the office exercises a governing function then the state can require that you be a citizen of that state. i.e. Missouri requires that you be domiciled in MO to be a MO judge**
   d. **Political Function Exception** – have to be a citizen to hold certain offices
3. Corporations are not citizens under Art IV
4. You must be a state citizen for this to apply – you can be a US citizen and not a state citizen, does not apply to non-US citizens b/c non-citizens cannot be state citizens

ii. **Dormant Commerce Clause**
1. Sometimes need to travel to engage in commerce – when that's impeded, struck down by giving strict scrutiny under this clause
2. Apply Dormant Commerce Clause review
3. *Edwards v. California* - CA passed a law during the dustbowl called the anti-Okie law, struck down under DCC, which is about the movement of capital across state lines. Here the capital moving across state lines was human capital in the form of labor

iii. **Equal Protection Clause**
1. *Shapiro v. Thompson* – had to live in NY 1 year before getting welfare benefits – struck down by court as impairment of right to travel; Brennan does note that legitimate domicile requirements would be constitutional
   a. This was a mere method of testing/ascertaining bona fide domiciliary intent – not allowed
2. Bona Fide Continuing Residence Requirements – these are okay, it's when you must live there for a certain duration that it's not allowed
   a. *Dunn v. Blumstein* – when they find something a restriction on travel is it per se unconstitutional
   b. You can restrict the bona fide requirements – i.e. you can require that someone be a current resident of the state, but you can't say they have to be a resident for X amount of time before they can have certain rights

iv. **14th Amendment P or I - Saenz v. Roe**

c. **Saenz v. Roe -** CA statute limited welfare benefits to new residents. Residents of less than a year could only receive the benefits they would have had in their old state.
   i. **Court applies Strict Scrutiny** – durational residency requirements get strict scrutiny
      1. Exception – portability – states can require residency for divorce
   ii. **Three Components of Right to Travel**
      1. **State cannot put up "barriers at the border" Right of citizen of one state to enter and leave another state**

2. **Right to be treated as welcome visitor rather than an unfriendly alien when temporarily present in the second state**
3. **For travelers who elect to become permanent residents, the right to be treated like other citizens of that that**

iii.   **Right to Travel is like 13ᵗʰ Amendment in that it does not require government action – only restriction of rights is required**

PROCEDURAL DUE PROCESS

I.   **A fair process (notice or hearing) is required for a government agency to individually take a person's life, liberty or property. Only intentional deprivation of these rights violates Due Process**

II.   **Analysis (could be either)**
a. **Property**
     i. **STEP 1: Is there a property interest?**
     ii.   **STEP 2: What process is due?**
b. **Liberty Interests**
     i. **STEP 1: Is there a liberty interest?**
     ii.   **STEP 2: What process is due? (what sort of remedy does it get?)**
       1. **Constitutional rights**
         a. **Do I have a right?**
         b. **Make whole relief**
       2. **Reputation**
         a. **Can I show harm?**
         b. **Name clearing hearing**

III.   PROPERTY
a. **Step 1: Is there a property interest at stake?   Definition of "property interests"**
     i. not created in constitution, but exist external to it
     ii.   property interests exist in state substantive law (state statute or C/L) and by statutory entitlements such as welfare benefits, business licenses, etc. – a govt. job is property (Roth)
     iii.   must have more than abstract need or desire for it to be property interest – **interest must be presently enjoyed and not merely an entitlement to a future interest to which one is an applicant or a potential holder of**
       1. our own property interests include 401k, licenses to practice law/medicine or to drive, our jobs, pensions, retirement plans
     iv.   *Roth v. Board of Regents* – professor sues claiming he was denied his property interest in a 1yr. renewal option – **court said he had no property interest in the renewal option since this was not a right to continued employment (not a presently enjoyed security interest)**
       1. Roth's govt. job is property but it had a 1yr. contract – his property interest was that one year of employment
       2. Roth would have been entitled to procedural due process had he been terminated in the middle of his contractual term of employment – University merely just failed to renew contract
     v.   *Perry v. Sindermann* – there is no property interest in the hope for future employment only a property interest in current employment
       1. *Cleveland Board of Ed. V. Loudermill* – state cannot give a property interest and then take it away without due process. I.e. you cannot be disbarred without due process
       2. *Arnett* – had held that the state imposed procedure were part of the property

interest itself – **must take the "bitter with the sweet" – Loudermill OVERRULES this – state can't give entitlement and then force person to give up due process rights through unfair procedural mechanisms**

3. Application for the bar is not a property interest it is an expectation of a property interest

4. Once admitted to the bar you have a property interest and it can only be taken away without procedural due process

5. *Paul v. Davis* – court says with damage to reputation, we don't want constitution to become a fount of tort law, so it's not enough to just show damage to reputation you have to show something additional that the government has deprived you of – loss of reputation plus loss of your job.

    vi. *Amer. Mfg. Mutual Ins. v. Sullivan* – Pennsylvania dodges Loudermill - workers compensation was deemed property right – Penn workers comp. law defined the benefit, a statutory right to workers comp. but defined injury on the job as a)work-related injury and b)med treatment must be shown reasonable and necessary – but Sullivan had not yet established no property right since didn't show reas. and necessary

b. Step 2: Proceed to Matthews Balancing

    i. 3 Part Balancing Test that weighs

1. **The importance of the interest and**

2. **The value of specific procedural safeguards to that interest - <u>1 & 2 AGAINST 3</u>**

3. **The government interest in fiscal and administrative efficiency**

    ii. *City of LA v. David*

1. City towed illegally parked car – David claimed it was deprivation of property without due process – took him $134.50 to get his car back – he argues no parking sign was covered by trees – took him 30 days to get a hearing

    a. Supreme Court performed Matthews balancing – struck balance in favor of city

        i. mere monetary interest here (not a case of prisoner being put in solitary)

        ii. accuracy – won't be affected by having hearing 5 days or 30 days after deprivation

        iii. city argues that it needs more time (5 days would be too hard for such trivial matters)

    iii. *Parratt v. Taylor* – inmate order game and had it delivered, but guards stole it – inmate sued for deprivation of property without due process; but Court held prisoner only had process due from the prison's internal system for filing a claim

IV. LIBERTY

a. Liberty Interests

    i. includes:

1. **fundamental rights (retaliation)**

2. **reputation damage**

3. **freedom from bodily restraint**

    ii. Damage to reputation

1. *Paul v. Davis* – **need damage to rep. plus something more** (con law requires more showing than tort law on this reputation damage issue) - damage to reputation alone not enough – need some other material loss (K not renewed, etc.) to show alteration in legal status

    a. *Roth* – his reputation argument is a loser – nonrenewal without further

comment doesn't create negative stigma
2. not entitled to a name-clearing hearing
  iii. Fundamental Rights (retaliation)
    1. Substantive constitutional rights – free speech, etc.
    2. You get "make whole" relief – govt. took something from you in retaliation and you want it back; you don't want more process – you want your liberty back and want to be restored to prior condition (money substitute sometimes necessary)
  iv. Freedom from Bodily Restraints
    1. *Sandin v. Conner* – "real substantive test"
    2. *Town of Castle Rock v. Gonzalez* - sues for deprivation of property in that the CO statute and the protective order she was issued under the CO statute was not sufficiently enforced by the police and the result was the murder of her children. Property interest is in the statutory defined police protection
      a. Court says she doesn't even get past step 1 – she does not have a property interest in police enforcement of a restraining order – the police have discretion to grant or deny protection – there is no mandatory duty
      b. **She claims she has a right to more process, more procedure, you cannot have a property interest in more procedure – you either have property or you don't, have a contract or don't have a contract, have a license or you don't – that is step 1**
      c. FN 20 – the enforcement of the restraining order is not discretionary it is a substantive act – the discretionary call however is whether or not the restraining order is being violated
    3. *Daniels v. Williams* – prisoner trips on pillow on steps and injures himself; sues officials claiming negligence in leaving it there; state claims sovereign immunity; prisoner claims deprived of property interest within meaning of Due Process Clause – and claims officer's negligence deprived him of liberty interest in freedom from bodily restraint
      a. "where a govt. official's act causing injury to life, liberty or property is merely negligent, no procedure for compensation is constitutionally required:"
        i. *Must show intent – negligent not enough*
      b. **Historically deprivation of due process had to be deliberate deprivation**
      c. *Washington v. Davis* – intent required in substantive due process context as well
      d. *Davidson v. Cannon* – negligence won't do for deprivation of liberty interest, some sort of higher level of fault or culpability must be shown

V. **What Substantive Due process is due when**
  a. **What constitutes a deprivation?**
    i. **Mere negligence is not enough – must show intent**
    ii. **Deprivation of due process has to be deliberate deprivation**
  b. **What Process is due and when?**
    i. **The Fundamental requirement of due process is the opportunity to be heard and it is an opportunity which must be granted at a meaningful time and in a meaningful manner. Pre-deprivation vs. post-deprivation.**
    ii. **If Property: three part balancing test;**
      1. **importance to the individual**

        2. **risk of erroneous deprivation**

        3. **government interest in efficiency (cost)**

    iii. **If reputation: government must give you a name-clearing hearing**

    iv. **If constitutional right/bodily integrity**

        1. **constitutional right: want your right back**

        2. **bodily integrity: want pre-deprivation Hearing – damages**

c. *Connick v. Meyers* - redefinement of Roth and Perry

    i. Facts – assistant prosecutor fired w/o process after circulating questionnaire about office greviances; Question 11 was about whether any other assi. Dist. attorneys had been pressured to support political campaigns (involves elections and free speech – fundamental rights) – so this was a matter of public opinion

    ii. **2 part test for Free Speech**

        1. **Speech must be on matters of public concern**

            a. *Givhaus* – speech on racisim probably going to be matter of public concern

            b. *Pickering* - teacher's complaints about school expenditures are a matter of public concern

            c. Pickering test:

                i. A public employee has a protected right under the First Amendment to comment on "matters of public concern," no matter what the employer thinks.

                ii. If the employee's comments aren't on a "matter of public concern," those comments are not protected.

                iii. If the employee's comments are on a matter of public concern, then the employer must demonstrate that the speech would "potentially interfere with or disrupt the government's activities, and can persuade the court that the potential disruptiveness" outweighs the employee's First Amendment rights.

        2. **Balancing test**

            a. Must balance government's interest in maintaining discipline and loyalty against employees free speech rights

                i. Cannot destroy close working relationships

                ii. High loyalty needed in some govt. jobs

            b. Burden is shifted to the government – government has an interest in lack of insubordination at the work place

    iii. *Garcetti v. Ceballos*

        1. Step 1: the court says this is not a matter of public concern – when statements made pursuant to official duties they are not speaking as citizens and thus don't have 1st Amendment protection

        2. The court rejects the notion that the 1st Amendment shields form discipline that expressions employees make pursuant to their professional duties

            a. When a government employee steps outside of their role as a government employee they are a citizen and have rights

            b. When a government employee is acting w/in the course of their employment they are acting as the government – thus it is a state action

STATE ACTION

I. **Intro**

    a. The state action requirement stems from the fact that the constitutional amendments protect individual rights. Because of this requirement, it is impossible for private parties (citizens or corporations) to violate these amendments, and all lawsuits alleging constitutional violations of this type must show how the government (state or federal) was responsible for the violation of their rights.

  i. **Constitution does not apply unless there is State Action – if there is an action between two individuals in civil society but the government is not involved the constitution does not engage**

  ii. **Exceptions – 13th Amendment or Right to Travel**

  iii. **If dealing with first 8 amendments we need Federal Action**

b. not really a right – kind of like justiciability – threshold issue

c. it's a prerequisite to 14th and 15th amendment rights

d. **Goal – to determine whether an action "can fairly be attributed to the State**

e. **"Federal Action" required for federal govt. to violate Bill of Rights** (only federal govt. can violate Bill of Rights. per *Barron v. City of Baltimore*)

f. **"State Action" required for state or local govt. to violate the parts of bill of rights incorporated through 14th amendment**

II. **Seven Constructs for Determining State Action**

a. **Color of Law**

b. **Conspiracy**

c. **Compulsion Test**

d. **Public Function (sovereign function)**

e. **Joint Action**

f. **Symbiotic Relationship**

g. **Pervasive Entwinement**

III. **Color of Law**

a. **Discriminatory acts by state officials – court relies on Enabling Clause**

b. Federal legislation can reach private conduct interfering with 14th amendment rights when that conduct contains sufficient indicia of state action

  i. *Screws v. U.S.* – police officer beat a prisoner to death, claimed he was violating the law so not operating under it – **ACTING UNDER COLOR OF LAW**

c. covers acts done "under the imprimatur of state law"

d. *Monroe v. Pape* –reaffirmed color of law in the civil side

IV. **Conspiracy**

a. **Discrimination by private individuals collaborating with state officials in state action**

  i. *US v. Price* - private citizen becomes state actor when conspires with government action – the all actions of the conspiracy are state action

b. Discrimination by private individuals alone is not state action

  i. Must show state involvement and not just the customs or social habits of a community

  ii. This deals with local custom/social convention

V. **Compulsion**

a. Government Regulation of Private Activity

  i. *Moose Lodge No. 107 v. Irvis* – state was indirectly ***compelling*** the club to discriminate by demanding bylaws be followed in order to get a liquor license and the bylaws prohibited blacks

b. *Jackson v. Metropolitan Edison Co.* – termination of utility services using the procedures allowed by state law does not constitute state action

  i. **mere fact that a business is regulated does not convert its action into State Action even if business is extensively regulated**

  ii. insurance company does not become state actor simply because state law requires private industry to purchase such insurance from the insurance company

VI. Public Function (or Sovereign Function)

    a. Sovereign Function test

        i. Private actor is doing a function which government usually does

        ii. Must also be that which exclusively a government does

        iii. Examples

            1. Parks and schools not traditionally public – there are private parks and private schools

            2. Operation of parks – public function

                a. *Evans v. Newton* – park ran by private trust; conveyance said no blacks – this was later limited to its facts

            3. *Rendell-Baker v. Kohn* - Operation of private schools is not a traditional govt. function

    b. Racial Discrimination - White primary cases – election of candidates is a public function and thus state action

        iii. Courts treat this as state action because **election officials are serving a public function in running primary elections**

    c. *Steel v. Louisville* – treating union activity as a public function and thus state action, but not good law anymore – now its interpreted mostly as wholly private conduct

    d. *Marsh v. Alabama* - company - **running a town is a public function**

        i. Operation of shopping malls NOT state action – originally held public function (*Amalgamated 1968*) but not anymore (*Lloyd, 1972*)

    e. Olympic organizers

        i. *SF Arts v. US Olympic Committee* – world athletic competitions not traditionally govt. function

VII. Joint Action Test

    a. *Luger v. Edmonson Oil* – Joint Action Test – 2 part Test

        i. **Action is done pursuant to a state law or right – connect the act of deprivation with state law**

        ii. **State official participated in the deprivation**

            1. distinguish from conspiracy – in conspiracy, state actor know s he is doing something wrong, under joint action he is doing what the law is telling him to do

    b. *Flagg Bros v. Brooks* -– warehouse keeps P's goods and plans to sell them off under UCC 7-210 to pay off her missed payments on the storage costs

        i. court held no public function - settlement of disputes between debtors and creditors is not traditionally an exclusive public function

        ii. no compulsion - state merely acquiesced in the private act by not prohibiting it

        iii. no joint action - first element met since deprived of property, but 2nd element not met since there was no public official jointly acting

    c. Peremptory Challenges to exclude jurors on account of race – Batson Rule these only make sense chronologically (court used to find state action easily now its harder to find it)

        i. Polk Cty. v. Dodson – public defender NOT state actor (since hired to be independent of state)

        ii. Powers v. Ohio – prosecutor is state actor

        iii. Edmonson v. Leesville Concrete –(civil) – court found state action

            1. Joint Action – court cheated on first element, which was in actuality not met – 1st part of joint action test requires facial challenge to the state law (but here law was facially neutral)

2. Georgia v. McCollum – private defense lawyer was state actor *in role of picking jury*, -which is a quintessential govt. function

VIII. Symbiotic Relationship (only one case has found it) – very narrow

   a. *Burton v. Wilmington Parking Authority* – lessees of state property whose leases further state interest and form an integral part of a state operation are required to comply with the 14th Amendment

   i. 2 part test

   1. private activity appears public (common location)

   a. looked public since it was part of public, govt. owned garage

   2. government is profiting from its wrongful conduct

   a. City of Wilmington could charge higher rents from having segregated restaurantso state is profiting from its wrongdoing

IX. Pervasive Entwinement

   a. not really a test but a collection of factors

   b. *Brentwood Academy v. Tenn. Secondary School Athletic Assn.*

   i. Facts – Athletic association collected money from 84% of the schools and were ran by paid employees of the public schools

   ii. HELD: There was pervasive entwinement between the Athletic Association and the public officials/teacher no public function and no compulsion, but court creates a new rule, which Court holds is met

   1. though court does note that entwinement is somewhat based on coercion/encouragement

   iii. They wouldn't have been a state actor if the staff had been private but because the staff was administrators and teachers at the schools it was entwined

   iv. NCAA is not state actor because NCAA has member schools spread across all the different states.

   c. **Acquiescence or mere approval is NOT enough** – i.e. extensive regulation, tax benefits, subsidies, licensing, etc. are mere approval or acquiescence and not alone good enough to constitute state action

X. Non-State Actors

   a. *Blum v. Yaretsky*

   i. Govt. had been paying for nursing home care but orders cost reduction through downgrading care levels; physicians are sued for depriving property benefits

   ii. No compulsion b/c physicians are exercising independent, private judgment and aren't being compelled to downgrade

   b. *Rendell-Baker v. Kohn* – **government funding NOT part of state action formula**

   i. schools are NOT exclusive, traditional govt. function

   ii. school in this case was 90-99% govt. funded, licensed teachers, students referred by govt. but court held still no state action

   iii. govt. funds almost every aspect of civil society in some way – to allow funding to be source of state action would be to subject all of civil society to the rigidity of the Bill of Rights

FREEDOM OF SPEECH

I. Mode of Analysis

   a. **Is this speech or is it merely conduct involving no or very little expressive conduct**

   b. **Is this a category of "disfavored speech"?**

   i. Advocacy of illegality

   ii. **Fighting words**

   iii. **Obscenity not including pornography which is fully protected**

             iv.   **Defamation**

   c. **If not disfavored, is this fully protected speech or is it commercial speech? (getting intermediate protection)**

   d. **If this is fully protected speech, then are any of these factors present**

       i. Time, place, manner, restrictions

       ii.   **Content-based or viewpoint based discrimination**

       iii.   **Public forum analysis**

       iv.   **Hostile or captive audience**

   e. **Is the law unconstitutionally vague**

II. Considerations - Vague, Overbroad or Prior Restraint

   a. **Overbreadth**

       i. *US v. Stevens – crush porn* -depictions of animal cruelty are not as a class, categorically unprotected by the First Amendment

          1. Dissent - The speech was the act , the act was the speech– to rape a child is speech, this is the same thing, the act of crushing the animal is speech.

             a. Had this been a simulation this would not have constituted speech

             b. The only difference for Alito is there are degrees of immorality – it is a greater immoral act to rape a child than to crush to death a small animal – both are illegal

             c. Any Overbreadth is tiny – the doctrine of Overbreadth does not apply and Stevens only has an "as applied" attack and not a facial attack

          2. Majority -

             a. Substantial Overbreadth – the facial attack on the code is that it is too overbroad to be applicable and is contrary to the constitution. Section 48 of the US Code was overbroad and thus contrary to the 1st Amendment

             b. **For a facial attack to survive MUST show that there is no possible constitutional application of the statute**

                i. Stevens obtained status to argue for turkey hunting videos, and then was allowed to argue the dog fighting videos. Once you argue a hunting video case (which they had done) then the dog fighting and crush videos were allowed to be argued

                ii.   First rate speech is so easily chilled that we allow others 3rd party standing to argue their case. The remedy is to strike down on its face, in total, whatever statute stops chilling the speech of the fully protected speaker.

       ii.   *Broadrick v. Oklahoma* – OK statute proscribed partisan political activity by state civil servants – couldn't support candidates while on the job but needed 3rd party standing. They were soliciting money on behalf of a candidate so they needed 3rd party standing and court said nope

          1. Court held that the statute is not overbroad as the state has the power to regulate partisan activities of civil servants

       iii.   *Brockett v. Spokane Arcades, Inc.* – defined obscenity in terms of the word lust because the term lust sweeps too broad as normal sexual arousal could be called lust.

          1. Normal sexual arousal is protected so the statute swept in a huge portion of fully protected speech

   b. **Vagueness**

       i. A statute can be stuck down as being void for vagueness as it is too vague to

apply to the constitution

ii.   *Herndon v. Lowery* – Georgia statute (pre Civil War) that was passed b/c of a fear of slave insurrection. Here it's being used to prohibit speech

    1. "the statute as construed and applied in the appellant's trial does not furnish a sufficiently ascertainable standard of guilt"

       a. As a result this statute is attempting to predict future activity of others based upon your persuasion and not prohibit current activity. Basically you would be executed for your speech that incites future events.

iii.   *Coates v. Cincinnati* – statute that prevented people from assembling in groups of 3 or more whose actions would annoy people.

    1. The ordinance is vague – conduct that annoys some people does not annoy others "men of common intelligence must necessarily guess at its meaning"

c. Injunctions and Prior Restraint

i. *Pittsburg Press Co. v. Pitt. Comm's on Human Relations* - prior restraints to speech are disfavored especially when it comes to institutional press

    1. Rarely can get an injunction against a newspaper

ii.   Prior restrains are disfavored

iii.   Prior restraints are common in some areas

    1. Parades, demonstrations – cities often require permits which are forms of prior restraints to speech

       a. Can only apply to streets, parks and side walks

       b. Must see a municipal official – official cannot be given unbridled discretion

iv.   Permit law probably must provide for judicial review

    1. Appeal should be rapid

    2. Procedure must spell out precisely what is needed – clerk needs to know exact basis to use in deciding whether to grant – can't make content based restrictions

    3. A modest fee can be required but cannot be excessive such that it is prohibitive

v.   What if permit is denied? Must exhaust the administrative means before just violating the law claiming it's unconstitutional

vi.   *Forsythe Cty. V. Nationalist Movment* - Court held invalid an ordinance that allowed administrator to adjust the amount to be paid for a permit as it gave him unbridled discretion

** *Note: Vagueness and substantial overbreadth do not apply to commercial speech* **

III. **DISFAVORED SPEECH** – rational basis review - speech is *per se* disfavored.

  a. Types of Disfavored Speech

    i. Advocacy of Illegality

    ii.   Obscenity

    iii.   Fighting Words

    iv.   Defamation

  b. Advocacy of Illegality

    i. **THE BRANDENBURG TEST** – *Brandenburg v. Ohio* - Establishes the clear and imminent danger test - **state cannot forbid "advocacy of the use of force or of law violation except where such advocacy is directed to inciting or producing imminent lawless action and is likely to incite or produce such action"**

1. **Elements of Brandenburg Clear and Imminent Danger Test:**
    a. **Imminence** – look to the time elapsed between the speech and when the fear of harm begins
    b. **Probability** – it must be "likely" that the advocated acts will occur – which implies must be greater than 50% chance – causation element
    c. **Magnitude of Feared Harm** – how big is the harm that was threatened
        i. Brandenburg does not make a violent/non-violent distinction – thought it would seem that nonviolent would be a lower "magnitude of feared harm"
    d. **State of Mind** – advocating the use of force or lawlessness must be directed to inciting the acts, there must be intent to incite the acts
2. Dissent – Douglas and Black - speech needs to be protected overt acts do not need to be protected because they are not speech

IV. **Obscenity**
    a. **Miller Test for Obscenity (three part test, must meet all 3)**
        i. **Whether the average person, applying contemporary community standards would find that the work, taken as a whole, appeals to the prurient interest**
            1. *US v. Thomas* – the "community" for purposes of this test is where the audience is – i.e. where the material is downloaded and viewed.
            2. Jury determines what the average member of the community would find obscene
        ii. **Whether the work depicts or describes, in a patently offensive way, sexual conduct specifically defined by the applicable state law**
            1. "Patently offensive"
                a. Patently offensive representations or descriptions of ultimate sexual acts, normal or perverted, actual or simulated:"
                b. "patently offensive representations or descriptions of masturbation, excretory functions and lewd exhibition of the genitals"
        iii. **Whether the work, taken as a whole, lacks serious literary, artistic, political, or scientific value.**
    b. *Jenkins v. Georgia* – court held that occasional scenes of nudity alone was not enough to make it obscene; a jury's verdict on obscenity is not immune from review; Justices used their own view and said movie was not obscene – **obscenity is not entirely left to the jury -** state must create standards that limit it to "patently offensive" materials.
    c. Child Porn – even though not obscene, state may restrict this
        i. *NY v. Ferber* – okay to allow adult porn but restrict child porn – **state has compelling interest in preventing the sexual exploitation of children**
            1. based on consent – 15 yr old legally cannot consent even though they may actually consent
            2. this means that "virtual child porn" is protected since children are not actually engaging in the acts (their faces are pasted over adults') so state's interest is not present
        ii. *Ashcroft v. Free Speech Coalition*- virtual child pornography is protected speech
        iii. *US.* v. Williams – if the seller is telling the buyer or trying to make the buyer the child pornography is real as opposed to virtual – the buyer must only believe that he was purchasing child porn to be prosecuted (even thought "he got duped")

d. **"secondary effects"**
  i. SCOTUS has upheld zoning restrictions on adult pornography (bookstores, strip clubs, porn shops.) – municipalities have been allowed to do one of two things:
    1. ghettoize them – put them all in one place
    2. spread them out (no adult establishments within 5000 ft. of each other) to try to minimize their effect
  ii.   this is allowed in order to minimize the secondary effects of these establishments: crime, reduced property values
e. Secondary Effect Cases
  i. *Young v. American Mini Theatres-* municipality didn't want adult businesses and passed ordinance prohibiting licensure of adult businesses unless the location was at least 1000 ft. from another sexually oriented business or 1000ft from school/library/church. This was upheld saying this is not a violation of freedom of speech b/c target is not the speech but the secondary effects of the speech
    1. Secondary effect of the speech is crime, drugs, prostitution
  ii.   *Renton v. Playtime Theaters* – secondary effects same holding

V. Fighting Words
  a. Fighting words are not protected speech – non-fighting gets full protection
    i. *Chaplinsky v. New Hampshire* - **"fighting words" are those which by their very utterance inflict injury or tend to incite an immediate breach of the peace – does not require intent to cause harm**
      1. **Some words have no essential part of an exposition of ideas and/or otherwise harmful and ought to be suppressed.**
    ii.   <u>**HATE Speech**</u> – is fully protected, unlike fighting words (which are disfavored)
      1. govt. cannot ban messages simply because it does not approve of the ideas of class hatred that are being expressed
      2. *Virginia v. Black* - Virginia statute banned cross burning "with an intent to intimidate" – this was constitutional (but the provision allowing cross burning to be prima facie evidence of intent was NOT constitutional)
        a. 2 consolidated cases:
          i. *Eliot Case*- cross burned in the front yard of black family that had recently moved in
          ii.   *Black Case* – KKK cross burning in an open field with other houses in range to see it – conviction overturned
        b. **directness** – cross in the Eliot case was directed at the homeowner to threaten him; cross in KKK was a general amorphous threat to all blacks – **hate speech is generally fully protected, so long as it does not become fighting words by being directed at someone to threaten**
        c. Cannot become an object of symbolic protest like burning the American Flag
        d. *Texas v. Johnson* – burning the flag is absolutely protected speech
      3. *R.A.V. v. City of St. Paul* – ordinance that said that any hate speech directed at a class was punishable, this was held unconstitutional.
        a. **it's okay to punish only the most harmful/pernicious of speech in the category – <u>so long as its for the reason the category is proscribable in the first place</u>**
        b. If the government only punished obscenity or fighting words when the content was critical of government policy that would be unconstitutional – viewpoint discriminatory.

        c. if you're going to punish hate speech or obscenity you must punish it without regard to view point – cannot be viewpoint discriminatory.

        d. Is Black case consistent with *R.A.V.? p. 1471.*

            i. 6 justices say so – Virginia statute targeted speech that was especially likely to threaten, the reason the speech is proscribable in the first place; the St. Paul ordinance merely based on content (race, gender, etc.) and the content is not the reason why the speech was proscribable (reason was b/c threatening, etc.)

    iii. HATE CRIMES

        1. Wisconsin v. Mitchell – if a crime is directed at a certain class then the penalty is doubled

            a. if all we have is the perpetrators own words we let that in to help convince the trier of fact that the motive was driven by hatred of a certain class

VI. Commercial Speech

    a. not fully protected, but not disfavored – gets quasi-protected or intermediate protected status

    b. Commercial Speech - speech which does no more than propose a transaction in goods or services

    c. *Virginia State Board of Pharmacy v. Virginia Consumer Council* - gave birth to protected commercial speech (prior *Christian v. Ballentine* would not have protected commercial speech) – though it is protected, State still has interest in ensuring that it flows cleanly as well as freely (meaning state can require it be truthful)

    d. Why protect it at all?

        i. Although it gets less protection than fully protected speech, it's still vigorously protected b/c our free market system depends on the free flow of economic information in order to support efficient allocation of resources

    e. Why not protect if fully?

        i. FN 24 – its objective and hardly speech capable of verifying accuracy; so we won't let commercial speech be false or misleading

            1. Durability – more hardy, less subject to chilling

            2. Verifiability - govt. can determine whether it's a lie and punish if it is

        ii. **False or misleading commercial speech can be restricted**

        iii. Doctrine of substantial Overbreadth does NOT apply to commercial speech (because it's hardy and not susceptible to being chilled)

    f. **Central Hudson – 4 part test** (really just 2 parts: purpose – means end)

        i. Is it commercial speech?

            1. Content must not be misleading and must concern lawful activities

        ii. **What is the purpose?**

            1. The asserted governmental interest served by the speech restriction must be substantial

        iii. **The speech restriction must directly and materially advance the asserted governmental interest**

        iv. **The speech restriction must not be more extensive than necessary to serve the interest that support it.**

    g. *Lorillard Tobacco Co. v. Reilly* - congress trying to regulate tobacco advertising

        i. Court takes up preemption of the supremacy clause –

        ii. Outdoor advertising regulations prohibited smokeless tobacco or cigar ads w/in 1000 ft. radius of school or playground – struck down by the court b/c it fails step 4 of the Central Hudson test – the 1000 foot rule is more extensive than necessary to serve the interest to support it.

    iii. The 5 foot rule – advertisement's must be at least 5 feet high to avoid pandering to children – court strikes this down for failing the 3rd and 4th prongs of the Central Hudson test

    iv. Having cigarettes behind the counter and out of reach of minors passes the Central Hudson test

FULLY PROTECTED SPEECH

I. Resctictions on Time, Place or Manner of Expression
  a. Even fully protected speech can be subjected to time, place and manner restrictions if supported by substantial reasons and are content and viewpoint neutral, and there are adequate alternative channels for the speech
    i. Content-based discrimination is given strict scrutiny unless in non-public forum
    ii. Viewpoint discrimination is unconst. unless in the rare instance when justified by compelling govt. interest
  b. **Public Forum Analysis – only on government-owned or operated property**
    i. The government has title to the property, we the people are the government so it's our property and the default mode should be "I get to use our property for my civil society speech" unless there is good reason for the government to keep me out.
    ii. 3 categories: traditional public forum, designated public forum, and non-public forum ; and there is also govt. property that is non-for a (not a forum at all)
    iii. **Traditional public forum** – places that by long tradtion have been devoted to public debate such as stress, parks sidewalks
      1. All content based, view-point based, and speaker-class restctions get strict scrutiny
      2. Content-neutral, place or matter restrictions must serve substantial governmental interest and leave open ample channels for communication – sounds like intermediate
    iv. **Designated Public Forum** - most difficult analysis – govt. has chosen to open up its property for expressive activity even though not required to in the first place. 2 types:
      1. **open to general public -** open to all subjects and speakers so same standard of review as traditional public forum
      2. **limited – govt. makes distinctions as to:**
        a. **class of speakers allowed**
        b. **class of topics/subject matter allowed**
        c. exclusion of speakers of like character and like topics within favored classifications will be given strict scrutiny, but other speakers and other tops may be excluded – **these classifications must be reasonable in light of the nature and purpose of the property**
        d. content-neutral time, place, and manner restrictions are permitted if reasonable in light of the nature and purpose of the property – sounds like rational basis
      3. **viewpoint discrimination receives strict scrutiny in either kind of designated forum**
    v. **Non-Public Forum**
      1. Govt's restriction need only be reasonable in light of the nature and

purpose of the property

2. Content-based allowed if reasonable – rational basis
3. **viewpoint discrimination still receives strict scrutiny**

vi. **Non-Forum – not open to speech**

c. *Schneider v. NJ* – ordinances prohibited distribution of handbills in the streets- court strikes down – traditional public forum

d. *Frisby v. Schultz* - ordinance prohibited picketing in front of a residence

i. this is still traditional public forum since its streets even though it is residential – apply strict scrutiny

ii. **Test: regulation is necessary to serve a compelling state interest and narrowly drawn to achieve that end**

iii. Ordinance upheld under a saving construction – ordinance did not suppress speech so long as picketers walked up and down street and were not squatting stationary in front of one house – ordinance construed so only prohibited in front of one house – this was sufficiently tailored according to the court

iv. These are content-neutral place restrictions – but they meet the test

1. Substantial govt. interest – privacy and tranquility of neighborhood
2. Ample alternative channels – could picket at the docs office, park, etc.

v. **A statute is narrowly tailored if it targets and eliminates no more than the exact source of the evil it seeks to remedy**

e. **Types of designated limited public forum**

i. **State fair grounds, charity drive, public amphitheatre for rent – if city is not using it you can rent it**

ii. **Classroom used to be a limited designated public forum (*Widmore v. Vincent*)**

f. **Types of Non-Public Forum**

i. **Mailboxes, light poles, postal premises, lobby inside post office**

g. *Krishna v. Lee* – fairground in MN, designated forum of a limited sort.

i. If you wanted to sell things or ask for money etc you are confined to a booth at the fair for which you had to pay a modest rent

ii. Court upheld this statute – designated forum of a limited sort

h. *Arkansas Education Television Commission v. Forbes* – **if you have to ask each time you want to use it then it's a *non-public forum***

i. Facts: state-owned public TV station did not want to allow acces to debate to every candidate on the ballot; editor's discretion in choosing candidates was speech

ii. Holding: state owned TV station hosting candidate debate was a nonpublic forum

1. AETC made candidate-by-candidate determinations – this was a "have to ask permission each time" case nonpublic forum
2. excluding fringe candidates for their fringe views – they were relying on poll data which indicated they had little support

iii. state fair booths you have to ask for and classrooms at night are now non-public forum

iv. this gives govt. power to down-grade forum from designated limited forum down to non-public forum by requiring permission for use of the forum

II. **Unconstitutional Conditions – Government as a Speaker** –, govt has provided funding and attached certain speech related conditions to it

a. **Considerations**

i. **Government speech or private speech?**

ii. **Is it in a forum?**

iii. **Is it religious? (Special consideration)**

b. Govt doesn't have rights – so can't be protected by 1ˢᵗ Amendment – nonetheless govt does speak and need not be neutral usually

c. *Pleasant Grove City of Utah v. Summum* - city park, city had put a dozen items relating to pioneer heritage, Summum wanted to have a monument of their own, Government said no.

    i. Supreme Court held that this was Government Speech and not a first amendment question

    ii. **When the government adopts it for its own it becomes government speech, and it is no longer a 1ˢᵗ Amendment issue** – if it become religious it shifts over to the establishment clause

d. **Exception – government must be neutral in its speech in 2 instances:**

    i. **Religion**

    ii. **politics-voting (most branches are not to take sides of Republican or Democrat)**

        1. can say "go vote", but not "go vote republican"

e. **RULE - Govt. can choose which programs to fund and which not to fund; but govt. cannot make funding contingent on the recipient giving up right to engage in other protected speech**

    i. look at whether the condition is on the *recipient* of the funding as opposed to on the *program or service*

f. *Russ v. Sullivan* - congress funds "family planning" under Title X which congress defines as not counseling on issue of abortion

    i. Held constitutional – Govt can selectively fund a program to encourage certain activities it velieves are in the public interest without at the same time funding an alternative program which seeks to deal with the problem in a different way

    ii. **Govt. has not discriminated on the basis fo viewpoint – rather it has simply chosen to fund one activity over the other** - congress chose to implement its own definition of "family planning" that is all – it was choosing what program it would fund

g. *Reagan v. Taxation w/o Rep.* – Congress could refuse to subsitide the lobbying activities of tax-exempt charitable organizations, so long as such organizations remain free to receive deductible contributions (subsidized contributions) to support non-lobbying activities

    i. "you have freedom of speech, but the govt. does not have to buy you a soapbox"

h. *FCC v. League of Woman Voters* – law said that a recipient of federal funds for public broadcast radio stations could not "editorialize" or no more funding; Court said that's an unconstitutional condition; station should be able to use private $ to editorialize (under statute they couldn't)

    i. Govt. can say no tax deduction for donors to stations to use for lobbying purposes; govt can force it to be charitable instead of funding political mouth piece

    ii. Govt. can't prohibit the recipient from engaging in protected conduct outside the scope of the federally funded program

i. *US v. American Library Assn.* – government put filters on all library computers to prevent viewing pornography on them.

    i. Held – Congress has the authority to require libraries to censor internet content in order to receive federal funding.

    ii. Libraries are government entities

    iii. 2 programs, E-Rate and LSTA provided funding to libraries; but CIPA says no federal funding unless you have internet safety policy to protect minors from porn and use software to block access to porn

  iv. but this potentially blocked access to adults too

  v. Plurality opinion:

    1. Holding – (plurality) – govt. need not fund libraries, but it does – and library must select materials to purchase (traditionally they have not bought porn) – so govt. is just making a selection to not buy porn

      a. (but didn't they buy everything from their ISP and then just take some of the books off the shelf in effect?)

    2. saving construction – Ted Olson says adults will be given porno access if they show proof of ID (Souter doesn't buy it) but the plurality does

  vi. Dissent

    1. Souter – calls this censorship rather than just selection

 j. **<u>Look for links between the federal funding and constitutional rights</u>**

III. Symbolic Speech

 a. On the borderline of overt acts and speech

 b. **Govt is given leeway in regulating the conduct portion of the speech so symbolic speech gets intermediate review unless purpose of law is to suppress expression then gets strict scrutiny**

 c. Apply Spence to determine if symbolic speech; if not symbolic then its not speech at all and is just conduct

 d. **TEST FOR SYMBOLIC SPEECH - 2 Part Test – test of whether conduct was expressing a message as speech rather than just being an overt act** (*Spence v. Washington* – "*Spence Test*" – from a flag burning case) – test of whether it's symbolic speech or just conduct which govt can regulate under its public power – must satisfy both parts

  i. **Did speaker intend to convey a particularized message?**

  ii. **Was the likelihood great that the message would be understand by those who viewed it?**

  (Did they understand the speaker was trying to communicate something as a message?)

 e. *U.S. v. O'Brien*

  i. **O'Brien Test (**it's just purpose and means end)

    1. **Purpose**

      a. **If the purpose is censorship then give it strict scrutiny – cannot ban the speech because of its expression (purpose must be unrelated to suppressing expression)**

      b. **Otherwise must further a substantial govt. interest (this is just intermediate review here)**

      c. **If action is aimed at conduct or an act give it intermediate review**

    2. **Means to end**

      a. **Incidental restriction on speech is not greater than needed to further the govt. interest**

  ii. The actual O'Brien Test Language by the court

    1. If its within the constitutional power of the govt. (disregard this step for speech purpose)

      a. Congress has power to raise army – so yes there is power here

    2. If it furthers an important or substantial govt. interest

    3. If the govt'l interest is unrelated to the suppression of free expression and

    4. If the incidental restriction on alleged First Amendment freedom is no

greater than is essential to the furtherance of that interest.

      iii.   Facts – burned his draft card; court held the law prohibiting this was constitutional

      iv.   Analysis – purpose here was not to suppress expression and there was substantial govt. interest in having a ready army and having functioning draft system (burning the cards harmed this interest) – law was held constitutional

      v.   **can't strike down the statute because of an improper motive – question is whether the law, on its face, targets expression or targets conduct** - from O'brien

  f. *City of Erie v. Pap's A.M.* - city ordinance bans public nudity, court upholds ordinance

      i. Analysis – court applies **secondary effects analysis to support govt interest in restricting expressive conduct**; this secondary effects was essentially imported by the court from cases dealing with zoning regulations of adult clubs (Stevens calls them on this)

          1. Dancers are conveying an erotic message which of course the audience understands

          2. Scalia says laws such as these have always been based on morals – but court is running from morals and finds govt'l interest in minimizing secondary effects

          3. Majority notes that it bans all public nudity, the conduct alone, rather than just the nudity used to express an erotic message

          4. Majority: state's interest in banning secondary effects is not related to the suppression of expression; and there is minimal effect on the expression by making the dancers wear "pasties and g-strings"

      ii.   *Barnes v. Glen Theatres* – public nudity law in Indiana upheld against strip club because it was a police power law (health, safety, morals and general welfare) – Scalia says it's a morals law and that's good enough

IV. Freedom of Association

  a. Freedom of Association is not expressly mentioned in 1st Amendment, but it is considered implied in the amendment

      i. freedom of association is instrumental in ability to effectively speak – "an indispensable means of preserving the other individual liberties" protected by the first amendment

          1. so association is protected when its necessary to support the other protected liberties of the 1st amendment

      ii.   **Association that is <u>fundamental</u> to freedom of speech, press, assembly, or petition is protected association**

      iii.   standard of review – strict scrutiny - compelling govt. interest / least restrictive means

  b. 2 types

      i. Freedom of intimate association (but Court has never actually found it and has largely abandoned it now)

      ii.   Freedom of expressive association

  c. case often involve state public accommodations laws being applied to organizations/clubs

  d. Test

      i. **Does the club/organization/association engage in expressive activity?**

      ii.   **What is the message?**

      iii.   **Is the message significantly burdened?**

          1. **Are they being forced to express views they do not want to express?**

  e. *NAACP v. Alabama* - did not have to turn over its membership list to the state (they feared their lives would be endangered) – disclosure would deter memberships; Alabama failed to provide justification for deterring NAACP's potential members

f. *NAACP v. Claiborne Hardware*

    i. Holding: **nonviolent** elements of boycotters expression was protected by 1st amendment; violent elements can be punished as legitimately proscribable conduct

g. *Roberts v. U.S Jaycees*

    i. forcing Jaycees to allow women did not impede their ability to engage in their protected expressive activities nor did it force the Jaycees to express views they did not want to express

    ii.   court mentions two types – intimate association and expressive association (but intimate not important)

h. *Rotary Int'l v. Rotary Club of Duarte* - had to admit women to rotary club; being male was not bound up in club's purpose – they were commercial orgs to do business/charity and network – not politically expressive so not being forced to espouse a certain view by allowing women

i. *BoyScouts of America v. Dale* - gay man wanted to be scout leader BSA would not allow it – man claimed it violated NJ public accommodation la*w*

    i. Holding – law violated BSA's freedom of association (5-4)

        1. BSA's purpose is to build character in youth BSA does engage in expressive activity (scout oath and scout motto) as to how its members should act, values they should have, etc. – they claim that being gay is not "morally straight" – they are allowed to define themselves

            a. scoutmaster argues that BSA never had a policy against homosexuality before and they are "making it up" now

        2. BSA doesn't want to speak about homosexuals (Irish parade didn't want to talk about gays in *Hurley*); they just want to tie knots

        3. Jaycess and Rotary would probably still lose even if *Dale* was applied

j. *Rumsfeld v. FAIR, Inc.* – law school prohibits Military Recruiters b/c of "don't ask don't' tell" violates antidiscrimination policies of law schools.

    i. Article I § 8 – congress has the right to force military recruiters on to campus under the "raise an army" clause of Art. I

    ii.   Court looks to see if there is a significant burden on the message of FAIR – the expressive component of a law school's actions is not created by conduct itself but by the speech that accompanies it.

    iii.   The Solomon Amendment does not violate law schools' freedom of speech nor their freedom of expressive association.

    iv.   Recruiter was not part of the law school so it does not speak on behalf of the law school – unlike Dale case in that Dale was part of BSA and spoke on behalf of them.

CONGRESSIONAL POWER

I. Commerce Clause

    a. Background

        i. 4 relevant time periods for commerce clause

            1. Early republic – 1840's – late 1800's: federal govt. is night watchman and commerce clause is used primarily to strike down state legislation (through Dormant Commerce Clause)

2. Late 1800's – 1937 – Lochner Era (legislation struck down in the service of laissez-faire)
3. 1937-1995 – Congress has expansive commerce power
4. 1995-present – Lopez changes everything – **modern federalism revolution**
   a. Commerce Clause
   b. §5 of 14th amendment
   c. 11th amendment

ii. *MCCulloch v. Maryland* - necessarily implied power to regulate the creation of a national bank plus Art I Sec 8 Cl 18 "necessary and proper clause"

b. **Growth of Commerce Power**

i. *Wickard v. Filburn* – **confirms Congress' broad commerce power (aggregation -> substantial effect on interstate commerce**

1. Test case – you can set up a test case (regardless of no case or controversy non justiciable) if the parties genuinely disagree and there is a constitutional issue – this is justiciable it's not an advisory opinion
2. Facts
   a. New Deal legislation uses commerce power robustly – Congress passes agricultural regulation act regulating price and sale of ag products
   b. farmer had grown wheat in his own home and not sold it; this violated the law b/c farmer could not grow and consume wheat personally; Farmer claims this is not *interstate commerce*
3. Court held that the effect of farmers' personal consumption, ***when aggregated***, would have **substantial effect on interstate commerce** – the home grown wheat competes with the wheat in commerce
4. rejects old distinctions courts' made (Congress' commerce power would now reach all these)
   a. indirect/direct effect on interstate commerce
   b. production/labor

ii. *Heart of Atlanta Motel v. US*

1. Congress can now use its commerce power to not just regulate highly localized events (farmers' home consumption of wheat) but even crimes and morals
2. committing a crime **"while crossing state line"**
   a. i.e. Mann Act – taking woman across state lines for prostitution purposes
3. Civil Rights Laws NOT based on 14th amendment (sec. 5), but rather the commerce power
   a. remember, 14th amendment can only reach state action and NOT wholly private conduct

c. **THE LOPEZ TEST**

i. **Congress Can Regulate Three Categories under Commerce Clause**

1. **CHANNELS - the power to regulate the use of the channels of interstate commerce**
   a. Channels - roads, canals, railways, airways, pipelines, etc.
2. **INSTRUMENTALITIES, PERSONS, THINGS - the power to regulate and protect the instrumentalities of interstate commerce, or persons or things in interstate commerce, even though the threat may come only from intrastate activities**
   a. Instrumentalities - trucks, barges, trains, airplanes
   b. Persons – pilots, drivers, passengers
   c. Things – cargo

      3. **SUBSTANTIAL EFFECT OR AGGREGATION - the power to regulate those activities having a substantial relation to interstate commerce - those activities that substantially affect interstate commerce**
         a. **aggregation test** – this is the hard category
   ii. *Lopez* – first time congressional legislation stuck down as exceeding commerce power since 1937; dealt with gun-free school zones act
   iii. ***Morrison v. U.S.*** – VAWA; 2 football players at UVA convicted for beating and raping girl and making vulgar gender-based remarks about her – Was this authorized under Commerce Power?
      1. Why not supported under §5 of 14th amendment?
         a. no state actor here – this occurred at public university, but university was not a party; this merely involved two football players and a girl (thus, private actors)
         b. so, if VAWA is to survive, must do so under Commerce Power
      2. **The Four factors from Lopez – WHEN YOU HAVE A CATEGORY 3 SITUATION**
         a. **Is the statute related to an economic enterprise?**
         b. **Is there a saving jurisdictional limitation that limits it to things having connection with or effect on interstate commerce?**
         c. **Are there congressional findings regarding the effects on interstate commerce?**
         d. **Is the link between the activity and interstate commerce too weak to be enforced?**
      3. In Lopez, Congress had not linked guns in schools to commerce (i.e. dangerous learning environment harms economy)
      4. In Morrision, Congress had made all kinds of findings as to the negative economic impact that gender-motivated violence has – reduces productivity of workforce, women feel intimidated to join, domestic violence's impact on women)
      5. **Court rejects the link because otherwise almost anything could be found to in some indirect, attenuated way to effect commerce – would give Congress power to regulate anything under guise of regulating interstate commerce**
   iv. *Reno v. Condon* – Drivers Privacy Protection Act – prohibited state DMV officials from selling drivers license info to private sources; this was upheld under commerce power
      1. it was a "thing" in interstate commerce – its intellectual property that can be bought and sold, so don't have to apply the Lopez test for category 3 aggregate

II. **Dormant Commerce Clause**
  a. **a restriction prohibiting a state from passing legislation that improperly burdens or discriminates against interstate commerce. The restriction is self-executing and applies even in the absence of a conflicting federal statute.**
  b. Two Step TEST for DCC
   i. **STEP 1: Intentional Discriminatory Regulation**
      1. State is protecting its own commerce – form of protectionism
      2. In the course of a state protecting its own commerce does it impose an undue burden on interstate commerce?
      3. YES – unconstitutional; NO – proceed to step 2
   ii. **STEP 2: Discriminatory Impact – balancing burden on interstate commerce with the value of local regulation**

1. State did not INTEND to discriminate but nonetheless does it have that impact
2. Some of the strongest values are health or safety, and while burdensome to commerce the these values are great
3. Instrumentalities or channels in interstate commerce –major impediments on transportation. Regulations requiring trains/trucks/planes entering one state from another and have to substantially change parts or function = DCC applies - *Navajo Freight Lines*
4. Restricting importation and insulating in-state business from out-of-state competition – undue regulation
5. Requiring business operations to be performed in the home state – undue regulation
6. State does not own the commodity but wants to hoard it – undue regulation
7. Limits on business entry – undue regulation – i.e. hostile takeover law in Indiana made it next to impossible for takeovers

c. *Pike v. Bruce Church Inc.* – AZ wanted to brand cantaloupe but they had to be processed, and the fruit was processed in CA, there was no intentional protectionism – court uses balancing test to determine that AZ did not have to process the cantaloupe to brand them.
   i. there is a debate within the court as to whether they should be doing STEP 2 at all
   ii. judiciary has virtually unguided discretion in to an area by which judges have no apptitude

d. Exceptions to the DCC
   i. Analysis applies to regulations which burden interstate commerce – they do not apply to state subsidies – direct state subsidies are okay (i.e. tax credits) -*New Energy Co of Indiana v. Limbach*
      1. State money is limited and that is sufficient to avoid DCC Analysis
   ii. State owned resources – state wants to hoard its resource in a manner that favors in-state business – Do not apply DCC

e. Why the DCC Exists
   i. Congress could regulate in this area but has been passive, a state has regulated, and an out of state industry is complaining of protectionism, congress could have passed a law but didn't, so the court extends a right to sue because of the pecuniary injury of the out of state industry
   ii. Court infers the right to the industry that is harmed by the protectionism to sue
   iii. Court has not done this in any other area – taking a delegated power and turned it into a right

III. **TAXING AND SPENDING POWER**
   a. **Taxing Power [Art. I, §8]**
      i. **Use as Regulation**
         1. *Sonzinsky v. U.S.*
            a. National Firearms Act puts $200 annual tax on dealers of firearms; dealer argues that true motive was to discourage sale of certain types of firearms
            b. it does regulate, but every tax regulates in some manner
            c. **Congress is allowed to raise revenue and we won't question their motive**
      ii. **Uniformity clause – Art. I., §8[1]**
         1. *U.S. v. Ptasynski*
            a. Windfall profit tax was a federal tax on oil but it exempeted Alaskan oil
            b. exemption is challenged under the **Uniformity clause**
            c. Holding: **uniformity clause gives Congress <u>wide latitude</u> in**

deciding what to tax and does not prevent congress from considering "geographically isolated problems"

b. **SPENDING POWER**
   i. ART I Sec 8 Cl. 1 – Congress has the power to "lay and collect taxes, duties, imposts and excises to pay the debts and provide for the common defense and **general welfare** of the United States."
   ii. Initial limits on spending power
      1. *U.S. v. Butler* – the *last* case to strike down a law in violation of the spending clause – its **partly overruled** later
         a. Agricultural adjustment act of 1933, part of new deal, imposes tax upon the first processing of certain crops; designed to raise farm prices; revenue devoted to crop control – Sec'y of Ag. entered into contracts with farmers to reduce acreage
         b. 2 competing views
            i. Madisonian – tax and spend power limited to the other enumerated powers of section 8
            ii. Hamiltonian – confers a separate and distinct power not restricted to section 8 powers – **Court picks Hamiltonian**
         c. Court holds that the act violates the reserved rights of the states – violates 10th amendment
            i. it seeks to regulate and control agricultural production
         d. Court said Congress could not purchase compliance from states – this was a purchase of compliance rather than a **conditional appropriation** (which court implies would be okay)
      2. *Chas Steward v. Davis* - social security program involved states administering program with money from feds – argued that this resulted in the **coercion of the states in violation of the 10ᵗʰ amendment**
         a. **Court upheld law – program was not voluntary – State could choose not to participate and tell fed govt "we don't want your money" – this was not coercion**
   iii. **"General Welfare" – Congress defines**
      1. **It's not a limiting of power – it's a grant of power**
      2. *Helvering v. Davis* – court upholds the age old benefits of Social Security Act are authorized under the general welfare clause
         a. "whether it be wisdom or unwisdom that is for Congress to say"
      3. *Buckley v. Valeo* - **congress is to say what the "general welfare" is**
   iv. ***SOUTH DAKOTA V. DOLE* - TEST of 1) Notice to States and 2) Germaneness**
      1. Facts – federal highway funding states made condition on state adopting a 21 year old drinking age
         a. 21ˢᵗ amendment puts regulation of production sale of alcohol in power of states; but court says state voluntarily gave up its 21ˢᵗ amendment power – Congress can circumvent it by using conditional spending
      2. **4 General Restrictions on Spending Power – 2 and 3 are the test (Notice and Germaneness)**
         a. must be in pursuit of the "general welfare" (but this does Nothing)
         b. **NOTICE – if Congress conditions federal funds it must do so unambiguously enabling the states to exercise their choice knowingly; cognizant of the consequences of their participation**

> c. **GERMANENESS – conditions on federal grants might be illegitimate if unrelated to "the federal interest in particular national projects or programs"**
> d. No unconstitutional conditions - There are rights which trump the spending power – congress can't make your federal funds conditional on you agreeing not to exercise free speech
>> 3. Dissent: O'Connor would give the Germaneness element more bite – she does not see a close enough link in federal highway funding and the dirnking age
>>> a. Majority says Congress has interest in its highways being safe – O'Connor says ththn law is both over and under inclusive
> v. Congress has BROAD spending power which can be used to sort of indirectly regulate in areas by using conditional spending even though Congress could not directly regulate in those areas
> vi. **10th Amendment DOES NOT limit conditions that Congress can put on federal funding**
> vii. Congress can essentially circumvent limits of Commerce Clause by spending money and attaching conditions to it – must only satisfy 4 part Dole test – make conditions clear and make the funding conditions somewhat related to the projects being funded
> viii. *US v. Comstock* - civil commitment under Federal Law for sexually dangerous individuals
>> 1. Majority says this civil commitment is allowed under the necessary and proper clause
>>> a. Necessary and proper clause is not a source of power – it is a means to an end

IV. **Supremacy Clause**
  a. **ART 6 Sec 1 Cl 2 - This Constitution, and the Laws of the United States which shall be made in Pursuance thereof; and all Treaties made, or which shall be made, under the Authority of the United States, shall be the *supreme Law of the Land*; and the Judges in every State shall be bound thereby, any Thing in the Constitution or Laws of any State to the Contrary notwithstanding...**
    i. Not a grant of power – just a choice of law clause
    ii. If there is a conflict between state law and federal law, federal law always wins out
  b. Trend in Congress to put in comprehensive legislation that the "federal government is occupying the field" in order to invoke the supremacy clause
  c. <u>**Nowhere in the constitution does it say that congress has power over immigration**</u>
    i. <u>**Closest thing is Art I uniform rule of naturalization**</u>
V. **Necessary and Proper Clause**
  a. Not an independent power – means to an end
  b. *McCulloch v. Maryland* (1819)– upheld the creation of a national bank and said state could not tax it
    i. Marshall interpreted the "necessary and proper" clause **broadly** – it's not a restriction on Congress' powers
      1. **necessary" does not mean necessary, but really just means "reasonable"**
      2. national bank is "any reasonable means" in order for Congress to utilize its delegated power to lay and collect taxes, borrow money, regulate commerce, etc.
      3. state cannot tax the federal government
  c. Congress may use any reasonable means in using its expressed or implied powers granted to it by the Constitution

VI. **STATE SOVEREIGNTY AND FEDERAL REGULATION**
   a. Historical basis for Federalism
      i. fear of centralist govt. had to be balanced with the utter lack of power the central govt. had under the articles of conf.
         1. cultural and religious heterogeneity
         2. geographic dispersion and slow communication
         3. economic factors - wealthy states and not as wealthy states
         4. local jealousies: states were absolutely sovereign before federal govt. formed
   b. **Interpretations of the 10th Amendment – MERE TRUISM!**
      i. **"mere truism"** – Congress cannot violate 10th amendment – it merely states that if federal govt. does not have the power then it cannot exercise it over the states – **majority of US Sup Ct takes this view today**
         1. **When Congress exceeds its power then the 10th Amendment is violated – DO NOT SAY THE 10TH AMENDMENT HAS BEEN VIOLATED SAY CONGRESS HAS EXCEEDED ITS POWER**
      ii. **10th can be violated** – *Maryland v. Wirtz* FN - "while the 10th amendment has been characterized as a mere truism it is not without significance – it expressly declares the constitutional policy that Congress may not exercise power in a fashion that impairs the states' integrity or their ability to function effectively in a federal system"
      iii. **majority vote of US Sup Ct. today is TRUISM – 10th amendment is merely a "mirror image" of the scope of Congress' power under its limited delegated powers**
      iv. **The 10th Amendment has no force of its own – 10th Amendment has no penetrative force it is merely a mirror image of Federal Power (i.e. a mirror image of the commerce clause or spending power)**
   c. Constitution does not allow Congress to directly require the states to govern according to Congress' instructions
   d. *Garcia v. San Antionio Metro-Transit Authority* - states as states can be regulated by congress – the sovereignty of the States is limited by the Constitution itself
   e. **New York v. US (Lexington/Concord of the Revolution of Lopez)-** Congress cannot simply **commandeer the legislative processes of the states by directly compelling them to enact and enforce a federal regulatory program. – violates the Commerce Clause**
      i. 2 Ugly Choices - states were given "choice" to either regulate toxic waste according to fed'l policy or take title to the waste and get tort liability from all the waste – this was "no choice at all" and amounted to coercion of the states
      ii. **Congress can't use commerce power to "grab the state generally assembly and order them to pass law in accordance with federal guidelines**
      iii. States CANNOT consent to Congress' improper usurpation of power by "choosing" one of the 2 ugly choices given to them in this case – govt's don't have rights that can be waived; this is a structural violation (violation of federalism)
      iv. Conditional federal funding is okay because states are given a choice of whether or not to satisfy the govt.'s conditions to get the money – this is appropriate use of Spending Power
         1. if states don't' want to do this they don't take the money. If they take the money they have to pass the law
      v. Congress can invite the states to regulate a certain problem area
   f. **"Cooperative Federalism" – THREATS TO PRE-EMPT ARE OKAY**
      i. Constitution gives Congress the power to regulate directly (on individuals) and to pre-empt contrary state regulation

      ii.   **Congress may give state choice of regulating itself or being pre-empted by federal law**

g. **POLICY IS *ACCOUNTABILITY***
      i. O'Connor wants the citizens to know who the right target is to speak out against
      ii.   Citizens will be going after state legislators when its really Congress who is forcing them to act – citizens should be going to Congress then
      iii.   this waste law makes citizens strike back and miss the mark (they complain to NY legislature instead of Congress) – **we need responsive government**
      iv.   O'Connor – when there is pushback we want the pushback directed at the institution that imposed the burden – Esbeck says this is brilliant, representative govt.
           1.   If congress invites some states to pass a law and no states pass the law, then congress passes the law so those affected by the law are angry with Congress.
           2.   The pushback should be at those who were responsible – O'Connor makes sure it is

h. *Printz v. U.S.* - **Congress may not conscript state governments as its agents**
      i. Facts: Brady Handgun law – state officials had to do background checks in the interim while FBI database was being set up; Congress was **commandeering** these state officials
      ii.   this portion of Brady Act was struck down
           1.   Madisonian constitutional adopted the Virginia plan (NOT the NJ plan) which says the federal govt. acts directly on individuals and not on states (fed. govt. and states both directly act on people)
      iii.   **Art II Sec 3 Take Care Clause – the President shall take care that the laws be faithfully executed**

VII.   **STATE SOVEREIGN IMMUNITY AND THE 11th AMENDMENT**
   a. Generally, govt. has no rights and only has powers and duties – state sovereign immunity is an exception; state does have a right in this context
   b. **Structure is absolute – either its honored or its not; We don't look for a compelling govt. interest to justify a structural violation like we do with rights (balance of liberty against power)**
   c. "State sovereign immunity"
      i. existed at common law and predated US Constitution
      ii.   before *Alden v. Maine*, it was thought that 11th amendment was source of sovereign immunity, but **state sovereign immunity existed prior to U.S. constitution**
      iii.   therefore, **Commerce Power could not have created Congress' ability to abrogate state sovereign immunity (when it expresses <u>clear intent</u> to do so) – must have been something post-Civil War when state sovereignty shrunk – 14th Amendment SECTION 5 allows for abrogation**
      iv.   sovereign immunity preexisted the constitution and is not abrogated by it
   d. **Stripping Doctrine** - private parties can sue state officers in their official capacity for injunctive relief.

State Sovereign Immunity & Eleventh Amendment Handout

   a. A State sovereign immunity means that a state cannot be sued in its own name without its consent. Such immunity from suit preexisted the formation of the union and continues to inhere in the federalist system in the Constitutions structure. **Alden v. Maine** (1999).
   b. The 11th Amend. recognizes that states generally have sovereign immunity when sued in federal court. Hence, the 11th Amend. confirms rather than creates sovereign immunity. The scope of

state sovereign immunity is broader than that set out in the 11th Amend. **Alden.** The Bankruptcy Clause, Art. I, § 8[4], is said to be an exception whereby sovereign immunity was waived when a state joined the union. **Central Va. Comm. College v. Katz** (2006).

    a. Sovereign Immunity does not come from the 11th Amendment – it preexisted the Constitution and was not abrogated or superseded by it

c. The 11th Amend. does not apply to claims filed in state court. However, states often have sovereign immunity when sued in their own courts as a matter of state law.

    a. Speaks only to Federal Court subject matter Jurisdiction – when you sue a state in its own courts it has sovereign immunity unless it waives that immunity

    b. States give limited waivers of their immunity – MO gives narrow waiver, you can sue the state for certain defects in roads/highways/bridges should they cause injury

d. State sovereign immunity and the 11th Amend. do not apply to claims against local govern-ments or other political subdivisions of a state. Rather, the immunity applies only to claims against the state and its departments and agencies.

e. The 11th Amend. does not apply to claims brought by a state against a sister state or a claim by the federal government against a state.

f. State sovereign immunity and the 11th Amend. apply whether plaintiff is a citizen of the defendant-state or of another state. **Hans v. Louisiana** (1890).

g. Neither state sovereign immunity nor the 11th Amend. bars federal claims against state officials for injunctive and/or declaratory relief. Although the official is sued in his or her own name, the claim must be for actions taken in his or her official capacity. *Ex Parte* Young (1908). In **Young,** the Court reasoned that because a state could never authorize one of its officers to violate the Constitution, therefore the officer must have been acting on his own. The rationale for the legal fiction is two-fold: to be able to enjoin continuing violations of federal law and to allow federal courts to have a definitive role in interpreting federal law.

    a. FICTION – the court says to itself, well here's a state official enforcing a state statute which is unconstitutional – if we enjoin this official we're not really enjoining the state but enjoining this person who's off on a frolic of their own – legal fictions are instrumental

    b. Rational Purpose Behind the Fiction – gives you someone to sue i.e. the Attorney General of the State

    c. If you can prove your case you get injunctive relief but not damages

h. The fiction applies only to prospective relief, not to damages. **Edelman v. Jordan** (1974). That future compliance with an injunction will cost the state money does not, however, make the claim one for damages. **Milliken v. Bradley** (1977).

i. Neither state sovereign immunity nor the 11th Amend. bars a federal claim for damages brought against a state official sued in his or her personal capacity. However, any monetary judgment in these personal-capacity suits can be collected only from the individual, not the state.

    a. State can waive its sovereign immunity – when it adopts a state tort claims act partially waives the immunity but only to sue in state court not federal court

j. A state may refuse to waive its sovereign immunity when sued in state court, even when the claim is on a federal right that cannot be pursued in federal court because of the 11th Amend. **Alden.** This may leave a plaintiff with a federal right but no judicial venue to enforce it.

k. A state may waive its sovereign immunity and the 11th Amend. However, any such wavier must be clear and knowing. A state may waive its immunity from suit in its own courts without waiving 11th Amend. immunity when sued in federal court.

l. Under its 14th Amend. powers, Congress may abrogate a state's sovereign immunity and the 11th Amend. However, the intent to abrogate must be clear in the text of the statute.

m. Congress lacks power under Art. I of the Constitution to abrogate a state's 11th Amend. immunity when sued in federal court. **Seminole Tribe v. Florida** (1996). Congress also lacks power under

Art. I to abrogate a state's sovereign immunity when sued in state court; and this is so even when the claim is on a federal right that cannot be pursued in federal court because of the 11th Amend. **Alden**.

    a. Congress by legislation can enforce the 14th Amendment
    b. One means of enforcing the 14th Amendment is to impose liability on a state for violation of the 14th Amendment

    e. *US v. Morrison* – court held that 42 USC 13981 could not be sustained under section 5 of the fourteenth amendment
        i. The language and purpose of the 14th Amendment place certain limitations on the matter in which Congress may attack discriminatory conduct
        ii. Limitations are necessary to prevent 14th Amendment from obliterating the Framer's balance of power between states and Federal Govt.
        iii. 14th Amendment by its very terms prohibits only state action
        iv. Breyer's Dissent: Commerce Clause provides adequate basis for the statute

VIII. **14th Amendment Sec 5 - The Congress shall have power to enforce, by appropriate legislation, the provisions of this article.**
    a. This is a remedial power – this does not give Congress the power to alter 14th Amendment rights
    b. *City of Bourne v. Flores* - the legislature does not have the power to expand substantive rights, but does have the power to provide remedies or enforce substantive rights
        i. **Congress cannot create new substantive rights under this section**
        ii. Religious Freedom Restoration Act Enlarged upon the Free Exercise Clause – SCOTUS says this is unconstitutional by half, still applies to the Federal Govt. but not to state and local governments
        iii. This is federalism – the states' won sovereignty
    c. **Congruence and Proportionality Test – apply this test to determine if the Congressional Action goes too far or is proportional and congruent to the evil it seems to remedy - requires congruence and proportionality between the evil to be prevented and the means/law/statute adopted to that end.**
        i. <u>Because the Fourteenth Amendment allows Congress to take "appropriate" action to enforce rights, the Court has determined that such action must be congruent and proportional to the deprivation of the right that the Congress is seeking to remedy.</u>
        ii. <u>Tough test to get a grip on and difficult to apply</u>
        iii. **Congruence**
            1. **The means between the means and the evil that the law intends to target must be congruent**
        iv. **Proportionality**
            1. **The means and the ends must be proportionate**
    d. **Prophylactic law - Prevent the problem before the consummation of the evil**
    e. *Kimel v. Florida Board of Regents* – Age Discrimination in Employment Act essentially gives intermediate review to alleged age discrimination
        i. HELD: ADEA was not authorized by §5 of the 14th Amendment, found unconstitutional when applied to state and local governments because of disparate levels of review
        ii. **Age does not get intermediate review under equal protection, only rational basis – FL. says the law enlarges upon the equal protection clause**
    f. *Board of Trustees of U of Alabama v. Garrett* – ADA prohibits discrimination against disabled, Title I applies to employment discrimination to state and local govts.
        i. HELD: the law goes beyond enforcement (mere effectuation) and have expanded into

intermediate level of review, this is unconstitutional
    ii. **Title I gives intermediate review to discrimination in employment for the disabled, but EP Clause gives rational basis (maybe Rational Basis w/ Bite) to the disabled**

g. *Nevada Dept. of HR v. Hibbs* - (turning point case) attack on congressional statute, FMLA (family medical and leave act) – could take up to 12 weeks off for medical leave or to care for family and not be punished by employer
    i. Women discriminated against, sex discrimination so intermediate review
    ii. HELD: We believe Congress had the power to impose the FMLA on states under Amend. 14 § 5. FMLA does not go beyond intermediate review, it was a mere effectuation of the Equal Protection right against intentional sex discrimination
    iii. **§ 5 can be used to do away with sovereign immunity so long as you have appropriately used the section – state sovereignty is not affirmed**
    iv. Rehnquist wrote the opinion – out of character for him, here he undermines the revolution, but he knew that he didn't have 5 votes so he assigned himself the opinion to write it super narrow so do damage control to keep the revolution going – pretty smart move

h. *Tenn. v. Lane* - - "the ground has eroded out from under the revolution, including Field General Rehnquist"
    i. Facts – ADA Title II questioned under § 5 of 14th Amendment. When you build a new building, sidewalk, etc you have to comply with ADA Title II. P was accused of a crime, wheelchair bound, and P cannot access the courthouse because it is not wheelchair accessible (crawled up the stairs and in to the court room to be heard)
    ii. *Garrett* reaffirmed but distinguished (Garrett was Title I this is Title II – pretty simple stuff)
        1. A clean ruling would have been to overrule Garrett, but not overruled probably to maintain the necessary votes
    iii. **Lane is a criminal matter so fundamental rights are at stake – any time you are accused of a crime you are dealing with fundamental rights – Due Process not just EP**
    iv. Courthouses must be handicap accessible there are more events there than just trials, i.e. weddings
    v. Scalia's Dissent – what does the word "enforcement" mean – heart of the matter - not an invitation by Congress to expand the law it is only to put in to execution or to cause to take effect.

i. **Comparing Garrett/Boerne and Lane**
    i. Not sure which way is the general rule and which is the exception
    ii. The "Field Generals" for state sovereignty are gone – O'Connor and Rehnquist
    iii. Roberts hasn't shown "fire in the belly for state sovereignty"

PRESIDENTIAL POWERS

I. President's Powers [list these by Art. Sec. Cl]
    a. Commander-In-Chief – Art II, Sec 2, Cl 1
    b. Receive Ambassadors – Art II Sec 3
    c. Appoint Ambassadors – Art II Sec 2 Cl 2
    d. Make Treaties – Art 2 Sec 2 Cl 2
    e. Take Care Clause – Art II Sec 3 (congress has to pass a law before president can take care to enforce it)
    f. Vestiture Clause - Art I Sec 1 – grant of power not a definition of the office
    g. Appointment Clause – Art II Sec 2 – power to appoint principal officers that must be appointed by congress, as well as inferior officers

II. Congress's Powers
    a. Declare War – Art I Sec 9 Cl 11
    b. Regulate Interstate Commerce
    c. Raise/Support Armed Forces – Art I Sec 8 Cl 11-13
    d. Power of the Purse (Taxing and Spending Power) – Art I Sec 8 Cl 11
    e. Approve Treaties
    f. Approve Appointment of Principal Officers

III. Article II – The Executive
    a. The executive power shall be vested in the President
    b. Modern presidency is different than what you see in a fair read of Art II
        i. Political initiative and policy generation is not so much with congress as it is with the president – i.e. tax cuts, president is involved in negotiating
        ii. It has evolved and enlarged beyond Art. II
        iii. 12th Amendment changed Art II

IV. President's Power to Determine National and Foreign Policy
    a. *United States v. Curtiss-Wright Export Corp* - arms embargo on Bolivia and Paraguay issued by the president, question
        i. **Power of the executive to conduct foreign affairs**
        ii. Treaty of Westphalia – ended the 30 years war, acknowledged expressly certain nation states and attributed to them the beginnings of modern sovereignty
        iii. Justice Sutherland – no here does the constitution say that congress or the executive has the power to deal with foreign relations, what we have are little bits and pieces of foreign relations
        iv. **HELD:** while the Constitution may not explicitly say that all ability to conduct foreign policy on behalf of the nation is vested in the President,

193

it is nonetheless given implicitly and by the fact that the Executive, by its very nature, is empowered to conduct foreign affairs in a way which Congress cannot and should not.

        v.   *Fong Yue Ting v. United States* – power to expel undesirable aliens – not stated in Constitution but comes to federal government by being a matter of sovereign nations

        vi.   *Altman & Co. v. United States* - Power to make such international agreements as do not constitute treaties

   b. *Youngstown Sheet &Tube Co. v. Sawyer* (Steel Seizure Case) – President Truman attempted to seize steel for the war effort in Korea, also tried to seize businesses that produced steel.

        i. President did not have the inherent authority to seize property in the absence of either specifically enumerated authority under Art II or statutory authority

        ii.   President cannot seize property/businesses for the purposes of war production

        iii.   **Jackson's Concurrence – breaks down the issue into three categories (Jacksonian Tripartite Categorization)**

            1. **President has the power if congress has authorized – highest power of president**

            2. **The Zone of Twilight - Where Congress is Silent president's power is in-between**

            3. **When the president takes measures incompatible with the expressed or implied will of congress – power of the president is at its lowest**

   c. Medellin v. Texas – Bush memorandum that a decision of the International Court of Justice would be followed by the courts of the US – Separation of Powers Issue – Court holds president does not have the power to bind the federal and state courts like this

        i. HELD: this is a Jackson Level 3 - while an international treaty may constitute an international commitment, it is not binding domestic law unless Congress has enacted statutes implementing it or unless the treaty itself is "self-executing"

        ii.   The Take Care Clause by its very plain text infers that congress makes the law and the president enforces it – there was no law here just the Bush memorandum

V. Appointments Clause

   a. Art II Sec 2 Cl 2 - by and with the Advice and Consent of the Senate, shall appoint Ambassadors, other public Ministers and Consuls, Judges of the supreme Court, and all other Officers of the United States

        i. All others are called "Principal Officers" as opposed to inferior officers

   b. Inferior Officers – Art 2, Sec 2, Cl 2 - but the Congress may by Law vest the Appointment of such inferior Officers, as they think proper, in the President alone, in the Courts of Law, or in the Heads of Departments

        i. President

        ii.   Courts

        iii.   Heads of Departments

   c. Power to remove is the power to control – congress cannot give itself the power to appoint and it cannot give itself the power to remove

   d. Mistretta v. US - the appointments of the sentencing commission required there be

3 judges appointed by the president– Court allows coordinate branches to seek help from one another

    i. While sitting on the sentencing commission the judge is acting at the direction of the president – this seems to give complete judicial independence

    ii.   Because they act

  e. Free Enterprise Fund v. Public Company Accounting Oversight Board –

    i. Humphrey's Executor Case - Congress can, under certain circumstances, create independent agencies run by principal officers appointed by the President, whom the President may not remove at will but only for good cause

    ii.   Morrison v. *Olson* - Congress can, as to a principal executive officer, appoint an inferior officer but couldn't remove that officer – i.e. Congress can appoint Special Independent Counsel and the Attorney General (or whomever) cannot fire them w/o cause

    iii.   Here we have the combination of Humphreys and Morrison – Board members of the PCAOB are also members of the SEC and that is unconstitutional, because they are double insulated from removal of the PCAOB

    iv.   Inferior Officers – are officers whose work is directed and supervised at some level by superiors appointed by the President with the Senate's consent.

VI. Presidential Immunities

  a. US v. Nixon - President Nixon invoked "executive privilege" to prevent release of Watergate Tapes – executive privilege is not in the text of the constitution

    i. Could have said - ***the text doesn't address it so it's not a constitutional question***

    ii.   There is a Presidential Executive Privilege and it extends to presidential aids

        1. Qualified Privilege For the aids - It can be overcome if good cause is shown

  b. *Clinton v. Jones* – President Clinton claims executive privilege to delay the deposition until the end of his term as president – Court denies this delay because you cannot be immune altogether from the deposition

  c. *Cheney v. US Dist. Ct. of DC* - civil case over documents about energy policy Cheney is preparing, invokes Vice-Presidential Privilege

    i. Civil proceeding so far less important and Cheney had to turn over the information

  d. Impeachment – Art II Sec 4 - The President, Vice President and all civil Officers of the United States, shall be removed from Office on Impeachment for, and Conviction of, Treason, Bribery, or other high Crimes and Misdemeanors.

  e.

CRIMINAL LAW

INTRODUCTION TO THE CRIMINAL LAW SYSTEM & BASIC PRINCIPLES OF CRIMINAL LIABILITY

I. **Federal Perjury Statute**
   a. Makes it a felony for one who has taken an oath in a federal proceeding to "willfully" make a statement "which he does not believe to be true."
   b. "Willfully" = to do an <u>act</u> voluntarily and purposely, with the specific intent to do something the law forbids.

II. **What is a crime, and who decides?**
   a. Legislatures bear the primary responsibility for deciding what is and isn't "crime."
   b. Whatever conduct the legislatures categorize as criminal is "crime."
   c. There are two themes/theories of lawmaking:
      i. We can say, as a theoretical matter, that you can't really have a crime without a culpable mental state that tells us it's blameworthy.
      ii. On the other hand, we can say that a crime is whatever the legislature says it is. Legislatures have passed laws that impose criminal liability without culpable mental state.

III. **Components of "Crime"**
   a. *Act*
   b. *Harm*
   c. *Culpable Mental State*
   d. *Causation*

IV. **A Criminal Case: The Suspect's Journey**
   a. Arrest
   b. Bail or Detention (question of whether or not D must stay in custody)
   c. Charges filed = *indictment* (by a grand jury is required in federal court) OR information (where prosecutor makes determination based on complaint)
   d. Arraignment (accused brought before judge and must enter a plea)
   e. Discovery Process
   f. Plea (?) (possibly a way to resolve case by lessening charges if D pleads guilty)
   g. Trial (with three possible outcomes = acquittal, conviction, hung jury)
   h. Sentencing (only happens if D is convicted)
   i. Appeal

V. **The American Criminal Trial**
   a. Select & swear in jury
   b. Opening statements by counsel
   c. Presentation of prosecution's case
   d. Defense motion to dismiss [FRCrP 29(a)]
   e. Defense case (if any)
   f. Prosecution rebuttal case (if any)
   g. Defense motion to dismiss [FRCrP 29(b)]
   h. Closing arguments

     i. Jury instructions
     j. Jury deliberations and verdict

MENTAL STATES (MENS REA)

I. **General Considerations**
    a. Nature of "Mens Rea":
        a. *Mens rea* = a guilty mind; a guilty or wrongful purpose; a criminal intent
        b. Culpable mental state is important in order to:
            1. Determine whether D is liable at all
            2. Grade the seriousness of the offense
        c. Broad (culpability) meaning = morally culpable state of mind, where D is guilty of a crime if she commits the social harm of the offense with *any* morally blameworthy state of mind.
        d. <u>Narrow (elemental) meaning</u> = the mental state D must have had with regard to the "social harm" elements set out in the definition of the offense, where D is not guilty of an offense if she lacks the mental state specified in the definition of the crime.
        e. A person may possess *mens rea* in the *culpability* sense but lack the requisite *elemental* mental state.
    b. Possible Categories:
        a. D *desires* to cause the harm he does in fact cause
            1. *Cunningham*
            2. MPC - Purposely
        b. D *desires* to cause a harm very similar to the harm he does in fact cause
            1. *Latimer*
            2. MPC – Purposely (transferred intent)
        c. D *desires* to cause some harm, but a harm different from and dissimilar to the harm he does in fact cause
            1. *Pembliton* – throws at person, but hits window
            2. MPC – No liability, or liability based on CMS for actual harm done
        d. D *foresees* that his illegal conduct will probably cause the harm he does in fact cause, but acts anyway
            1. *Cunningham, Martin*
            2. MPC – Knowingly
         e. D *actually foresees* that there is a *substantial and unjustifiable risk* that his conduct will cause the harm it does cause, but proceeds anyway
            1. MPC - Recklessly
         f. D *should have foreseen, but did not foresee*, that his illegal conduct would cause the harm he does in fact cause
            1. *Faulkner* ?
            2. MPC – Negligently
    c. ***Regina v. Cunningham***: D stole a gas meter from the cellar of a house, fracturing a gas pipe and injuring a woman, who was sleeping in the house and inhaled the gas, in the process. The trial judge instructed the jury that the meaning of "malicious" under the Offenses Against the Person Act (under which D was being charged) means wicked, or something which he has no business to do and perfectly well knows it. He says that it is not part of the offense that D intended to poison the lady, as he did an action which he should have known would result in her harm. The appellate court held that the judge's instructions were incorrect, as <u>some form of *mens rea* is required</u>, and D must have either

intended to injure Mrs. Wade or have foreseen that the removal of the meter might cause injury to someone but nevertheless removed it.

d. ***Queen v. Martin***: D put out the gaslights along a stairway at a theater and placed iron bars across the doorways at the bottom, causing the audience to become panicked as they attempted to leave and resulting in injury to many people. The court held that D had "maliciously" wounded or inflicted grievous bodily harm upon others, as he must be taken to have intended the natural consequences of what he did, which was an unlawful act calculated to injure (and did injure).

e. ***Regina v. Faulkner***: D lit a match in the process of attempting to steal some of the rum on a ship, and the rum caught fire, causing an explosion and destroying the entire ship. In considering the issue of whether the trial court erred in instructing the jury that D was guilty if the fire took place in the manner stated, even if he had no intention of burning the vessel, the court held that the instructions were erroneous, as the proposition stated in the earlier case was too wide. The law imputes to a person who willfully commits a criminal act an intention to do everything which is the probable consequence in the act constituting the body of crime which actually ensues.

II. <u>MPC General Requirements of Culpability</u>

a. Person isn't guilty of an offense unless he acted purposely, knowingly, recklessly, or negligently.

b. Purposely

    a. *A desire to cause the prohibited result; A purpose to engage in conduct of that type*

    b. MPC - Person acts <u>purposely</u> when:

        1. The element involves the nature of his conduct or a result thereof, it is his conscious object to engage in conduct of that nature or to cause such a result; and

        2. The element involves the attendant circumstances, he is aware of the existence of such circumstances or he believes or hopes that they exist.

    c. Note: Purposely in the MPC is what other statutes refer to as intentionally. Not all jurisdictions distinguish between knowledge and purpose/intent.

c. Knowingly

    a. *Consciousness of the practical certainty that the bad result will happen*

    b. MPC - Person acts <u>knowingly</u> when:

        1. If the element involves the <u>nature of his conduct or the attendant circumstances</u>, he is <u>aware</u> that his conduct *is* of that nature or that such circumstances *exist*; and

        2. If the element involves a *result* <u>of his conduct</u>, he is aware that it is <u>practically certain</u> that is conduct *will* cause such a result.

    c. Note: The distinction between purpose and knowledge involves the difference between knowing the nature of a conduct or the attendant circumstances and knowing the result of conduct; it's knowledge of past experience vs. a predicate knowledge.

d. Recklessly

    a. *Distinguished from knowledge because of the degree of certainty*

    b. MPC - Person acts <u>recklessly</u> when he *consciously disregards a substantial and unjustifiable risk* that the material element <u>exists or will result</u> from his conduct. The **risk must be of such a nature and degree** that…its disregard involves a **gross deviation** from the standard of conduct that a law-abiding person would observe in the actor's situation.

    <u>c.</u>Note: The distinction between knowledge and recklessness is that, with knowledge, you are *practically certain* with regard to future events, whereas recklessness involves less certainty with regard to future events.

  c. Negligently
- **a.** *Doesn't involve a conscious disregard*
- **b.** MPC - Person acts <u>negligently</u> when he **should be aware** of a substantial and unjustifiable risk. The risk must be of such a nature and degree that the actor's **failure to perceive it**…involves a **gross deviation** from the standard of care that a reasonable person would observe…
- <u>c.</u>Note: The difference between recklessness and negligence is like the difference between purpose and knowledge, as it involves the difference between presence and intent.

III. Intent, Purposefulness, and Knowledge
- **a.** Intent in general
  - **a.** "Intent" may be used broadly to refer to the required mental state for a crime or narrowly as a <u>term of art</u> to refer to a particular <u>category</u> of culpable mental state.
  - **b.** Even when used as a term of art, "intent" is of two types:
    1. "general intent" =
       - **a.** a recognition that one's conduct is highly likely to cause a prohibited result, OR that a circumstance exists (class)
       - **b.** May be denominated when no particular mental state is set out in the definition of the crime and the prosecutor need only prove that the act was performed with a morally blameworthy state of mind.
       - **c.** Is designated as *any* mental state in the definition of the event that relates *solely* to the events that constitute the criminal offense (e.g. battery = applying force on another)
    2. "specific intent" =
       - **a.** a *desire* to cause a prohibited result, OR actual subjective awareness that a circumstance exists.
       - **b.** Used in an offense in which a mental state *is* expressly set out in the definition of the crime
       - **c.** Designates a special mental element which is required above and beyond any mental state required with respect to the act of the crime, including:
         - **i.** Intention by the actor to commit some future act separate from the act of the offense (e.g. possession of marijuana with intent to sell)
         - **ii.** Special motive or purpose for committing the act (e.g. offensive contact with intent to humiliate)
         - **iii.** Actor's awareness of the attendant circumstances (e.g. selling obscene lit. to a person under 18)
    3. The categories are not well defined, and it's often difficult to tell the difference in practice.
  - <u>c.</u>It is ordinarily defined to include not only those results that are the conscious object of the actor but also those results that the actor knows are virtually certain to occur from his conduct.
- **b.** *People v. Conley*: D struck V in the mouth with a wine bottle after swinging at V's friend with the bottle, and the injuries to V included mucosal mouth. D was convicted of

aggravated battery, which required in IL that the offender <u>intentionally *or* knowingly</u> caused great bodily harm, or permanent disability or disfigurement. The appellate court upheld the conviction, holding that the evidence was sufficient to support a finding of intent to cause permanent disability beyond a reasonable doubt. The court allowed application of the <u>transferred intent doctrine</u> (although it might not have been necessary to meet the statute) and found that D's intent could be inferred from the circumstances.

IV. Knowledge

a. ***State v. Nations***: The police found a 16-year-old girl "dancing" for "tips" in D's club, and D hadn't seen the girl's identification. The issue was whether D *knew* that the child's age was less than 17 and therefore committed the crime of endangering the welfare of a child, which requires that one knowingly encourages, aids or causes a child less than 17 to engage in conduct which is injurious to her welfare. The court held that the state failed to prove that D knew the child's age was less than 17, as they had to show actual awareness, not a high probability of awareness or recklessness (in seeking to avoid knowing).

b. <u>Doctrine of Willful Blindness</u>: If D had facts that would cause any reasonable person to believe that a certain fact existed but D did something to avoid learning that the fact did, in fact, exist, it is treated as if D had actual knowledge. (In such cases, an "ostrich instruction" is provided, whereby the judge instructs the jury that a defendant acted knowingly if he deliberately closed his eyes to what otherwise would have been obvious, like an ostrich burying its head in the sand.)

V. Recklessness and negligence

a. ***State v. Hazelwood***: D ran his ship aground a reef, causing 11 million gallons of oil to pour into Prince William Sound and cause an ecological disaster. D was convicted of negligent discharge of oil under an Alaska statute, and the court held that the <u>ordinary negligence standard</u> (as opposed to a criminal negligence standard) was <u>adequate to protect D's interests</u> and did not deny his due process rights, <u>as the conduct at issue is something which society could reasonably expect to deter</u>. Criminal negligence is usually denoted, and ordinary negligence is acceptable in civil cases, and we impose criminal sanctions for strict liability.

b. A number of states define criminal negligence as "something more" or "gross" for some or all criminal offenses.

c. <u>Principle of lenity</u>: a maxim that the court sometimes observes that says evidence and/or any ambiguity should be construed favorably to the defendant and unfavorably toward the government.

d. ***State v. Larson***: While driving through a construction zone, D crossed over the center line and struck and instantly killed two construction workers. The court held that there was sufficient evidence to sustain the jury's finding of *recklessness* and to uphold the convictions of manslaughter. Although the majority reasoned that D's speed in the presence of a visible road construction crew could be evidence from which the jury could conclude that he was aware of, yet disregarded, the risk of an accident, the dissent stated that the majority confused recklessness with ordinary negligence (gross deviation), and "conscious disregard" is a subjective standard resting on D's state of mind.

e. ***People v. Smith***: D (parents) took their son and his friend in their car while visiting friends and consuming alcohol and drugs. They left the boys in the car "camping out" in sleeping bags with the backseat folded down, and when they drove home, they discovered that the boys were dead. They had died from carbon monoxide poisoning, and the car hadn't had an inspection in a while. This was a real CO case where the conviction was for criminally negligent homicide (although FB isn't sure he'd pursue the same charge now).

f. The difference between criminal negligence and recklessness involves looking at what a reasonable person would have done and what D in fact consciously recognized and disregarded.

VI. Strict liability

a. Two principles identifying the contours of the **public-welfare offense doctrine** (*United States v. Cordoba-Hincapie*):

    a. If punishment of the wrongdoer far outweighs regulation of the social order as a purpose of the law in question, then *mens rea* IS probably required.

    b. If the penalty is light, involving a relatively small fine and not including imprisonment, then *mens rea* probably is NOT required.

b. **"Public welfare" offenses** share certain characteristics (*Staples v. U.S.*):

    a. They regulate "dangerous or deleterious devices or products or obnoxious waste materials"

    b. They "heighten the duties of those in control of particular industries, trades, and properties"

    c. They "depend on no mental element but consist only of forbidden acts or omissions"

c. Strict liability is criticized on two grounds:

    a. SL legislation does not deter, since an actor, by hypothesis, is unaware of the facts that render his conduct dangerous.

    b. It is unjust to condemn a person who is not morally culpable.

d. *Staples v. United States*: An AR-15 rifle (civilian version of the military's M-16) was recovered at D's home, and it had been modified to be capable of fully automatic fire, which made it a "firearm" that needed to be registered. D argued that it must be proven beyond a reasonable doubt that he knew the gun would fire automatically, and the court held that, if Congress had intended to make outlaws of gun owners who were wholly ignorant of the offending characteristics of their weapons, it would have spoken more clearly to that effect, and offenses punishable by imprisonment cannot be understood to be public welfare offenses.

    a. This is a case of statutory interpretation where the court read the statute as requiring a culpable mental state, even though it didn't mention it.

    b. D claims he was ignorant of the facts, not the law, as he doesn't say he didn't know the law or that machine guns had to be registered.

    c. The dissent says the statute is one of public welfare, as the absence of an express knowledge requirement suggests that Congress didn't intend to require proof that D knew all the facts that made his conduct illegal.

e. *Garnett v. State*: D, a 20-year-old retarded man, was convicted of statutory rape after engaging in sexual intercourse with a 13-year-old girl who had told him that she was 16 years old (and ended up giving birth to his baby later). The court held that, although modern scholars generally disapprove of statutory rape as a strict liability crime, Maryland's statute is a creature of legislation, and any new provision introducing an element of *mens rea* should come from the Legislature.

f. **Strict Liability Offenses:**

    a. Questions:

        1. Are they consistent with criminal law theory?

        2. Are the Constitutionally permissible?

        3. Who has the power to create strict liability crimes?

        4. How do we know if something is a strict liability crime?

        5. If a statute is ambiguous, what factors do we look to in determining whether strict liability was intended?

b. Factors to consider in construing facially ambiguous statutes:
1. Legislative history
2. Is crime of "public welfare" or "regulatory" type?
3. How do we know if crime fits in these categories?
    a. Nature of activity being regulated
    b. Severity of penalty imposed

VII. Legality, Notice, Vagueness & Mistake of Law

a. The Doctrine of Legality

a. Condemns judicial crime creation, is considered the first principle of American criminal law jurisprudence, and has foundations in both the *Ex Post Facto Clause* and the Due Process Clause

b. Has <u>three interrelated corollaries:</u>

1. *Statutory Clarity*: Criminal statutes should be understandable to reasonable law-abiding persons.
    a. Statute must give sufficient warning that men may conduct themselves so as to avoid that which is forbidden, and a person is denied due process of law if she is convicted and punished for violation of a statute that lacks such clarity.
    b. Courts are slower to hold that an ordinary criminal statute is unconstitutionally vague, as they don't want to reward ignorance.
    c. Due Process clause isn't violated unless a law-abiding person would still have to guess as to the meaning after his/her attorney conducts research.

2. *Avoiding Undue Discretion in Law Enforcement:* Criminal statute should be crafted so as not to delegate basic policy matters to policemen, judges, and juries for resolution on a subjective basis.
    a. Supreme Court observed that a statute or ordinance must establish minimal guidelines to govern law enforcement.
    b. Constitutional doctrine of *void for vagueness* forbids wholesale legislative delegation of lawmaking authority to the courts.

3. *The Lenity Doctrine:* Judicial interpretation of ambiguous statutes should be biased in favor of the accused.
    a. *Rule of strict construction* directs that judicial resolution of residual uncertainty in the meaning of penal statutes be biased in favor of the accused.
    b. Doctrine comes into play only if a statute is ambiguous.
    c. MPC does NOT recognize the lenity principle.

c. *Commonwealth v. Mochan*: D repeatedly called a married woman, harassed and embarrassed her, and solicited intercourse. Although D's actions were not specifically defined as criminal under PA's Penal Code, the court held that D's actions identify the offense as a common law misdemeanor (which was included in a "savings clause" of the code).
1. FB: You almost have to read this case as one that gives the courts the power to define a crime under the common law.
2. To the extent judges have common law lawmaking power, their power is *retrospective*, so it's always something of a surprise to D.
3. Legislatures, on the other hand, legislate prospectively.

d. *Keeler v. Superior Court*: D and V were in the process of divorcing when they met each other on the road, and D beat V, causing the fetus she was carrying to die. D was charged with murder, but the court held that the Legislature intended to exclude the killing of an unborn fetus in adopting the definition of murder, so it would have been unforeseeable to D and thereby deny his due process rights if he were convicted.

e. The uses of the "common law":

    1. An ongoing grant of lawmaking power to judges – a power to define new crimes

    2. A shorthand way of referring to and retaining offenses defined by early American and English judges

    3. A method of determining legislative intent regarding old legal terms of art

f. Legality and Notice: Three principles:

    1. Preference for legislative, rather than judicial, creation of crime. Little common law is left.

    2. Due process in criminal law requires fair **_notice_**, which includes:

        a. Prior enactment (*Nullum crimen sine lege*, or "no crime without law")

        b. Clarity

g. Regardless of who's doing the lawmaking, we want the application to be prospective:

    1. It is morally hard to condemn/punish people who are unaware that their choice is prohibited (when we value the exercise of free will).

    2. If we want people to conform behavior, they have to know what's prohibited.

b. The Vagueness Doctrine

    a. **_In Re Banks_:** D contended that GA's "peeping tom" statute (which punished any person who "shall peep secretly into any room occupied by a female person") was unconstitutionally vague, but the appellate court held that the statute was sufficiently definite to give an individual fair notice of the conduct prohibited, violates neither the state constitution nor the Due Process Clause, and is not unconstitutional for overbreadth.

        1. FB: The statute gives us no indication as to what it prohibits and is "utterly lunatic."

        2. This case illustrates a court trying to impose limited construction on an over-broad statute to limit its application and avoid having to declare it unconstitutionally vague.

    b. **_City of Chicago v. Morales_:** The court held that the Gang Congregation Ordinance, prohibiting "criminal street gang members" from "loitering" with one another or with other persons in any public place, afforded too much discretion to the police and too little notice to citizens who wish to use the public streets.

c. Mistake of Law

    a. There's a difference between culpable mental state with respect to the conduct and being aware that the conduct was actually prohibited, or a difference between knowingly engaging in conduct and knowing the conduct is against the law.

    b. **_People v. Marrero_:** D, a guard at a federal prison, was arrested in a NY social club in possession of an unlicensed pistol and moved to dismiss his indictment on the ground that, under NY law, peace officers were exempt from criminal liability under the firearm statute. The court held that D's misunderstanding of the statute was not a defense that could excuse his criminal conduct. Basically, the court said ignorance is no excuse.

    1. Dissent says that the use of the "ignorance is no excuse" doctrine was more appropriate during a time when most offenses were *malum in se* (wrong in and of itself) but is not so appropriate when many acts are *malum prohibitum* (wrong simply because they are prohibited).

    2. This is truly a case of MISTAKE, as D had researched the statute.

c. *Cheek v. United States*: D refused to file federal income tax returns and eventually claimed that he was exempt from federal income taxes. The crimes he was charged with required that *D acted willfully*, and D claimed that he sincerely believed that the tax laws were being unconstitutionally enforced and that his actions were lawful. The Supreme Court held that it was error to instruct the jury to disregard evidence of D's understanding, as a good-faith belief doesn't have to be objectionably reasonable to negate evidence purporting to show D's awareness of the legal duty.

    1. FB: They're *not* saying D can't be convicted; they're just saying that evidence as to his subjective understanding is relevant.

    2. This case probably doesn't mean much in a broad context, as it involves a very specific type of situation.

d. *Lambert v. California*: The Supreme Court invalidated an LA law that made it unlawful for "any convicted person" to remain in the city for more than 5 days without registering and said that they believe that actual knowledge of the duty to register is necessary.

    1. FB: If the Court had decided to employ this kind of thinking to other types of statutes, this could have been a sweeping decision, but it actually turned out to be a dead end.

    2. Except in cases that almost exactly match this statute, the idea that there's a Constitutional right requiring notification in these types of crimes hasn't been seen.

THE REQUIREMENT OF AN ACT (ACTUS REUS)

I. **In General**

    a. Why an act requirement?

        i. Difficulty of proving evil thoughts

        ii. Difficulty of deterring evil thoughts

        iii. Coercive power of gov't. should be limited to occasions when real harm occurs or at least seriously threatens

        iv. Choice to act has a moral component

    b. *Actus reus* = The physical or external part of the crime, which includes both the conduct and the harmful result; to be interpreted as the comprehensive notion of act, harm, and its connecting link, causation, with *actus* expressing the voluntary phsyical movement in the sense of conduct and *reus* expressing the fact that this conduct results in certain proscribed harm.

        i. With a conduct crime, the *actus reus* won't involve a harmful result

        ii. Speech can constitute an act. (e.g. "Take this gun and kill someone.")

        iii. A muscular contraction can be an act (e.g. Finger pulling trigger).

    c. Act MUST occur at the same time as the culpable mental state.
Act must be voluntary.

II. **Voluntariness**

a. ***Martin v. State***: D was arrested at his home and taken to the highway, where he allegedly manifested a drunken condition, and was convicted of being drunk on a public highway. The court held that the conviction was contrary to the principle that a voluntary appearance is supposed by the statute.

   i. *Both* components of the prohibited conduct had to be voluntary.

   ii. D was voluntarily drunk but did not choose to be in public.

b. ***State v. Utter***: D (formerly in the armed services) had been drinking all day, stabbed and killed his son when he came home, and had no recollection of the event. D was convicted of manslaughter and appealed, alleging that his evidence regarding conditioned response should have been allowed. The court held that, even though an act committed while one is unconscious is no act at all, the evidence presented was insufficient to present the issue of D's unconscious or automatic state at the time of the act .

   i. There *can* be a defense of automatism; it just can't be used in all cases.

   ii. Courts are particularly reluctant to recognize automatism in two cases:

      1. Claims with voluntary intoxication

      2. Claims where D was consciously aware of his act but driven by some type of internal compulsion (i.e. psychological disorder)

III. Omissions

   a. In General:

      i. There is NO criminal liability for failure to act.

      ii. Exceptions:

         1. Statute imposes a duty to act (e.g. taxes, hit and run driving)

         2. Duties arising from relationships

            a. Parent – minor child

            b. Husband – wife

            c. Other family relations

            d. Contract

               i. With victim

               ii. Third party

               iii. Employer – Employee

         e. D created risk of harm in the first place

   b. ***People v. Beardsley***: D invited a woman to come to his apartment while his wife was away. She ingested morphine in his presence, and D took her to his neighbor's apartment, where she died. The court held that D was under no legal duty which required him to make an effort to save the woman, even if the omission to perform made him responsible for her death.

      i. FB: Court's decision is surprising, as he HID her. They basically don't want to impose a legal duty to care for a floozy.

      ii. Although there might be a common law duty to aid, there's no statutory duty, and the common law duty will only be imposed in certain situations.

   c. ***Barber v. Superior Court***: When a man suffered a cardio-respiratory arrest after undergoing a successful surgery, his doctors (D's) took all life-sustaining machines off him and removed his IV tubes after his family gave permission. The court held that, although D's omission to continue treatment under the circumstances was intentional and with knowledge that the patient would die, was not an unlawful failure to perform a legal duty.

   d. Justifications offered for the common law rule of permitting harm (book):

      i. "Non-doings" (omissions) are inherently more ambiguous than wrongdoings (acts)

      ii. Difficult line-drawing problems arise in omission cases

iii.   Well-meaning bystanders often make matters worse by intervening

iv.   There is an issue of freedom

IV. Possession

   a. Kinds of Possession:

      i. A person who has direct physical control of something on or around his person is then in ***actual possession*** of it.

      ii. A person who is not in actual possession, but who has both the power and the intention to later take control over something, either alone or together with someone else, is in ***constructive possession*** of it.

      iii. If one person alone has possession of something, possession is ***sole***.

      iv. If two or more persons share possession, possession is ***joint***.

   b. ***People v. Gory***: An officer found marijuana scattered loosely in a metal box where D stored his possessions, and D admitted that the marijuana was taken from his box but stated that he had never seen it before. The court held that the jury should have been instructed that D was guilty if he "knowingly ha[d] in his possession the objects charged in the information," although whether D had a "guilty knowledge…and intent" was irrelevant. **Although D could possess the object without knowing the nature of it, he couldn't possess it if he didn't know it was there at all and didn't show intent to exercise physical control over it.**

   c. ***Commonwealth v. Lee***: D received a package at work, and police officers approached her about it before she opened it. When asked, she opened the package (which contained marijuana) and said, "I know what they are." The court held that the evidence was sufficient to support possession.

      i. FB: The court is basically saying that one can be found in possession of the contents of a package without knowing what they are before opening it. It should have to be proven that you knew of the contents.

   d. ***Commonwealth v. Rambo***: It was discovered that two parcels, en route to D, contained hashish, so a "controlled delivery" of the packages was arranged. D accepted the packages, and an agent seized them while D was out and left a note for D, who reported to the police station and was arrested. The court held that the evidence was sufficient to support a conviction, as it could be inferred that D was expecting the packages and expected them to contain hashish.

   e. ***State v. Flaherty***: D and his wife spent the day with Giles, whose gun ended up in D's car. When D discovered the gun, he started to drive back to give the gun to Giles but was stopped by a police officer, who removed the gun and charged D with theft. The court held that D could be **convicted of possession if he had been in control for "a sufficient period to have been able to terminate his possession."**

   f. ***Wheeler v. United States***: The police went to D's room after being informed that its occupants were selling heroin and found some heroin in the room. D admitted that she lived in the room, and the court held that the evidence, albeit circumstantial, was sufficient for a trier of fact to determine beyond a reasonable doubt that D was guilty of the charged offense. Although courts are sometimes reluctant to hold an individual responsible for substances found in a home absent proof he's something other than a visitor, D admitted she lived in the room.

THE REQUIREMENT OF CAUSATION

I. In General

   a. *Causation* = the relationship between the voluntary act(s) [*actus reus*] of the defendant and the prohibited harm.

    b. Two types:

        i. Cause-in-fact: "But for" causation (If D hadn't acted, would the harm have occurred?)

        ii.   **Legal cause** (sometimes called "proximate cause"): "but for" causation + foreseeability (will be the correct analysis most of the time)

    c. Intervening Causes (must independently satisfy "but for" and occur after D's act but before the harm):

        i. "Direct" cause: A significant, *foreseeable*, "but for" cause with no intervening cause between act and harm.

        ii.   "Intervening" causes: Independent "but for" cause which occurs after D's act, but before the harm:

            1. *De minimis* relation to the harm – no defense

            2. "Foreseeable" intervening causes – no defense

            3. "Responsive" (or dependent) intervening causes – no defense [Ex. Bad doctor]

            4. Coincidental (independent) intervening causes – Possible defense

            5. Defendant's *mens rea*

                a. "intended consequences" doctrine – any intended consequence of an act is proximate

                b. Ex. *Regina v. Michael* – You tried to poison one, so the other being poisoned is your fault.

            6. Victim's choice (Ex. *Velasquez* – uncertain results)

    d. When a person reaches a position of safety, the original wrongdoer is no longer responsible for any ensuing harm ("Apparent safety" doctrine).

    e. The "negative act" of an omission will not cut off liability of an earlier "positive act," as "nothing" can never supersede "something."

    f. Contributory negligence by V is NOT a defense in criminal cases.

II. Actual Cause (Cause-in-Fact)

    a. *Oxendine v. State*: D's girlfriend pushed his son into the bathtub, causing microscopic tears in his intestines which led to peritonitis. The next morning, D beat the child, who ended up dying that night en route to the hospital. At trial, medical experts varied on their opinions as to which beating was the underlying cause of death, and the State put forth a theory of "acceleration." The court held that the evidence was insufficient to establish hat D's conduct accelerated his son's death. Contribution without acceleration is insufficient to establish causation.

        i. Causation in homicide often has to do with two things:

            1. Showing that death resulted from contact

            2. A timing question (as all of them really just accelerate death)

        ii.   Here, they failed to show that D's actions were a cause-in-fact of the child's death.

III. Proximate Cause ("Legal" Cause)

    a. Doctrine serves the purpose of determining who or what events among those that satisfy the "but-for" standard should be held accountable for the resulting harm.

    b. The analysis is an effort by the factfinder to determine, *based on policy considerations or matters of fairness*, whether it is proper to hold D criminally responsible for a prohibited result (whereas cause-in-fact is a *fact* question)

    c. *A person or event cannot be a proximate cause of harm unless she or it is an actual cause,* *but a person or event can be an actual cause without being a proximate cause.*

    d. ***Kibbe v. Henderson***: D and his friend met V at a bar, where he became drunk, and they decided to rob him later (after offering him a ride home). They abandoned him on the side of an unlit, two-lane, rural highway, and he was struck by another driver 30 minutes later, suffered massive injuries, and died. The appellate court held that the trial court's failure to instruct the jury on the issue of causation deprived D of his right to due process, as a determination of whether the intervening force was a sufficiently independent or supervening cause of death was one for the jury.

        i. Most of the time, foreseeability is key when you are considering the question of legal cause.

        ii. The real issue here wasn't "but for" causation, as that's obvious; it was whether D's should be held accountable.

    e. ***Velazquez v. State***: D and Alvarez met and decided to drag race. Alvarez completed the course, turned around, and drove 123 mph (while drunk and not wearing a seatbelt) toward a canal. Both drivers crashed through the guardrail, and Alvarez died. D was convicted of vehicular homicide, but the appellate court held that D's participation in the subject "drag race" was not a proximate cause of the deceased's death, as the deceased participated and himself drove recklessly. Policy considerations are against imposing liability on D.

IV. Concurrence of the Elements

    a. ***State v. Rose***: D hit V with his station wagon, after which the body rolled off the hood, and D drove off. An expert couldn't testify whether V died upon impact or after being drug, and D was charged with both leaving the scene of an accident and manslaughter. The court held that D was entitled to a directed verdict on the manslaughter charge, as the testimony lacks reasonable medical certainty as to the time of V's death, so one couldn't conclude D's guilt beyond a reasonable doubt.

        i. There's no evidence D was being negligent before hitting V, so he's not guilty of anything for hitting the man who ended up dying.

        ii. However, if D's dragging is definitely what killed him, there's culpability.

        iii. There's no doubt D left the scene of an accident.

HOMICIDE

I. Common law malice

    a. Murder was defined as the unlawful killing of another human being with "malice aforethought." Four consistent states of mind are given to "malice aforethought":

        i. Intent to kill

        ii. Intent to cause grievous bodily harm

        iii. Depraved-heart murder

        iv. Intent to commit a felony

    b. Homicide =

        i. "…every mode by which the life of one man is taken by the act of another" – *Commonwealth v. Webster*

        ii. "the killing of a person by another" – CO statutes

        iii. A criminal homicide is essentially the taking of a human life without some legal justification.

    c. ***Commonwealth v. Webster***: D was indebted to V, and after the two had an interview, V disappeared, and parts of a human body were later discovered in D's medical lab at Harvard.

      i. Court distinguishes between murder and manslaughter.

      ii.   D was found guilty and sentenced to death.

      iii.   At trial, he'd said he didn't do it at all, but he later confessed and described what he did as heat of passion (to try to avoid death).

      iv.   Court says that the *implication of malice arises in every case of intentional homicide.*

      v.   Malice aforethought = Doing a voluntary act whose likely and probable consequence is the death of another person with the *absence of heat of passion.*

   d. **Murder v. Manslaughter (at common law):**

      i. Murder = "the killing of any person…with malice aforethought, either express or implied by law."

      ii.   Manslaughter = "the unlawful killing of another without malice, and may be either voluntary…or involuntary."

      iii.   "The characteristic distinction between murder and manslaughter is malice, express or implied."

   e. *People v. Eulo:* D shot V in the head, and V was taken to a hospital in an unconscious state, where he was later declared dead and had his artificial respiration terminated. The court recognized a principle of "brain death" as a definition of death after D challenged the jury instructions as to death.

II. "Heat of Passion" Doctrine

   a. **Common Law**

      i. Sufficient Provocation

         1. Blow to D from V

         2. Angry words followed by assault

         3. Sight of friend or relative being beaten

         4. Sight of citizen being unlawfully deprived of liberty

         5. Sight of man in act of adultery with D's wife (but not reverse?)

      ii.   Insufficient Provocation

         1. Words alone

         2. Gestures

         3. Trespass to property

         4. Misconduct by servant or child

         5. Breach of contract

   b. "Heat of passion" is NOT a defense; it only mitigates the seriousness of the crime and therefore lessens the sentence. It doesn't justify or exonerate the crime.

III. Deliberate and premeditated homicides: Murder & Manslaughter

   a. **Murder vs. Manslaughter**

      i. The first subdivision of homicide crimes

      ii.   A **murder** is a death resulting from voluntary acts the natural and probable consequence of which is death.

      iii.   A **manslaughter** is a murder mitigated by the presence of heat of passion

   b. Murder is sometimes subdivided by the existence of premeditation or deliberation

   c. *Girouard v. State:* Husband D and wife V got into a fight, during which D continually made taunting comments to D. He went into the kitchen, got a knife (which he hid behind his pillow), and asked V if she'd meant all the things she said before. When she responded in the affirmative, he stabbed her 19 times, after which he slit his own wrists and called the cops. In considering whether the taunting words uttered by V were enough to inflame the passion of a *reasonable* man so that the man would be sufficiently infuriated so as to strike out in hot-blooded blind passion to kill her, the court held that the provocation in this case wasn't enough to cause a reasonable man to stab his provoker 19 times. D's conviction of second-degree murder was upheld.

- **i.** Rule of Provocation:
    - **1.** There must have been adequate provocation
    - **2.** The killing must have been in the heat of passion
    - **3.** It must have been a sudden heat of passion – that is, the killing must have followed the provocation before there had been a reasonable opportunity for the passion to cool
    - **4.** There must have been a causal connection between the provocation, the passion, and the fatal act.
- **ii.** FB: This court says that not having a cooling-off period helps the cause of manslaughter, although other jurisdictions may be friendlier to those who've been provoked over a long period of time.
- **iii.** Some argue that it's never *reasonable* or justifiable to murder someone, so we shouldn't even have a provocation defense.

d. *Attorney General for Jersey v. Holley*: D and V were both alcoholics who lived together and had a "stormy" relationship. While D was drunk and chopping wood one day, V came home and told D that she'd just had sex with another man. D picked up the axe, intending to leave, and V said, "You haven't got the guts." D then struck her seven or eight times. The court held that, although it was correct to leave out the account of D's alcoholism, the appellate court's decision to set aside the conviction of murder and instate one for manslaughter should stand.

e. *People v. Casassa*: After V informed D that she was not "failing in love" with him, he broke into both her apartment and her neighbor's. One night, he brought several bottles of wine and liquor to offer to V as a gift. When she refused, he stabbed her several times in the throat with a steak knife he'd brought with him. He then submerged her in a bathtub full of water. The appellate court held that the trial court had correctly applied the statute regarding extreme emotional disturbance, and the conviction of murder in the second degree should stand.

- **i.** Extreme emotional disturbance has two components:
    - **1.** D must have acted under the influence of extreme emotional disturbance
    - **2.** There must have been a reasonable explanation or excuse for such extreme emotional disturbance

f. *State v. Guthrie*: D and V worked together as dishwashers. One night, V was taunting D, and D pulled a knife from his pocket and stabbed V in the neck. After D was found guilty of first degree murder, the appellate court reversed and remanded for a new trial, holding that there was a failure to inform the jury of the difference between first and second degree murder, and premeditation and deliberation should be defined in a more careful but still general way to give juries both guidance and reasonable discretion.

- **i.** Court overrules *Schrader*, which said an intention to kill need exist only for an instant.
- **ii.** Court said that *Hatfield* may instead be used, and it states that "murder in the first degree consists of an intentional, deliberate and premeditated killing [that is] done after a period of time for prior consideration."
- **iii.** FB: This rule may not be helpful to a jury. (Is two "instants" enough?)
- **iv.** *People v. Morrin* provides a standard: "To premediate is to think about beforehand; to deliberate is to measure and evaluate the major facets of a choice or problem…premeditation and deliberation characterize a thought process undisturbed by hot blood. While the minimum time necessary to exercise this

process is incapable of exact determination, the interval between initial thought and ultimate actions should be long enough to afford a reasonable man time to subject the nature of his response to a second look."

g. The doctrine of "lesser included offenses": A defendant has the right to a jury instruction upon request that he may be found guilty of an offense "included" within the offense charged, as long as the factfinder could reasonably conclude from the evidence introduced at trial that the defendant is guilty of the lesser, but not the greater, offense. A defendant may *not* be convicted of a *more serious* degree or offense than that charged.

h. *People v. Anderson*: D lived with a woman and her three children, including V. D diverted V's brother and mother from finding V and made up stories about the blood they discovered being from various people cutting themselves. Eventually, V's body was discovered in her room with over 60 wounds. After two juries found D guilty of first degree murder, the court held that the evidence was insufficient to support a verdict of first degree murder on the theory of premeditated and deliberate murder. The court listed categories for the types of evidence the court has found sufficient to sustain a finding of premeditation and deliberation and set forth cases that it found to be both analogous and distinguishable.

> **i.** FB: The court essentially reconstructed the statute, making it very difficult to sustain charges of first degree murder. Essentially the only thing that's happening here is that the Supreme Court of CA is trying to cut down on the number of people who receive the death penalty.
>
> **ii.** The Legislature basically overturned this case later.

i. *Midgett v. State*: D father abused V son over a period of time. V died ~4 days after a beating consisting of four blows. D brought the body to the hospital, where the examiner found that V died as a result of intra-abdominal hemorrhage caused by a blunt force trauma consistent with having been delivered by a human fist. D was convicted of first degree murder, but the appellate court found that there was no evidence of "premeditated and deliberated purpose of causing the death of another person" required for the conviction of first degree murder, although a conviction of second degree murder could stand.

> **i.** FB: Court's reasoning might make sense, as one who abuses another over a long period of time might not have intent to kill; however, it forgives long-term abusers over those who have a brief period of anger.
>
> **ii.** FB: The court may have just decided not to be activist in order to prompt the legislature to enact a relevant law (which it did).

j. *State v. Forrest*: After admitting V father to the hospital and watching his condition worsen, D son fired four shots into his father's head while alone in the hospital room with him. Jury found D guilty of first degree murder, and the appellate court upheld the conviction, as there was substantial evidence that the killing was premeditated and deliberate.

IV. Unintended (reckless or negligent) homicides: Involuntary Manslaughter & Criminally Negligent Homicide

a. "Unintentional killings" In general

> **i.** Any killing in which D does not subjectively desire the death of the victim
>
> **ii.** However, they do NOT include wholly accidental killings (which aren't criminal)
>
> **iii.** Include a range of seriousness, from lowest to highest
>
> > **1.** "Abandoned and malignant heart" or "extreme indifference" homicides can be first degree murder

2. Jurisdictions distinguishing between **"knowing"** and **"purposeful"** killings make killings without purposefulness, but with knowledge of virtual certainty of death, second degree murder.
3. Many jurisdictions define <u>involuntary manslaughter</u> as some form of **reckless** killing (i.e. killing by acting with conscious recognition that one's conduct presents substantial and unjustifiable risk of death)
4. Many jurisdictions have **"criminally negligent homicide"** as their least serious form of criminal homicide.

b. ***People v. Nieto Benitez***: CA court says that malice can mean TWO things: *Express* malice is an intentional killing, but *implied* malice is when one does an act with a high probability that it will result in death and with an antisocial motive and *wanton disregard for human life*. The last phrase is most important in fitting CA in with the rest of the country, as they are saying that a person's acts, while not necessarily intentional, can rise above the level of negligence and even recklessness (like intent). They say that this "wanton disregard" can demonstrate implied malice and support a conviction for second degree murder (not manslaughter).

c. ***Berry v. Superior Court***: D's pit bull killed a 2 ½ year old. The dog had never attacked a human being, but he was bred and trained to be a fighting dog, and he was "protecting" D's marijuana plants.
  i. If you're D, you argue that the dog has never attacked anyone, and you have no reason to believe he would.
  ii. If you're the state, you argue that putting him near the marijuana plants supports the theory that you think he *would* attack someone.
  iii. Court found that sufficient evidence existed for trying D for second-degree murder and finding that implied malice existed.

d. ***State v. Hernandez***: D was driving a van which struck a truck carrying three men, one of whom died as a result of the accident. D was traveling in the wrong lane and told ambulance employees that he'd been drinking. At trial, stickers, pins, and a sign with various slogans printed on them were admitted as evidence. The appellate court found that the trial court erred in admitting evidence of the drinking slogans, as D's knowledge of the effect of alcohol on him was not at issue, and evidence must logically tend to support or establish a fact or issue between the parties.

e. ***State v. Williams***: D's were aware that their baby was sick but thought he had a toothache and gave him aspirin and did not take him to a doctor. The baby died because an abscessed tooth developed into a gangrenous infection, and he caught pneumonia. A doctor testified that the baby might have been saved if he'd had medical attention in the last week of his life. The court found that there was evidence to support the finding that D's were put on notice and required to obtain medical care for the child, so a charge of manslaughter could stand.

V. Felony murder
a. **Generally:**
  i. In looking at this rule, you must <u>ALWAYS identify the predicate felony</u>!
  ii. Operated to impose liability for murder based on the culpability required for the underlying felony without separate proof of culpability with regard to the death. The homicide was thus a strict liability offense.
  iii. <u>**The Rule at Common Law:**</u> *D is guilty of murder if he kills another person during the commission of, or during the attempt to commit, any felony.* (However, the list of felonies was much smaller at common law.)
  iv. It was hard to claim the doctrine worked injustice in an age that recognized

only a few felonies and that punished each as a capital offense, but modern legislatures have created a wide range of statutory felonies, many which concern relatively minor misconduct.

> **v.** **The Rule in Most Modern Statutes:** D is guilty of the highest degree of murder if death results from the commission of a *specified* felony.
>> **1.** Limitations:
>>> **a.** Many states limit the felony murder rule to deaths resulting from the commission of "inherently dangerous felonies."
>>>> **i.** Sometimes the list is in the statute;
>>>> **ii.** Sometimes it's imposed by courts.
>>> **b.** The Merger (or "Anti-Bootstrapping") Rule: Many states prohibit the use of predicate felony which is a "lesser included offense" of 1st degree murder, or which is an "integral part" of, or is "included in fact" in the homicide.
>>>> **i.** Judges say that *any* offense can't be turned into felony murder.
>>>> **ii.** Prevents prosecutors from charging D with 1st degree assault with a deadly weapon and then saying it's a felony murder.
>>> **c.** The Death must occur <u>during the commission</u> of the felony or in <u>direct flight therefrom</u>.
>>>> **i.** Time starts when "attempt" to commit underlying felony is legally complete;
>>>> **ii.** Time ends when D reaches pace of temporary refuge.
>>> **d.** Must be <u>causal relationship</u> between felony and death.
>>> **e.** Generally, *but not always*, a <u>felon is not liable for a death caused by one opposing the felony</u> (i.e., bystander, police officer). A minority of states impose liability for *any* death proximately caused by the events of the underlying felony.
> **vi.** We're really attempting to focus on the high-risk, underlying felony. By imposing the punishment of murder on felons who commit more dangerous felonies and kill, we're trying to deter the felony itself.

b. *People v. Fuller:* A police officer observed D's rolling tires toward a car before getting into it and driving away, after which a high-speed chase ensued. D's ran a red light, struck another car, and killed its driver. The court held that the CA felony-murder rule could apply to an unintentionally-caused death during a high-speed automobile chase following the commission of a nonviolent, daylight burglary, and D's can be prosecuted for first-degree murder.
> **i.** CA's first-degree felony murder rule lists burglary as a predicate felony.
> **ii.** The court noted that it would hold differently if working with a clean slate, as this type of burglary is different than breaking into a dwelling at night.

c. *People v. Howard:* After a police officer saw D driving a Tahoe without a rear license plate, he signaled him to pull over. D stopped but restarted the engine and sped to a nearby freeway when the police officer and his partner got out of their patrol car. Many officers then took up the chase, during which D turned off the car's headlights, ran two stop signs and a red light, and drove on the wrong side of the road. After D's gave up the chase, D ran a red light, collided with a car, and killed its driver. The court found that the predicate felony with which D was charged, driving with a willful or wanton disregard for the safety of persons or property while fleeing from a pursuing police officer, was not an inherently dangerous felony, so D could not be charged under the state's second-degree felony murder rule.

> **i.** The court used the fact that the statute's subdivision included a definition encompassing lesser offenses as support for its decision.
>
> **ii.** In many states with the "inherently dangerous" limitation, the problem becomes whether the class of crime is always dangerous or whether it's dangerous in the way this D committed it. The majority of courts fall into accord with this opinion and say that they need to look at the class of crime in the abstract instead of the instance at hand.
>
> **iii.** FB: Even if the court's result seems crazy, their application of the doctrine (in theory) wasn't necessarily bad.

d. ***People v. Robertson***: Two men, after driving around drinking and doing drugs with others, approached D's automobile (parked in front of his residence) and began removing the vehicle's hubcaps. D emerged onto the porch and fired shots at them, shooting one in the foot and shooting the other fatally in the back of the head. The court held that the merger doctrine did NOT preclude application of the second degree felony-murder rule in this case, which involved the predicate offense of discharging a firearm in a grossly negligent manner.

> **i.** Rule: The felony-murder instruction is not proper when the predicate felony is "an integral part of the homicide" and "included in fact with the offense charged."
>
> **ii.** The dissent doesn't like the result, as the doctrine *can't* be applied if the person were trying to kill.
>
> **iii.** FB: The problem is trying to figure out when the causal relationship is close enough to satisfy the causation requirement but not so connected that the predicate felony is no more than a part of the homicide.

e. ***State v. Sophophone***: D and three other individuals broke into a house. Police responded and ran down D and handcuffed him. One of his accomplices fired at an officer, after which the officer returned fire and killed him. The court held that the lawful act of the law enforcement officer was sufficient to insulate D from criminal responsibility, so the felony-murder rule isn't applicable here.

> **i.** FB: We need focus on two points from this case: the timing, and the liability of the co-felon.
>
> **ii.** A few states allow application of the felony-murder rule in this instance.
>
> **iii.** The fact that D was in custody doesn't necessarily get him off, as some states permit liability as long as what the co-felon does is part of committing the underlying felony or in flight therefrom.

VI. Capital Punishment

a. **The Death Penalty and Theories of Punishment:**

> **i.** Deterrence:
>
> > **1.** General – The abolitionists argue that capital punishment is no more than judicial murder, while those in support of the death penalty argue that the abolitionists are exhibiting too much concern for the killers and devaluing the victims and society.
> >
> > **2.** Specific – It's a great specific deterrent, but some people who engage in crime aren't very risk-averse.
>
> **ii.** Incapacitation: Capital punishment is the perfect incapacitator.
>
> **iii.** Rehabilitation: Capital punishment doesn't really do this at all.
>
> **iv.** Restitution: Dead people have a hard time making restitution.
>
> **v.** Retribution: Many people want killers to "pay" and feel a need for

retribution and "just desserts." Imposing retributive punishment may also be justifiable on the ground that it can prevent future crime (esp. retaliatory), as people won't feel the need to avenge wrongs.

b. In ***Furman v. Georgia* (1972),** the Supreme Court set aside death sentences in four GA cases, and the effect of the case was to end executions nationwide, because all death penalty statutes were constitutionally inform under the reasoning of the case. Thereafter, 35 states reformulated their sentencing provisions.

> **i.** Two justices concluded that capital punishment is unconstitutional in all circumstances.
>
> **ii.** Three justices reasoned that there was too great a risk that the death penalty was being imposed arbitrarily, capriciously, or in a discriminatory manner.
>
> **iii.** Four dissenters rejected the *per se* and procedural attacks on the death penalty.

c. **Post-*Furman* Death Statutes:** Attributes of (presumptively) valid death penalty statute:

> **i.** D guilty of highest available degree of homicide in the jurisdiction.
>
> > **1.** Capital punishment for rape ruled unconstitutional (*Coker v. Georgia*)
> >
> > **2.** D need not be person who actually did killing. Accomplice murders OK. (Compare *Enmund v. Fla.* With *Tison v. Arizona*)
> >
> > **3.** Open question whether any non-homicide offense is constitutionally punishable by death.
>
> **ii.** Automatic death penalty for highest degree of homicide impermissible (*Woodson v. N.C.*)
>
> **iii.** Applicability of death penalty narrowed by statutory list of aggravating factors.
>
> **iv.** Sentencer (jury ONLY) must find:
>
> > **1.** Existence of at least one aggravator, and
> >
> > **2.** Aggravating factor(s) outweigh mitigating factor(s)
>
> **v.** State cannot limit mitigating factors (*Lockett v. Ohio*)
>
> **vi.** Automatic right of appeal.

d. ***Gregg v. Georgia* (1976):** D was convicted of intent-to-kill murder and armed robbery. At a post-conviction sentencing hearing, the jury imposed the death penalty after it found beyond a reasonable doubt that D was guilty of two statutory aggravating circumstances. In determining whether the sentence of death for murder is a per se violation of the Eighth and Fourteenth Amendments, whether it comports with the basic concept of human dignity at the core of the amendments, and whether the punishment of death is disproportionate in relation to the crime for which it is imposed, the Supreme Court held that the death penalty is not a form of punishment that may never be imposed, and the statutory system under which D was sentenced to death does not violate the Constitution.

e. **Development of Capital Punishment Law Post-*Gregg* & Post-*Furman*:**

> **i.** The three concepts of proportionality (imposition of death isn't proportionate to any crimes other than murder), consistency (procedural), and individuality (procedural) are considered.
>
> **ii.** Courts have grappled with which crimes are eligible: Treason, murder (not always), rape (not death-eligible), child rape (still a question).
>
> **iii.** Basically, surviving statutes designate a particular degree of justified homicide and then go on to say that the jury must consider whether one of many listed aggravating factors exist, then whether one of many mitigating factors exist, and finally do a balancing test between the two.

f. ***McClesky v. Kemp*:** D, a black man, was convicted of the murder of a white police officer during the course of a robbery, and was sentenced to death after the jury found the existence of two aggravating circumstances and no mitigating factors. D petitioned for a writ of habeus corpus, alleging multiple claims, one of which was that the Georgia capital sentencing process is administered in a racially discriminatory manner in violation of the Eighth and Fourteenth Amendments. He presented a statistical study, the Baldus study, that purports to show a disparity in the imposition of the death sentence in GA based on the race of the murder victim and the race of the defendant. The court held that the Baldus study was clearly insufficient to support an inference that any of the decisionmakers in D's case acted with discriminatory purpose, and the study does not demonstrate a constitutionally significant risk of racial bias affecting the GA capital sentencing process.

g. ***Payne v. Tennessee***: D murdered his girlfriend's neighbor and her daughter and seriously injured her son. In considering whether "victim impact" evidence of the son's experience could be presented at trial, the Supreme Court held that the Eighth Amendment erects no per se bar to such evidence.

RAPE

I. **Generally**
  a. **Who?**
    i. Defendant = formerly only men; now men and women
    ii. Victim = formerly only women not married to D; now both men and women, including women married to D
    iii. Spouses can now rape one another.
  b. **What kinds of sexual behavior?**
    i. At common law, only general intercourse
    ii. Most modern rape statutes include sex acts involving the mouth or anus
    iii. In general, *penetration*, however slight, constitutes *actus reus*.
    iv. Emission is not required.
    v. Sexual offenses that are NOT "rape":
      1) Sometimes forcible sodomy (e.g., MO 566.060)
      2) MPC sexual assault – unpermitted "sexual contact," meaning touching for purpose of arousing or gratifying sexual desire
      3) "Statutory rape" – sexual relations with an underage person, even if that person consents.
  c. **Non-Consent:**
    i. Victims incapable of consent (two categories):
      1) Those victims who subjectively don't consent
      2) Those who don't have a subjective state of mind that they don't want to participate (two subgroups):
        a. People who subjectively consent but are deemed legally incapable of doing so.
        b. People who aren't aware in some way or have been incapacitated in some way that they're not capable of having a subjective state of mind of consent.
    ii. Examples of passive non-consent:
      1) **CA Code** – It's rape if victim:
        a. Is incapable, because of a mental disorder or developmental or physical disability, of giving legal consent
        b. Person is prevented from resisting by any intoxicating or anesthetic substance, or any controlled substance
        c. and this is known or reasonably should be known to the person

committing the act
- **d.** Is at the time unconscious of the nature of the act, and this is known to the accused
  - **i.** Victim was unconscious or asleep
  - **ii.** Victim was not aware the act occurred
  - **iii.** Victim was not aware of the essential characteristics of the act due to the perpetrator's fraud in fact
- **iii.** Victim's inability to give legal, as opposed to subjective, consent (refers primarily to statutory rape)
- **iv.** Used to be a requirement that V fight, which made proof easier; however, we've realized it might not be a good policy to require that women resist their attackers to the utmost. It still helps with proof but isn't required.
- **d. MPC 213.1 – Rape:** "A male who has sexual intercourse with a female not his wife is guilty of rape if:
  - **i.** he compels her to submit by force or by threat of imminent death, serious bodily injury, extreme pain or kidnapping, to be inflicted by anyone; or
  - **ii.** he has substantially impaired her power to approase or control her conduct by administering drugs, intoxicants, or other means for the purpose of preventing resistance; or
  - **iii.** the female is unconscious; or
  - **iv.** the female is less than 10 years old."

II. Resistance & Force:

- **a. *State v. Alston*:** D and V had been involved in a consensual sexual relationship, which sometimes involved violence. After D hit V, she moved out of their apartment and didn't have sex with him for over a month. One day, he came to see her at school, grabbed her arm, and took her for a walk. V told him the relationship was over, but D said he had a "right" to "make love" to her again and walked her to a friend's house. Even though V said "no," the two had intercourse. V made a complaint, but the two had intercourse again before trial. D's conviction was reversed on appeal, as the court found that absent evidence that D used force or threats to overcome the will of V to resist the sexual intercourse alleged to have been rape, such general fear was not sufficient to show that D used the force required to support a conviction of rape.
  - **i.** Court said that although V had NOT consented, she was NOT forced.
  - **ii.** FB: This opinion is probably outdated, as most courts would reach a different conclusion.
  - **iii.** *Constructive force* = modern statutes typically provide that nonconsensual intercourse obtained by *threat* of force constitutes forcible rape.
- **b. *Rusk v. State*:** V met D at a bar, and he requested a ride home. When she refused to come up to his apartment, D took her keys, and she went up. While in D's room, V said she begged him to leave and asked if he'd let her go without killing her if she did what he wanted. When she started to cry, he started to "lightly choke" her, and he said that he'd let her go if she did what he wanted. She then performed oral sex, and they had sexual intercourse. At trial, D was convicted of rape, but the Court of Appeals reversed. Although the dissent agreed with the appellate court, the MD supreme court reversed and remanded with directions that D's conviction be affirmed.
  - **i.** Court of appeals and dissent said that V didn't resist the acts, and the facts and circumstances of the case were insufficient to cause a reasonable fear which likely overcame her ability to resist.
  - **ii.** The supreme court of MD found that the reasonableness of V's

apprehension of fear was plainly a question of fact for the jury.

    c. ***Commonwealth v. Burkowitz*:** V went to D's dorm room to leave a note for his roommate, and D asked her to stay. D pushed her, kissed her, fondled her, and tried to put his penis in her mouth. V said "No" repeatedly, but D put her on the bed, removed her pants, and began engaging in sexual intercourse with her. On appeal, D's conviction for rape was discharged, as PA law requires evidence of "forcible compulsion," and the court believed that evidence of verbal protestations was not sufficient evidence of such.

III. Mistake of Fact & the Law of Rape

    a. **Mistake of Fact Generally**

        i. Genuine mistake of fact is, or can be, an effective way to defend against the prosecution's case.

        ii. TEST: If the facts were as D believed them to be, would those facts constitute a defense?

        iii. AS TO MENTAL STATE: A mistake of fact may be an effective defense when the mistaken belief, if honestly held, would negate or disprove the existence of the required mental state.

    b. ***DPP v. Morgan*:** D, a senior officer in the R.A.F., invited 3 men in the R.A.F. to go back to his house and have sex with his wife. He told them that his wife might put up a show of struggling, but, in reality, she'd welcome intercourse with them. V claimed that she struggled when the 4 men awakened her and drug her into another room to engage in sexual intercourse with her, but she was held down on the bed by 3 men while the 4th had intercourse with her. She drove to a hospital and complained of being raped as soon as her husband went to bed. The oral and written statements of the 4 accused amounted to complete confessions of multiple rapes, but all asserted the wife was a willing party.

        i. Judge's Instructions at Trial: "If they came to the conclusion that Mrs. Morgan had not consented to the intercourse in question but that D's believed or may have believed that she was consenting to it, they must nevertheless find D's guilty of rape if they were satisfied that they had no reasonable grounds for so believing."

        ii. Issue on Appeal: Whether in rape D can properly be convicted notwithstanding that he in fact believed that the woman consented if such belief was not based on reasonable grounds.

        iii. Lords are choosing between three mental states:

            1) No intent/strict liability: if V doesn't consent, you're guilty.

            2) Purposely/knowingly: Aware V doesn't consent but proceed.

            3) Negligence: Based on whether or not your belief as to consent was reasonable.

        iv. Result: The instruction was improper. The Crown must prove <u>D actually believed V did not consent.</u> Conviction upheld anyway.

IV. Policy from Susan Estrich Article:

    a. In concluding that "non-traditional" rapes are not criminal and that the woman must bear any guilt, the law has reflected, legitimized, and enforced a view of sex and women which celebrates male aggressiveness and punishes female passivity.

    b. The law should be understood to prohibit claims and threats to secure sex that would be prohibited by extortion law and fraud or else false pretenses law as a means to secure money.

    c. The law should evaluate conduct of "reasonable" men, not according to a *Playboy*- macho philosophy that says "no means yes," but by according respect to a woman's words.

PROPERTY CRIMES

I. Larceny

    a. <u>LARCENY</u> = "the trespassory taking and carrying away of the personal property of another with the intent to steal the same."

        i. Courts gradually broadened the offense by manipulating the concept of possession to embrace misappropriation by a person who w/ the consent of the owner already had physical control over the property (*Lee v. State*).

    b. Consists of <u>SIX ELEMENTS</u>:

        i. Personal Property

        ii. Of another [which must be]

        iii. Taken

        iv. By trespass [and]

        v. Carried away [with]

        vi. The intent to steal.

    c. Actus Reus (Trespassory taking and carrying away):

        i. A person can take possession of property without carrying it away, and one can carry away without taking possession. One needs to do both to commit larceny. The slightest "carrying away" movement suffices.

        ii. ***Rex v. Chisser***: D asked shopkeeper to show him two ties. She showed them to him and placed them in his hands. He asked the price. She answered 7s. He offered her 3s and ran out of the shop with the goods. The court held that D's acts were a felony. Even though the goods were delivered to D by the owner, they weren't out of her possession.

            1. D had <u>physical</u> possession (custody), not <u>LEGAL</u> possession. The owner still had <u>constructive</u> possession.

        iii. ***United States v. Mafnas***: D was employed to deliver money and, on three occasions, opened the bags and removed money. The court held that D's acts constituted larceny. D had <u>custody</u>, not possession, of the bags, and a bailee who "<u>breaks bulk</u>" commits larceny. When D broke open the bags, it was trespassory.

        iv. ***Topolewski v. State***: D planned to steal meat from his employer with Dolan as his accomplice. Dolan got their employer involved and worked to stage a set-up. D picked up meat from the platform, and the person in charge of the platform let him take it (as he'd been instructed to do). The court held that the taking was not trespassory and D was not guilty, as the owner had aided in the commission of the offense by performing some act in the transaction essential to the offense.

            1. The court said that the setting of a trap must not go further than to afford the would-be thief the amplest opportunity to carry out his purpose.

            2. FB: Whether a taking is trespassory has nothing to do with real estate but is instead about whether possession was obtained with the lawful possessor's <u>permission</u>.

        v. ***Rex v. Pear***: D hired a horse from Finch and said he'd return that night. However, he did not return and instead sold the horse that same day. It was proven he'd provided a false address. The court found that D was guilty, as the parting with the property had not changed the nature of the possession, which remained unaltered at the time of conversion.

            1. This type of offense came to be known as "*larceny by trick*."

            2. This deals with a situation where the owner ultimately gives consent to the possession of the object in the beginning, but the object was obtained by result of a misrepresentation and was trespassory from the very beginning.

    vi.   ***Brooks v. State***: Newton lost money, discovered it was missing, and published notice of the loss. D found the package of money, put it in his pocket, spent part of it, and left town. D was convicted of larceny, and it was affirmed, as the property in question could be the subject of larceny.

        1. Rule: When a person finds goods that have actually been lost, and takes possession with intent to appropriate them to his own use, really believing, at the time, or having good ground to believe, that the owner can be found, it is larceny.

        2. FB: At some point, it really is just "finders keepers," but you should at least make reasonable efforts to find the owner.

d. Personal Property of Another:

    i. ***Lund v. Commonwealth***: D was a grad student who required the use of computer operation time and services for the preparation of his dissertation. His faculty advisor neglected to arrange for D's use of the computer, so he used it without obtaining proper authorization. The court found that labor and services and the unauthorized use of the University's computer could not be construed to be subjects of larceny.

    ii. Things which are NOT personalty:

        1. Realty

            a. Crops (unless harvested)

            b. Lumber (unless already chopped, etc.)

            c. Wildlife (unless already killed by owner)

        2. Intangibles

            a. Labor or services

            b. Contractual rights

            c. Securities, bank notes, stocks (although currency IS)

            d. Electricity (although natural gas IS)

e. Mens Rea (With the Intent to Steal the Property):

    i. ***People v. Brown***: D took a bicycle to get even with a boy who threw oranges at him but took the wrong bike. He did not intend to keep it but got caught before he could return it. The court found that D's conviction of burglary could not stand, as felonious intent must be to deprive the owner of the property permanently.

        1. A mere borrowing is not larceny, as one would only intend to temporarily deprive the owner of the thing.

        2. FB: The law requires that the intent to steal be coexistent in time with the taking.

    ii. ***People v. Davis***: D entered a department store, took a shirt, and tried to "return" it. The court found that D's intent to claim ownership of the shirt and to return it to the store only on condition that the store pay him a "refund" constituted larceny, as D showed an intent to permanently deprive the store of the shirt within the meaning of the law of larceny, and his conduct constituted a trespassory taking.

        1. The court says this is like three relevant categories of cases:

            a. D intends to "sell" the property back to its owner

            b. D intends to claim a reward for "finding" the property

            c. D intends to return the property to its owner for a "refund"

    iii. "Continuing Trespass" Doctrine: The initial trespass continues as long as the wrongdoer remains in possession of the property that is the subject of the prosecution.

        1. Fills in gaps in logic

        2. Applies to situations where there was no initial intent to steal.

       iv.   <u>"Claim of Right" Rule</u>: A person is not guilty of theft if she takes and carries away another's property believing that it belongs to the actor or that she has some other legal right to take possession, as the intent to steal is lacking.

           1. Example: Man thinks his missing dog is hooked to a post. He unhooks the dog, its true owner comes out, and he shows the owner his gun. This was NOT armed robbery, as the element of taking the personal property of *another* wasn't intended.

II. **Robbery**

    a. Consists of all SIX LARCENY ELEMENTS, plus:

       i. <u>Property taken from the person or presence of another</u>

       ii.   <u>Taking accomplished by force or fear.</u>

           1. Weapon or excessive force not required

    b. A common law felony that is today a statutory felony, regardless of the amount taken; may be thought of as aggravated larceny.

    c. There must be concurrence of conduct and state of mind, and D's acts of violence or intimidation must occur either <u>before</u> or <u>at</u> the time of taking; if the force is used to retain possession, carry away the property, or resist apprehension, the acts are sufficient.

    d. Earlier cases hold that it is robbery where one strikes another with no intent to steal but then takes the latter's property, but modern cases disagree.

    e. <u>Aggravated Robbery</u>: Most modern robbery statutes distinguish, for purposes of punishment, between simple robbery and aggravated robbery. The most aggravating factors are:

       i. Robber armed with dangerous or deadly weapon

       ii.   Robber used dangerous instrumentality

       iii.   Robber actually inflicted serious bodily injury

       iv.   Robber had an accomplice

    f. **Trespassory**

       i. Victim's consent will negative the trespass

       ii.   The fact that the victim, acting as a decoy, voluntarily enters the robber's den and is robbed there, does not constitute such intent as vitiates the trespass.

    g. **Taking and**

    h. **Carrying away of the**

       i. Robbery under the traditional view requires asportation

       ii.   Modern statutes often reflect the MPC position that asportation is not required for the underlying theft and that it suffices that the theft was merely attempted.

    i. **Personal Property**

       i. May include money and any property which can be taken by larceny.

       ii.   Items which cannot be stolen, like labor or services, cannot be the subject of robbery.

    j. **Of another**

       i. May be one who has possession or custody of property, though he is not the owner.

    k. **With intent to steal it**

       i. Is the same as the intent required for larceny.

       ii.   Can be negated by:

           1. An honest, though mistaken, claim of ownership

           2. An honest, but mistaken, belief that the latter owes him the property being taken

3. An intent to return the property within a reasonable time

4. Intoxication sufficient to make it impossible to entertain the specific intent to rob

5. Perpetrating a practical joke

6. Coercion

iii. Intent to steal need not include an intention to convert the property to one's own use.

l. From the person or presence of the other and

i. The taking must be from the person or presence of the victim as well as from his possession.

ii. Property is on the victim's person if it is in his hand, the pocket of the clothing he wears, or is otherwise attached to his body or his clothing.

iii. A homicide victim is still a "person" within the meaning of the robbery statute, at least when the interval of time between the infliction of the fatal blow and the taking of the property is short.

iv. "Presence" is not so much a matter of eyesight as it is one of proximity and control: the property taken in the robbery must be close enough to the victim and sufficiently under his control that, had the latter not be subjected to violence or intimidation by the robber, he could have prevented the taking.

1. A robber takes property from the victim's presence if he locks or ties the victim up in one room of a building and then helps himself to valuables located in another room of the same building.

2. It would not be robbery to use force or fear to immobilize a property owner at one place while a confederate takes the owner's property from a place several miles away.

v. Most modern robbery statutes do not contain this requirement.

m. Accomplished by means of force or putting in fear (by means of violence or intimidation)

i. *Violence*

1. There is not sufficient force to constitute robbery when the thief snatches property from the owner's grasp so suddenly that the owner cannot offer any resistance to the taking, but when the owner, aware of an impending snatching, resists it, or when, the thief's first attempt being ineffective to separate the owner from his property, a struggle for the property is necessary before the thief can get possession thereof, there is enough force to make the taking robbery.

2. To remove an article of value, attached to the owner's person or clothing, by a sudden snatching or by stealth is not robbery unless the article in question is so attached to the person or his clothes as to require some force to effect its removal.

3. MPC's position is that only an infliction of "serious bodily injury" will suffice, but the modern codes have consistently rejected such a limitation.

4. One may commit robbery by striking his victim with fist or weapon or by rendering his victim helpless by more subtle means (e.g., administering intoxicating liquors or drugs), but one may not commit robbery by hypnotizing his victim.

5. Some require that the taking be by force; some require that the force be used for the purpose of the taking; and some merely require that the force occur "in the course of" the theft.

ii. *Intimidation*

<ol start="1">
<li><u>**1.**</u> The threat of immediate bodily injury may be made to a member of one's family or even to someone in the company.</li>
<li><u>**2.**</u> The threat must be one of IMMEDIATE harm, not future harm.</li>
<li><u>**3.**</u> It is loosely said that the threat may be of injury to the property, but this aspect is limited to a threat to destroy a dwelling house.</li>
<li><u>**4.**</u> There must be a causal connection between D's threat of harm and his acquisition of the victim's property.</li>
<li><u>**5.**</u> The threat of harm must be such as would, under the circumstances, arouse in the victim a reasonable fear of harm, or cause a reasonable man to be apprehensive of harm, or induce a reasonable person to part with his property.</li>
</ol>

<u>**iii.**</u> These elements of violence and intimidation are ALTERNATIVES. There need only be one.

III. Embezzlement

<u>**a.**</u> EMBEZZLEMENT = "The fraudulent conversion of property by a person to whom it was entrusted either by or for the owner."

<u>**i.**</u> A statutory creation designed to deal with holes in common-law larceny

<u>**ii.**</u> Applies to things other than personalty (unlike larceny)

<u>**iii.**</u> One obtains both possession and *title* in embezzlement

<u>**b.**</u> Consists of FIVE ELEMENTS:

<u>**i.**</u> Fraudulent

<u>**ii.**</u> Conversion of

<u>**iii.**</u> The property

<u>**iv.**</u> Of another

<u>**v.**</u> By one who is already in lawful possession of it.

<u>**c.**</u> ***Rex v. Bazeley***: D was a bank teller who received bank-notes and cash from a customer. He credited the customer's account but placed a bank-note in his pocket, which he later appropriated to his own use. The court found that the bank never had constructive possession of the notes, so D was not guilty of larceny. The notes had never been in their custody or control.

<u>**i.**</u> None of the larceny situations fits this case, as the note was obtained with permission, and there's no misrepresentation.

<u>**ii.**</u> After this case, a statute was enacted to protect masters against embezzlement by their servants.

IV. False Pretenses

<u>**a.**</u> FALSE PRETENSES = "Knowingly and designedly obtaining the property of another by means of untrue representations of fact with intent to defraud."

<u>**b.**</u> The crime contains SIX ELEMENTS:

<u>**i.**</u> A false representation of a material present or past fact

<u>**1.**</u> Must actually be false
<u>**2.**</u> Must be of fact, not merely puffery or opinion
<u>**3.**</u> Can be present or past (NOT predictions of future event, etc.)
<u>**4.**</u> Can be written, oral, or physical
<u>**5.**</u> Intent involves two things (at the time the representation is made)
  <u>**a.**</u> KNOWLEDGE of the falsity of the representation
  <u>**b.**</u> An intention to CHEAT
<u>**6.**</u> Victim must actually be deceived or have relied on the representation

ii.   Which causes the victim

iii.   To pass title to his property (not just possession)

iv.   To the wrongdoer

v.   Who knows his representation to be false, and

vi.   Intends thereby to defraud the victim

c. *People v. Whight*: D discovered that the ATM card connected to his default checking account could still be used to obtain cash at local stores and continued to use the card. Safeway, the store at which he used it, treated each transaction as a "stand-in" without verification or approval when a "no response" code was returned. The court held that D's conviction of grand theft by false pretenses could stand, as Safeway relied on D's representation that his card was valid.

     i. CONDUCT can constitute an implied false representation.

     ii.   This case illustrates the reliance component of the false pretenses crime.

V. Federal Mail, Wire, and Computer Fraud

a. Mail Fraud, 18 U.S.C. §1341: " Whoever, ***having devised or intending to devise any scheme or artifice to defraud***, or for obtaining money or property by means of false or fraudulent pretenses, representations, or promises…**for the purpose of executing such scheme or artifice or <u>attempting</u> so to do,** <u>places</u> in any *post office* or authorized depository for mail matter, any matter or thing whatever…<u>or deposits or causes to be deposited</u> any matter or thing whatever to be sent or delivered by any *private or commercial interstate carrier…*shall be [punished]."

     i. Congress was given power to govern mail by Constitution.

     ii.   The essence of the crime is devising a scheme to or artifice defraud, which is very broad and has been used to reach all types of activity (from promising to send the elderly money and not doing it to depriving people of the honest services of various officials).

b. Wire Fraud, 18 U.S.C. §1343: "Whoever, having devised or intending to devise any scheme or artifice to defraud, or for obtaining money or property by means of false or fraudulent pretenses, representations, or promises, **transmits or causes to be transmitted by means of wire, radio, or television communication in interstate or foreign commerce** any writings, signs, signals pictures, or sounds *for the purpose of executing such scheme or artifice*, shall be fined…or imprisoned..."

c. 18 U.S.C. §1346 - Honest Services Statute: For purposes of this Chapter, the term "scheme or artifice to defraud" includes a scheme or artifice to deprive another of the intangible right of honest services.

d. *United States v. Czubinski*: D was employed by the IRS and was able to retrieve income tax return information regarding virtually any taxpayer, but he was permitted from doing so outside the course of his official duties. D carried out numerous unauthorized searches of files but did not do anything other than observe the confidential information he accessed. The court found that the government failed to prove beyond a reasonable doubt that D willingly participated in a scheme to defraud within the meaning of the wire fraud statute. There was no evidence that D did anything more than mere browsing.

e. Points to Remember About Mail & Wire Fraud:

     i. The "unit of prosecution" = each mailing or wiring in furtherance of the scheme. (If you have 58 units of mail, you can have 58 counts.)

     ii.   Mailing or wiring need not contain fraudulent information. May be entirely innocent.

     iii.   D need not mail or wire something himself; it is sufficient that he causes it to happen OR that mailing or wiring could reasonably be foreseen as a result of or in the course of the scheme.

    iv.   Mailings may be local. Wirings must be interstate or foreign.

    v.   D must know or be able reasonably to foresee that interstate wiring(s) would occur and

        1.   Gov't. must show that such interstate wiring(s) did occur.

        2.   Gov't. need not show that D knew or foresaw they'd be interstate.

DEFENSES TO CRIME: JUSTIFICATION AND EXCUSES

I. Generally

    a. "Defense" = any set of identifiable conditions or circumstances which may prevent a conviction for an offense.

        i. *Failure of proof defenses* = instances in which, because of the conditions that are the basis for the "defense," all elements of the offense charged cannot be proven (i.e., mistake)

        ii.   *Offense modification defenses* = real defenses in the sense that they do more than simply negate the elements of the offense and apply even where all the elements of the offense are satisfied (i.e., even where elements are satisfied, actor hasn't caused the harm the statute meant to prevent)

        iii.   *Justifications* = Not alterations of the statutory definition of the harm sought to be prevented or punished by an offense. Harm caused remains a legally recognized harm which is to be avoided whenever possible; However, under special justifying circumstances, that harm is outweighed by the need to avoid an even greater harm or to further a greater societal interest. (e.g., Setting fire to a field located between a forest fire and the town is arson, but it serves as a fire break and saves 10,000 lives.)

        iv.   *Excuses* = Defenses applicable to all offenses even though the elements of the offense are satisfied. Admit that the deed may be wrong, but excuse the actor because conditions suggest that the actor is not responsible for his deed.

        v.   *Nonexculpatory public policy defenses*: Statute of limitations may bar a man's conviction for robbery despite his clear culpability because by foregoing that conviction society furthers other, more important, public interests. Other public policy-based bars to prosecution include diplomatic immunity, judicial, legislative, and executive immunities, and incompetency.

    b. *Patterson v. New York*: D shot and killed a man after seeing him through the window of his father-in-law's house with his wife in a state of semi-undress. In determining whether NY's allocation to D of proving the mitigating circumstances of severe emotional disturbance in a second-degree murder trial is consistent with due process, the court held that D's conviction under NY law did not deprive him of due process of law and declined to adopt as a constitutional imperative that a state must disprove beyond a reasonable doubt every fact constituting any and all affirmative defenses related to the culpability of the accused.

        i. At common law, D had to prove that the killing occurred in a heat of passion, while the government had to prove malice aforethought.

        ii.   *Winship* established the basic principle that the government has the burden of proving beyond a reasonable doubt every basic element of a crime, as that burden is a critical element of due process for the purpose of criminal cases.

        iii.   In ME, *Mullaney v. Wilbur* held that its statute was inconsistent with *Winship* and shifted an affirmative obligation of disproving one of the elements to the defendant, making it unconstitutional; however, in ME's statute, absence of heat of passion is an element (unlike in NY).

    iv. The effect of both statutes is the same, as D must prove heat of passion if he doesn't want to be convicted of murder.

II. Self-defense

    a. Use of deadly force is justifiable when:

        i. There is a threat, either actual or apparent, of the use of deadly force against the defendant;

        ii. The threat must be unlawful (possibly also if you perceive it's unlawful, but not when you're under "attack" from police officers, etc.)

        iii. The threat is *immediate*;

        iv. Defendant must believe that his use of deadly force is necessary to save himself from the threat;

        v. Defendant's beliefs (both in his imminent peril and in the necessity of deadly force) must be objectively reasonable.

    b. Caveats:

        i. Self-defense not available to the "aggressor."

        ii. It may sometimes be available to defend against rape or kidnapping, even if all the above requirements aren't completely satisfied.

        iii. Depending on the state, there may be an obligation to retreat, if it can be done safely. (Obligation to retreat is more prevalent in the east.)

    c. *United States v. Peterson*: Three guys drove to the alley behind D's house to remove the windshield wipers from his wrecked car. After a verbal exchange, D went to obtain a pistol from in the house, loaded it, and shouted to V, who got out of his car, yelled at D, and got a lug wrench. When he advanced toward D, D shot him (after warning him not to take another step). In considering whether the jury should have been instructed to consider whether D was the aggressor in the altercation that preceded the homicide in determining whether he had the right to use deadly force in self-defense, the court determined that the evidence plainly presented an issue of fact as to whether D's conduct was an invitation to and provocation of the encounter which ended in the fatal shot, and the trial judge's action in remitting that issue for the jury's determination is sustained. In considering whether D was required to endeavor to retreat, if he could have done so, from D's approach with the lug wrench, the court held that, although the doctrine of retreat has never required a faultless victim to increase his assailant's safety at the expense of his own by retreating, D wasn't faultless here. The "castle doctrine" can also only be invoked by one who is faultless.

        i. Although D probably could have proven the elements, there's an issue of provocation here. If the justification for self-defense is necessity, it's hard to say that it was necessary for one who created the threat.

        ii. The court talks about *Laney*, where a man was convicted after failing to evade a mob. FB thinks that decision was ridiculous.

    d. *People v. Goetz*: Four youths were on a subway with screwdrivers. D was on the subway with a loaded, unlicensed pistol. One or two of the youths approached D and stated, "Give me five dollars." D fired four shots in rapid succession, striking three of the youths. He surveyed the scene and then fired another shot at the fourth (after saying, "You seem to be alright, here's another"). In determining whether the test for justification of deadly force to protect a person should be subjective or objective, the court held that the reasonableness requirement retained by the legislature requires an objective test.

        i. NY statute expands the list of felonies to which you can respond with deadly force to include robbery. This might not entirely have solved D's "problem," as we're not certain a reasonable person in his situation would have believed he was about to be robbed. Also, he must believe the *use* of deadly force is necessary (not that pulling out the gun would prevent it).

<u>**ii.**</u>　　It's tough to justify the fifth bullet, but the NY jury acquitted him of every charge except carrying a firearm.

<u>**iii.**</u>　　The jury was allowed to take his previous experiences of being mugged into account, but they also had to consider everything else.

<u>**e.**</u> One negative implication of the reasonable-belief rule is that a person who acts on the basis of a genuine, but *unreasonable*, belief that deadly force is necessary for self-protection cannot successfully claim self-defense. Many states recognize "imperfect"/"incomplete" justification defenses where one harbors a genuine (but unreasonable) belief or uses deadly force in response to a non-deadly threat.

<u>**f.**</u> ***State v. Wanrow***: D's children were at Hooper's home when one of them came inside and told her that a man tried to pull him off his bicycle and drag him into his house. The man came to the house to say he didn't touch the kid, and Hooper's daughter confessed that he was the man who'd molested her months earlier. When Hooper called the police, they said she needed to "swear out a warrant," and they wouldn't arrest him until Monday. She'd noticed someone prowling around her house at night, so she called D and others to stay with her. D's brother-in-law went to V's house, and V then returned to the residence with him to get things "straightened out." When he entered the house, D (5'4", on crutches) shot him after he startled her (and had approached a child). In considering whether the instructions to the jury regarding self defense were erroneous in that they excluded circumstances predating the killing and stated that one who was met with a naked-hands assault was prevented from using a deadly weapon in a deadly manner, the court held that the instructions were erroneous, as circumstances predating the killing were deemed essential to a proper disposition of the claim of self-defense, and the language utilized suggested that D's conduct must be measured against that of a reasonable male individual finding himself in the same circumstances.

<u>**i.**</u> FB thinks they had to work pretty hard to find the first error in the instructions, although the major point is that you can take information into account other than that which you obtained at the moment at which you decided to kill.

<u>**ii.**</u>　　FB doesn't buy the second argument either, although it does raise an issue as to whether the self-defense requirements should apply differently to people of different genders.

<u>**g.**</u> ***State v. Norman***: D and V had been married for 25 years, and V had begun to drink and beat D five years after they were married. He forced her to prostitute herself, told others he'd kill her, and abused her in other ways. After a particularly violent series of events over a two-day period, during which a police officer was dispatched twice to D and V's home, D shot V while he was napping. At trial, D testified that she didn't leave V, take out a warrant, or have him committed, because she believed he'd kill her, and two expert witnesses testified that D suffered from abused spouse syndrome. In determining whether the victim's passiveness at the moment the criminal act occurred precludes her from asserting self-defense, the court held that the evidence was sufficient to submit an issue of self-defense to the jury, and a jury could find that D merely took advantage of her first opportunity to protect herself and did not use more force than necessary to protect herself from death or great bodily harm. On appeal from a new trial, the court held that the evidence introduced in this case wouldn't support a finding that D killed her husband due to a reasonable fear of imminent death or great bodily harm, as is required before a defendant is entitled to jury instructions concerning self-defense.

<u>**i.**</u> The legal requirement of *imminence* is most at issue here.

ii. Recently, courts have been more receptive to the idea that, in determining immediacy, the nature of domestic violence should be taken into account.

h. Battered Woman's Syndrome:

i. Cases may be divided into three categories: confrontational homicides, near confrontational homicides, and cases in which the woman hires a third party or plots with a relative to kill the batterer.

ii. Syndrome evidence, according to Morse, may be relevant to an objectively reasonable assessment of the need to use deadly force, as it may dispel myths or correct seemingly sensible but erroneous inferences that might affect assessment, and battering syndrome sufferers may be especially acute observers of cues that presage imminent violence from the abuser. The law is simply taking advantage of fresh evidence to apply old doctrine.

III. Necessity

a. *Nelson v. State*: D got his truck stuck. In determining whether the jury had been properly instructed on the defense of necessity, the court held that the instruction given adequately describes the requirements of necessity for the jury, and D failed to prove the elements anyway, as his fears about damage to his truck roof were no justification for his appropriation of sophisticated and expensive equipment.

i. Judge instructed the jury that the necessity defense was only available when 1) natural forces create a situation; 2) the harm to be avoided is greater harm (than the harm caused in violating the law); 3) the harm to be avoided is immediate and dire; and 4) No reasonable alternative other than violating the law is available.

ii. AK Sup. Ct. added: Necessity is available based on the actor's reasonable belief about the situation, and actions should be weighed against what was reasonably foreseeable, rather than what actually happened.

b. *The Queen v. Dudley and Stephens*: Four men were stranded at sea without much food, and Dudley and Stephens thought they should sacrifice one to save the rest. One man dissented, but the other two decided to kill the young boy. They did so, and the three fed upon him for four days until they were rescued. In a trial for murder, the court held that D's act was willful murder, and the facts as stated are no legal justification for the homicide.

i. The jury wasn't allowed to render a verdict, just to find facts.

ii. Panel of judges said necessity defense didn't exist in England at the time.

c. *United States v. Schoon*: D's gained admittance to the IRS office in Tuscon, where they chanted ("Keep America's tax dollars out of El Salvador!" and splashed simulated blood everyone. The court held that the necessity defense is inapplicable to cases involving indirect civil disobedience.

IV. Duress

a. Duress: The General American Rule:

i. Duress does not excuse the killing of an innocent person.

ii. For lesser crimes than murder, duress may be a defense if the coercion was:

1. Present, imminent, and impending

2. Fear of death or serious bodily injury

3. Well-grounded

4. And if there was no reasonable opportunity to avoid doing the crime without undue exposure to death or serious bodily injury.

b. *United States v. Contento-Pachon*: Jorge proposed that D swallow cocaine-filled balloons and transport them to the United States. Jorge said that failure to cooperate would result in the death of D's wife and child, and D was informed he'd be watched at all times during the trip. In determining whether the defenses of duress and necessity were applicable, the court held that D presented credible evidence that he acted under an immediate and well-grounded threat of serious bodily injury with no opportunity to escape, so the defense of duress should have been presented (but it was correct to disallow use of the necessity defense).

> i. Note: The threat need not be one of serious bodily injury to oneself.
> ii. Dissent says there was a lack of immediacy and an opportunity to escape.
> iii. Some courts require an additional element in cases involving drug circles, which states that D didn't place himself in the situation. Otherwise, they could always say, "Jorge made me do it."

c. *People v. Unger*: D was assaulted and molested by inmates at an honor farm. Five days later, he got a call on an institution telephone threatening him with death, because the caller had heard that D had reported the assault to prison authorities. D left on that day and said he planned to return once he found someone who could help him. The court held that D's testimony was sufficient to raise the affirmative defense of necessity.

> i. Prison cases usually require D to report himself to the authorities.
> ii. FB has found that courts take somewhat lenient approaches to these types of claims, although many courts are not favorable to the necessity defense in prison escape situations.

d. *People v. Anderson*: D and others suspected V of molesting two girls who resided in a camp, and one of the girl's fathers allegedly told D that he'd "beat the shit out of [him]" if he failed to help kill V. In determining whether duress is a defense to murder, the court held that duress is not a defense to any form of murder. In determining whether duress can reduce murder to a lesser crime, the court held that a new form of voluntary manslaughter should not be created for duress. A malicious, premeditated killing, even under duress, is first degree murder.

V. **Competence to stand trial**

a. Generally:

> i. Incompetence is not a "defense" to criminal charges. It is only a decision about whether D is able to participate in the trial of criminal charges.
> ii. The focus of a competency determination is on the D's mental state *at the time of trial, not at the time of the offense.*
> iii. The test of whether D is competent to stand trial is if:
> > 1. He is oriented as to time and place and has a rational understanding of the nature of the proceedings (*Dusky v. U.S.*), and
> > 2. He is able to consult with his own attorney "with a reasonable degree of rational understanding" (*Dusky*) and to assist in his own defense.
> iv. The sticking point is often the *degree* to which the D is able to assist in his defense. Some courts say a D should be able to assist with trial *strategy*; others say that is not required.
> v. The practical result of a finding of incompetence is usually "hospitalization."
> > 1. The Supreme Court says that an incompetent D "cannot be held more than the reasonable period of time necessary to determine whether" he can be restored to competence "in the foreseeable future." (*Jackson v. Indiana*).
> > 2. If restoration of competence is improbable, gov't. must use civil commitment procedures (Which usually turn on dangerousness or need for care or treatment).

b. *Pate v. Robinson*: D had a long history of disturbed behavior and had shot and killed his 18-month-old son after spending time in the state mental hospital. His mother had sworn out a warrant for his arrest and made multiple complaints to the authorities. One day, he went to the restaurant where his live-in-girlfriend was working and shot her. In determining whether D was entitled to a hearing on the issue of competence, the Supreme Court said that, where the evidence raises a bona fide doubt as to a defendant's competence to stand trial, the judge on his own motion must impanel a jury and conduct a sanity hearing.

> **i.** D's lawyers say he was insane at both the time of the murder and trial, but state says that Haines would testify that D knew the nature of the charges against him and was able to cooperate with counsel when he examined him two or three months before trial (although court didn't permit them to get additional evidence regarding his opinion).
>
> **ii.** Even if D's did raise the issue of incompetency, they stipulated to the testimony of Dr. Haines. Otherwise, it can be said D waived the issue when his lawyers didn't bring it up (although the court says it's contradictory that an incompetent person could waive an issue).
>
> **iii.** Competence to stand trial is different from insanity.
>
> > **1.** There's a difference in timing.
> >
> > **2.** There's a different standard to be applied.
>
> **iv.** D is entitled to a legal determination of BOTH issues, so long as there are facts sufficient to merit the inquiry.
>
> **v.** If D's lawyers ask for a competency hearing, D's entitled to one.
>
> **vi.** The trial court has some independent obligation to initiate a competency inquiry if the facts suggest it, even if there is no such request from either party.
>
> **vii.** FB doesn't think the district court made ANY error.
>
> **viii.** Also, saying D "waived" the issue of incompetence is wrong, because INCOMPTENCE IS NOT A DEFENSE (unlike insanity).

c. *Jackson v. Indiana*: D is deaf, mute, and mentally retarded. After a court-appointed hearing, D was found incompetent and committed until restored to competency. The Supreme Court held that by subjecting D to a more lenient commitment standard and to a more stringent standard of release than those generally applicable to all others not charged with offenses, and by thus condemning him in effect to permanent institutionalization without the showing required for commitment or the opportunity for release, Indiana deprived D of equal protection of the laws under the Fourteenth Amendment. Furthermore, Indiana's indefinite commitment of a criminal defendant solely on account of his incompetency to stand trial does not square with the Fourteenth Amendment's guarantee of due process.

> **i.** It appears D will never be competent, so he'd just be incarcerated forever.
>
> **ii.** A state can commit a person indefinitely, but it must be done civilly by a set of procedures.
>
> **iii.** He hasn't been convicted, so we can't commit him criminally.
>
> **iv.** Court doesn't say how long he can be held while his competence is in question; they just note that there IS a limit.

VI. Insanity

> **a. Generally:**
>
> > **i.** *Insanity* is a "defense." Whereas a finding of "incompetence" means only that the gov't. cannot try D, a finding of "insanity" means exoneration from criminal

liability.

    ii.   <u>Assertion of the Insanity Plea:</u>

        1. D must often assert a special plea rather than or in conjunction with the general plea of "not guilty."

        2. Insanity is an affirmative defense

            a. Until the 1980s, most jurisdictions required the prosecutor to carry the burden of proof regarding D's sanity

            b. Today, a majority of states place the burden of persuasion on D.

        3. If issue isn't raised, D is presumed to be sane.

    iii. If the moral justification for imposing penalties for crime rests on the supposition that we have free will, or the capacity to choose between good and evil, and it is on the exercise of that choice to do bad rather than good on which the right to punish rests, we shouldn't punish those who lack the capacity to make the choice on which moral punishment rests.

    iv. <u>Catch 22:</u> Those who are deemed insane might be found not guilty by reason of insanity, but they are still going to be in a locked room in a building (albeit in a different one with a different name).

    v. The time focus for insanity is the TIME OF THE CRIMINAL CONDUCT.

    vi. There are at least <u>three types of mental illnesses:</u>

        1. A failure to appreciate the nature of the conduct

        2. A failure to appreciate the difference between right and wrong

        3. An inability to control one's actions

b. **M'Naghten Rule**

    i. ***Daniel M'Naghten's Case***: D thought Peel, the head of the British police force, was the head of a conspiracy trying to kill him. He shot one of Peel's aids, thinking he was shooting Peel. He gets off originally, but the charge is later reversed.

    ii. <u>Prong I:</u>

        1. <u>At the time</u> of the criminal act

        2. D was laboring under such a <u>defect of *reason*</u>

        3. From *disease of the mind* (not drunkenness, etc.)

        4. As to not know the *nature and quality* of the act; OR

    iii. <u>Prong II:</u>

        1. If he did know it [the nature and quality of the act],

        2. He <u>did not know it was wrong</u>.

    iv. <u>Comments/Explanation:</u>

        1. Prong I is about capacity to perceive reality.

            a. Implies an organic condition, not a self-induced one

            b. The delusion must be relevant

        2. Prong II is about moral sense.

            a. "Wrong" means something D knew "he ought not to do."

            b. It does not mean knowledge of illegality.

    v. <u>What did people find wrong with the M'Naghten Rule?</u>

        1. Problem with being able to say whether someone knows if something is right or wrong.

        2. Medical people were being asked to give legal opinions

        3. It doesn't include anything about impulse control…

c. **"Irresistible Impulse" (a.k.a. "control" test)** (*Parsons v. State*)

    i. At the time of the crime, D suffered from a disease of the mind "so as to be either idiotic, or otherwise insane";

      ii.   If D was insane, did the insanity prevent him from knowing right from wrong "as applied to the particular [criminal] act"? <u>OR</u>

      iii.   Even if D knew right from wrong:

          1. Had the mental disease deprived D of the *power to choose* not to do the wrongful act?

          2. Was the mental disease the sole cause of the wrongful act?

      iv.   <u>Comments/Explanation:</u>

          1. The *M'Naghten* rule is about "capacity for intellectual discrimination," i.e., the ability to perceive the physical world accurately and to make basic moral judgments. It was criticized because it failed to account for persons who accurately perceive physical reality and can distinguish right and wrong, but who are said to be unable to control themselves.

          2. How far down the road to extreme determinism does "irresistible impulse" take us?

  d. **The "Product" Test** (*Durham v. U.S.*)

      i. Excuses D's from criminal liability whose acts "were the product of a mental disease or defect."

      ii.   Comments:

          1. This formula eliminates the "sole cause" requirement of "irresistible impulse."

          2. The "product test" also eliminates the requirement that D be deprived of the "power to choose." It suggests that so long as the mental disease *affected* the choice between good and evil, it may be sufficient for exoneration.

          3. How far down the road to complete determinism would this take us?

          4. Criticized for giving too much deference to medical expert

  e. **Model Penal Code**

      i. At the time of the conduct

      ii.   The D as a result of mental disease or defect (not alcohol)

      iii.   Lacks <u>substantial capacity</u> either:

          1. To *appreciate the criminality of his conduct*

          2. Or to *conform his conduct to the requirements of the law.*

      iv.   <u>Comments:</u> The MPC differs from the "product" test only in degree. It attempts to ensure that the mental condition was a major ("substantial") factor in the defendant's choice to do wrong. Of course, this sort of wording leaves considerable room for interpretation by judges and juries.

  f. <u>**18 U.S.C. §17: Insanity Defense**</u>

      i. Affirmative Defense – It is an affirmative defense to a prosecution under any Federal statute that, at the time of the commission of the acts constituting the offense, the defendant, as a result of a severe mental disease or defect, was unable to appreciate the nature and quality or the wrongfulness of his acts. Mental disease or defect does not otherwise constitute a defense.

      ii.   Burden of proof – The defendant has the burden of proving the defense of insanity by clear and convincing evidence.

  g. *State v. Green*: D thought people in NY were talking to him, sending messages to his brain, and "directing him" and that a machine called an "ousiograph" could detect these matters. He shot a police officer and put a note on his back addressed to an FBI agent and containing reference to an "ousiograph." D had a prolonged history of psychiatric issues. At trial, experts testified that D was delusional and a paranoid schizophrenic, but the state's witnesses testified that they didn't notice anything out of the ordinary when they encountered D. When he was eventually found competent to stand trial, the court held that the state's rebuttal evidence was not sufficient to refute the overwhelming proof of D's insanity, because although the acts of D at or near the time of the killing were arguably "consistent with sanity," they were not "inconsistent with insanity."

    i. FB: Evidence presented might have been enough to show he didn't meet the MPC standard for insanity, but it's strange that the state couldn't find even one person to come in and say he's sane.

h. Other General Points:

    i. Sup. Ct. held that D who raises psychiatric-related defense has right to a psychiatric exam (not a private prof., though), assuming he's indigent.

    ii. Sup. Ct. said you can't execute someone who doesn't understand why he's being executed, although medication is allowed.

    iii. If you're found NGRI but determined to be sane at the time of the trial, the court has no jurisdiction to monitor you afterwards.

VII. Diminished capacity

a. Doctrine allows a criminal defendant to introduce evidence of mental abnormality at trial either to negate a mental element of the crime charged or to reduce the degree of the crime of which he may be convicted.

b. How Do We Treat People Who are Mentally Ill but not Insane?

    i. Allow evidence relevant to the existence of the mental state required for conviction (at all phases)

        1. Some jurisdictions say it's only admissible to negate *specific* intent crimes (not general intent crimes, anything other than purposeful)

    ii. Any mental evidence short of insanity could be allowed to reduce the degree of the offense (mitigation)

    iii. We could exclude this evidence at the guilt phase of the trial altogether but allow it in at sentencing

    iv. We could completely exclude the evidence and say that if you're legally sane you're getting convicted and punished (allow nothing at all).

c. Federal law doesn't recognize diminished capacity as a defense, but it is recognized as a factor in mitigating sentencing.

    i. Only applies when D is suffering from "significantly reduced" mental capacity

    ii. Doesn't cover voluntary use of drugs or intoxicants

    iii. Doesn't apply to violent crimes

    iv. If D's history indicates a need to incarcerate D to protect the public, it doesn't matter.

d. *Clark v. Arizona*: D (17) thought his town was populated with aliens, and he shot a cop when pulled over for playing his music loudly while driving his truck around. A psychiatrist testified that D was from paranoid schizophrenia with delusions when he shot the cop. D was found incompetent to stand trial and committed for two years, after which he was found restored to competency and ordered to be tried. A verdict of first-degree murder was issued (as he's being charged with knowingly killing a police officer). Trial court denied D's motion for j.n.o.v. grounded on failure of prosecution to show that D knew the victim was a police officer. D moved to vacate the judgment arguing that AZ is violating his due process rights.

    i. Issue – Whether due process prohibits AZ's use of an insanity test stated solely in terms of the capacity to tell whether an act charged as a crime was right or wrong, and whether AZ violates due process in restricting consideration of defense evidence of mental illness and incapacity to its bearing on a claim of insanity, thus eliminating its significance directly on the issue of the mental element of the crime charged.

ii. Holding – There was no violation of due process, as the reasons for requiring the evidence to be channeled and restricted are good enough to satisfy the standard of fundamental fairness required by the process.

iii. FB: AZ basically says that if you're not straight-up insane by their definition, you can't introduce evidence of mental disease or defect to negate mental state or for other purposes. You're either legally insane (and exonerated), or you only get evidence to come in on narrow grounds in order to negate mens rea or mitigate liability.

iv. On one hand, AZ has defined insanity and shouldn't have to allow evidence that doesn't rise to that level; on the other hand, the observational evidence may relate directly to the other evidence, and it's hard to distinguish between the two.

VIII. Intoxication
a. Voluntary

i. Treatment of intoxication is similar to that of diminished capacity.

ii. Approaches:

1. Some jurisdictions say evidence isn't admissible to show presence or absence of mental states, and D will be treated the same regardless of whether he's drunk or not.
2. Others say evidence can be allowed to negate specific intent.
3. Some say it can only be admitted to mitigate serious offenses (i.e., homicide).

iii. *Montana v. Egelhoff*: Montana says intoxication isn't a defense, and the Supreme Court says excluding such evidence was okay, even if some argued that it spoke directly to the mental state.

1. Dissenters said whether or not someone is intoxicated is plainly relevant to mental state, so due process demands evidence.
2. Scalia (4-person plurality) says it's an evidentiary rule that is allowable, so the state can make the policy choice.
3. Ginsberg (1-person plurality) says the Montana legislature has the ability to exclude drunkenness as a defense.

iv. ***Commonwealth v. Graves***: D and his cousins, pursuant to a prior conceived plan, burglarized the residence of a 75-year-old man and robbed him. At trial, D testified he had consumed wine and taken LSD on the day of the incident. He said he had no recollection of the occurrence. On appeal from a conviction for first degree murder, robbery, and burglary, the court held that it was error to refuse to permit evidence and to charge the jury as to the possible effect of D's consumption of alcohol and ingestion of drugs upon his capacity to form the requisite intent required in the charges of robbery and burglary.

1. Dissent: The end result of allowing intoxication to bear on one element of the defense is the same as allowing a complete defense. It has long been held that voluntary intoxication neither exonerates nor excuses a person from his criminal acts.

v. SEE MPC 2.08

vi. Some jurisdictions recognize "settled insanity" in cases of long-term use.

b. Involuntary

       i. Successful claims of this sort are rare.

       ii.   Four different kinds of involuntary intoxication have been recognized:

          1. Coerced intoxication (involuntary induced by reason of duress or coercion)

          2. Pathological intoxication (grossly excessive in degree, given the amount of the intoxicant, to which the actor does not know he is susceptible)

          3. Intoxication by innocent mistake (resulting from an innocent mistake by D about the character of the substance taken, as when another person has tricked him into taking the liquor or drugs)

          4. Unexpected intoxication resulting from the ingestion of a medically prescribed drug.

       iii.   Exculpates in two ways:

          1. Entitles individual to acquittal if he doesn't form the mens rea for the offense as a result of the condition.

          2. If rendered "temporarily insane," individual is entitled to acquittal of any offense.

ATTEMPT CRIMES (& Assault)

I. Generally

    f. **MPC 5.01 – Criminal Attempt:** A person is guilty of an attempt to commit a crime if, **acting with the kind of culpability otherwise required for commission of the crime,** he:

       i. **Purposely engages in conduct** that would constitute the crime if the attendant circumstances were as he believes them to be; or

       ii.   **When causing a particular result is an element of the crime,** does or omits to do anything with the **purpose of causing or with the belief that it will cause such result** without further conduct on his part; or

       iii.   Purposely does or omits to do anything which, under the circumstances as he believes them to be, is an act or omission constituting a substantial step in a course of conduct planned to culminate in his commission of the crime.

    g. **Policy:**

       i. When is it okay for the law to intervene? We have a balancing problem.

       ii.   We don't want to punish thought crimes, so we want to make sure the person is well on the way to committing the harm.

       iii.   We also don't want to let things escalate to the point at which the act actually occurs, so we want to intervene in time to prevent possible crimes.

       iv.   We may conclude that people who have both had bad thoughts and engaged in a certain amount of planning activity are dangerous to the community and can justifiably be punished.

VI. Mental State

    a. Generally:

       i. D must intend to cause the prohibited result OR

       ii.   D must have CMS required for completed crime, *and* D must have intentionally engaged in the conduct constituting the substantial step.

    b. ***People v. Gentry***: D and his girlfriend were arguing, and D spilled gasoline on her. It ignited, and she was severely burned, despite D smothering the flames with a coat. The girlfriend testified that the gasoline had only ignited after she'd gone near the stove in the kitchen. In deciding whether the trial court erred in including all culpable mental states for murder in its definition of attempt murder, the court found that the jury was misinstructed, as only the specific intent to kill satisfies the intent element of the crime of attempt murder.

> **i.** If D had actually killed, the mental state would be different, as intent to cause great bodily harm, knowledge would substantial certainty that death would occur, etc. would suffice.
>
> **ii.** The usual rule is that D can't be found guilty of an attempt to commit a crime unless he was actually intending to cause the prohibited result.
>
> **iii.** Under the MPC provision above, (b) could be read more liberally, and D might have been convicted.

c. ***Bruce v. State***: Three men entered V's shoe store. D, masked and armed with a handgun, demanded that V open the cash register and, when V said it was empty, he aimed the gun at his head and said he was going to kill him. When V "banged into" D, he shot him. On D's appeal of a conviction of attempted first degree felony murder, the court found that attempted felony murder is not a crime in Maryland.

> **i.** Conviction of felony murder requires no specific intent to kill, but a criminal attempt is a specific intent crime.
>
> **ii.** An attempt at an intentional killing may form the basis of a crime, but an unintentional killing may not form the basis of a criminal conviction for attempt.

VII. Act – Six Possible Tests
a. The "Last Act" Test

> **i.** D must have done everything that he believes necessary to bring about the criminal result (probably the most restrictive test)
>
> **ii.** ***Commonwealth v. Peaslee***: D constructed and arranged combustibles in a building in such a way that they were ready to be lighted, and if lighted would have set fire to the building and its contents. D offered to pay a man to carry out the plan, but he refused. Later, D and the man drove toward the building, but when they were a quarter of a mile away, D said that he had changed his mind and drove away. The court found that D could not be held liable for attempt to burn a building.
>
> > **1.** Holmes: "Mere preparation" is not enough, even though the mental state had been formed, and some steps had been taken.
> >
> > **2.** D needed to have set events in motion where the act would happen, barring the occurrence of some unforeseen event.

b. The "Dangerous Proximity" Test

> **i.** Focuses upon what D has done and how close he thereby came to succeeding in his criminal objective
>
> **ii.** ***People v. Rizzo***: D and 3 others planned to rob a man while he was carrying a payroll from a bank. They drove around and went to the bank from which he was supposed to get the money. They were arrested as D jumped out of the car and ran into the building, although they hadn't found or seen the man they intended to rob. The court found that D's acts did not constitute a crime. They had made plans and were looking for an opportunity, but it never came, as they never even found the man.
>
> > **1.** Rule: There must be dangerous proximity to success.
> >
> > **2.** FB can think of no modern court that would find an attempt here.

c. The "Indispensible Element" Test

> **i.** Focuses instead upon what remains to be done in order to accomplish the criminal objective

236

d. **The "Probable Desistance" test**

    i. A judgment must be made as to whether D had reached a point where it was unlikely he would thereafter abandon his efforts to achieve the criminal objective

e. **The "Equivocality" Test**

    i. Question is whether D's actions manifest the intent to achieve the criminal objective (without considering any statements made)

    ii. *People v. Miller*: D, drunk and carrying a gun, came to the hop field where Jeans was working. He walked toward Jeans' boss, stopped, and appeared to be loading his rifle. After Jeans fled, his boss took the gun, which was found to be loaded. The court found that D's acts did not constitute an attempt to commit murder.

        1. Rule: Whenever the design of a person to commit a crime is clearly shown, slight acts done in furtherance of this design will constitute an attempt.

        2. Up to the moment the gun was taken from D, no one could say with certainty whether he had come to carry out his threat to kill Jeans or for some other reason.

f. **The "Substantial Step" Test**

    i. D's acts must be strongly corroborative of his criminal purpose

        1. Has been adopted by the MPC

        2. Is probably the majority test, to the extent there is one

        3. "Substantial step" is a more expansive reading of the act requirement, allowing more people to be convicted.

    ii. *State v. Reeves*: Two 12-year-old girls spoke on the phone and decided to kill their homeroom teacher. One of them brought rat poison to school, and they planned to steal their teacher's car after killing her. After one girl told another of their plan, she told her teacher, who told the principal. D's purse, containing the rat poison, was lying next to the teacher's coffee cup on her desk when the teacher came into the room. On appeal, the court found that the jury was justified in finding D guilty, as the issue of whether D's conduct constitutes a substantial step is one for the jury.

        1. Rule: When an actor possesses materials to be used in the commission of a crime, at or near the scene of the crime, and where the possession of those materials can serve no lawful purpose of the actor under the circumstances, the jury is entitled, but not required, to find that the actor has taken a "substantial step" toward the commission of the crime if such action is strongly corroborative of the actor's overall criminal purpose.

VIII. Punishing Pre-Attempt Conduct

a. In recent years, legislatures have sought to criminalize a broader range of threatening but pre-attempt conduct (even entering the realm of "virtual" threats).

b. *United States v. Alkhabaz*: Two men exchanged email messages over the Internet, the content of which expressed a sexual interest in violence against women and girls. One man posted a story describing the torture, rape, and murder of a woman who shared the name of one of his classmates at the University of Michigan. He was charged with violating 18 U.S.C. § 875(c), under which a communication containing a threat must be proven. The court held that the communications did not constitute a threat, as threats must be employed to have some effect, or achieve some goal, through intimidation.

c. *Stalking* = the willful, malicious and repeated following and harassing of another person; a course of conduct directed at a specific person that involved repeated visual or physical proximity, nonconsensual communication, or verbal, written or implied threats (or a combination) that would cause a reasonable person fear.

d. *Luring* is an inchoate offense, and one could be convicted of a *double* inchoate offense if he were convicted of something like *attempting* to lure a child into a car, presumably with the intent to commit some further harm.

IX. Defenses

a. Impossibility

i. Factual impossibility is not a defense

ii. Legal impossibility can be a defense

iii. Test: If the defendant had completed the course of conduct he intended, and if the facts were *as he believed them to be*, was a crime committed?

iv. *People v. Thousand*: A deputy posed as a 14-year-old girl on the Internet, and D approached him in a chat room. The conversations became sexually explicit, and D sent "Bekka" a picture of male genitalia and invited her to come see him at his house for the purpose of engaging in sexual activity. The two planned to meet, and D was apprehended at the location they decided upon. The court held that "legal impossibility" was not a defense, as the nonexistence of a minor victim does not give rise to a viable defense to the attempt charge in this case.

b. Abandonment

i. *Commonwealth v. McCloskey*: D was serving a sentence in a prison when the alarm went off, indicating that someone was attempting an escape in the recreation area of the prison. Guards found a piece of barbed wire near the recreation area that had been cut, along with a laundry bag full of civilian clothing (later identified as D's). D later approached a guard voluntarily and explained that he was going to make a break but changed his mind and returned after thinking of his family. The court held that D exonerated himself from criminal liability by abandoning the criminal offense of attempted prison breach voluntarily.

ii. You may only be eligible for the defense of abandonment if you've gotten to the point where the crime of attempt is complete.

iii. Some jurisdictions say that backing out is just evidence as to whether you're actually guilty of the completed crime of attempt. Then, if you have gone far enough to be guilty of attempt, abandonment can be a defense.

iv. This defense shows a contradiction between the law of attempts and the law of completed offenses.

v. However, FB thinks we allow this, because the harmful result hasn't yet occurred, and we want to encourage people not to go all the way.

X. Burglary

a. The Common Law

i. A breaking

ii. And entering (only requires that some part of the burglar enter the building)

iii. Of the dwelling

iv. Of another

v. In the nighttime

vi. With the intent to commit a felony (doesn't matter which felony: murder, rape, property crime, etc.)

b. District of Columbia (1973)

i. Unlawful breaking

<u>ii.</u>   And entering
<u>iii.</u>   Into the dwelling
<u>iv.</u>   Of another
<u>v.</u>   While a person was present therein
<u>vi.</u>   With the intent to commit a criminal offense

<u>c.</u> Colorado (present) 2d Degree Burglary

<u>i.</u> Knowingly breaks an entrance into,
<u>ii.</u>   Or enters, or remains
<u>iii.</u>   Unlawfully
<u>iv.</u>   In a building or occupied structure
<u>v.</u>   With intent to commit therein a crime against a person or property

<u>XI.</u> Assault

<u>a.</u> *Common law assault* = attempt to commit battery; "an unlawful attempt, coupled with a present ability, to commit a violent injury on the person of another."

<u>i.</u> "Present ability" imported an even stricter notion of proximity to the completed act than characterized the law of criminal attempt

<u>ii.</u>   Some say "attempted assault" doesn't exist, as assault is an attempt, but others say it could be an attempt to commit battery without present ability

<u>b.</u> Assault is usually committed in one of two ways:

<u>i.</u> An actual or attempted battery

<u>ii.</u>   An intentional scaring (some act undertaken by D with an intent to cause fear or imminent bodily injury and in fact causes the victim to experience apprehension of imminent bodily harm)

<u>c.</u> *Battery* = unlawful application of force to another.

<u>i.</u> Force must be applied directly or indirectly

<u>ii.</u>   Mental element of crime may be either an intent to injure or criminal negligence

<u>iii.</u>   Harm can be either an actual physical injury or an unpermitted touching

<u>d.</u> SEE MPC 211

<u>i.</u> Merges scaring and hurting someone

<u>ii.</u>   Grading will usually be on the degree of injury

<u>iii.</u>   "Scaring" assault = inchoate crime

<u>GROUP CRIME</u>

<u>I.</u> <u>Complicity (aiding and abetting)</u>

<u>a.</u> Generally

<u>i.</u> There is NO SEPARATE CRIME OF AIDING AND ABETTING. It is a *theory* used to charge someone with a crime.

<u>ii.</u>   An accomplice is not guilty of the crime of "aiding and abetting" but instead is guilty of the substantive offense committed by the perpetrator because of the accomplice's complicity in the crime.

<u>iii.</u>   Aiding and abetting is NOT an inchoate theory, as a crime MUST be committed in order for one to aid and abet.

<u>iv.</u>   Common Law Categories:

<u>1.</u> *Principal in the first degree* = one who actually commits a crime, either by his own hand (e.g., trigger man), or by an inanimate agency, or by an innocent instrumentality (e.g., pit bull attack)

<u>2.</u> *Principal in the second degree* = one who is guilty of felony by reason of having aided, counseled, commanded or encouraged the commission thereof in his presence, either actual or constructive; one who intentionally assisted the principal in the first degree in committing the act and was actually or constructively present (i.e., located where he could assist).

3. *Accessory before the fact* = One who is guilty of felony by reason of having aided, counseled, commanded or encouraged the commission thereof, *without* having been present either actually or constructively at the moment of the commission of the act

4. *Accessory after the fact* = One who, with knowledge of the other's guilt, renders assistance to a felon in the effort to hinder his detection, arrest, trial or punishment
   a. Occurs after the commission of the crime
   b. Today, such a person wouldn't be liable for the offense as a complicitor but might be guilty of a different crime.

5. These categories have, for the most part, been abolished, although they sometimes still show up.
6. Their primary function was procedural.
7. The penalties for people in different categories was no different.
8. The accessory couldn't be convicted unless the principal was either simultaneously or previously convicted (no longer the rule)

v. 18 U.S.C. § 2. Principals
1. Whoever commits an offense against the United States or aids, abets, counsels, commands, induces, or procures its commission, is punishable as a principal.
2. Whoever willfully causes an act to be done which if directly performed by him or another would be an offense against the United States, is punishable as a principal.

vi. *State v. Hoselton*: D was with several friends who stole items from a storage unit on a barge and was convicted for entering with intent to commit larceny. On appeal, the court held that it had not been proven that D was a lookout, so the conviction under a theory of aiding and abetting could not stand. D didn't seem to know they were going to steal.

b. **The Act**
   i. General Requirements:
      1. Must be one of assistance
      2. The act may be either
         a. Physical conduct, or occasionally an omission
         b. Psychological encouragement (see 18 U.S.C. 2)
      3. "Mere presence" is not enough
      4. There is no causation requirement (i.e., not necessary to show that my act was necessary for the successful completion of the underlying crime).
   ii. *State v. Vaillancourt*: D and Burhoe were outside of a house, and D allegedly stood by and watched Burhoe attempt to break into a basement window and talked to him while he was doing it. In ruling on whether D's conviction for accomplice liability could stand, the court ruled that accompaniment and observation are not sufficient acts to constitute "aid."
      1. Dissent: D was furnishing moral support and encouragement.
      2. FB: Under the traditional rules, the majority has it right, as we have no idea what D was saying.
      3. We're twice removed from the crime being charged, as the principal was

charged with attempted burglary.

iii. ***Wilcox v. Jeffery*:** Hawkins, a U.S. saxophone player, visited England, and D was among the people who greeted him at the airport. Although Hawkins did not have permission to land, D attended his concert as a spectator and did not "get up and protest in the name of England that Mr. Hawkins ought not be here competing with them and taking bread out of their mouths or the wind out of their instruments." The court held that there was evidence on which it could be found that D aided and abetted.

    1. This wasn't an accidental presence, and D didn't protest.

    2. FB: This is a silly case.

iv. ***State v. Helmenstein*:** A group of young people got into D's car, and someone suggested they drive to another town and break into the store there. They did so, drove back to down, and agreed on a cover story. D was convicted of burglary. On appeal, the court held that the record clearly shows that the burglary was the result of a plan in which each of the parties had a part, and there's no evidence connecting D with the commission of the offense, other than that of persons who are also accomplices. The owner's testimony didn't connect D with the offense.

    1. Rule: A conviction may not be had upon the testimony of an accomplice unless it is corroborated by such other evidence as tends to connect D with the commission of the offense.

    2. FB isn't sure that "many" states have a corroboration rule.

    3. The others' conduct rose to accomplice liability for:

        a. Saying she wanted bananas and going to the place where they get them

        b. Agreeing and going along

        c. Actually taking part in the burglary with D and Clem

        d. Being asleep when the burglary was committed but helping make up the story later

            i. Here, court of appeals seems to be substituting their judgment about the inferences drawn at trial

            ii. Under any conventional view, this guy is NOT an accomplice

            iii. Under common law, he might have been an accessory after the fact.

            iv. Court knows this guy wasn't an accomplice but is making something up

    4. Many states have a corroboration rule requiring a jury instruction cautioning jurors to treat accomplice testimony with caution.

v. ***People v. Genoa*:** An undercover agent met with D an proposed that if D gave him $10,000 toward the purchase of cocaine, he'd repay D the $ plus profits. D later returned with $10,000 and was arrested. In determining whether D could be held liable for committing the underlying offense, although he believed he was giving money for an illegal enterprise, when the police agent never intended to commit the contemplated crime and never did commit it, the court held that, absent the underlying crime being committed, it was legally impossible for D to have committed any offense.

    1. Under Michigan law, *someone* had to commit the crime.

    2. The MPC would allow conviction here, and FB thinks that most courts would too.

vi. Entrapment: Every jurisdiction in the U.S. recognized the defense of entrapment by a law enforcement officer.

1. "Subjective" test = entrapment is proved if a government agent induces an innocent person to violate the law

2. "Objective" test = focuses on the police conduct used to ensnare the defendant; entrapment occurs when the police conduct falls below standards for the proper use of governmental power

c. Mental State

i. General Requirements

1. Accomplice must intend to assist principal, in the sense of desiring to aid his criminal endeavor. *No agreement between complicitors is required.*

2. Split on whether D must desire that the crime be committed, or only be aware that it will and that his own actions will assist. Former is probably the better (and majority) rule.

3. Accomplice need not know all details of principal's criminal plans. Intention to help principal carry out the basic substantive offense is enough (e.g., knowledge of gun in robbery).

4. If accomplice desires to assist principal in carrying out one criminal objective, accomplice probably liable for other foreseeable crimes committed during the criminal episode (see *Linscot*).

ii. *People v. Lauria*: Three prostitutes were using D's telephone answering service to further their trade. When arrested, D admitted that he knew some of his customers were prostitutes. On appeal from the trial court's setting aside of an indictment for conspiracy to commit prostitution, the court held that there was insufficient evidence that D intended to further the prostitute's criminal activities. Although proof of D's knowledge of the criminal activities of his patrons was sufficient to charge him with that fact, it was not enough to prove intent to assist them in their crime.

1. One must actually prove a desire to assist.

2. FB doesn't think this would be hard to make the leap in this case.

iii. *Riley v. State*: D and another opened fire on an unsuspecting crowd of people around a bonfire, seriously wounding two of them. The evidence did not reveal which of the two weapons fired the wounding shots. In considering what the legislature meant when requiring proof that the accomplice acted with intent to promote or facilitate "the offense," the court held that D could be convicted of first-degree assault under the statute either upon proof that he personally shot a firearm into the crowd or upon proof that, acting with intent to promote or facilitate the other man's acts of shooting into the crowd, D solicited, encouraged, or assisted him to do so.

1. D needed to promote or facilitate the *conduct* constituting the act.

2. D's mental state need only be recklessness, as that's the one required for the underlying crime.

iv. *State v. Linscott*: D's friend suggested that they and two friends drive to the house of a reputed cocaine dealer in order to take him by surprise and rob him. D broke the window, and his friend fired a shot through the broken window, hitting the dealer in the chest. D testified that he knew it was not unusual for his friend to carry a firearm but stated that he had no knowledge of any reputation for violence his friend may have had and had no intention of causing anyone's death in the course of the robbery. D appealed from a conviction of murder and robbery, and the court affirmed, holding that the foreseeable consequences rule was constitutional.

v. <u>Natural-and-Probable-Consequences Doctrine – Four Requirements:</u>

1. Primary party committed the target offense

2. Secondary party was an accomplice in the commission of the target offense (and intended to promote the *primary offense*)

3. Primary party committed *another* crime or crimes, beyond the target offense.

4. The latter crimes, although not necessarily contemplated at the outset, were *reasonably foreseeable consequences* of the original criminal acts encouraged or facilitated by the aider and abettor.

vi. ***Bailey v. Commonwealth***: D and Murdock had been arguing over their CB radios. D knew that Murdock had a "problem with vision," was intoxicated, owned a handgun, and became easily agitated (especially if someone insulted Patton). D told M that he and Patton were homosexuals and demanded that M arm himself and wait on his front porch. D made a first anonymous call to the police department to tell them a man at M's address was on his porch waving a gun around. When the police didn't see anything, D called M to taunt him and told him he'd be coming in a blue and white car. D called the police again, M eventually came out and opened fire when the police advanced, and the police retaliated and fatally wounded M. In determining whether D's conviction of involuntary manslaughter was proper when the victim was killed by police officers responding to reports from D concerning M's conduct, the appellate court held that a jury question was presented on these issues, and the jury could have determined that the fatal consequences of D's reckless conduct could reasonably have been foreseen and, accordingly, that M's death was not the result of an independent, intervening cause but of D's misconduct.

1. D WASN'T an accomplice here; he was the PRINCIPAL, and the police officers were basically innocent agents.

2. A reasonably foreseeable intervening act can't be relied upon in breaking the chain of causal connection between D and the act.

d. Principal's Effect on Accomplice Liability

i. ***United States v. Lopez***: McIntosh landed a helicopter on the grounds of a prison in order to effect the escape of his girlfriend, D, whose life allegedly was unlawfully threatened by prison authorities. D and M indicated their intent to raise a "necessity/duress" defense. In considering whether Lopez committed a criminal offense if her necessity/duress defense succeeds, the court found that necessity would be a justification to the alleged crime of prison escape IF she could prove it. If D is acquitted, M would be entitled to raise the defense as well.

ii. ***People v. McCoy***: McCoy and Lakey were tried together and convicted of first degree murder arising out of a drive-by shooting. M shot to death the victim but claimed self-defense. Review was granted to decide whether an aider and abettor may be guilty of a greater homicide-related offense than the actual perpetrator committed. The court found that when a person, with the mental state necessary for an aider and abettor, helps or induces another to kill, that person's guilt is determined by the combined acts of all the participants as well as that person's own mens rea. If that person's mens rea is more culpable than another's that person's guilt may be greater even if the other might be deemed the actual perpetrator.

1. EX: Iago tells Othello that O's wife is having an affair, hoping O will kill her in a fit of jealousy. O does so. O might be guilty only of manslaughter (heat of passion), but I's criminal liability might extend to murder, as he was acting with malice.

    2. FB: It's at least possible for the aider and abettor to be more guilty than the one who actually commits the crime.

e. Limits to Accomplice Liability

    i. *In Re Meagan R.*: D broke into a home with Oscar in order for the two to have sexual intercourse. The court found, given D was the victim of statutory rape under the circumstances of this case, the juvenile court cannot rely on that crime to serve as the predicate felony in a true finding she committed the burglary.

        1. FB: This is rare, as courts aren't usually going to charge people as accomplices to conduct of which they are the victim.

        2. The court basically decides as a matter of policy that they're not going to use aiding and abetting to penalize this victim.

f. Withdrawal

    i. For withdrawal to be effective in a case of accomplice liability, D must:

        1. Communicate to his accomplice his intention to withdraw from the criminal undertaking, AND

        2. Make an attempt to "neutralize the effect of the previous support" (e.g., call the cops)

    ii. *People v. Brown*: D and two others went to a car dealership, and D and one of the others went to the back of the building and kicked the door in. After that, they went to the front of the building and told the third that they were leaving and not going forward with the burglary. D appealed from his conviction for attempt burglary, arguing that the evidence established that he voluntarily abandoned his criminal activity and purpose. The court held that withdrawal was not applicable to the attempt burglary charge in that the evidence supported a finding that the offense had occurred prior to the time of D's withdrawal (although it would be effective for burglary).

        1. FB: D actually met the above requirements for withdrawal. It was just too late to avoid the attempt charge, as knocking open the door was enough.

II. Solicitation

a. Generally

    i. Solicitation = counseling, commanding, or encouraging another to commit a crime [see aiding and abetting] but the party of the second part does no criminal act in response

    ii. In effect, an "attempt to conspire" or an "attempt to aid and abet" (a double inchoate offense)

    iii. Is a freestanding crime, but you can't generally be convicted of both solicitation and the underlying crime (which is true of conspiracy)

    iv. Is a *separate* offense, not just a theory (like aiding and abetting).

    v. If successful, it merges with the completed crime.

    vi. Solicitor conceives the criminal idea and furthers its commission via another person by suggesting to, inducing, or manipulating them (and is seen as more morally culpable than a conspirator, who's not hiding)

b. *State v. Cotton*: D was arrested as a result of misconduct involving his stepdaughter. While in jail, D discussed with his cell mate his desire to persuade his stepdaughter not to testify against him, and he wrote two letters (which were never mailed) to his wife stating that she should help him convince the girl not to testify against him. The court held that D could not be convicted of solicitation where his wife, the intended solicitee, never received the letters.

  i. The offense of solicitation requires some form of actual communication from the defendant to either an intermediary or the person intended to be solicited, indicating the subject matter of the solicitation.

III.Conspiracy
  a. Generally
    i. *People v. Carter*:
      1. *Conspiracy* = a partnership in criminal purposes; a mutual agreement or understanding, express or implied, between two or more persons to commit a criminal act or to accomplish a legal act by unlawful means.
      2. The gist of the offense lies in the unlawful agreement, and the <u>crime is complete upon formation of the agreement</u>.
      3. Conspiracy is a crime that is <u>separate and distinct from the substantive crime</u> that is its object. The <u>guilt or innocence</u> of a conspirator <u>does not depend upon the accomplishment</u> of the goals of the conspiracy.
      4. A conviction of conspiracy does not merge with a conviction of the completed offense. A defendant may be convicted and punished for both the conspiracy and the substantive crime.

    ii. Rationale – <u>The Dual Function of Conspiracy</u>:
      1. In its aspect as an inchoate crime, it has been employed to fill the gap created by a law of attempt too narrowly conceived.
      2. In its role as a weapon against group criminal activity, conspiracy has been used to combat the extraordinary dangers allegedly presented by multi-member criminal undertakings.
        a. Criminal groups are self-reinforcing.
        b. Criminal groups might be more dangerous.
    iii. Conspiracy is an <u>inchoate</u> offense; however, in most jurisdictions the existence of a conspiracy also constitutes the basis for holding a person accountable for the *completed* crimes of co-conspirators.
    iv. <u>Procedural Features of Conspiracy Law – Why it's a Powerful Tool</u>:
      1. Evidence
        a. Rules of evidence generally bar introduction of hearsay evidence at trial, but an exception to the rule is that an out-of-court statement made by a conspirator, while participating in the conspiracy, may be introduced in evidence against all of her co-conspirators (regardless of whether they knew about it, endorsed it, or even knew the other co-conspirator existed).
        b. The existence of the conspiracy need only be proven by preponderance of the evidence in order for hearsay statements of co-conspirators to be introduced, and as long as it can be established the co-conspirator was part of the same conspiracy as the defendant, the statement is admissible.
      2. Trial Practice
        a. Persons charged in a conspiracy are typically tried together rather than separately.
        b. Evidence is heard relating to all of the defendants, and it's easier to prove conspiracy than if one was confined to a single trial and could introduce evidence solely related to each defendant.

3. **Reach of the Offenses of Which People can Be Convicted**

    a. Most states and federal law permit the government to bring a conspiracy prosecution in the jurisdiction in which *either* the alleged conspiracy itself was formed or *any* act in furtherance of that conspiracy allegedly occurred.

v. The Supreme Court has held that, under federal law, a conspiracy does not automatically terminate simply because law enforcement officers have defeated the object of the conspiracy.

vi. *Pinkerton v. United States*: Two brothers were indicted for violations of the Internal Revenue Code. There was no evidence that D participated directly in the commission of the substantive offenses on which his conviction for conspiracy and six substantive counts was sustained (and he was in prison while at least some of them were committed). The Supreme Court let D's conviction stand, as there was a continuous conspiracy, and both were responsible for the substantive offenses committed by the other in the course of furtherance of the conspiracy.

    1. Rule: So long as the partnership in crime continues, the partners act for each other in carrying it forward. "An overt act of one partner may be the act of all without any new agreement specifically directed to that act."

    2. The acts needed to be foreseeable.

    3. There's no evidence of affirmative action on the part of D to withdraw.

b. **Mens Rea**

    i. A twofold specific intent is required for conviction:

        1. Intent to combine with others (agreeing with another to accomplish an illegal objective).

        2. Intent to accomplish the illegal objective (having a state of mind necessary for the commission of the substantive offense).

    ii. *People v. Swain*: D's were convicted of conspiracy, the target offense of which was murder in the second degree, after a drive-by-shooting death of a 15-year-old boy. In determining whether intent to kill is a required element of the conspiracy to commit murder where the target offense is determined to be murder in the second degree (unintended), the CA Sup. Ct. held that a conviction of conspiracy to commit murder requires a finding of intent to kill and cannot be based on a theory of implied malice.

        1. The prosecution must show not only that the conspirators intended to agree but also that they intended to commit the elements of that offense.

        2. Although conspiracy could be found in regard to express malice murders, the same is not true for those where malice is implied.

        3. FB thinks that abandoned and malignant heart theories would support conspiracy, so he's not sure he agrees with CA.

        4. This will NOT be a problem most of the time, as you can usually convince a jury that D's agreement was enough to show intent.

    iii. *People v. Lauria*: [See aiding and abetting for additional information.] The court finds that there's insufficient evidence to convict D of conspiracy, as there was no evidence of direct action to further or encourage the activities or an interest in the venture. There needs to be evidence of an agreement to show the first intent prong, and if that had been found, we'd also need D's intent to promote prostitution.

    iv. Some courts hold that conspiracy cannot be proven unless the parties have knowledge of the attendant circumstance which makes their actions a crime, even if such knowledge is not required for the underlying crime. Other courts believe that the policies relating to the underlying offense should apply to the conspiracy charge: if the underlying offense is strict liability as to the attendant circumstance, the same rule should apply to conspiracy to commit that offense.

    v. "Corrupt Motive" Doctrine: Provides that, beyond the usual mens rea requirements, parties to an alleged conspiracy are not guilty unless they had a corrupt or wrongful motive for their planned actions.

c. **Actus Reus**

    i. The *formation of the agreement* signifies the point at which matters have gone far enough for the law to consider it okay to punish the conspirators.

        1. Sometimes the mere formation of an agreement satisfies the act requirement.

        2. Sometimes, an agreement PLUS an overt act in furtherance of the conspiracy is required (only *one* overt act by *one* conspirator).

            a. Probably less than a "substantial step" in an attempt case

            b. Can be something really minor

            c. Doesn't have to be criminal in and of itself (i.e. phone call)

    ii. It is improbable that the parties will enter into their illegal agreement openly, and it is not necessary that all the parties ever have direct contact with one another, or know one another's identity, or even communicate verbally their intentions to agree.

    iii. It is therefore unlikely that the prosecution will be able to prove the formation of the agreement by direct evidence, and the jury must usually infer its existence from the clear co-operation among the parties.

    iv. *Commonwealth v. Azim*: D drove a car in which two other men were passengers. D stopped the car, and one of the men called V over to the curb, after which the two men got out of the car, inflicted bodily injury on V, took his wallet, and left the scene in the car driven by D. In determining whether D's convictions for conspiracy, assault and robbery could stand, the court held that a rational factfinder could find that D conspired with the others to commit assault and robbery, and once conspiracy is upheld, a member of the conspiracy is also guilty of the criminal acts of his co-conspirators.

        1. Rule: Although a conspiracy cannot be based upon mere suspicion or conjecture, a conspiracy "may be inferentially established by showing the relationship, conduct or circumstances of the parties, and the overt acts on the part of the co-conspirators have uniformly been held competent to prove that a corrupt confederation has in fact been formed.

    v. *Commonwealth v. Cook*: V went to visit some friends and see her boyfriend, who wasn't home. D and his brother attempted to engage her in conversation, and she accepted their second invitation to socialize. She sat with the two for a while, and D's bro later suggested that the three walk to a convenience store, as he was out of cigarettes. V agreed but fell as they walked along a wooded path. D's bro jumped on her and forcibly raped her, and D was overheard laughing and made a comment. The court held that the evidence was insufficient to warrant a conviction of conspiracy (although it was established that D was an accomplice).

        1. "The gist of conspiracy rests in the agreement between the conspirators to work in concert for the criminal or corrupt or unlawful purpose, and it is the **agreement** which constitutes the criminal act *and* which generally serves to manifest the requisite criminal intent."

        2. The existence of an agreement must be proven, in addition to it being shown that D was aware of the objective of the conspiracy, and the circumstances under which the rape happened were not indicative of a preconceived plan between D and his bro.

    3. To warrant a conviction for conspiracy, the evidence must show more than participating in the offense, and D's accomplice liability does not substitute for the agreement needed for conspiracy.

d. Bilateral or Unilateral?

    i. *People v. Foster*: D approached Ragsdale in a bar and asked him if he was "interested in making money" and told him of an elderly man who kept many valuables in his possession. D returned to the bar the next day and discussed his plan in detail with R, who decided to feign agreement in order to collect more information. After D went to R's residence to find out if he was "ready to go," R informed the police, who later apprehended the two at the elderly man's residence. In determining whether the IL legislature intended to adopt the unilateral theory of conspiracy, the Sup. Ct. of IL held that the statue encompassed a bilateral theory of conspiracy.

    ii. Pros of Unilateral Theory: A person who believes he is conspiring with another to commit a crime is a danger to the public regardless of whether the other person in fact has agreed to commit the crime.

    iii. Cons of Unilateral Theory: The unilateral theory does not further the purpose of punishing the special dangers inherent in group activity, as there is no "group" criminal activity when there is only one conspirator. The unilateral theory also does not further the purpose of permitting preventative steps against those who show a disposition to commit a crime, as the punishable conduct in a unilateral conspiracy will almost always satisfy the elements of either solicitation or conspiracy.

    iv. "Recurrent Problems" in Bilateral Conspiracy Jurisdictions:

        1. In *Commonwealth v. Byrd*, D sought to overturn his conviction for conspiracy after his co-conspirator was later acquitted. The PA Sup. Ct. rejected this claim, stating that it is error to assume that the failure of a jury to convict one conspirator necessarily invalidates the Commonwealth's verdict on a separate trial.

        2. The general rule in bilateral conspiracy jurisdictions has been that a conviction of a single conspirator cannot stand if the alleged co-conspirators are acquitted *at the same time*.

        3. Federal law has a bilateral conspiracy theory.

        4. In bilateral jurisdictions, there can still be a conspiracy when an undercover guy is involved, as long as at least two people are aware of the existence of some other person involved.

e. Scope of An Agreement: Party & Object Dimensions

    i. The "object" of a Conspiracy:

        1. At common law, the object didn't itself have to be a crime.

        2. The general rule in the U.S. is that it must be a crime (although 18 U.S.C. §371, the federal conspiracy statute, is an exception).

        3. A single conspiracy may have MULTIPLE objects (*Braverman*).

    ii. Concerns With the Scope to be Accorded:

        1. In most cases, it is clear that D has committed or conspired to commit one or more crimes.

        2. The question then revolves around to what extent he is a conspirator with each of the persons involved in the larger criminal networks to commit the crimes that are their objects.

    3. This inquiry is crucial for a number of purposes:

        a. Defining each D's liability

        b. The propriety of joint prosecution

        c. Admissibility against a defendant of the hearsay acts and declarations of others

        d. Questions of multiple prosecution or conviction and double jeopardy

        e. Satisfaction of the overt act requirement or statutes of limitation

        f. Rules of jurisdiction and venue

        g. Liability for substantive crimes executed pursuant to the conspiracy

    4. This problem is central to a concern based on the conflict between the need for effective means of prosecuting large criminal organizations, and the dangers of prejudice to individual defendants.

iii. ***Kilgore v. State*:** D was convicted for the murder of Norman. At trial, the state introduced evidence of three previous attempts on Norman's life. The first attempt involved Oldaker and Benton. D and Berry were connected with the second attempt, and D and Chambers were connected to the third attempt, which was presumably successful. D argued that the trial court erred in admitting the hearsay testimony of Oldaker, who said that Benton told him who wanted Norman killed (as the man's identity was brought up again in relation to the other attempts), as the exception to the hearsay rule would only apply if D, Oldaker, and Benton were co-conspirators. In deciding whether D, who did not know of or communicate with Oldaker and Benton, and Oldaker and Benton, who likewise didn't know of or communicate with D, can be considered to have agreed to and become co-conspirators in the murder of Norman, the court held they could not have and therefore were not co-conspirators.

    1. FB: These were successive agreements to commit different crimes, which can be contrasted with a single agreement to commit multiple crimes (like in *Braverman*).

iv.   Types of Conspiracies:

    1. *Wheel* = involves an individual – the hub, who transacts illegal dealings with the various other individuals – the spokes. The most common evidentiary issue in a wheel conspiracy is whether the separate transactions between the hub and individual spokes can be merged to form a single conspiracy (as in *Kilgore*). If there's no rim connecting the spokes, it's hard to find a wheel conspiracy.

        a. If there's no rim, we have multiple conspiracies.

    2. *Chain* = involves several layers of personnel dealing with a single subject matter, as opposed to a specific person. A single conspiracy can be proven if each link knew or must have known of the other links in the chain, and if each defendant intended to join and aid the larger enterprise (like with drug trafficking). The people need not have actually met one another.

v.   ***Braverman v. United States*:** Evidence showed that D's and others collaborated in the illicit manufacture, transportation, and distribution of distilled spirits involving the violations of various statutes. The trial judge submitted the case to the jury on the theory that the seven counts of the indictment charged as distinct offenses the several illegal objects of one continuing conspiracy, and D's appealed. In determining whether a single agreement to commit acts in violation of several penal statutes is to be punished as one or several conspiracies, the

Supreme Court held that it is the agreement which constitutes the conspiracy that the statute punishes, so the one agreement cannot be taken to be several agreements and hence several conspiracies because it envisages the violation of several statutes rather than one.

vi. *Albernaz v. United States*: Supreme Court held that D's could be convicted and punished under two drug conspiracy statutes, even though the government did not prove the existence of separate conspiratorial agreements to import and to distribute the drugs. The Court distinguished *Braverman* on the ground that it charged under a general conspiracy statute.

f. Completion, Renunciation, Withdrawal

i. Conspiracy technically complete once there has been an agreement and (when required) an overt act; however, it's a continuing offense.

1. Although complete when an agreement, not OVER then.

ii. Crime exists until either the objective is obtained or it's abandoned.

iii. <u>Withdrawal</u> is possible if:

1. D notifies other co-conspirators, AND

2. D takes affirmative action to frustrate designs of conspiracy.

g. Defenses

i. *Iannelli v. United States*: D's were charged with conspiring to violate and violating a federal gambling statute making it a crime for five or more persons to conduct, finance, manage, supervise, direct, or own a gambling business prohibited by state law. On appeal, the Supreme Court was required to consider whether <u>Wharton's Rule</u>, a doctrine of criminal law enunciating an exception to the general principal that a conspiracy and the substantive offense that is its immediate end are discrete crimes for which separate actions may be imposed, applied. The Court held that the history and structure of the Organized Crime Control Act of 1970 manifest a clear and mistakable legislative judgment that more than outweighs any presumption of merger between the conspiracy to violate the statute and the consummation of that substantive offense.

1. <u>Wharton's Rule</u>: When to the idea of an offense plurality of agents is logically necessary, conspiracy, which assumes the voluntary accession of a person to a crime of such a character that it is aggravated by a plurality of agents, cannot be maintained.

2. The rule traditionally applied to adultery, incest, bigamy, and dueling, in which the parties to the agreement are the only persons who participate in the substantive offense, and the consequences of the crimes rest on those parties, not society.

3. The rule applies only to offenses that *require* concerted criminal activity, a plurality of criminal agents. In such cases, a closer relationship exists between the conspiracy and the substantive offense because *both* require collective criminal activity.

ii. In <u>jurisdictions that still apply Wharton's Rule</u>, it is typically only invoked in cases in which the target offense of the conspiracy has been committed or attempted; thus, the rule only serves to require merger of the conspiracy into the completed or attempted offense.

iii. *Gebardi v. United States*: D's, a man and a woman, were indicted for conspiring to transport the woman from one state to another for the purpose of engaging in sexual intercourse with the man. The woman consented to go on each journey, and there was no evidence that any other person had conspired. In considering whether, admitting that the woman by consenting, has not violated the

Mann Act, she may be convicted of a conspiracy with the man to violate it, the Supreme Court held that the woman is not guilty of a conspiracy.

<u>**1.**</u> A woman can't be punished for transporting herself, so there's evidence of the legislature wanting her acquiescence to be left unpunished.

h. **Punishment**

<u>**i.**</u> Majority rule: Once can be convicted of both conspiracy and the underlying substantive offense(s).

<u>**ii.**</u> ALSO, one can be punished for both conspiracy and underlying substantive crime(s).

<u>**iii.**</u> ALSO, *Pinkerton* renders conspirators liable, <u>and punishable</u>, for the foreseeable offenses committed by co-conspirators in course and furtherance of conspiracy.

PROPERTY

Concepts in Property and Its Parameters
I. Right to Exclude
   a. Property Rule v Liability Rule
      i. Property Rule
         1. property is taken w/o permission
         2. punitive damages allowed
            a. protecting legitimate expectation of exclusion
            b. promotes respect for boundaries
         3. promotes feeling of control of property/line
         4. permitting trespass may discourage investment and efficient reallocation of resources (ensures dominion/control over asset)
         5. *Jacques v Steenberg Homes*- trailer cuts across land
            a. Jacques has exclusive veto over use, except with Jacques' permission
            b. Protected by injunctive relief
            c. Should have been awarded compensatory damages- the reasonable value of one-time access to the Jacques' land
      ii. Liability Rule
         1. Jacques could have allowed Steenberg to cross, had Steenberg paid the fair market value of the right to cross the land
   b. Restrictions on right to exclude- *State v Shack*- (I want to come talk to your immigrant workers)
      i. Advocating a right to exclude
         1. promote individual security
         2. efficiency (protect and encourage economic investment in land)
         3. certainty- to guide future behavior
      ii. Against a right to exclude
         1. public health concerns
         2. migrants' unawareness of available services may implicate significant dignity concerns
      iii. Land owner must absorb costs in conducting this type of farming operation
      iv. Other concerns in *Shack*
         1. 1st amendment right to free association vs. state trespass law
         2. common law- workers are tenants w/ rights to receive visitors
II. A community's interest in property- *US Steel*
   a. Community (union) argument for such a property interest
      i. long relationship w/ town and employees has contributed to US Steel's well-being; severance will destroy town
      ii. ct should reallocate partial ownership of US Steel to workers, based on their detrimental reliance (i.e. reallocation of property upon divorce)
   b. US Steel's argument against such a property interest
      i. no constitutional provision, statute, or ct ruling permits such a reallocation
      ii. Is the ct the proper institution to make this decision?
         1. Economic impact of reallocation would be profound
         2. Far more complex than a marriage dissolution
         3. Could have significant (and unknown) impact on capital markets
            a. cts may not be competent to properly analyze such a dispute

        b. should be handled by more accountable legislature
- iii. WARN Act now in place to warn town of impending closing
  1. WARN doesn't protect based on a property rule- actually militates against a property interest in plant
- iv. Estoppel Argument
  1. Requires
     a. Conduct (acts/statements/omissions)
     b. Reliance by another party that is *reasonable* and *detrimental*
     c. Irreparable harm or great injustice unless estoppel is granted
  2. If ct had granted injunction (to not close the plant) based on estoppel
     a. Would *not* have been a "property" right
     b. Basically a "contract" (to not close the plant if it wasn't profitable) would have been breached
     c. US Steel could close later if it did become unprofitable
     d. Or, US Steel could compensate employees for reliance-based expectations in order to close, move the plant
  3. Rejected because
     a. Statements weren't promises
     b. Workers couldn't rely on statement of lower-level US Steel spokespersons

III. Limits of property rights- *Moore v Board of Regents*
   a. Spleen is removed, cells taken and used for profitable research
   b. Sue for conversion and lack of informed consent
   c. Conversion- reasons for rejection
      i. His cells are not "unique"
         1. bad argument- plenty of things are not unique, but are property (cash, casebooks)
      ii. UAGA statute reduces patient control over cells to the point that what is left does not amount to property
         1. UAGA gives power to designate donor
      iii. Golde's patented cell line is both factually and legally distinct from Moore's cell line
         1. bad argument- Moore isn't claiming that the cell line is his property, only that his cells were used to create it
      iv. conversion liability could discourage research by restricting access to raw materials- Why?
         1. patients might hold out for share of profits
         2. risk of litigation increases
         3. relieving researchers from risk of conversion liability may indirectly subsidize needed and socially valuable medical research
   d. Informed consent
      i. Unlikely to win- have to prove he would have refused treatment w/ full disclosure
         1. may not be a great argument- full disclosure would satisfy "dignity-based" expectations
   e. Property or tort?
      i. Ct says tort of informed consent better covers this
         1. Moore's expectation is a "dignity" interest (to be able to make informed decisions), not a commercial interest
         2. decision should be left to legislature
         3. BUT- ct is confusing conversion and commercial expectations

      a. Law could protect right to say NO (based on property), but forbid profitability

      b. Could have awarded

          i. Nominal damages (violation of property right)

          ii. No compensatory damages (he couldn't expect to profit on those cells)

          iii. Punitive damages (for Golde's knowing conduct)

   ii. Ct says Recognizing property in tissues risks a marketplace for bodily tissues

      1. moral issues

      2. BUT- we already *have* a marketplace for bodily tissues, and people *are* profiting; why shouldn't the donor share?

Acquiring Interest in Property: The Significance or "Possession"

IV. First-in-Time, First-in-Right

   a. *Pierson v Post*- fox hunting

      i. Post argues: pursuit + reasonable prospect of capture = possession

         1. support

            a. foxes are scourge, rules should encourage hunting

            b. hunters may not hunt if they aren't protected

         2. dissent

            a. too unclear a "rule"

            b. Pierson needs clear signal of Post's claim (possession is a clear act that signifies possessor's claim)

            c. Rule of physical capture (or mortal wounding + continued pursuit) needed for certainty

      ii. Why not apply custom?

         1. For custom

            a. Customs have a sufficient "signal" effect to enable 3rd parties to adjust their behavior

            b. Use of custom promotes strong respect for law (as common practice shapes the law)

         2. Against custom

            a. Customs aren't always universal

            b. Society as a whole should evaluate if custom is welfare-maximizing

            c. Resolution of dispute via common law process may influence future disputes over "possession"

   b. Prepossessory interests- *Popov v Hayashi*

      i. Popov had pre-possessory interest based on significant but incomplete steps to get possession- both Popov and Hayashi have equal interest

      ii. Ball is to be sold and proceeds split

      iii. Use prepossessory right to vindicate right to catch ball without fear of assault?

         1. Pros- Yes, as they are fighting over the actual ball

         2. Con-

            a. not if Popov didn't certainly catch the ball

            b. could also be protected via tort and criminal law

      iv. Result really doesn't make sense

         1. If Popov had possession, he should win

         2. If Popov didn't establish possession, it isn't clear how his claim is of equal dignity with that of Hayashi

   c. *Cujus est solum*- Possession of subsurface- *Edwards v Sims*

i. Edwards explored and exhibited cave- entrance is on Edwards' land

ii.   Both parties claim first ownership of portion of cave supposedly under Lee's land- survey desired here

iii.   Why apply cujus est solum?

1.   strong public interest in settling possibly similar disputes with large mining industry

2.   easiest to draw line

iv.   Dissent

1.   don't apply mining rules

2.   cave was empty space until Edwards explored, exhibited it

3.   Lee's expectation of control of cave is less deserving of protection than his expectation of the surface boundary, as Lee has no access to cave (can't enjoy it)

   a.   3 Problems with that- 1. Lee could cut new opening to cave

   b.   2. Ct could grant Lee an "easement" for access

   c.   3. Lee can benefit via rent paid by Edwards to exhibit Lee's portion of cave

4.   Lee would get windfall, since cave was empty before Edwards made it beautiful (Laboring theory)

   a.   Problems- cave has natural beauty

v.   Remedy

1.   portion of net profits- due to cave's own beauty

2.   Edwards saves invested money

d.   Property interests in ideas- *Joyce v GM*

i. Employee discusses cost-saving suggestion w/ boss, submits it to drop-box, along w/ another employee, who heard about it from the same boss; employee #2 is given award ($12K)

ii.   Copying in common law- no property rights in ideas

1.   evidentiary and/or administrative problem: who was first?

2.   property in ideas would create monopoly (control) problems with respect to ideas

   a.   may stifle creativity

   b.   negative market effects in recognizing monopoly rights

iii.   Why does Congress recognize patent and copyright protection for ideas/expression (intellectual property)?

1.   people won't innovate w/o protection

   a.   Linux?

2.   Allocation property rights may encourage people to innovate at a greater level

3.   *Joyce* leaves recognition of such right to legislature, not cts

   a.   Competence

   b.   Administrative concerns- w/o system for recording evidence of "title" claims, f.i.t principle is unworkable for ideas

iv.   Patent Law, briefly

1.   Fed patent law provides blueprint for legislative recognition of intellectual property

2.   Patent office award of patent provides surrogate f.i.t

3.   Awardee receives time-limited monopoly in idea (need consent from patent holder to explore idea)

   a.   Antitrust goes against this

4.   after monopoly period ends, idea goes into public domain

255

v. Domain Names
  1. concerns
     a. is there a risk of confusion to the public
     b. will "celebrity" be embarrassed by being associated w/ undesirable
     c. is this cybersquatting as blackmail
  2. cannot act in bad faith
  3. cts, when deciding if infringing on rights, can consider if user
     a. has an intention to divert traffic
     b. has made an offer to sell domain name
vi. Identity protection- *Midler v Ford, White v Samsung*, Elvis, & The Three Stooges
  1. Why protect wish to control use of identity
     a. Celebrity has commercial value
     b. Value is exhaustible (no value added by association w/ her name if everyone could associate products w/ her name)
     c. Fans could be misled
     d. May be embarrassed by an association
  2. general rule: if a reasonable person would think impersonation was of that celebrity, or was that celebrity- using that person's celebrity for commercial purpose w/o consent
  3. *Vanna*
     a. Vanna's expectation
        i. Her expectation of controlling the commercial use of her identity- **right of publicity**
        ii. Personal dignity interest (a robot could do her job)- tort law
     b. Question of Samsung's intent
        i. Relevant? Not usually in regards to property rights
        ii. Only consider if a reasonable person would associate Vanna and Samsung
  4. Elvis
     a. First amendment probably protects this, as there is no risk of confusion
     b. Such impersonation actually promotes musical and artistic creativity in a positive way
  5. First amendment protection of expression
     a. 1st am protects inasmuch as it contains significant transformative elements or that the value of the work does not derive primarily from the celebrity's fame (Three Stooges tshirts)
     b. if not, it violates right of publicity
     c. Transformative
        i. Do literal or creative elements dominate?
        ii. Does marketability/value of challenged work derive primarily from celebrity's fame?
  6. Publicity v 1st am
     a. Distinguish (a) whether a celebrity has a conceivable publicity claim and (b) whether such a claim must "give way" to 1st am concerns
     b. E.g., Vanna may have a claim for appropriation of publicity rights, but for the intervention of 1st am rights
     c. Or, the ad was protected by "transformative" analysis, or by characterizing as "parody"

V. "First-in-Time" and Finding Disputes
  a. background

i. bailment = rightful possession by one who is not its TO

ii.   bailee has absolute duty to redeliver card to bailor

    1. liable for FMV if this is breached

b. *Armory v Delamirie*- discovers stone, jeweler won't return

    i. Why let Armory recover jewel (or its value), if he isn't TO?

        1. protecting possession is efficient way to protect ownership (difficult to prove ownership, easier to prove possession)

        2. protecting possession discourages trespass by 3rd parties

    ii.   Does full market value of jewels overcompensate Armory?

        1. yes- jewels are not worth that much to him (must be returned to TO if reclaimed)

        2. but, ct could find the value of his interest

        3. also, can't avoid windfall associated w/ possession of a lost object, we can only allocate it- better to choose Armory than to give Delamirie an incentive to steal

c. The false jus tertii defense

    i. Def *jus tertii*- neither P nor D, but a third party, is TO, and only TO can bring suit

    ii.   If D has to pay damages to A, then TO can show up and be able to recover damages from D- wrong

    iii.   Risk of double liability is unavoidable, either A or D must bear the risk of losing two lawsuits

    iv.   Ruling for D wouldn't avoid risk of losing 2 lawsuits; it would just shift that risk to A

    v.   If TO later sues D, TO will recover damages against him

    vi.   D's protection from risk of double liability lies in doctrine of subrogation

        1. once D pays second judgment to TO, D becomes subrogated to rights of TO

        2. D can then assert those rights (TO) against A and recover value of the jewels

d. Landowner v finder: *Hannah v Peel*- brooch found by soldier

    i. Arguments

        1. Hannah: as finder, I have possessory claim better than all but true owner (Peel is not true owner)

        2. Peel: I should be considered as having superior possessory right to brooch

            a. It was in my home

            b. Ct should treat me as having "constructive possession" of the brooch prior to H finding it

    ii.   Precedents

        1. *Bridges*: salesman finds banknotes in bag on floor of store; disp for finder

        2. *Sharman*: pool cleaner discovered gold rings in pool; disp for LO

            a. Law should protect security of a landowner's expectation of control of activities on land

                i. Manifestation of control over land = signal of control over land and objects

                ii.   Pool cleaner had a limited purpose (invitation) on land

            b. Allowing LO to recover possession of the rings should avoid temptations of dishonesty

            c. Law should facilitate return of lost objects to TOs

                i. Usually, if TO has lost something, they will come back for it- LO best to facilitate the return

    iii.   So why did ct follow *Bridges*?

        1. Hannah acted honestly

        2. Hannah's honesty should be rewarded

a. For its own sake
b. Honesty is first step in reuniting objects w/ TOs
c. Hannah wasn't trespassing
iv. Policies in Finder v LO disputes
1. protect LO's legit expectation of dominion/control over land
2. discouraging trespass/encouraging respect for boundaries
3. facilitating return of objects to TO
4. determination of any finder/LO dispute in English law was likely explained by ct's ad hoc balancing of these concerns
e. Lost/Mislaid/Abandoned
i. **Lost**: unintentionally dropped and subsequently forgotten- awarded to **finder**
ii. **Mislaid**: intentionally placed and subsequently forgotten- awarded to **LO**
iii. **Abandoned**: TO is presumed to have given up search- awarded to **finder**
iv. **Treasure trove**: cash/coin that is "antiquity"- awarded to **finder** (not used in all states)
v. Classification often made after deciding who should get the property
vi. Many hypos for this in q/a and notes

When is Prior Possession Not Enough? The Estoppel Concept
VI. Estoppel and Finding Statutes- estopping TO from recovering after time determined by statute
a. Policy encourages finders to be honest and report finds, so as to facilitate return of objects to TOs
b. Vigilant TO should be able to react w/in 1 yr to find filed affidavit
c. Need for "repose"
d. Finding Statute and *Benjamin* (money in plane wing)
i. Maj- statute doesn't apply to mislaid property, only lost property
1. statute didn't abolish common law lost/mislaid standard
2. b/c cash was "mislaid," statute is inapplicable
ii. Dissent: statute suggests cash now "abandoned"
1. even if statute doesn't abolish lost/mislaid distinction, that should become moot when TO doesn't reclaim w/in 1 yr (statute basically presumes abandonment after 1 yr)
e. **Derivative Title** Principle UCC 2-403(1)
i. resolution method alternative to first-in-time
ii. **purchaser gets same title as transferor had**
iii. purchaser gets voidable title of transferor even if
1. (1) transferor was deceived as to ID of purchaser
2. (2) delivery was in exchange for a check with is later dishonored
3. (3) it was agreed that the transaction was to be a cash sale
4. (4) delivery was procured through fraud punishable as larcenous under criminal law
5. ALSO, purchaser can then transfer good title to good faith purchaser
iv. So
1. B steals object from A, sells it to C- C gets rights of B, which were bad, so A can recover from C
2. A sells object to B for counterfeit $5; B sells to C for $5 (w/o knowledge of B's actions)- A is estopped from recovery from C- B received voidable title from A, good title could be conveyed to good faith purchaser
v. Why have 2-403(1) if A can't recover from C in above hypo?
1. in #2, A voluntarily sold to B, thus A's conduct, in part, caused the

258

misimpression that B had power to sell
2. C's good faith reliance on A's conduct justifies estoppel (A estopped from asserting derivative title rule to reclaim object)
3. Hypo: A lets B borrow object, and B sells it to C- A can recover from C
a. B was only a bailee of object, w/o authority to convey A's title to C
b. Sale passed only B's rights as bailee
f. Merchants
i. Entrusting possession (any delivery and any acquiescence in retention of possession) to a merchant gives him power to transfer all rights of entruster to a buyer in ordinary course of business
1. ordinary course of business
a. pay value (need not be FMV)
b. not know defect in title
c. act in good faith
d. buy in ordinary course of business
i. may not be ok outside of business
e. buy from someone who sells goods of that kind
ii. Why?
1. Encourages buyers to rely on merchant's appearance of title
2. facilitates merchandising (merchant doesn't need to keep title records to everything)
3. Entruster has cause of action v merchant (breach)
VII. Adverse Possession
a. Elements of adverse possession- must establish all for entire statutory period
i. Open and notorious
1. *Mullis v Winchester*- used land for cutting timber, had land surveyed, paid taxes- objectively seen as owner
2. "Minor" encroachments
a. along common boundary is not open and notorious, unless TO has actual knowledge of it- *Mannillo v Gorski*
b. "Discovery Rule"
i. Possession of chattels not "adverse" until TO knows or should know location of chattels and ID of AP
ii. Consistent with estoppel principle
iii. If encroachment is minor, possession is not open, unless TO knows of encroachment
iv. REJECTED by most cts
1. vague standard
2. presumption that TO will know visible boundaries
3. Must be not only typical, but typical and alerts owner that AP is APing and acting as TO
ii. Continuous
1. can be seasonal use, if typical possession would be seasonal- *Lilly v Lynch*
iii. Exclusive
1. doesn't mean AP must have precluded other from using land- *Lilly v Lynch*
2. TOs often customarily allow neighbors to use land (boat ramp)
3. neighbors are acting as if AP is TO
iv. Actual
v. Hostile
1. **Objective** standard- maj- were AP's acts typical of acts engaged in by owners

of similar land?
- a. Avoids inquiry into actor's state of mind
- b. Subj may encourage AP to lie
2. **Subjective**
- a. *Good faith*- was AP in possession based on honest mistake? Yes, Then, hostile
- b. *Intent to claim*- did AP intend to possess land as her own, w/o regard to location of true boundary? Yes, Then, hostile
3. Possession w/ permission of TO is not "hostile," cannot ripen into title by AP
4. *Norman v Allison*- triangle of land from built road/fence
- a. 2 interps
  - i. (1)Norman knew he planned to build fence on land, was seeking permission
  - ii. (2) Norman thought he was building a division fence on true boundary line
- b. rule: exclusive use and possession of another's land is presumed adverse, absent positive proof to contrary
  - i. presumption is made to clear up encroachments ASAP, to place risk of silence on TO, and gives TOs strong incentive to be vigilant and confront possible boundary encroachers
- c. uses intent to claim standard, although Norman put fence there both with permission and believing it was the true boundary line
5. Hostility and Permission
- a. If permission is given by TO, then permissive APer transfers title to new owner, then new owner must be informed of permission by permitting party, if not by transferor
- b. Also applied to change in use

b. Color of title- document that purports to convey title to land, but that is legally ineffective to do so
c. Why recognize AP
- i. Protects expectations that possession will continue w/o interruption in future
- ii. Good faith possessor
- iii. Reliance becomes strong
- iv. Avoid harsh economic and emotional consequences
- v. Gives TOs incentive to resolve potential title disputes quickly
- vi. Theories
  1. **Sleeping theory**: AP should operate to punish TOs who sleep on their rights and do not promptly seek to resolve disputes over possession of land
  2. **Earning theory**: AP should operate to reward possessors who behave consistently with true ownership for so long that their expectations become deserving of legal protection
d. "Open lands" Rule
- i. on open lands, acts of AP need only be exercised "in such manner as is consistent w/ the use to which the lands may be put, w/o actual residence of occupancy"
- ii. For open lands
  1. even minimal acts, if consistent w/ expected use, should alert vigilant TO as to existence and nature of AP's claim
  2. AP shouldn't have to occupy and develop land that is not presently suited for it
- iii. Against open lands
  1. why force TO to expend comparable resources to avoid loss of title? (only

period assertion needed, really)
- e. Constructive Adverse Possession
  - i. i.e., building home on 5 acres of 250 acres AP thinks he owns, has color of title to entire parcel
    1. What would you want to know?
       - a. Size of tract
       - b. Physical characteristics (for common usage)
       - c. Location of improvements
       - d. Tax paid?
  - ii. Why recognize this?
    1. AP's good faith- if he claims under color of title, he has no reason to realize he needs to exercise control over all 250 acres (he thought he owned it)
    2. Signal to TO that he should know he owns entire parcel, so AP's possession of part of the parcel should sufficiently "signal" AP's claim as to all of the land
  - iii. If land if further subdivided
    1. A builds home on small part of B's 130 acres, under color of title, but has color to those acres and 120 owned by C.
       - a. A can't establish constructive possession of C's land
       - b. A's color of title may show C's land, A doesn't "signal" C that he is claiming any of C's land
       - c. A isn't trespassing against C
       - d. a reasonable person in C's position wouldn't see A's action as adverse/hostile
    2. A has color to 250 acres; land had been divided into 25 acre lots; A occupies one lot
       - a. S.C. statute says constructive possession via color of title doesn't apply to subdivided tracts
       - b. However, minimal acts (paying taxes) may be sufficient to find "actual" possession by A
  - iv. Color of title is *necessary* for a constructive adverse possession claim, but not *sufficient*????
    1. must "signal"
- f. Equitable Estoppel
  - i. Must prove
    1. reasonable, detrimental reliance on conduct by other party
    2. unjustifiable injury if ct lets other party recover possession
  - ii. "Good faith improvement" statutes
    1. good faith improver can recover value of improvements even if it might not have been protected under equitable estoppel doctrine
    2. or, occupier may have to buy land on which she is sitting
    3. or, occupier has to pay rent to TO, and (obviously) AP period would not run during this time

Transferring Property by Gift
VIII. Personal Property
- a. Requirements
  - i. **Intent** to make an immediately effective gift of property to the donee
  - ii. Donor must make **delivery** of object of gift
  - iii. Donee must **accept** object of the gift
    1. if gift is beneficial, law presumes acceptance

b. **Delivery**
   i. Usually, actual physical (manual) delivery of object of gift, if at all possible
      1. objective act corroborating the donor's subjective intent
      2. manual delivery corroborates donor's intent with regard to timing of gift
         a. places object beyond donor's dominion and control, making gift effective at that time
   ii. sometimes, manual delivery is impossible
      1. symbolic delivery of land by delivery of deed, car by key
   iii. *In re Estate of Evans*- safe deposit box key and "I want you to have the contents" not enough
      1. contents of box weren't beyond dominion and control, b/c "donee's" name is not on box
      2. contents capable of manual delivery
      3. ct doubted Evans' intent- illegitimate argument
         a. donor's subjective intent is a question of fact- appellate ct can't reverse unless trial ct finding was clearly erroneous, ie no reasonable person could have reached that conclusion
c. Kinds of gifts
   i. Inter vivos- immediately effective gift between living persons
   ii. Testamentary- taking effect at death of testator
      1. takes effect only upon donor's death
   iii. Causa mortis- special kind of inter vivos gift, made in contemplation of imminent death (deathbed)
      1. immediately effective, subject to implied condition
      2. donor can revoke before dying; revoked if donor recovers; gift is absolute at death
      3. still require intent, delivery, and acceptance
d. *Scherer v Hyland*
   i. Suicide note is not a sufficient "symbolic" delivery of all her assets to make a valid causa mortis gift. Why?
      1. language of note ("bequeathed") suggests she had *testamentary* intent
      2. law doesn't want to allow "end run" around will statute and its requirements, because of the risk of fraud
   ii. check is a valid causa mortis gift, but not other assests
      1. "surrender of possession" was complete when she endorsed check, left it on table
      2. check was beyond her dominion and control prior to death
   iii. compared to *Evans*
      1. *Evans*- "traditional" (policy-driven) view: delivery requirement should be interpreted strictly, even if that frustrates subjective intent (it is a good policy to promote gifts to be made in a way that leave less doubt/no doubt about intent)
      2. *Scherer*- "intent"-driven view: if donor's intent is clear, *any action by donor in furtherance of that intent is sufficient delivery* if that action objectively corroborates that donor's intent to make an immediately effective gift
e. Gifts and Remainder Interest
   i. *Gruen v Gruen*- dad wants to give son painting for bday, but keep possession of it for his life- declared a valid inter vivos gift of a remainder interest in painting
      1. dad had present right to possession for life
      2. son had future interest in painting

          a. it is a present property right, but one that would not entitle son to possession of the painting until after his father's death

     3. Why is letter sufficient delivery?

          a. Manual delivery inappropriate

          b. Sufficient objective manifestation of dad's intention to make a presently effective gift (of future interest)

  ii. Testamentary gift v inter vivos gift of remainder

     1. testamentary- if painting is willed, son has no property right prior to dad's death

          a. will can be changed until death

          b. dad can sell or give away painting

     2. inter vivos- dad gives son remainder interest

          a. remainder interest can be sold or mortgaged by son

          b. dad can't transfer right to possession after his death

  iii. Beneficiary Deeds (Testamentary Deed)

     1. characteristics

          a. deed must expressly provide that it will take effect only at donor's death

          b. deed must be recorded (can't be kept hidden)

          c. deed has exactly same effect as will during donor's life (none); during donor's life, donee does not have a remainder interest

          d. if donor still owns land at time of donor's death, deed passes title to donee

     2. *Ferrel v Stinson*- deed to give farm to 3 people to be put in lock box in closet, asks housekeeper to deliver it to grantees at death- dies 10 mnths later

          a. ct says grantor lost dominion and control (couldn't get to lock box)

          b. deed was thus delivered- as if placed in escrow- objective manifestation of intent to make inter vivos gift of a remainder interest in the farm

          c. intent-drive policy decision here- if intent is clear, *any* act that objectively manifests intent is sufficient

     3. counter- *Bergi*- deed to land given to son, w/ oral agreement that dad possesses and operates til death (20 yrs later)

          a. ct: dad intended to make gift only effective on death, so deed was invalid

f. Conditional Inter vivos gifts

  i. Typically, inter vivos gifts are absolute

  ii. Oral conditions are typically invalid absent uncontroverted proof of intent to make conditional gift

  iii. *Lindh v Surman*- engagement ring, engagement broken by man

     1. gift treated as impliedly conditional upon actual marriage

     2. counter- conditional upon donee's willingness to marry

          a. characterized as "fault-based"

     3. probably a case of gender-bias

     4. if she had spent $15K in reliance on the promise of a wedding, then she could recover those costs

The System of Freehold Estates

IX. Vocabulary/background

  a. "Estate" in land- one's legal right to *possession* of land

    i. present estate or

   ii. future estate

 b. Estates have "quantum" (duration)

   i. Fee simple absolute (freehold)

   ii. Fee simple defeasible (freehold)

   iii. For life (freehold)

   iv. For a term of year, at will, or from period to period (nonfreehold- landlord/tenant)

 c. Creation of estates

   i. By **conveyance**- inter vivos transfer of deed

   ii. By **devise**- testamentary transfer by will

   iii. Deed or will contains operative "granting language" that indicates that estate(s) the grantor/testator is creating

   iv. Inheritance- die w/o will; state decides you get property

 d. Folks receiving benefits of estates

   i. Heir- person to receive estate, w/o will of deceased (no one has an heir while living – only people who may be heirs (apparent) when I die) *see Inheritance*

   ii. Devisee/Beneficiary- person to receive estate w/ will

   iii. Issue- lineal descendants

 e. Conveyance vocab

   i. *Words of purchase*- who takes estate conveyed- "To X"

   ii. *Words of limitation*- quantum of estate conveyed to grantee- "and his heirs"

Present Estate	Corresponding Future Estate
Fee simple absolute	None
Fee simple defeasible Fee simple determinable Fee simple subject to condition subsequent Fee simple subject to executory limitation	 Possibility of Reverter Right of Entry (or Power of Termination) Executory Interest
Fee tail	Reversion (if retained by grantor) or Remainder (if created in grantee)
Life Estate	Reversion (if retained by grantor) or Remainder (if created in grantee)

Possessory Estates in Land

X. Fee Simple Absolute Estate

 a. Three characteristics

   i. *potentially infinite in duration* (FEE)

   ii. *freely inheritable* by heirs of person who owns estate(SIMPLE)

   iii. not subject to any condition or limitation that will terminate the owner's estate (ABSOLUTE)

   iv. any estate w/ all 3 must be an estate in fee simple absolute

 b. If Blueacre is conveyed from O "to X and his heirs,"

   i. X's heirs have **no** estate, because heirs don't exist until X dies

   ii. X could sell or give BA to someone else inter vivos

   iii. X could devise it to someone else by will

 c. If Blueacre is conveyed from O "to X's heirs"

i. X has no estate

ii.   If X is dead, X's heirs can be ID'd, and they have a present possessory estate in BA

iii.   If X is alive, we would say:

1.   O has fee simple, subject to an executory interest (a future interest that may divest O's title)

2.   X's heirs have an executory interest

XI.   Life Estate

a.   Restraints Against Alienation

i. Cannot place direct, absolute, perpetual restraint on alienability of land

1.   unreasonable restraint on alienability

2.   ct's policy decision against deadhand control

ii.   *White v Brown*- dividing future interest and present interest

1.   leaves home to White "to live and not to be sold" w/ personal property to Perry; heirs argue White has life estate to home, and home should be later reverted, then to heirs; trial ct holds life estate and home sold, proceeds split between White and heirs

2.   Better solution: heirs get portion of proceeds now

a.   Each interest should be valued and transferred separately

b.   Cts could value those interests and distribute accordingly

3.   Trial minority/SC holding- will is ambiguous, so use rules of construction

a.   1: conveyance presumed to grantor's entire estate, unless specific limitation appears

b.   2: will construed to avoid partial intestacy

c.   So, no express limitation, White has fee simple

i. Sale restraint on fee simple is void (unreasonable)

b.   Powers of Life Tenant

i. During life estate, life tenant holds present right to possession and may exercise that right as he sees fit. Life tenant may:

1.   exclude all others from possession, including person(s) holding a future interest

2.   lease the land and collect rents

3.   make improvements

4.   harvest products or extract minerals (and deliver clear title to them to 3rd parties)

5.   take any other action that might be taken by a holder of a fee simple absolute estate

ii.   Law of Waste

1.   life tenant has a duty to keep land unchanged in its nature, character, and improvements for the benefit of holder of future interest

a.   "externality" risk: life tenant could use his control to harm land, with cost of his behavior ultimately borne by holder of remainder interest

b.   remainder interest is protected by tort of legal waste

2.   remedies for legal waste

a.   damages to compensate for reduction

i. some states allow for multiple liability, once from each remainder interest

b.   value raised?

i. Unlikely damages

ii.   May be able to get injunction against destruction of property

3. Disagreements between use of land
   a. Co-ownership- partition available to co-owners as a matter of right
   b. divided ownership- partition-like remedy is not available as a matter of right
      i. instead, ct will order sale only as last resort, and only if consistent w/ best interest of all owners
      ii. thus, division of land into present/future estates creates significant (and perhaps serious) burdens on alienability of land
4. *Baker v Weedon*
   a. J dies, will has W (life estate), A's kids- none then (remainder in fee simple absolute), J's grandkids by 1st marriage (remainder in fee simple absolute if A died w/o kids); W used or rented farm for yrs, now wants to sell, J's gkids protest
   b. Appellate ct makes suspect argument about harm to gkids
      i. Sale not in best interest of all parties
      ii. Expected FMV to double in 4 yrs
      iii. Land probably overestimated
   c. Typical of CL decisions that did now allow life tenant to compel sale of fee interest over objection of holder of future interest (vice versa)
   d. J's intent matter?
      i. Intended to create life estate
      ii. Probably thought that this would be sufficient to provide for A during her life (wrong)
      iii. Separation of ownership into present and future estates created inflex and thus complicated future decisions regarding the land (burden on alienability)
   e. Trust would solve these problems
      i. Trustee: *legal* FSA; A: *Equitable* life estate; GKids: *equitable* remainder interest
      ii. If J's places land into trust, trustee has fiduciary duty to invest the land prudently for support of beneficiaries
         1. legally accountable to beneficiaries
         2. legal power to sell land, even if beneficiaries object

XII. FEE TAIL?
XIII. Defeasible Estates
   a. Defeasible Estate Corresponding Future Interest
      i. Fee Simple Determinable "to A so long as used for school purposes" possibility of reverter (retained by grantor)
      ii. Fee simple subject to condition subsequent "to A, but if land ceases to be used as a school, grantor may reenter" Right of entry or Power of termination (retained by grantor)
      iii. Fee Simple subject to executory interest "to A, but if land ceases to be used as school, then to X" executory interest (created in grantee)
   b. Fee simple Determinable
      i. "to A so long as alcohol is not consumed on the land"
         1. Terminates <u>automatically</u> once the stated restriction (*special limitation*) is violated
         2. <u>Possibility of reverter</u> in fee simple absolute
         3. "So long as..."- words of limitation that reflect O's intent to place a <u>durational</u> limit on A's estate

       ii.   "to A, but if alcohol is consumed on the land, O may reenter and recover estate"

           1. A has *fee simple subject to condition subsequent*

           2. estate may last forever, but if condition is breached, O can terminate A's estate (but it doesn't happen automatically)

           3. "but if…O may reenter" = words of limitation showing O's intent to create estate subject to condition subsequent

           4. O retains a *right of entry* in fee simple absolute

c. *Roberts v Rhodes*

     i. O deliver deed to School and heirs to be used to school or cemetery purposes only; land stops being used for school; School sells to X; O's successors sue X

       ii.   possible estates created?

           1. Defeasible fee simple (determinable or subject to condition subsequent)

              a. O would have future interest

           2. Fee simple absolute (Ct's decision)

              a. Language was wishful

           3. Fee simple absolute, but subject to covenant

              a. O could sue for damages or injunction if breached, but couldn't forfeit School's title

       iii.   Ct decided FSA is product of statutory rule of construction applied to ambiguous deeds

           1. In absence of intent to limit title, grantors pass all interest they own in the real estate

           2. Mere statement of purposes of a conveyance will not limit the extent of the grant

d. *Humphrey v CG Jung Educational Center* p282

     i. H deeds lot to R- "agreement as a convenant that land to be used for residence only" with reversion clause, should they so elect

       ii.   Ct says deed is ambiguous

           1. Some lang reflects intent to create a covenant (only injunctive relief available)- K right

           2. Some lang reflects intent to create defeasance (reversion clause)- property right

           3. Ambiguity means covenant, not defeasance

       iii.   deed not necessarily ambiguous

           1. ct implies that restriction must constitute either a defeasance or a covenant

           2. however, nothing prevents H from using same restriction as BOTH a defeasance AND a covenant

              a. should be able to reserve alternative remedies for violation of same restriction

           3. influenced by fed ct sitting in diversity, trying to interpret law as state ct would

       iv.   Some use restrictions typically take the form of Kal agreements or "covenants" that run w/ an estate in land

           1. Subdivision restrictive covenants

           2. If breached, these restrictions can be enforced

               a. At law: by action for damages caused by violation

               b. In equity: by injunction to enforce compliance with the covenant

           3. If a restriction constitutes a covenant, violation does not result in a forfeiture of title (in a defeasance, violation does/may result in a forfeiture of title)

       v.   *Johnson v City of LA*- land to be used for dam, w/ reversion clause for violation

           1. Ct enforces

           2. Wants to encourage public gifts

       3. If grantor owns surrounding land, that land would be worth more now

    vi. Efficiency explanation- *Humphrey*

       1. If area is being developed for residential purposes, commercial use of the restricted land could diminish value of land w/in the area

       2. This might justify creation and enforcement of defeasance

e. *Falls City* and *Cast*

    i. *Falls City v MO Pacific RR*

       1. FC deeds land to RR, reversion clause if not used for HQ

       2. ct: deed completely restricted alienability of land to other grantees, condition is void b/c unreasonable restraint on alienation

       3. RR has land in FSA

    ii. *Cast v Nat'l Bank of Commerce*

       1. W devised farm to nephew, subject to 2 conditions:

          a. He live on farm for 25 yrs

          b. Change last name to W

       2. ct: unreasonable restraint, thus void

    iii. Compared

       1. condition in *Cast* is private, idiosyncratic, and would provide no benefit to its enforcement

       2. condition in *FC* is public in nature and serves public purpose

          a. city acted to ensure responsible use of publicly-owned land (jobs, taxes)

          b. this would seem sufficient to justify condition

f. Marriage as a Condition/Restriction

    i. "to S in FS, but if S gets married, title reverts to grantor"

    ii. historically, cts enforced some such restrictions, depending on grantor's motive

       1. conditions tending to encourage divorce or marriage generally treated as void

       2. conditions motivated by desire to provide support often treated as valid

g. Lawyering

    i. Be aware of unforeseen consequences- changing area around land in question

    ii. Ct can stretch purpose of client to include selling land

h. Statutory Time Limits on Defeasible Estates

    i. Some states make defeasance restrictions unenforceable after a fixed period of time (30-40 yrs)

    ii. Why

       1. Caters to grantor intent to some extent (limits deadhand control)

       2. takes acct of risk of change in circumstances and avoids risk of perpetual "suboptimal" use

       3. takes acct of risks due to "fragmentation" of ownership after "old" defeasance is triggered

XIV. Future Interests in Land

a. Types of Future Interests

    i. Interests retained by the grantor (as part of a conveyance/devise creating a present estate in favor of a grantee)

       1. reversion

       2. possibility of reverter

       3. right of entry (also called power of termination)

    ii. Interests created in favor of a grantee

       1. Remainder

          a. Vested remainder

        b. Contingent remainder

    2. Executory interest

b. Future Estates Retained by Grantor

    i. Reversion

        1. future interest retained when the grantor (a) conveys a present estate of a lesser quantum than she has, and (b) does not create a vested future interest in favor of a 3rd party following that present estate

        2. O to A for life

            a. A=life estate; O=reversion in FSA

        3. O to A and heirs of his body

            a. (at CL) A=fee tail; O=reversion in FSA

    ii. Possibility of reverter

        1. estate retained by grantor when she conveys a determinable estate of the same quantum (duration) as she possesses

        2. O to A so long as used as a home

            a. A=FSdeterminable; O=possibility of reverter in FSA

        3. O (life estate) to A so long as used as home

            a. A=life estate determinable *pur autre vie* (measured by O's life); O=possibility of reverter for life

    iii. Right of entry

        1. estate grantor retains when grantor conveys an estate of same quantum (duration) as grantor possesses, but subject to a condition subsequent

            a. O to A, but if not used as a home, O may reenter and terminate the estate

                i. A=FSsubject to cond subsequent; O=right of entry in FSA

            b. O (life estate) to A, but if not used as a home, O may reenter and terminate the estate

                i. A=life estate subject to cond subsequent *pur autre vie*; O=right of entry for life

c. Future Interests Created in Grantee

    i. Remainder

        1. future interest created in a grantee that may become possessory at the natural end of the preceding estate that was created in the same conveyance/devise

            a. O to A for life, then to B

                i. A=life estate; B=remainder in FSA

            b. O to A for life, then to B for life, then to C

                i. A=life estate; B=remainder for life; C=remainder in FSA

    ii. Executory Interest

        1. estate created in a grantee that can become possessory only by divesting the preceding estate

            a. O to A when A graduates from school (A is in school)

                i. O=FSsubject to executory interest; A=executory interest in FSA (will divest O's estate when A graduates); A's interest is *springing executory interest* (title will "spring out" of grantor, to A, when divesting event occurs)

    iii. Classes of Remainder Interests

        1. Vested

            a. Created in an identifiable person AND

            b. Not subject to a condition precedent

         2. Contingent

   a. Created in an unascertainable person OR
   b. Subject to a condition precedent
3. exs
   a. O to A for life, then to B
       i. A=life estate; B=vested remainder in FS (B is IDfiable, and B's right to exercise control at A's death is not subject to condition precedent)
       ii.   Note: B surviving A is *not a condition precedent*
   b. O to A for life, then to B if B is then alive
       i. A=life estate; B=contingent remainder in FSA (express condition precedent of survival); O=reversion in FSA
   c. O to A for life, then to B's first child (B has no children at time of conveyance)
       i. A=life estate; B's first child has a contingent remainder in FSA (contingent b/c B's first child is not capable of being ID'd); O=remainder in FSA
   d. O to A for life, then to B's first child (at time of conveyance, no children)
       i. B has child (C)
           1. A=life estate; C=vested remainder in FSA (C now ID'd)
       ii.   C dies before A
           1. b/c C has vested remainder in FSA, it will pass under terms of C's will (or to heirs)
       iii.   Why isn't C's survival of a A (life tenant) considered a cond precedent (making this a contingent)?
           1. **grantor must make survival an express condition precedent, if that is grantor's intent**
           2. vested interests pass by will or inheritance (if not inter vivos)
   d. *Kost v Foster*
       i. MK executes deed conveying to RK for life, at death to his kids, the lawful child or children of any dead child of RK to have and receive its or their parents share
       ii.   Children's interest is remainder (possessory at end of Ross's life estate)
       iii.   Child Oscar goes bankrupt
           1. trustee sells O's interest to Foster
           2. R dies, survived by 7, F claims 1/7 of land, sues
       iv.   If O's remainder was vested, trustee sold it to F; If contingent, trustee's sale was void (contingent remainders inalienable in IL)
           1. CL- contingent remainders, right of entry, and possibilities of reverter could not be transferred inter vivos- expectancy, not property
           2. today, generally alienable in most states
       v.   O argues interest is contingent on surviving RK
           1. If O doesn't survive RK, deed says my interest passes to my kids
           2. This means I can't control how land would be disposed of at my death
           3. If I can't control how the land would be disposed of at my death, then my remainder interest can't be vested
       vi.   O loses
           1. his remainder is vested, subject to divestment (in favor of his surviving children, if he dies before RK)
           2. Two explains

a. There is *no express condition of survival* and the law doesn't imply one

b. It is technically possible that O could control what happens to the land at his death

   i. If O dies before RK, but has no kids, deed does not specify what happens to O's interest

vii. Was ct right to split remainder into 7 shares between RK's surviving children?

    1. No, should have been 8

    2. RK's 6 or 7 child (X) died as an infant, but that child had a vested remainder in FS, subject to divestment *only if X died before RK and left surviving kids* (which didn't happen)

    3. Thus, X's interest was not divested at X's death

    4. This interest would've passed to X's heirs (X's parents and older siblings, *but not* any younger siblings)

viii. Ex

    1. H to C for life, then to N's children and their heirs

        a. N has no kids at devise

            i. C=life estate; N's kids= contingent remainder in FSA (can't be ascertained)

            ii. If will has no residuary clause: H's estate has reversion in FSA, inherited by H's heirs

            iii. If will has residuary clause: residuary devisee takes alternate contingent remainder in FSA (will vest in N never has kids)

        b. At devise, N has 2 kids (S & A)

            i. C=life estate; S, A=vested remainder in FSA (ID's, there is no cond prec), *subject to open*

                1. class will "open" if N has more kids, who will share ownership of remainder (as co-owners)

            ii. H's estate: no future interest (interest of two living gkids is vested in FSA; H has given away his entire interest and retains nothing)

        c. At devise, N has 2 gkids

            i. C=life estate; S, A=vested remainder in FSA (ID'd, no cond prec), *subject to open*

            ii. 2 yrs later, A is killed.

                1. A's interest was vested FSA

                2. if A has not already conveyed that interest inter vivos, A's interest will pass under terms of will; if no will, to heirs

        d. 5 yrs since H's death

            i. C dies, ending life estate- N has 3 kids (S, A, J)

            ii. 2 yrs later, N has kid, B

            iii. At B's birth, S, A, and J have present estate in FSA

                1. B gets no interest at all- **Rule of convenience**

                2. Rule- class will close, even before the time it would have closed naturally, *when any member of the class is entitled to demand possession*

                3. rule of construction (can be avoided by writing explicitly in will)

e. Contingent Future Interests

    i. Destructibility rule (CL)

1. if a remainder is still *contingent* when the immediately prior estate ends, it is destroyed
   a. To A for life, then to B's heirs
      i. When A dies, if B is alive, remainder in B's heirs is destroyed
      ii. Land reverts to O in FSA
2. rule was necessary b/c law did not recognize springing future interests
   a. also, land is alienable sooner

ii. Merger Rule
1. if one person holds a present estate and *next vested future interest*, present estate merges into future estate and is terminated
2. O to A for life, then to B's heirs [B is alive]
   a. A=life estate; B's heirs=contingent remainder in FSA' O=reversion in FSA
   b. 10 yrs later: B is alive, and Comp. wants to buy for big $
   c. O could convey his reversion to A, which merges w/ A's life estate, remainder in B's heirs is still contingent, and would be destroyed, giving A FSA
3. Should it apply?
   a. No longer necessary, now that law recognizes springing executory interests
   b. Rule does not promote alienability, but is not needed for that purpose, as the RAP already serves that function

iii. Restraining Alientation and "deadhand" control
1. Fee Tail
   a. Created by words of limitation "and the heirs of his body" (O to A and the heirs of his body)
      i. A can transfer possession, *but only for A's life*
      ii. At A's death, A's lineal heir took possession of land (even if A had transferred possession)
      iii. Estate lasted til A's lineal heirs ran
   b. Abolished in nearly all states
      i. Burden on alienability of land
      ii. Encouraged a land aristocracy

f. Rule Against Perpetuities
   i. No interest is good unless it must vest, if at all, within some life in being at the time of the conveyance, or w/in 21 yrs thereafter
      1. Addresses inalienability caused by "remote vesting" (possibility that interests may remain contingent for a very long period of time, or perpetually)
      2. Period ("life in being" + 21 yrs) reflects balancing of interests (grantor intent v promoting alienability of land)
   ii. Applying RAP
      1. "Measuring life"
         a. he/she was alive at time the interest you're testing was created (when transfer took effect) AND
         b. the interest you're testing MUST vest OR fail during his/her life, or w/in 21 yrs of his/her death
      2. O to A for life, then to B for life, then to B's children [B had no children at time]
         a. A=present life estate (satisfies RAP, vested at time of creation)
         b. B=vested remainder for life (satisfies RAP)

    c. B's kids=contingent remainder in FSA (no class members yet ID'd)

        i. satisfies RAP

        ii. Last moment remainder could be contingent is at B's death- will be vested or fail then

        iii. B is a valid measuring life

    d. O=reversion in FSA (will take effect if B dies w/o children)

        i. Satisfies RAP

        ii. O's reversion is vested future interest @ creation

            1. At time of conveyance, O had *vested* FSA

            2. If O conveyed any part, whatever retained is vested in O

    e. **VESTED ≠ "WILL BECOME POSSESSORY"**

3. H to L for life, then to P's kids who reach 21 (at time of conveyance, none 21)

    a. L=life estate (vested, satisfies)

    b. P's kids=contingent remainder in FSA

        i. satisfies RAP

        ii. P is measuring life (class of his kids will close at his death; any born must reach 21 (or die) w/in 21 yrs of P's death)

    c. H=reversion in FSA (vested at time of creation, satisfies)

4. W to B, but if land ceases to be used as temple, then to T

    a. B=FSsubject to exec interest

    b. T=exec interest in FSA

        i. interest is void (RAP)

        ii. interest won't vest until land ceases being used as temple, but that could be 500+ yrs from now (after T's death, and death of everyone alive at time of W's conveyance)

    c. Why can't T be "measuring life"?

        i. If T is still a temple @ her death, T's interest will not fail when she dies

        ii. T's interest is contingent *only* on the land ceasing to be used as a temple, *not on her surviving until that happens* (survival is not presumed to be cond precedent!)

        iii. If T's interest were valid, she could transfer it inter vivos or at death (but interest wouldn't vest until land no longer a temple)

        iv. interest could vest more than 21 yrs after T's death (or any other "life in being"

    d. now, "to B, ~~but if land ceases to be used as temple, then to T~~

        i. b/c T's interest is void, B has FSA

        ii. T's exec interest would have placed profound practical burden upon the alienability of this land (effectively would have been perpetual burden on B and its successors)

        iii. App of RAP renders land immediately alienable by C (which holds vested FSA interest)

5. W to B for so long as used as a temple, then to T

    a. W has attempted to create exec interest in FSA in T, but this interest in void (as in (d), above)

    b. T=FSdeterminable

    c. W=possibility of reverter in FSA (will become possessory when land ceases to be used as a temple)

        i. satisfies RAP

ii. *vested* at time of creation

iii. retained by W, who had held vested FSA

iv. W's interest may never be possessory (if land is always temple), but it is still vested

v. gaping loophole in RAP's effectiveness

    1. W's retained interest has just as big a burden on alienability

    2. This explains state statutory time limits on the enforceability of defeasances (p283, note 4)

d. Try "W to B so long as used as a temple, then to T *if she is then living*"?

    i. T's exec interest now satisfies RAP

    ii. T is measuring life- at her death, either interest has vested (no temple) or it will fail (still temple)

e. For one to be a measuring life, their living or dying *must have some impact on whether the interest being tested will vest or fail at their death or w/in 21 yrs thereafter*

6. B to S for life, remainder to first son of S who reaches 25 yrs

    a. S has 3 teen sons

    b. Remainder in 1st son to reach 25 would be contingent remainder (reaching 25 in cond prec) in FSA, if valid

        i. void

        ii. after conveyance, S may have another son, J (not a "life in being")

        iii. next day: B, S, 3 sons die, class closes, J is <1yr

        iv. J's interest can't vest w/in 21 yrs

        v. remote vesting is *possible* (not likely, but possible), and thus contingent remainder is void in violation of RAP

    c. now, "to S for life, ~~remainder to 1st son of S who reaches 25 yrs~~"

        i. S=life estate

        ii. S's first son to reach 25=nothing; attempted contingent remainder interest is void in violation of CL RAP

        iii. B=reversion in FSA (takes effect in possession at end of S's life estate)

7. H to F for life, then to F's children who reach 25 yrs of age (at conveyance, F has 1 child, 26)

    a. 26 yr old has vested remainder, subject to open

    b. future children have contingent interest

    c. remainder **violates** RAP

        i. could vest too remotely in other children of F

        ii. A class gift must vest in *every member of class* w/in the perpetuities period to be valid!

    d. H to F for life, ~~then to F's children who reach 25 yrs of age~~

        i. F has life estate

        ii. F's children have nothing

        iii. H has reversion in FSA, to take effect at end of F's life

    e. Variation: H to F's children who reach 25 (at conveyance, F is dead, survived by 3 teen sons)

        i. H has attempted to create springing exec interest in FSA in F's kids

ii. **satisfies** RAP
iii. F's kids are measuring lives
1. Alive at time of conveyance
2. Will reach 25 or die w/o reaching 25
8. H to F for life, then to F's kids for life, then to P's children
   a. F's kids?
      i. satisfies RAP; class will close at F's death
      ii. F is measuring life
   b. P's kids?
      i. satisfies RAP, class will close at P's death
      ii. P is measuring life
9. H to F for life, then to his children for life, then to P's children then living [at time, F and P are both alive]
   a. F's kids? Valid
      i. F is measuring life
   b. P's kids? Violates RAP
      i. P's death won't cause interest to vest
      ii. class will close, but P's kids must survive F's kids (cond prec- "then living")
      iii. prob- thus, "vesting interest" is death of last child of F, but this could be an afterborn child
         1. after conveyance, F and P could have new children, F1 and P1
         2. 1 wk later, F, P, and all other lives in being die; F1 could then live for 90 yrs before P's interest could vest (if P1 survives F1)
   c. now, H to F for life, then to F's children for life, ~~then to P's children then living~~
      i. F has life estate
      ii. F's children have remainder for life
      iii. P's children=nothing
      iv. H=reversion in FSA
iii. *Merril v Wimmer*
1. N Merril's will devises land to trustee
   a. Trustee holds for benefit of N's kids (J, D, W) for their lives
   b. Trust was to terminate, and trust corpus (principal) to be distributed, as follows:
      i. when youngest gkid reached 25, trust to terminate w/ respect to 2/3 of trust assets, to be distributed between J, D, and their kids
      ii. when W died, trust to terminate w/ respect to 1/3 of trust assets, to be distributed between W's issues and N's then-living gkids
2. what interests do the trust beneficiaries have?

Merrill v. Wimmer

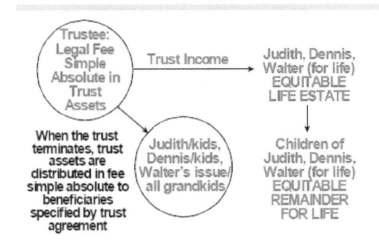

    a.
3. Interest in corpus (upon termination of trust) is an exec interest
    a. For duration of the trust, trustee has legal FSA (which it holds for benefit of equitable beneficiaries)
    b. When trust terminates, trustee's life as to trust property is divested; title to trust property shifts in fee simple to ultimate beneficiaries
    c. Thus, interest of beneficiaries in corpus upon termination of trust is exec interest
4. Do the exec interests satisfy RAP? No
    a. J/D/their kids
        i. Trust to terminate when youngest gkid is 25
        ii. Class of N's gkids is still open
            1. J could have new child, Bart, 2 yrs after N's death
            2. 1 wk later, J, D, W, and all other gkids die
            3. it would take >21 yrs before Bart could reach 25 and trust would terminate
    b. W's issue/N's gkids
        i. interest would vest at W's death, and W was life in being
        ii. appears to satisfy RAP
        iii. ct invalidates it anyway, under "infectious invalidity" doctrine:
            1. if ct had only partly invalidated the trust, W would've gotten not only his intended share (1/3 life interest) but also 1/3 of what was meant to go to J and D (by inheritance)
            2. N likely wouldn't have intended that; better to let residuary estate pass by inheritance equally
5. What is the intended meaning of "when my youngest gkid reaches 25"?
    a. Options
        i. Youngest of all, whenever born (invalid)
            1. SC interprets it this way
        ii. Youngest of gkid living at time of death (trust would terminate during their lives)
            1. appeals ct uses "equitable approximation" doctrine to

construe the language in this fashion in order to preserve trust

  b. Which makes more sense?

    i. as a matter of intent, appeals probably has it right

      1. N expected that J and D might still be alive when trust terminated

      2. But, if "my youngest gkid" includes afterborn gkid, you'd have to wait until J and D die before you could be certain who that was—in which case, there could be no distribution directly to J and D

      3. Trust terms only makes sense if we read them to mean "when my youngest living gkid is 25"

 iv. Applying RAP—Furthering Grantor's intent, or defeating it?

  1. Common law

    a. Shown in *Merril*; Remorseless; Cts applied RAP in intent-defeating way

    b. Traditionally, cts specifically refused to exercise equitable power to modify or "reinterpret" conveyances to avoid violations of RAP (even inadvertent/unintended ones)

    c. Promotes alienability of land; constrains deadhand control by defeating intent of grantors who violate RAP; encourages care/precision in drafting of conveyances/wills

  2. "Wait and See"

    a. explain/rationale

      i. RAP not applied at time of conveyance; rather ct waits to see if interests actually vest w/in life in being +21 yrs

      ii. We would wait to see if trust terminates w/in lifetimes of all N's descendants alive when he died (when his will took effect), or w/in 21 yrs thereafter

      iii. If we're willing to tolerate "life +21 yrs" of inalienability, what's the harm in waiting that long to see if a contingent interest will vest?

    b. H to F for life, then to F's kids who reach 25 yrs of age (at conveyance, F has 1 kid, 26)

      i. if F dies w/o addl kids, remainder in 1st kid is valid

      ii. if F dies leaving a child under 4, remainder is invalid

      iii. if F has more kids, remainder will be valid unless any are < 4 when F dies

  3. *Cy Pres*

    a. Cts reform deed/will so as to avoid RAP violation, *if reformation would be more consistent w/ grantor/testator's primary purpose*

  4. USRAP

    a. Adopts ct pres and wait and see

    b. Contingent interest satisfies USRAP if it:

      i. satisfies common law RAP, OR

      ii. actually vests w/in 90 yrs of its creation, OR

      iii. can be modified in a fashion that both carries out the grantor's primary intent and satisfies either the common law RAP or 90 yr wait and see period

    c. USRAP doesn't apply to interest created in nondonative (commercial)

transactions
- v. RAP applied to Trusts… good idea?
    1. No
        a. Not if RAP is concerned about the potential restraint on the alienability of land
        b. w/ most trusts, trustee has power to sell land in FSA (thus, alienability of land is not restrained, regardless of trust's duration)
    2. Yes
        a. If RAP is concerned w/ limiting deadhand control of assets, then applying RAP to limit time duration of trust makes sense
        b. Eventually, residual beneficiary gets to control investment of trust corpus, not trustor
    3. Increasing number of states have abolished RAP, by statute, as applied to trusts
        a. Reasons/Dynamics
            i. Allows creation of perpetual "dynasty" trusts in those states
            ii. Dynasty trust allows owner to place $1MM in trust for future descendants
            iii. Under dynasty trust, no federal estate tax levied on the trust as long as it exists
        b. Concerns
            i. what if, in future, all identified beneficiaries want to terminate trust?
            ii. American trust law is very inflexible, doesn't easily permit beneficiaries to terminate trust
- vi. RAP and Options to Buy Land
    1. CL
        a. Option w/o time limit violates RAP
        b. Option to buy land = equitable interest in land (enforceable by action for sp perf)
        c. Option = contingent (subject to condition prec- exercise of option)
        d. Orig owner's legal interest (legal title if he exercised option) could vest too remotely w/o time limit
        e. Concern- perpetual fixed-price option constitutes severe restraint on alienation/development of land
    2. USRAP
        a. Option arose in commercial transaction, RAP doesn't apply
- vii. Right of First Refusal and RAP
    1. def- having to give orig owner right to match any binding offer
    2. cts have almost uniformly concluded that RAP does not apply to a right of first refusal (no present equitable interest at time right granted)
    3. right of first refusal has no significant impact on alienability of land (still get full market value)

Concurrent Ownership
XV. Contenancy
- a. Types of concurrent estates
    - i. Tenancy in common (by the share)
        1. each tenant has coequal right to possession,
        2. no right of survivorship,
        3. may transfer his/her individual interest (his/her "share" of cotenancy)

278

      ii.   Joint tenancy (by the share & by the whole)
         1. each tenant has coequal right to possession,
         2. right of survivorship,
         3. may transfer his/her individual interest (his/her share of cotenancy)
      iii. Tenancy by the entirety (only in marriage)
         1. coequal right to possession,
         2. right of survivorship
         3. no right to partition or (generally) transfer his/her interest

b. Common characteristic- *unity of possession*
      i. Each coowner may enjoy possession of the entire land, subject only to same right of other coowners
      ii. Problems must be resolved 1) by agreement or 2) by partition; ct won't resolve it for them

c. Determining type of cotenancy
      i. Any coownership is **presumed** to create a **tenancy in common** *unless grantor expresses intent to create joint tenancy w/ right of survivorship*
         1. typical grantor wouldn't create right of survivorship between parties
         2. "jointly" doesn't indicate clear intention to create right of survivorship
      ii. "To N and E for their lifetime" N dies, devising everything to S. Interps?
         1. joint tenant for life (survivor would have individual life estate; N & S have nothing)
         2. Tenants in common for lifetime of survivor (N's share measured by E's life)
            a. N's share of tenancy in common for life would pass to S
            b. S and E would share right to possession as tenants in common, for E's life
         3. Most likely result: tenancy in common between N, E, for life, measured by both of their lives
            a. N's share passes to S
            b. S has undivided right to possession (concurrently w/ E) for duration of that estate (i.e. until E's death)
            c. After E's death, land reverts to grantor in FSA
            d. Life estate measured by last tenant to die
      iii. *Palmer v Flint*
         1. "Bank to N and A as joint tenants, and not as tenants in common, to them and their assigns and to the survivor, and the heirs and assigns of the survivor forever"
         2. options
            a. N and A joint tenants in FSA
            b. N and A joint tenants for life, w/ survivor holding an individual remainder in FS
         3. A's argument
            a. N and A joint estate for their lives, w/ contingent remainder in survivor
            b. Rationale: Language "to them and to the survivor, and the heirs and assigns of the survivor forever" suggested that *only survivor of them would have inheritable estate*
            c. A's contingent remainder was not transferred to N by virtue of A's quitclaim deed (contingent remainders were still inalienable at that time)
            d. Thus, A now owns land in FSA (having survived N)
         4. Holding

a. Joint tenancy in FSA

b. **Rule of construction**: deed passes grantor's entire estate (here, FS) unless grantor expressly or impliedly limits the estate granted

c. A's quitclaim deed upon divorce severed joint tenancy and transferred share to N (giving N FSA)

d. N subsequently deeded to himself and R as joint tenants in FSA

e. R now owns land as surviving joint tenant

5. Critique of holding

   a. Words "and to the survivor" are also consistent w/ joint tenancy

   b. Fact that deed didn't say "to N and A *and their heirs*" doesn't prove Bank intended to give them only a life estate

   c. If A is correct, Bank would have retained a contingent remainder, but there is not reason to expect Bank intended to retain any future interest

   d. Ct's interp avoids practical burden on alienability of land caused if deed had created a contingent remainder in survivor

d. Survivorship

   i. O to A and B as joint tenants in FS, and not as tenants in common

      1. coownership in FSA (right of survivorship is inherent characteristic of joint tenancy; *it is not a future interest*)

      2. either A or B can unilaterally sever by transfer, terminating right of survivorship

   ii. O to A and B for their joint lives, remainder to survivor of them forever

      1. creates in both A and B an individual future interest (a *contingent remainder* in FSA) which cannot be destroyed by unilateral action

   iii. Which of the above would A prefer?

      1. depends on circumstances

      2. imagine B has terminal illness, and attempts to deed her interest in land to her children

         a. #1: joint tenancy severed; B's children and A would hold as tenants in common in FSA (no right of survivorship if B dies before A)

         b. #2: B's children and A hold life estate as tenants in common; if B dies first, A will take land in FSA (survival contingency)

e. "Secret Severance"

   i. *Riddle v Harmon*

      1. execution of deed to self, "severing" joint tenancy w/ husband; husband does not know, only daughter

      2. Mr. Riddle argues deed was not valid, didn't sever joint tenancy or destroy right of survivorship

         a. Doesn't matter that Mrs. Riddle was grantor and grantee under deed

         b. Important legal distinction between Ms Riddle as grantor (joint tenant w/ right of survivorship) and Ms Riddle as grantee (individual who would hold her share as tenant in common)

         c. Delivery would be satisfied in this situation as long as deed was executed *w/ present intent to effect a severance*

      3. challenging secret severance

         a. lack of present intent

            i. fraudulent

            ii. If Mr Riddle dies first, Ms Riddle can destroy secret deed and claim title as surviving joint tenant

            iii. Lacked intent to make a present transfer

       b. Harmed parties under secret severance
          i. Mr Riddle- didn't know he was tenant in common, now needs a will
          ii.   Potential buyer- wouldn't know of severance deed
   ii.   Some states have statute mandating recorded severance deed to make it effective

f. "Four Unities"-
   i. necessary in joint tenancy
      1. unity of **time**- joint tenant had to receive interest at same time
      2. unity of **title**- joint tenant had to receive their interest by virtue of same instrument
      3. unity of **interest**- joint tenants had to have interest of the identical size and quantum
      4. unity of **possession**- joint tenants had to each have undivided right to possession of the land
   ii.   if **any** unity was broken, joint tenancy was severed and became tenancy in common

g. *Harms v Sprague* –mortgages and joint tenancy

Harms v. Sprague

1. Sprague obligated to repay loan to Simmons
2. John Harms mortgages his interest in his land (held as joint tenant w/brother, Wm. Harms) to secure payment of Sprague's debt to Simmons
3. John dies; will devises his land to Sprague

   i.
   ii.   Classic Mortgage Transaction Under **Title Theory** of mortgages

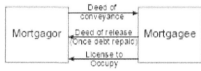

• Legal right to possession conveyed to mortgagee
• Mortgagor can occupy land as long as not in default on mortgage payments
• Upon default, mortgagee may retake possession, sell land, deliver mortgagor's title to purchaser

   iii.
   iv.   Sprague's view- John's mortgage transferred John's title to Simmons, severing unities of time and title
      1. After mortgage, state of title: W Harms and Simmons were tenants in common
         a. John retained an equitable interest (to redeem his share by paying off the mortgage)
         b. Simmons thus held his share subject to John's right to redeem title to the land, by repaying mortgage
      2. Mortgage thus terminated right of survivorship
      3. At John's death, Sprague took John's share as devisee under John's will (subject to Simmons' mortgage)
   v.   The Modern Mortgage Theory of Transaction Under **Lien Theory** of Mortgages

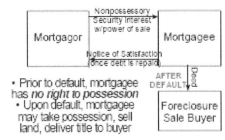

- Prior to default, mortgagee has *no right to possession*
- Upon default, mortgagee may take possession, sell land, deliver title to buyer

vi.

vii. Held: Mortgage did not sever joint tenancy
1. IL is "lien theory" state
2. mortgage is not a transfer of "title" to mortgaged land; title would not shift until John defaulted and Simmons conducted foreclosure sale to enforce Simmons' lien (nonpossessory security interest)
3. W Harms owns land as survivor
   a. Simmons' mortgage is now void (Simmons' right was derivative of John's now-extinguished right)

h. *Mann v Bradley*

i. Mr/Mrs Mann, joint tenants, divorce. Terms:
1. Mrs Mann would continue to live in home, w/ their 3 kids
2. House would be sold and proceeds split when
   a. Youngest child reached 21, or
   b. Mrs Mann remarried (whichever occurred first)

ii. Mrs Mann dies

iii. Ct: although 4 unities continued to exist at Mrs Mann's death, divorce agreement had already severed joint tenancy
1. Agreement reflected their intent to no longer own as joint tenants w/ right of survivorship
2. parties agreed to sell/divide land, putting off date of sale solely for benefit of kids
3. implausible that Mrs Mann would want joint tenancy after divorce
4. Manns are tenants in common; Mrs Mann's share passes by will or inheritance to her kids

iv. *Mann* and Four Unities
1. Mrs Mann's sole possession break unity of possession?
   a. Law should encourage these types of agreements
   b. Cts view these agreements as having no effect on unity of possession

v. *Harms* in a *Mann* jurisdiction
1. If John intended for mortgage to sever joint tenancy, Sprague would have ½ interest in the land, as a tenant in common w/ W
2. Credible evidence of John's subjective intent when he granted mortgage-
   a. Sprague's promissory note (co-signed by John) said load was to be repaid from sale of John's interest in joint tenancy, or after 6 months
3. Problems w/ a rule depending on John's subjective intent
   a. John is now dead, unable to testify about intent
   b. Sprague's testimony may be biased
   c. John's conduct may be only reliable evidence of his intention
4. Typical person in John's position probably would not have intended to sever joint tenancy
   a. Typical mortgagor doesn't expect to "lose" title, but for a loan to be repaid and mortgage released
   b. Probably would not expect this act to affect fellow joint tenant's

282

interest

i. Modern Role of Four Unities

    i. W/o credible proof of subjective intent to terminate joint tenancy (divorce agreement in *Mann*), "4 Unities" is plausible default rule

        1. *Harms*- under lien theory, mortgage is not transfer of title, no transfer of title = no severance

        2. had John clearly intended to sever, he should have manifested that by making effective transfer of title

        3. he could/should have made inter vivos conveyance of his ½ share to Sprague, subject to existing mortgage in favor of Simmons

j. Homicidal Joint Tenant- N and E are joint tenants; N kills E; E's will leaves all assets to C

    i. Four Unities Approach

        1. N would appear to be FS owner as survivor

        2. Alt: murder severed joint tenancy

    ii. *Mann* Approach

        1. N's intent to commit murder = constructive severance (at time of death, tenants in common)

    iii. Other cts

        1. N owns FSA, but subject to constructive trust (for benefit of E's devisees or heirs)

k. Exoneration

    i. At common law, specific devisee of land had right of *exoneration*- right to have any lien against the land satisfied out of decedent's residual estate

        1. Gates dies w/ land w/ $100,000 mortgage to E, remaining $100,000 cash to T

        2. E gets land in FSA, T gets nothing

    ii. Statutes overrule this- but common law *never applied as between joint tenants* (even though they are mentioned in statute)

        1. S, K own land as joint tenants, subject to $100K mortgage

        2. S dies, K is not entitled to have mortgage satisfied out of other assets in S's estate

        3. K received her interest by right of survivorship, not by devise from S's estate

    iii. Why mention joint tenants?

        1. Argument 1) avoids result from *Harms*

            a. statute meant that when John's interest (subj to mortgage) passed to W, W took it subj to mortgage

            b. this is contrary to common law derivative title rule

        2. Argument 2) statute "codified" CL rule that there was no right of exoneration between joint tenants for joint debts

    iv. Ct doesn't consider statute in *Harms*

        1. Under arg 2, statute doesn't apply, mortgage was extinguished by John's death

        2. Under arg 1, statute's application and interp should have been raised as an issue at trial

            a. Since it wasn't, issue was waived on appeal (civ pro)

    v. Attaching Co-owned Property

        1. Creditor w/ judgment v tenant in common or joint tenant has lien on the cotenant's *individual share* of co-owned property

        2. Fraudulent conveyances (to avoid attachment in anticipation of judgment)

            a. CL allowed creditor to invalidate such a transfer

            b. Attachment then allowed

        3. See *Sawada*, below

l. Tenancy by Entireties
   i. *Sawada v Endo*

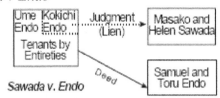

1. Mr. Endo has accident, injures Sawadas
2. Mr./Mrs. Endo transfer home, owned as tenants by entireties, to their sons
3. Sawadas get judgment vs. Mr. Endo
4. Sawadas seek to set aside deed to sons as fraudulent transfer

    1.
    2. held: conveyance by Endos to sons was not fraudulent
       a. tenants by entireties own "by the whole and NOT by the share"
       b. Mr Endo has no individual ownership in land, distinct from wife
       c. Mr Endo's *individual* creditors cannot attach lien v entireties property

  ii. Married Women
    1. at CL
       a. husband had a marital estate in all land owned by wife and over all marital interests
       b. H has complete dominion/control over H&W's and W's lands during marriage
    2. Married Women's Property Acts abolished this and removed disabilities that had existed on married women
       a. Maj: MWPA made H and W equal by taking away H's control; neither party can take unilateral action to affect the tenancy (*Sawada*)
       b. Min: MWPA made H and W equal by giving W the same rights H had at common law
          i. Either H or W could transfer right to possession;
          ii. other spouse would still have a right to possession and right of survivorship

  iii. Tenancy by Entireties and Individual Creditors
    1. Min- "Group II"
       a. voluntary transfer of right to possession, subject to co-tenant's rights of shared possession and survivorship
       b. if transferor outlives cotenant, transferee gets FSA; if cotenant outlives transferor, transferee gets nothing
       c. problem- risk of nonfamily member having possessory right is too disruptive of family harmony
    2. Min- "Group IV"
       a. Right of survivorship can be attached (no present right of possession during marriage)
       b. Gift in *Sawada* would be fraudulent
       c. Problem- lien against one spouse's survivorship right could prevent spouses from using home equity for family purposes
    3. Better solution-
       a. some states limit how much can be held by entireties
       b. some states abolished TBE altogether
    4. *Sawada* view
       a. Justification

     i. Protects spouse, children from improvident acts of one spouse

     ii. Makes entireties tenants take marital relationship seriously

     iii. Protection from individual creditors creates incentive to hold land by entireties

    b. Problems

      i. Tort creditors can't "adjust" to this rule

       1. don't choose to deal w/ debtors

  iv. Forfeiture and Entireties Property

    1. forfeiture- property involved in drug trade by one spouse, not other

    2. If tenants are joint or in common, govt can forfeit individual interest and sell it

    3. tenants by entireties

      a. in *Sawada* jd, no individual right to forfeit

      b. some cts hold govt can take right to survivorship only

  v. Creating Tenancy by Entireties

    1. conveyed "by the entireties" to unmarried couple. Options?

      a. 1) tenancy in common

      b. 2) joint tenancy

      c. 3) Joint life estate w/ contingent remainder in survivor

    2. cotenants are not by entireties automatically when later married (for coowned or individually owned property)

      a. new conveyance is required to create this separate legal person

XVI. Rules Governing Relationship Between Coowners

 a. Adverse Possession in cotenancy

    i. tenants in common- one occupies, one does not for 15 yrs; occupier then rents space; nonoccupier wants to move in and kick out renter

     1. renter and nonoccupier are cotenants w/ right of tenants in common during lease

     2. (same leasing in entireties tenancy would be void; only 1 spouse did it)

    ii. adverse possession must be hostile- will not be assumed to be hostile until some objective action is taken

     1. living in a home, paying taxes is not a sufficient "signal"

     2. disagreement over selling the home is not necessarily "ouster"

 b. Action involving coowners

    i. **Accounting** (equitable): one coowner asked to account for benefit he/she received that belongs to all coowners

     1. Does not terminate coownership

     2. From above (a)(i)(1) hypo, can nonoccupier demand rent for occupier's 15 yrs of occupation? (accounting)

      a. No, not w/o an agreement or ouster

      b. Only enjoying own right to possession

     3. Renting the land

      a. Must account to coowner for rents collected

     4. Rents and profits

      a. Must account for net rentals

      b. Can take credit for expenses incurred

       i. taxes

       ii. mortgage interest

       iii. repairs

       iv. improvements

     5. Farming and farm profits

    a. If one coowner works land, and the other does not, the worker need not account for profits

    b. Why not? He's not the owner of the farming operation

  ii. **Contribution** (legal): one coowner seeks to recover from other coowners expenses/costs that he/she incurred

    1. Does not terminate coownership

    2. Contribution for "carrying costs"

      a. Cotenant paying taxes has a right of contribution from other cotenants

  iii. **Partition** (equitable): ends cotenancy; land (or value) split among cotenants

    1. Ct can adjust shares based upon unaccounted-for benefits, expenses

    2. On agreement for one coowner to possess and pay expenses, with partition later, occupier cannot get contribution for expenses

    3. Partition can be sought as a matter of right

    4. Land can be split:

      a. **In kind**, giving each former cotenant ownership of separate portions, OR

        i. preferred type of split

        ii. dividing into sublots may diminish value

      b. **By ordered sale,** and division of proceeds between coowners

      c. Also split considering accounting and contribution

    5. "Right" to partition/ Agreement not to partition

      a. coowners (esp. multiple) need way to resolve disputes over how land will be used

      b. agreement not to partition is an unreasonable restraint on alienation

        i. not time-limited

        ii. voting allows maj to oppress min

        iii. min owners could be forced to sell out for less than what share is really worth

      c. some cts see agreements not to seek partition as reasonable

  iv. Meshing accounting and contribution- "Rental Value Offset"

    1. If A sues B for contribution of ½ of taxes:

      a. Maj- B can counter for accounting of rent value of A's sole possession

      b. Min- B gets no rental value against tax liability

    2. Maj is more sensible- nonoccupier would not expect to bear ½ cost of ownership

c. If ouster occurs

  i. Ouster must pay ousted ½ (or 1/3, or 2/3, etc) of FRV for use of other(s)' right(s)

d. Repairs

  i. Absent contrary agreement, no right of contribution for cost of repairs

  ii. Can try for accounting of repairs

  iii. Can get credit in partition

e. Improvements

  i. no right of contribution for improvements

  ii. can get credit in accounting or partition

  iii. improvement by one cotenant

    1. may have credit in partition *to extent improvement increases land's value*

    2. be careful of what increased the value- improvements or land value

f. Exploitation of Natural Resources

  i. extracting cotenant must account to other cotenants for (1/2 of) *net* revenue from extracting nonrenewable resources

      ii.   logic: land being severed and sold; normal coowners would agree to share proceeds

      iii.   availability of partition depends on type of natural resource taken and its value/availability on the other ½ of the land

  g. waste between cotenants

      i. CL- one cotenant could not sue other cotenant for waste

         1. In partition (equity), cts often took account of "waste" in adjusting shares

      ii.   today- statutes in many states let cotenant sue for waste w/o seeking partition

  h. Tax sales

      i. Maj- if coowners acquire interest at same time, law views them as *fiduciaries*

         1. A acquires land at tax sale on behalf of he and B

         2. B can reimburse A, reclaim share w/in reasonable time

         3. A can quiet title if B fails to reimburse him w/in reasonable time

      ii.   Min- coowners are not fiduciaries

         1. B could have paid taxes herself, A had no obligation to act to protect her interest

Landlord and Tenant

XVII. The Lease as a Conveyance v Lease as a Contract

  a. Traditional view- Conveyance

      i. Rent in exchange for possession of land

      ii.   Tenant's liability based on tenant's status as possessor of an estate in land

      iii.   "privity of estate"- liability for rent

         1. mutual relationship between L and T when L conveyed a possessory estate to T, retaining future estate in the land

         2. T's obligation to pay "rent" issued *directly from the land* itself

         3. if L evicted T, T's liability for rent ceased

  b. Lease as a Contract: Covenant of Quiet Enjoyment

      i. Leases today often contain covenant by T, ostensibly conditional, to pay rent for agreed term

      ii.   Covenant established T's liability via *privity of contract*

      iii.   *Covenant of quiet enjoyment* is implied into leases

         1. Def- T's liability for rent conditioned on L not interfering w/ T's right to possession

         2. presumed intent of L and T in making lease

      iv.   protects interference by

         1. L

         2. persons acting as L's agent or at L's direction

         3. persons holding "paramount title" to L

      v.   If CQE breached, T can

         1. seek damages/injunction OR

         2. can terminate lease (CQE is dependent covenant, breach excuses T's rental obligation)

      vi.   in case of even a partial eviction by L, T's obligation for rent is *entirely excused*

         1. if partial eviction has been made, and T continues to occupy the rest of the land, T is liable in quasi-K for reasonable value of that occupancy

      vii.   Damages for breach of CQE

         1. expectation damages: if FRV of leased premises > actual stated rent, then L's breach deprives T of benefit of the bargain

            a. measured = FRV – actual rent

         2. consequential damages: costs incurred by T in finding other premises, costs of

moving/storage
- a. consequential damages will be subject to K law's foreseeability requirement

viii. **Constructive eviction**
1. elements
    - a. Intentional
    - b. Substantial and
    - c. Permanent interference
2. legal equivalent of an actual eviction
3. T can declare rent terminated (must vacate); T is not liable for rent that would have accrued in future
4. Interference by Third Parties
    - a. Generally, CQE does not protect against acts of 3d parties, *if 3d parties are not acting at L's request or are not under L's control*
    - b. T is in a position to protect its own interest and can't hold L responsible for 3d party interference *unless the lease expressly or impliedly allocates that risk to L (Fidelity v Kaminsky* [abortion provider picketed])
5. Practical issues of constructive eviction
    - a. L must have duty
    - b. T must vacate first (if not, how bad is the problem, really?)
    - c. Is the problem bad enough?
        - i. Ct may not find it rose to CQE
        - ii. If so, T breached by not paying rent
        - iii. Documentation needed showing seriousness of interference
    - d. Alternatives/needs for T?
        - i. Pay rent, sue L for damages
        - ii. Sue L, pay rent into ct escrow (if permitted)

ix. Paramount Title
1. def-
    - a. rights in leased premises inconsistent w/ T's rights as purportedly created by lease
    - b. that are held by a 3d party when lease is made
    - c. and which the L cannot terminate by the time the T is entitled to possession
2. L has life estate, A remainder in FSA, T rents from L for 5 yrs, L dies after 2 yrs
    - a. L has breached CQE
    - b. Once A is entitled to possession, A has paramount title and T's right to possession is extinguished
    - c. A would have to authorize T's lease
    - d. T should have searched public records
    - e. Damages
        - i. L's estate can not hold T liable for future rent
        - ii. T has damages claim v L's estate
            1. T Can't recover rent from first 2 yrs
            2. T can recover money paid in advance for yr 3
            3. T can recover foreseeable consequential damages
            4. Expectation damages, if T lost benefit of a valuable lease

288

3. One day into term, T learns L has previously rented to X, who has not taken possession; T vacates and refuses to pay rent
   a. L has not breached CQE
   b. X hasn't interfered w/ T's possession
   c. **Mere Existence of paramount title doesn't breach CQE**
   d. CQE protects against *actual eviction*, not risk of eviction
 c. Lease as Conveyance and Contract
  i. Dependency
   1. Under K, Mutual promises are dependent (material breach excuses non-breaching party's performance)
   2. Traditionally, lease covenant were independent
    a. except CQE, which was central to bargain, was dependent covenant
  ii. Premises destroyed during lease
   1. Ts relieved of liability, lease terminated if premises destroyed
  iii. Liability of Prematurely Departed T
   1. anticipatory repudiation- recover $ for entirety of lease, rather than each month

XVIII. Discrimination in Leasing
 a. Traditional View of L-T bargain
  i. As owner of land (w/ power to exclude), L may choose not to lease to particular T *for any reason* (or none at all)
 b. **Fair Housing Act**
  i. Restricts discrimination-based decisions in housing
  ii. Legislative judgment that "protected classes" have suffered (or would suffer) exclusion from housing market w/o protection
   1. students, lawyers are not protected classes
   2. Congress needs to "find" systematic exclusion justifying protection
   3. localities can enact local ordinances to address local exclusion problems
  iii. Denial cannot be based on **family status**
   1. some families w/ kids have to rent (can't afford to buy)
   2. lack of access to housing for families w/ kids presents safety, health, and economic problems
   3. common law right to exclude outweighed by public interest in access to housing
  iv. FHA Exemptions
   1. **ONLY APPLIES TO RESIDENTIAL**
   2. doesn't apply to owner-occupied duplex
   3. single-family home sold or rented by owner, as long as owner doesn't own more than 3
   4. Why exempt?
    a. FHA focused primarily on those "in the business" of providing housing
     i. Public accommodation laws justified by Congress's power to regulate commerce, those engaged in activities affecting interstate commerce
     ii. Regulating "little guys" should be sufficient to open up access to protected groups
  v. Advertising Regulations
   1. "Small potatoes" exclusion for owners of 3 or fewer single-family homes *doesn't protect preferential ads*
   2. Ads/statements that express a preference based upon protected class status violate FHA

a. Denial decision of "small potatoes" will violate FHA by using preferential ad

3. Why?

   a. Ease of administrative enforcement (just scan the ads)

   b. L can't use instrumentality of commerce to publicize discriminatory preference

   c. Forces L to "look potential Ts in the eyes" before excluding them

4. interpreting

   a. cts tend to interpret language of ads through the eyes of a member of the protected class

   b. i.e. would a member of the class think the ad was expressing a preference?

vi. Discriminatory intent

1. L is liable if it intentionally denies lease applicant based upon applicant's status w/in a protected class

2. For prima facie case, P must prove *through direct evidence* that decision was based on an impermissible factor

vii. Disparate treatment

1. P must prove

   a. Belonged to protected class

   b. Applied and was qualified

   c. Was denied

   d. Similar applicants treated more favorably

2. burden shifts to L who must establish its denial was based on legitimate neutral justification

   a. can't just be pretextual

viii. Practical Issues

1. T must burden cost of discovery and investigation

2. public interest groups often do "testing"

XIX. Leasehold Estates: Their Creation and Characteristics

a. *David Properties v Selk*

i. Selk sells land and shack to DP

1. Selk takes "purchase money" mortgage to secure DP's obligation to pay $45K balance of price

2. Selk stays in possession of home (DP allegedly agreed)

ii. Immediately after sale

1. Selk has **tenant at will** status

2. either party can terminate tenancy at any time by giving notice to the other

3. one party or other can contract away right to terminate

iii. Selk & DP sign lease, renting for $1 the shack and land from Oct-Dec

1. now Selk has **tenancy for years** or **term of years**

   a. fixed beginning and ending dates

   b. no notice needed to terminate term of year

   c. can terminate "naturally" by end of term

iv. Selk stays in possession past term

1. Selk is now a **"holdover" tenant** or **tenant at sufferance**

   a. At CL, L could

     i. Reach new agreement w/ T OR

     ii. Treat T as trespasser and take action to evict T OR

     iii. "hold over" T for a new term (not longer than 1 yr) on the

same terms as old lease (even if T objects and doesn't want new term)
- b. Rationale for Holdover Rule
  - i. T signals intent to be bound to new term
  - ii. Punish T to make T account for external costs caused by holdovers
- c. Today
  - i. L no longer has unilateral option to hold "holdover" T to a new term
  - ii. T liable for damages = rental value of land for time of holdover (and foreseeable consequential damages)
- v. *Selk* ct- ***implied periodic tenancy***, which continued for following 22 mnths (product of holdover + DP's letter demanding removal or payment + Selk's continued holdover)
  1. renews for additional periods automatically, until *either L or T* gives one period's notice to terminate
  2. classically arises when T goes into possession under oral lease that violates SoF
- vi. Other ways to interpret DP's letter
  1. offer for a lease on different terms
  2. treat Selk as trespasser, sue for damages (FRV for holdover period)
  3. order to vacate inconsistent with language to pay rent
- b. ***Periodic tenancy*** (i.e. month-month)
  - i. Terminable upon 1 period's notice
  - ii. Traditional view- must give one period's notice, or be liable for full rent until proper notice is given (even if you vacate)
  - iii. Modern ("Intent") view- manifestation of intent to terminate is enough, liable for last full period's rent

XX. Modern Lease—Problem areas in negotiation, drafting, and interpreting leases
- a. Lease creation
  - i. Creation of a lease is a matter of substance, not form
  - ii. If a possessory interest is created, then a lease is created
  - iii. Other remedies for breach: expectancy, reliance
- b. Possession at commencement
  - i. English (contract) rule
    1. L has duty to place T in actual possession on first day of term
    2. if prior T holds over, L is responsible (L has breached lease with T)
    3. rationale
       - a. L has greatest incentive to control/avoid holdovers
       - b. L better suited to know of prior T's plans
       - c. Ls typically more familiar w/ eviction process
  - ii. American (status) rule
    1. L has no such duty absent express covenant to do so
    2. once a term begins, T can/must protect itself by evicting holdover T
    3. rationale
       - a. conveyance view of lease
       - b. at commencement, T, not L, has estate and right to possession
  - iii. Contract should not be interpreted to allocate to T risk of *unreasonable* or unlimited delay
    1. express provision may allow a minor delay

2. cts are often more reluctant to "imply" unexpressed duties into commercial leases

    iv.   Delay and length of lease term

       1. traditional (conveyance) view: lease covenants independent

       2. modern (contract) view: *material breach* of covenant that was "part of the *essential consideration* for lease" excuses non-breaching party, even if termination right not expressed

c. Tenant Default

    i. Abandonment by T

       1. Three options

          a. leave it vacant, sue T for rent as it comes due OR

          b. accept T's surrender, terminating T's lease (T no longer liable for future *rent* payments) OR

          c. re-enter and re-let them on T's account, while still keeping T bound on original lease (liable for future rent payments as the come due)

       2. CL: L lets it sit vacant, sue T for rent as it came due

          a. Lease is a conveyance

          b. T has estate, T can use it or not

          c. L should be able to get sp perf of lease

          d. If L is in business of leasing, harm to L isn't "mitigated" by finding replacement T (L could've leased other space to the replacement)

       3. Trend: L has duty to mitigate

          a. Lease is K

          b. law shouldn't award "avoidable damages

       4. Now:

          a. Many states continue to hold that L has no duty to mitigate

          b. Some states, L has general duty to mitigate, parties *in commercial leases* are free to contract around that rule

       5. L's options for re-letting

          a. (1) Accept T's surrender, which terminates T's lease, and re-let on L's account

             i. T no longer liable for future *rent* payments

          b. OR (2) Re-enter premises and re-let them *on T's account*

             i. T remains bound on original lease (and liable for rent payment as they come due)

             ii. Re-entry and re-letting would be an *implied sublease or assignment* of T's estate

Transfer of Tenant's Interest

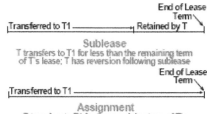

          c.

          d. If L re-lets to T1 after terminating T's lease, L is re-leasing on its own account

             i. T has no claim v each rent payment by T1

             ii. But, T is not liable for rent if T1 later defaults

  e. If L re-lets to T1 on T's account, T is still liable for rent if T1 doesn't pay
    i. But, absent contrary agreement, surplus rent belongs to T, not L
 6. Abandoning T's liability
  a. If L accepts surrender, terminates T's lease and liability for rent, *but not for damages for breach of lease*
    i. Damages for anticipatory repudiation = full term of lease x $/mnth lost bargain (from re-letting at lower rent), discounted to present value of money
    ii. L could recover this amount immediately from T
  b. If L re-lets on T's behalf, L can recover lost bargain from T in extra rent each month as it comes due
 ii. Rent Acceleration Clause
  1. clause that makes T liable for all of term's rent immediately in case of breach by T
   a. View 1: yes, L and T could've bargained for prepaid rent, so acceleration clause just converts deal into deal for prepaid rent once T defaults
   b. View 2: this is unenforceable penalty (T wouldn't have agreed to pay $60K in advance, but a discounted price)
  2. leaves open possibility for double recovery by L
   a. recover from defaulting T once, then re-let to T1 and recover again)
   b. Solution 1: L can't terminate lease if it wants judgment for accelerated balance
   c. Solution 2: Any amt L collects from "new" T must be applied to reduce judgment v T
 iii. Padlocking premises (and T's property inside)
  1. CL: L could use self-help if L didn't "breach the peace"
  2. Today: maj- prohibit self-help w/o T's consent (after default)
   a. L must resort to summary eviction process
   b. Eases risk of violence
  3. note: lease has to have started to limit self-help
  4. locking up property inside
   a. L's interest doesn't extend to T's personal property
   b. L would have no right to hold unless lease granted security interest
   c. L's act is conversion
 iv. Other protection clauses
  1. Survival clause
   a. expressly preserves L's option to re-let either on L's acct or on T's acct
   b. "re-entry and re-letting shall not be deemed acceptance of T's surrender, it being understood that surrender can be effected only by written agreement of L and T"
  2. "Recapture" clause
   a. any "bonus value" from re-letting belongs to L

XXI. Condition of Premises
 a. Trad: *caveat lessee*: L has no duty to maintain premises
  i. Lease is conveyance, as party in possession, T has responsibility to maintain land
  ii. T can inspect, decide whether to rent premises as is, maintain premises thereafter
 b. Now: cts in most states have held that *residential leases* contain ***implied warranty of habitability*** that L will maintain premises in a condition that is safe, clean, fit for human

293

habitation
- i. General rule: "defect is of a nature and kind that will prevent the use of the dwelling for its intended purpose"
    1. case-by-case analysis warranted
- ii. L must (a) place premises in habitable condition at beginning of term, (b) maintain them in such a condition throughout the term
- iii. IWH is treated as a "dependent" covenant; if breached, T may sue for damages, *but may also terminate lease/withhold rent payments*
- iv. IWH is immutable (unwaivable) rule. Potential issues:
    1. bargaining power
    2. paternalism (law should refuse to enforce waivers b/c Ts generally don't appreciate risks associated w/ waiver – Ts will undervalue benefit of IWN as compared to reduced rent)
    3. public policy (health/safety reasons for Ts in substandard housing)
- v. Commercial leases
    1. agreements as to how one party shall comply w/ a mandatory duty may be enforced if not "manifestly unreasonable"
    2. i.e. an agreement mandating 45 day period to fix (in 1 yr lease) may be unreasonable for residential (violating IWH), but not manifestly unreasonable for commercial; consider:
        - a. duration of "fix" period v period of lease
        - b. rent abatement clause during fix period?
- vi. Measuring damages: 3 options
    1. *Hilder*
        - a. FRV of premises as warranted – FRV "as is"
        - b. Pro:
            - i. standard expectation measure of K law
            - ii. gives L incentive to spend $ to get premises habitable
        - c. Con:
            - i. Low-income can't absorb rent increases
            - ii. L may pull out of market (making housing scarce)
            - iii. "FRV" is artificial, hard for juries to determine
    2. *Kline*
        - a. Agreed rent – FRV "as is"
        - b. Pro:
            - i. Easier to determine
            - ii. T can't recover more than agreed rent
        - c. Con:
            - i. De facto waiver of right to damages for beach of IWH
            - ii. T could still terminate lease, but most Ts don't want to terminate (no better options)
            - iii. Bad housing policy (incentive for L to improve bad conditions?)
    3. *Pugh*
        - a. Agreed rent x % reduction in use
        - b. Easiest for lay juries to comprehend and apply
        - c. Doesn't permit effective waiver of damages for breach of IWH (like *Kline*)
        - d. L has some incentive to improve conditions in order to avoid liability, but L's liability is capped by agreed rent

c. Commercial Leases and Condition of Premises
    i. No warranty of "fitness" implied in commercial leases
        1. more equal bargaining power than in residential leases
        2. public health issues underlying IWH not a significant factor in commercial context
        3. no "typical" bargain can be extrapolated
    ii. If L knows of condition problems that would prevent proper use
        1. T could rescind based on misrepresentation
        2. in commercial lease, L has no duty to disclose presence of such defects, unless unlikely to be discovered by inspection

d. Casualty/Unexpected Risks
    i. Trad rule: if premises destroyed during term, T not excused
        1. T bargained for possession of land, still has it
        2. exception: if T leased only *part* of a building, and *entire* building is destroyed, then lease is terminated, T excused
            a. presumed that T bargained for space, not underlying land
    ii. Modern rule: if lease silent, lease terminates if premises destroyed w/o fault of L or T
        1. reflects contract doctrines of impracticability, frustration of purpose (T really bargained for improvements)
        2. L in equal/better position to protect against such risks (insurance for casualty loss and interruption of rent)
    iii. Long term lease
        1. "Net lease"
            a. carrying costs of ownership (taxes, insurance, maintenance) are borne by T
            b. L shifts economic ownership risks/benefits to T
            c. Ct likely to fill a gap in a lease by assuming parties allocated economic risks of ownership to T (like casualty risk)
                i. Casualty clauses are often used to expressly allocate risk
    iv. Unexpected Expenses- *Hadian* (seismic retrofitting)
        1. Repair clause
            a. Provision requiring T to make repairs doesn't require T to bear cost of seismic retrofit
            b. Interping such a clause
                i. 1: literal language of repair clause in the lease "presumptively" controls
                ii.   2: look to surrounding circumstances to "conform" that literal language really was intended to allocate this particular risk to T
            c. Circumstantial factors relevant to scope of T's liability under Repair Clause
                i. Relationship of cost of repair to amt of rent reserved under the lease
                ii.   Length of lease term
                iii.   Benefit of repair to L compare w/ benefit to T
                iv.   Whether repair is "structural" or "nonstructural"
                v.   Degree to which repair will interfere w/ T's right to possession
                vi.   Likelihood that parties contemplated the particular repair in

question

2. "Compliance with Laws" Clause (ex- asbestos removal)

    a. allocates burden to T to comply w/ laws of general applicability regulating buildings and land use

    b. apply "repair clause" steps to these types of clauses

        i. does T have time, over term of lease, to pass through and recoup costs of work?

        ii. Cost of work v agreed rent?

        iii. Benefit of expenditure?

            1. if useful life of work >>>! remaining lease term, L gets significant benefit

        iv. interference w/ T's business while work is being done

XXII. Transfer of Leasehold Estate

    a. General rule: T's estate is "property" and thus T can freely transfer it

        i. However, most leases contain a "no-transfer" clause that forbids T from assigning or subletting its interest w/o L's consent

    b. Why isn't this an unreasonable restraint on alienation?

        i. **Trad view: L may withhold consent for any reason** (L's ability to choose Ts is absolute)

            1. Proponents say

                a. Allows L, which has a significant residual economic interest in the land, to protect that interest

                b. L may have justified concerns about proposed assignee's credit, or proposed use

            2. Opponents say

                a. Allows L to discriminate against persons L doesn't like (possibly race-based)

                    i. FHA would generally prohibit this today

                b. Does L have "L's remorse" over a bad bargain (now that rents have gone up)?

    c. *Kendall* and Bonus Value from Subletting

        i. T has long term, fixed-rent lease; market rates increase, making lease unfavorable to L; T wants to assign to T1; L wants all of lease's bonus value

        ii. **Modern Rule: L must have "commercially reasonable" basis for withholding consent**

            1. property: clause is unreasonable restraint on alienation (making it void) if reason for refusal is unrelated to L's economic interests as a landlord

            2. Contract: L has duty to perform and enforce lease in good faith

        iii. Ct: withholding consent to capture bonus value not "commercially reasonable"

            1. clause protects L as landlord, not L's "general economic interests"

            2. doesn't mean L can't object for economic reasons, just that the economic reasons have to be related to L's operation of the property

    d. **Subletting Rule: Whether T could have expected L would reject T1 on those grounds**

        i. Could be seen as an unreasonable restraint on alienation

        ii. "L" is subjective

            1. unless "L may not w/hold consent unreasonably" is in K- may indicate an *objective* estimation of business judgment

            2. (1.) may change interpretation of reason for denial

    e. Sublettors that are transferring from L's other property

        i. Could be seen either way

1. unreasonable restraint
   a. clause does not protect L's general economic interest
2. reasonable restraint
   a. maybe T has long-term, fixed-rent lease and protection from future increases in rent
   b. L is in business of leasing, shouldn't have to compete w/ T in leasing space (*Kendall* forces such competition)
   c. L should insist upon T giving up right to transfer, in order to capture long-term , fixed-rent right to possession

f. Due-on-Sale Clauses
   i. Def-
      1. borrower agrees not to sell land w/o mortgage lender's consent
      2. if borrower makes an unauthorized transfer, lender can accelerate, demand immediate payment of full mortgage balance
      3. due-on-sale clause would prevent borrower from selling land to Buyer and Buyer simply "taking over" borrower's mortgage payment, at least w/o mortgage lender's consent
   ii. Analogous to *Kendall*
      1. if lender can refuse, buyer can't simple "take over" existing loan, he must get new mortgage
      2. if interest rates have gone up, lender gets higher rate for new loan
      3. lender uses the clause to hedge against risk
   iii. Acceptance of this
      1. some states: this is unreasonable restraint on alienation
      2. Congress: reasonable, no matter what state law says

g. Acceptance of *Kendall*
   i. Maj of states have refused to accept *Kendall* result
   ii. In these states, L can w/hold consent under no-transfer clause, T cannot assign/sublet w/o L's consent, even to capture bonus value
      1. some have held this is permissible under trad rule (even if was viewed as arbitrary or unreasonable decision by L)
      2. others have held that L's refusal to consent in order to capture bonus value is commercially reasonable

h. Recapture Provisions
   i. Requires payment by T to L in the event that T assigns/subleases its interest during lease term (amt of payment dictated by terms of recapture clause)
      1. common in many leases, even non-*Kendall* jds
   ii. In *Kendall* jds, L must have recapture clause in lease in order to have claim against lease bonus value
   iii. How to avoid this if clause is for transfer of lease in sale of business
      1. one way
         a. If selling business, just sell stock to T1
         b. no transfer of lease, recapture provision isn't triggered
         c. Recapture clause should be written to prevent transfer of maj or all of ownership interest in T
      2. another way
         a. T and T1 could manipulate sale price to avoid clause
         b. Instead of selling equipment/goodwill to T1 for $X, and charging rent (bonus value $Y), sell assets for $(X+Y) and assign lease to T1 at current rate

297

        c. No excess rent, no obligations to pay L

i. Use of Premises

    i. Prohibitory v Authorizing constraints

        1. prohibitory- certain uses aren't legal

        2. authorizing- T can only make a particular use; preferable b/c:

            a. T's creditworthiness or business acumen to run other types of biz

            b. Operational concerns (proper tenant mix, preserve project's primary use, avoid interference w/ other T uses or exclusives

        3. T trying to weasel out of lease based on authorizing clause

            a. T: excuse based on impracticability or frustration of purpose (franchise out of business, K to run that type of biz)

            b. L: use restriction is there for L's benefit, so L can choose to waive breach and allow T to make another use

                i. Is it really only for L's benefit?

                ii. If authorizing restriction is too narrow, it will be difficult to counter frustration of purpose argument

        4. T has 25-yr term, builds waffle house, sued by neighbor for violating res-only covenant on land, injunction is granted. T liable for rent?

            a. Does lease **require** use of land as a waffle house or restaurant?

                i. If yes, then covenant is paramount title, deprived T of benefit of lawful possession

                ii. Breaches CQE, T excused

                iii. T doesn't have to argue frustration of purpose under K law

        5. same case, except "T may use premises for any lawful purpose" on lease

            a. not a CQE case

            b. T argues frustration of purpose

    ii. Duty to Operate (WAL*MART)

        1. factors in "going dark" inquiry

            a. relationship of fixed rent and relationship of % rent to fixed rent payments

            b. term of lease

            c. T's right to assign/sublet

            d. T's right to remove fixtures

            e. Presence of "noncompete" clause

            f. Whether T is "anchor" tenant

            g. Party drafting lease

        2. Conveyance model- absent restriction, T can use (or not) its estate as long as T pays rent

        3. Contract model- anchor T might have good business reasons to close store but keep paying rent

            a. If L wants T to have duty, should have bargained for it

            b. Silence reflects L's decision to assume this risk

        4. this is often seen by cts as a predictable, foreseeable risk if not bargained for

        5. Percentage rent- suggest mutual expectation that T would operate and generate sales?

            a. Yes, if expected % rent was "substantial" in relation to minimum rent payments and land's fair rental value

            b. No, if fixed rent was "substantial" or close to fair rental value of premises

        6. T's right to sublet/assign w/o L's consent- implied operating covenant?

a. *PigWig* ct- weighs strongly against requirement to operate

b. Arguments against this- does this mean sublessee can also go dark?

7. L Minimizing risk

a. Short term lease (unlikely T will agree)

b. L may cancel if T goes dark (unlikely)

c. Time limit

d. L can re-let to noncompeting tenant

e. Radius restriction for T opening another store

iii. "Exclusive" provisions

1. "True exclusive"- gives T right to be the only seller of a particular product w/in a defined area (selling food)

2. "limited exclusive"- gives T right to be only party conducting a particular type of business w/in a defined area (restaurant)

3. Interpreting

a. If items are listed, they may be treated as "exclusive," even if phrased to limit use

b. To limit use, lease should provide that T can't sell items that would violate another T's exclusive rights

4. Remedy for T

a. Damages will be T's only remedy unless ct treats "exclusive" as a dependent lease covenant

b. Damages will be hard to prove

c. T wants express right to terminate in case of breach

i. Many cts do treat breach of noncompete clause by L as excusing T's performance, but better if this is expressed

d. T should also record lease (to give notice of exclusive to later tenants, so T could obtain injunction vs them)

Nonpossessory Interests – Easements, Covenants, and Servitudes

Servitude—nonpossessory property interest in the land of another

-easements

-real covenants (covenants running at law)

-equitable servitudes (covenants running in equity)

Servitudes are either *affirmative* (permit holder to use land owned by another or compel owner of servient land to do something) or *negative* (permit holder to prevent another from using land in a particular way)

Easements

XXIII. Express Easements

a. Servitudes (and, particularly here, easements)

i. **Appurtenant**- benefits the ownership of a different parcel of land

1. e.g., owner of lot B has an easement to cross lot A in order to reach public road from lot B

2. easement on lot A (servient estate) is *appurtenant* to lot B (dominant estate)

3. ownership of easement "runs with " ownership of lot B

ii. **in gross**- benefits its holder individually, and not as a owner of land

1. not transferable

b. determining if *appurtenant* or *in gross* is by function of grantor's intent

i. differing language in paragraphs of lease in *Alft* case granting *in gross* access to lake, *appurtenant* access to driveway

ii. ambiguity resolved in favor of appurtenance- based on presumed intent

1. appurtenance raises value of dominant land

2. reasonable person would create appurtenant easement to command higher price (if selling dominant land)
3. easement in gross would create burden on servient parcel w/ a corresponding benefit on other land
4. promotes preservation of land values

iii. reasons for grating easement *in gross*
1. a favor
2. influence identity of transferee of dominant land (if easement is necessary for access to land—*Alft*)

iv. factors in favor of *appurtenance*
1. practical benefit to LAND in value, usefulness
   a. think resale value
2. long stated duration of easement

c. Restatement of Servitudes
   i. Change
      1. Trad- "in gross" = personal
         a. lake easement was "personal" to Alfts, it was "in gross"
      2. Rest- distinguishes "in gross" from "personal"
         a. *In gross/appurtenant* distinction focuses upon land-relatedness (is right tied to ownership of particular land?)
         b. "personal" focuses upon transferability ("personal" = not transferable)
   ii. Why change?
      1. more sensible to separate transferability of easement from its general character
      2. some easements should be treated as transferable, even if "personal" (e.g. utility easements for which the holder paid)
      3. but easements in gross were traditionally presumptively nontransferable
   iii. *Alft* under Rest.
      1. both driveway and lake easements are tied to Alfts' ownership of the lot (both appurtenant)
      2. driveway easement would "run" (transfer) with ownership of Alft lot
      3. lake easement, however, would not (it is personal) according to its terms

XXIV. Non-express Easements
a. Types
   i. Prescriptive Easement
      1. easement based on longstanding adverse use
      2. use is to prescriptive easement as possession is to adverse possession
   ii. Implied easement based upon **prior use** (quasi-easement)
   iii. Implied easement of **necessity**
   iv. Irrevocable license?
      1. typically, licenses are by nature revocable, but may be made revocable by estoppel

b. Prescriptive Easements
   i. "hostility" can be objective or subjective, depending on jd
   ii. Default rule
      1. use of another's land, w/o evidence as to how it began, is presumed hostile
      2. **TO has burden to show use was permissive** in order to avoid prescriptive easement
   iii. Exception
      1. shared use of another's driveway, **built and also used by TO for his own use**, is presumed permissive

2. circumstances justify conclusion that use arises out of neighborly accommodation

3. **user has burden of proof that use was hostile**

iv. *Melendez v Hintz*

1. looped driveway

a. "loop" was clear invasion of interest of owner of lot

b. owner of lot did not use "loop" portion

c. used Default Rule- fulfilled period of prescription by using time lot was occupied by previous owner

2. if driveway had not been looped, but used together

a. use "exception" rule

b. presumed permissive

c. no evidence of hostility

3. Public policy of this result

a. Ct's mistake

i. By focusing on loop, ct implies that use must be "exclusive"

ii. Generally, prescriptive use doesn't have to be exclusive

1. unlike possession, use not exclusive *by its nature*

2. Owner of dominant estate is not trying to prevent servient owner from using drive, just continue using it himself

iii. "exclusive" is NOT a characteristic of PE, but is of AP

b. Good

i. Neighbors view use differently from possession

ii. If detrimental reliance (building loop), that would be unmistakable evidence of hostility

c. Bad

i. We want TO to be vigilant and raise challenge to encroachments…

ii. Presumption of permissiveness would permit TO to remain silent in face of ambiguous conduct by neighbor using shared driveway

v. Prescriptive cross-easement?

1. shared (cost/use) driveway, new owner wants to fence his lot

2. depends on whether use is presumed permissive or hostile

a. permissive- "burdened party" can't overcome presumption

i. no express easement

ii. no extrinsic evidence sufficient to demonstrate claim of right

b. hostile- "burdened party" will likely prevail

3. allowing continued use comports better w/ policy underlying prescription doctrine (puts burden on "lot splitter" to object/clarify "burdened party's" status

c. Implied Easement of Necessity

i. If a lot is landlocked **due to transfer severing lots from common ownership**, an easement of necessity is implied

ii. Servient lot must have been part of original, common lot that created servient and dominant lots

iii. "Cartway" easements (allowed by statutes in some places)

1. allow owner of landlocked parcel to condemn an easement over adjacent parcel

       2. owner must pay fair value for easement

       3. cartway easement is perpetual

          a. even if holder subsequently acquires other means of legal access

          b. contrast- implied easement of necessity terminates when no longer necessary

  d. Implied Easements from Prior Use

      i. Factors relevant to grantor's intent, according to FIRST Restatement

          1. was use **apparent** (visible) at time dominant and servient parcels severed from common tract?

          2. was use **continuous** at time parcels were severed (manner or nature of use)?

          3. was use **necessary** (reasonably convenient) at time parcels were severed?

          4. is the easement an implied grant or an implied reservation?

          5. would "reciprocal benefits" accrue to both grantor and grantee from implying easement?

      ii. Why must it have been apparent, continuous, and necessary at time of severance?

          1. "**apparent**" std demonstrates that use was w/in contemplation of parties

          2. "**continuous**" and "**necessary**" stds show that aprties appreciated benefits of continuing pre-existing use (stds are thus a proxy for lack of express statement of intent in the deed)

          3. w/o these factors, there would be no reason to infer that parties would have intended for the use to continue after the severance of the parcels

      iii. *Bob's Ready to Wear*

          1. parking lot is bought, rear entrance to Bob's is fenced off

          2. ct says implied easement is not justified (Bob's has only permission/license)

             a. no reciprocal benefit *unless parcel remains in parking lot*

             b. as a parking lot, owner can raise funds to offset burden of easement

             c. but, would create a heavy burden that would impede future development for other uses

          3. Policy

             a. Pro: should be reluctant to imply easements

                i. Reluctance increases the incentive for parties to document their transactions carefully (get an express easement)

                ii. If there is ambiguity/doubt regarding parties' intent, this should be resolved against implication of an easement

             b. Pro: concern that implying quasi-easement will unduly impact on transferees of would-be servient land

                i. Would a subsequent transferee have realized there was an easement over the servient parcel where no easement appears in the deed?

             c. Con: "reciprocal benefit" may have been "premium" (increased price due to parking an access rights) sellers of lots got for parcels when they sold them to Bob's, parking owner

                i. Even if sellers may have constrained their future ability to develop the servient land, they were still benefited

             d. Con: seller's prior use (for parking and tenant access) and continued use by both Bob's and buyer suggest that all contemplated use would continue

      iv. Grant v reservation

          1. some cts will imply easement more readily by grant (servient owner deeds dominant estate to grantee) than by reservation (dominant owner deeds

servient estate to grantee)

2. rationale: if grantor wants to reserve easement across land it is conveying, grantor can do so expressly (grantor usually prepares deed)
3. factor operates similarly to contracts rule of interp that ambiguity is construed against party that drafted contract
4. would create easement by implied grant in *Bob's*

v. Comparison: Express Easement
1. no "reciprocal benefit" analysis
2. even if servient lot could better be used otherwise, that doesn't limit dominant estate's rights

vi. Restatement of Servitudes
1. Rule: Ct should imply easement from prior use when, upon severance of parcels from common ownership, "the parties had reasonable grounds to expect that the conveyance would not terminate the right to continue the prior use"
2. Factor
    a. Was prior use not merely "temporary" or "casual"
    b. Was continued use "reasonably necessary" to enjoyment of benefited parcel
    c. Was prior use "apparent or known to parties"
    d. Was prior use "for underground utilities serving either parcel"

vii. *Bob's* and **Irrevocable Licenses** (Equitable Estoppel)
1. licenses are generally revocable (licensee has no "real property" right to continue use)
2. theory in *Bob's* that license to use lot for customer access is irrevocable based upon equitable estoppel
    a. detrimental reliance (Expense of renovations to back door) upon conduct by seller
    b. *Bob's* will suffer irreparable harm (loss of investment) if buyer can revoke license
    c. *Bob's* reliance is reasonable under the circumstances (longstanding use, no objection)
3. "reasonableness" of reliance on only a license: a contextual judgment
    a. may have thought they had an easement, not just a license (i.e. use by right, not permission)
    b. buyer improvement of rear entrance on reliance of prior use
        i. buyer doesn't have "clean hands" in dispute
4. Ct: *Bob's* has irrevocable license
    a. Does not mean an easement
    b. Irrevocable to the extent needed "to prevent licensee from being unfairly deprived of the fruits of expenditures" (Old Rest.)
        i. Suggests *Bob's* can use license until they recoup cost of rear renovations
5. A licensee cannot extend a license beyond its original purpose
    a. Irrelevant to *Bob's*, though
    b. *Bob's* is making same use as before
    c. Buyer couldn't revoke license indirectly by changing use

XXV. Duty to Maintain Easement
a. Default rules
    i. Where easement holder uses road/way, but use is **not shared** by owner of servient

land, holder bears duty to maintain easement

        1. presumed intent: burden of maintenance more plausibly borne by party benefiting from its use

     ii. in contrast, **where use is shared w/ owner of servient land**, duty to maintain is shared between easement holder & owner of servient land

  b. multiple users of easement; lang "to help" pay?- *Elrod* lake access

     i. lang is at least consistent w/ shared duty

     ii. free-riding problem, risk of chaos, resulting poor maintenance of road

     iii. ct interprets agreement to avoid this problem by allocating duty/cost to servient owner

XXVI. Scope of Easement

  a. Use of easement/servient land is governed by "rule of reason"

     i. Easement holder can make reasonable use of servient estate

         1. can't unreasonably interfere w/ servient owner's possession and enjoyment

         2. owner of servient land can enjoin "excessive" use or recover damages caused by such use

     ii. servient owner can reasonably enjoy possession of servient estate, but can't unreasonably interfere w/ holder's use of easement

         1. easement holder may enjoin an unreasonable interference, or recover resulting damages

  b. Consider

     i. Was new use w/in contemplation of original parties when easement was created

         1. is so, then use is "reasonable" (w/in scope of easement)

         2. if not, then "excessive"

             a. CL: generally, servient landowner is entitled to an injunction against excessive use

  c. Utilities

     i. Does an *express easement* allow for underground lines to dominant estate?

         1. are they needed to provide meaningful enjoyment of dominant land?

         2. if so, "access" likely to be interpreted to include access for both people and utilities (Rest. Serv.)

     ii. What about *easement by prescription*?

         1. would use of surface have "signaled" the possibility of use of subsurface for utilities?

         2. servient estate owner might have objected to underground usage

  d. Transference/Division of easement

     i. Transference

         1. trad rule: easement in gross is personal to holder, not transferable

             a. exception: commercial easements in gross are transferable

             b. rationale: presumed that parties would expect holder could transfer easement to recoup its investment (otherwise, utility company wouldn't invest finds needed to establish infrastructure)

         2. *Henley v Cablevision*

             a. SWB could use its easement to install CATV lines and provide service

             b. w/in scope of orig easement ("telephone & electric light purposes"), not "excessive"

             c. used to bring power, communication, even though not foreseeable in 1922 (time of easement creation); no increase in intensity of use

     ii. Division & Exclusivity

         1. If grantee's easement rights are "exclusive," the grantor cannot make any use

of that strip of land to provide same service as in scope of easement

    a. If rights are "**exclusive**," they **can be divided**

  2. if grantor retained right to share right of use conferred to grantee, then grantee's easement is "**nonexclusive**" and **can't be divided**

 iii. *Henley* decided that easement was "exclusive" b/c trustees retained no interest or authority for using strip to provide utility service (and they never did so)

    1. Trustees aren't harmed if SWB licenses others to provide utilities

    2. Problem:

      a. trustees had right to provide services **and** grant easements

      b. does fact trustees haven't done so for 60 yrs suggest they intended to assign this right away in 1922?

    3. Pro: contrary ruling would require Cablevision to incur higher "infrastructure" expense of obtaining express easements

      a. Higher cost would be passed on to consumers

      b. Public benefit >>> nominal private burden on servient landowners

    4. Con: no, ruling is plainly anti-competitive

      a. If lower-cost competition is now possible, ct's decision frustrates that competition

e. Combining parcels

 i. Use of appurtenant easement to benefit land other than dominant estate is *per se* excessive use (beyond intended scope)

    1. if use is excessive, servient landowner has "property right" to exclude or prevent that use

 ii. *Brown v Voss*

    1. Brown combining 2 parcels, easement only to 1; above rule is used, but injunction denied b/c of inequity; ct is WRONG

    2. dominant landowners (now in error) put themselves in problem

    3. can condemn and pay for easement to benefit new parcel if it is landlocked (*see* cartway easement)

    4. could have denied injunction on equitable estoppel

      a. Voss knew Brown was constructing home

      b. V could have objected sooner, but didn't (17 months)

      c. Brown paid $11K in that time (detrimental reliance), which he can't if ct grants injunction

f. Relocation of Easements

 i. Trad rule

    1. if deed that created easement also specifically located it in that area, then servient owner can't unilaterally relocate

    2. rationale: by definition, any change would be unreasonable interference w/ easement holder's rights *in that location*

 ii. If servient landowner offered to pay?

    1. CL: no matter, dominant owner may still refuse

    2. New Rest: unilateral relocation would be possible *unless the easement expressly denied servient the power to relocate it* (see below)

 iii. Relocation under New Rest.

    1. owner of servient estate may make reasonable changes in location of easement, at servient owner's expense, but only if:

      a. change does not significantly lessen the utility of the easement

      b. change does not increase the burdens on the owner of the easement in its use and enjoyment

c. change does not frustrate the purpose for which the easement was created, AND

d. express terms of the easement do not deny servient owner the power to relocate easement

iv. if deed does not identify specific location for easement, ability to relocate is a fact question

1. will relocation of easement "unreasonably" interfere w/ dominant's ability to enjoy it?

Negative Easements, Covenants, and Equitable Servitudes (Promissory Servitudes)

XXVII. **Negative Easements, Covenants, and Equitable Servitudes (Promissory Servitudes)Covenants Running with Land**

a. Background

i. Trad, CL didn't recognize "negative easements," except in very limited circumstances (flow of light or air)

ii. Contract law's influence- agreement between two restricting use of land is enforceable between them, but what about to transferees?

iii. **Test for Covenant to Run "At Law"**

1. covenant **intended to bind successors** to original promisor

2. covenant "**touches and concerns**" the land"

3. **privity of estate** between orig promisor and transferee

4. transferee took land **w/ notice** of covenant

5. need ALL ELEMENTS

b. Privity of Estate Req

i. 3 yr lease for T; T transfers to T1 after 1 yr; T1 transfers to T2 w/ 6 months left; no money comes in for last 4 months

ii. most leases have express covenant to pay rent

1. L can recover remaining rent from **T** due to their **privity of contract**

2. Contractual liability is not excused, absent novation or release by L

iii. L can recover remaining rent from **T2** b/c they were in **privity of estate**

1. L and T were originally in privity of estate, based on mutual interest in premises (horizontal)

2. Privity was transferred to T1, then to T2, by subsequent assignments (vertical)

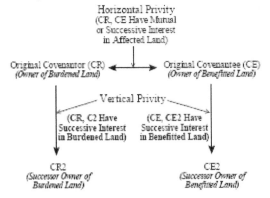

3.

iv. What about **T1**?

1. Covenant to pay rent to L "run" to bind transferee if T transfers leasehold estate?

a. Intent to bind successors- usually express on lease

b. Rent covenant "t & c" land- lease is "rent for possession" exchange

c. Notice? Unknown

d. Privity of estate?

i. when T1 assigned to T2, L and T1 no longer in privity of estate

ii. if he had sublet, then they would still be in privity of estate

iii. L should have had no transfer clause and had T1 guarantee rent

iv. T1 sublettor who grants full possession for his term to T2- L can't collect from T2, no privity of estate

v. Sublet v Assign distinction

  1. CL

    a. Transfer for balance of term- assignment

    b. Transfer for less than balance of term- sublease

    c. Parties can't contradict nature of transfer

  2. Modern

    a. Characterization should be based on parties' intent

    b. What shows intent

      i. Reversionary interest? Sublease

      ii. "sublease" lang, w/ reversionary interest? Could be argued either way

vi. Benefit/Burden distinction for horizontal/vertical privity

  1. A & B sign agreement that neither they, nor successors/assigns will operate business on respective land; A sells to C, who builds business; B sues C for damages (reduced value); privity of estate?

    a. If "privity of estate" is only vertical privity: yes

    b. If horizontal also req'd: no

      i. A & B just neighbors

      ii. Covenant not created as part of a transaction involving transfer of interest in land (e.g. a lease)

      iii. If A had transferred lot to B, with deed having restrictions, then sufficient horizontal privity

  2. Still, C can enforce against B

    a. C is asserting benefit of covenant, and is seeking to impose burden on B

    b. CL- only req'd privity of estate for **burden** or a covenant to run w/ land to bind a successor; privity not req'd for **benefit** to run to a successor

    c. Rationale: running a burden could impact alienability of land (not a problem w/ respect to benefit)

Privity of Estate and Enforcing Covenants at Law (for damages):

Plaintiff	Defendant	Enforce-able?	Rationale
CE	CR	Yes	Covenant enforceable based on privity of K
CE2	CR	Yes	Privity of estate not needed for benefit to run to CE2
CE	CR2	No	Horizontal privity lacking; burden doesn't run to CR2
CE2	CR2	No	Horizontal privity lacking; burden doesn't run to CR2

    d.

  3. Equitable Servitudes

    a. B can enforce against C in equity (injunction against business) if:

      i. Covenant **intended to bind successors** to A (orig promisor)

      ii. Covenant **t&c land** AND

      iii. C took land **w/ notice** of covenant

vii. Rejecting "privity" req

1. privity insufficient proxy for parties' expectation regarding enforcement
2. intent, t&c and notice are sufficient "checks"
3. if successor has notice of covenant, she can factor burden of covenant into price she is willing to pay
4. Rest of Servitudes rejects privity req

c. Touch and Concern Requirement

    i. *Neponsit*

      1. test

        a. covenant t&cs if it **imposes a burden upon an interest in land**, which

        b. **increases the value of a different interest in the same or different land**

      2. *Neponsit* test not really helpful

        a. just describes effect of enforcing the covenant:

        b. if covenant runs, it increases value of benefited land

        c. this test doesn't help decide whether or not any particular covenant *should* run w/ land

      3. Neponsit Home Owner's Assoc. covenant enforcement rationale

        a. covenant functions to ensure NPOA can preserve common areas

        b. such maintenance preserves value of each lot

        c. lack of funds would threaten value of lots

        d. while covenant is an indirect restraint on alienation, it is reasonable and efficient (which should be enforceable)

    ii. *Creager*

      1. gas station partnership dissolution; one has to buy gas from the other for 5 yrs, unless sold, in any event for at least 12 months

      2. test- did parties **intend** covenant to "run w/ the land" to bind successors

        a. covenant is "personal" to CE & CR, does not pass to CR2

        b. Rule: **if benefit of a covenant is personal (*in gross*), burden of covenant doesn't run** to bind successors

    iii. Affirmative Covenants (like in *Creager*)

      1. Trad- not enforced, in contrast w/ neg covenants

      2. concern- does enforcement create a unwarranted or unreasonable burden on alienability of land?

        a. Covenant may become obsolete w/ time

          i. Title burdened

          ii. *Creager* burden is brief

        b. Aff covenants often aren't needed to permit neighbors to accomplish mutual objectives

          i. Can Creager sell gas elsewhere, does it need to be tied to ownership of the gas station parcel?

      3. deed obligates paying developer $250/yr for water

        a. want to know if fee sustains neighborhood

    iv. *Caullett*

      1. S sells lot to C for $4K (bargain); "grantors reserve right to build" orig. home on lot- to bind "purchasers, heirs, assigns"; C sues to quiet title

      2. Touch and concern- relevant?

        a. Irrelevant- C is orig covenantor (not transfer); C's liability is a function of K law

        b. Relevant- establishing covenant isn't binding to successor would enable easier sale of land

3. Held: Covenant not enforceable
   a. Meaning is too "obscure" to be ascertained
   b. Doesn't t&c
      i. Doesn't limit uses to which may be put (not land-use-related)
      ii. Benefits S personally, not as the owner of other land
      (**benefit is in gross, so burden of covenant will not run so as to bind successors**)
v. Rest. of Servitudes
   1. Abandons t&c test
   2. Servitude is valid unless
      a. Arbitrary, spiteful or capricious
      b. Imposes an unreasonable restraint on alienation
      c. Imposes unreasonable restraint on trade or competition
   3. Servitude not invalid *merely b/c it indirectly restrains alienation* unless there is *no rational justification* for the servitude
   4. Rest. in *Caullett*
      a. Rational basis for covenant in *Caullett*
         i. C likely paid discounted price
         ii. S expected to "make up" that discount in building fee
         iii. any buyer from C can discover covenant (recorded) and factor that into price paid (covenant affects *value*, not *alienability*)
      b. comments in Rest. suggest contrary result in *Caullett*
         i. servitudes created in comm. transactions *rarely* lack rational justification
         ii. cts should be reluctant to find a servitude that has little impact on outsiders, and was agreed upon in an exchange for value, arbitrary b/c the parties are usually the best judge of what makes sense to them and for their property
   5. Rest. v CL
      a. CL: "if benefit is in gross, the burden won't run" rule is *prophylactic* pro-alienability rule
         i. even if enforcing otherwise personal covenant would have trivial impact on alienability, CL refused to enforce it *based on potential harm*
      b. Rest. focuses upon *actual burden upon alienability*, rather than focusing on potential threat/risk
   6. Donor-imposed covenants
      a. i.e. 1% of all future sales of this land will be donated to X charity
      b. cmts- donor-imposed covenants may be capricious since the creator of the servitude will not suffer the financial consequences of the servitude
      c. but, developer will suffer lower sale price if covenant is enforceable
   7. Criticism of Rest.'s abandonment of t&c req
      a. Even if t&c test is nebulous, covenant of X (above) wouldn't have been enforced under it (benefit is in gross, burden wouldn't run)
      b. Rest. std is much fuzzier (what is arbitrary? unreasonable?), makes decision-making unpredictable and increases cost of negotiating/transacting
   8. is *Caullett* result contrary to Public Policy?
      a. Fact that covenant is not related to land use planning does not make it

contrary to public policy (at least under Rest. view below)

  b. It could be contrary if it constituted an unreasonable restraint on trade

    i. If restriction created or maintained a monopoly

    ii. But, S is unlikely to have a monopoly on buying lots and contracting services

d. Limits of Home Owner's Associations' Regulatory Power

  i. political lawn signs ordered down

  ii. Can First Am. Protect homeowner?

    1. No-sign covenant t&cs land

     a. Signs have *potential* aesthetic impact that could affect value and enjoyment of benefited lots

     b. Same reason, covenant has rational basis

    2. **Trad view:** HOA is not a "govt" and thus isn't bound by 1ˢᵗ am

    3. But, **Rest.**- servitude invalid if it burdens fundamental constitutional rights unreasonably

     a. This suggests a more nuanced approach to sign problem:

     b. Covenant is rational on its face, and is generally enforceable

     c. Could be enforced against most signage

     d. May restrain "free speech" if it prevents political speech in pre-election period

      i. HOA might be unable to enjoin such signs during pre-election period (take down after election)

  iii. *Nahrstedt*

    1. Cats not allowed

    2. Ct: covenant enforceable b/c it is facially reasonable

     a. Pets can pose annoyance; "no pets" more efficient that "no problem pets"

      i. "problem" would produce disputes/litigation

      ii. litigation bad b/c it discourages HOA from enforcing and residents bear costs via assessment

     b. this result consistent w/ Rest.

      i. no-pet covenant imposes only indirect restraint on alienation and has "rational" justification"

      ii. not unreasonable

      iii. enforceable

       1. note: statute *could* make such covenant "illegal"

  iv. Regulating "problem uses"- two options for developer

    1. (1) Weak model: Strict CCRs, w/ little/no room for board discretion

     a. appeals to certain buyers who value certainty, are suspicious of democratic neighborhood governance

     b. enforcement cheaper

     c. problems

      i. no or limited flexibility for association to accommodate changes

      ii. doesn't foster "neighborhood citizenship" and shared est. of comm. norms

    2. (2) Strong model: CCRs that authorize board to establish rules or stds to address "problem" situations

     a. provides flexibility

      i. comm. can set rules geared to prevent actual harm

      ii. neighbors have increased responsibility

      b. risks of ad hoc decision making
          i. association must articulate stds.
          ii. potential for abusive comm. governance
          iii. risk of challenge to rulemaking (not same presumption of reasonableness as CCRs)

v. CC&Rs v "Rule" enforcement
    1. CC&R restrictions are generally presumed valid/enforceable
      a. HOA need not demonstrate actual harm from violation, only that covenant serves rational purpose and has been violated
    2. HOA rules/regs that are not specified in CC&Rs don't get presumptions of validity

vi. Transfer Restrictions
    1. Direct restraint on alienation
      a. Must be reasonable under the circumstances
          i. Find an objective reason to not allow transfer
    2. Indirect restraints need only be "rationalized"
    3. consider (for renting land)
      a. change in character of use ("time-share" characteristic)
      b. maintenance of land

vii. Interpreting Servitudes
    1. Trad- ambiguous covenants are interpreted narrowly, in favor of free use
    2. Rest.- restrictive covenant should be interpreted broadly to carry out the purpose for which it was created, consistent w/ public policy

viii. Recreational/Club Dues
    1. Arguments to get out of them
      a. Covenant is affirmative covenant (to pay money), doesn't t&c land, doesn't bind him
      b. Quality level expected is lacking
    2. Rest.
      a. Dues for *for-profit* clubs are rarely invalid as indirect restraint on alienation, b/c overall financial structure of development provides justification
    3. if actions of club are w/in scope of powers of CC&Rs, no basis for legal complaint
      a. go to HOA meetings
      b. still have to pay dues
      c. move

ix. Damages for HOA decisions
    1. "Business judgment" rule
      a. board not liable if:
          i. good faith belief
          ii. upon reasonable investigation
          iii. that decision was in residents' best interests
      b. highly deferential
      c. Pros
          i. Strong deference = good community policy
          ii. Residents get involved
      d. Cons
          i. Encourages incompetence and abuse

e. Termination of Covenants

      i. Estoppel
1. reasonable reliance
2. to detriment
3. on silence or inaction of neighbors
4. reliance actions must come **after** silence and inaction of neighbors
    ii. Abandonment of Covenant
1. *Fink* factors to determine abandonment
    a. Number, nature, and severity of violations of covenant?
    b. Any prior enforcement efforts?
    c. Still possible to realize, to a substantial degree, the benefits intended through the covenant?
2. Would average person (potential buyer) conclude neighbors no longer intend to enforce? (signaling intent to abandon)
    iii. Enforcement After Violations
1. association must "signal" intent to enforce the covenant in the future
2. communicate to owners in violation: when you next perform maintenance on violating characteristic of home, we intend to enforce covenant
3. place evidence on land record of association's intent to enforce covenant in future, despite existing violations

f. Termination of easement
    i. Abandonment
1. rare
2. lack of visible use of easement doesn't itself raise inference of intent to abandon
    ii. by Prescription
1. easement holder's failure to act to prevent interference AND
2. passage of time

g. Zoning and Covenants (continuation of termination of covenant discussion)
    i. Change of conditions won't necessarily justify conclusion that restrictive covenants are terminated and land can be re-zoned
    ii. Allow it and let violating owner pay damages for breach of covenant
1. Trad- No- each lot owner has property right in violating lot, can set his/her own "release price"
    a. Risk of undercompensation (for what is effectively private party eminent domain)
    b. Objective FMV may not reflect sentimental value
    c. Proof of damages is difficult
2. Std Economic Theory- no- if change is beneficial, then neighbors will "sell" their entitlement
3. problems with both of these
    a. not all people will sell
    b. some will hold out (Sanford & Son)

h. Establishing a Servitude Regime
    i. Developer's objective: establish covenants that are both workable and appeal to buyers
1. Developer could establish rigid declaration (only amendable by unanimous consent) or flexible (amendable by majority vote or supermajority vote)
2. Flexibility may allow for future changes to "suboptimal" covenants
3. Flexibility (and potential for amendment) may also make regime less certain (and perhaps less appealing to buyers who value certainty)
    ii. New v amended restrictions (case-based)

1. amendment to a covenant should be something owners would have fair notice of

iii. Timing of covenant amendments- can't be amended/added to outside of time provided in servitude for amendments, even if a long time (25+ years)

iv. Creating a proper servitude regime
    1. (1) divide land into numbered lots, as shown on subdivision map
    2. (2) execute declarations (CCRs), creating reciprocal restrictions as to each numbered lot
    3. (3) record declaration and map on public land records
    4. now, when buyer takes lot 1, it is subject to burden of CCRs, and benefit of CCRs vs. all other lots

v. Creating a crappy servitude regime
    1. deed lots to individual buyers, one at a time, subject to servitude regime
    2. buyers will not be able to enforce benefits against subsequent buyer(s), but is subject to burden of covenants
    3.

TORTS

I. INTENTIONAL TORTS
A. PRIMA FACIE CASE
   a. **Act by**
- i. Requires volitional movement
- ii. Hitting someone during a seizure does not count
  1. **Cohen v. Petty**
     - a. has seizure while driving, wrecks and hurts
- iii. Do not have to intend injury; liable for any consequence

   b. **Intent**
- i. **Specific**
  1. The goal in acting is to bring about specific consequences
- ii. **General**
  1. The actor knows with *"substantial certainty"* that these consequences will result
     - a. **Spivey v. Battaglia**
       - i. pulled into hug and <u>knew</u> she was averse to being touched, thus battery
- iii. **Transferred Intent**
  1. Applies when the intends to commit a tort against one person but instead commits:
     - a. A different tort against same person
     - b. Same tort against different person
       - i. **Talmage v. Smith**:
         1. threw stick to "scare" boy A, hit boy B
     - c. Different tort against different person
  2. May only be invoked if tort intended AND tort resulting are one of the following:
     - a. Assault
     - b. Battery
     - c. False imprisonment
     - d. Trespass to land
     - e. Trespass to chattels
- iv. **Everyone is capable of intent.**
  1. Incapacity is not a defense, even for:
     - a. young children
       - i. **Garrat v. Dailey**
         1. Child pulls chair out from under adult .
     - b. the mentally incompetent.
       - i. **McGuire v. Almy**
         1. Home nurse harmed by mentally disturbed
  2. Exceptions:
     - a. Institutionalized mentally disabled
     - b. Very young children
- v. Mistake does NOT negate intent.
  1. **Ronson v. Kitner**
     - a. was hunting wolves, mistook 's dog for wolf and shot it. Honest mistake yet still liable.

B. Causation
   a. Result must have been legally caused by 's act or something set in motion.

b. Satisfied if 's conduct was a ***substantial factor*** in bringing about the injury.

C. Battery
- **a.** Elements of Prima Facie case:
  - **i.** *Harmful* or*offensive contact*
  - **ii.**   To 's person
  - **iii.**   Intent; and
  - **iv.**   Causation
- **b. Harmful or Offensive Contact**
  - **i. Judged by Reasonable Person Standard**
    - **1.** Harmful or offensiveness are judged by a reasonable person is same or similar circumstances
      - **a.** Offensive means ***non consented***
      - **b.** Hypersensitivity does NOT count unless knew about it BEFORE
        - **i. <u>Wallace v. Ronson</u>**—Oversensitive who claims teacher committed battery while trying to get out of the way in a fire drill.
      - **c.** Crowded World Theory—
        - **i.** Normal bumps and brushes don't count
        - **ii.**   **<u>Cole v. Turner</u>**—If two people in small hallway and brush into each other without violence, no battery. With violence, battery.
    - **2. Direct or Indirect Contact**
      - **a.** Direct—striking the
      - **b.** Indirect—setting a trap for to fall into
  - **ii.**   **'s Person**
    - **1.** includes anything connected to the
      - **a.** purse, clothing, etc.
      - **b. <u>Fisher v. Carrousel Motor Hotel</u>**
        - **i.** at conference when plate is ripped out of his hands while being verbally abused

D. Assault
- **a. Elements of prima facie case:**
  - **i.** An act by creating a ***reasonable apprehension*** in
  - **ii.**   Of ***immediate harmful or offensive contact*** to 's person
  - **iii.**   Intent
  - **iv.**   Causation
- **b. Distinguish Fear**
  - **i.** Apprehension should not be confused with fear or intimidation
    - **a.** Weak person can cause apprehension in a bully
- **c. Apparent Ability Sufficient**
  - **i.** If has ***apparent ability*** to commit a battery, this will be enough to cause reasonable apprehension
    - **1. <u>Western Union Telegraph v. Hill</u>**—makes lewd suggestion and reaches to grab . acting outside employment and is behind counter. WU would have been liable if within scope of employment, plus he couldn't reach her. No apprehension.
    - **2. <u>I de S et ux. v. W de S</u>**—owns bar, tries to beat down door and hits it with axe after 's wife tells to stop. can recover although no physical harm to wife.
- **d. Effect of Words**

> **i.** Words alone not sufficient. For to be liable ,words must be coupled with conduct. HOWEVER, words can *negate* reasonable apprehension
>> **1.** Shake fist but state will not hit

 e. Requirement of Immediacy
>**i.** must be apprehensive that she is about to become victim of immediate battery

E. False Imprisonment
 a. Elements of Prima Facie case:
>**i.** An act or omission on part of that *confines or restrains*
>**ii.** To a *bounded area*
>**iii.** Intent
>**iv.** Causation

 b. Sufficient Methods of Confinement or Restraint
>**i.** Physical barriers
>**ii.** Physical force or Threats of force
>>**1. Hardy v. LaBelle's Dist. Co.**
>>>**a.** ∏ accused of stealing stays to clear her name, absent force or threat of force there is no FI
>**iii.** Failure to release
>>**1. Enright v. Groves**
>>>**a.** ∏ arrested for not producing ID, falsely arrested – arrest w/o proper legal authority is FI
>**iv.** Invalid use of legal authority
>>**1. Big Town Nursing Home v. Newman**
>>>**a.** ∏ escapes nursing home – direct restraint w/o legal justification is FI

 c. Insufficient Methods of Confinement or Restraint
>**i.** Moral pressure
>**ii.** Future threats (economic, employment threats)

 d. Time of Confinement
>**i. Doesn't matter**

 e. Awareness of Confinement
>**i.** Must *know* of the confinement or be *harmed* by it
>>**1. Parvi v. City of Kingston**—Police drop off drunk ∏ near a highway, ∏ wanders onto highway and is hit by a car

 f. What is a bounded area?
>**i.** Multidirectional, limited freedom of movement with **NO** *reasonable* means of escape *known* to
>>**1. Whittaker v. Sanford**—∏ not allowed to go ashore – physical barriers

F. Intentional Infliction of Emotional Distress
 a. Elements of prima facie case:
>**i.** Act by amounting to *extreme and outrageous conduct*
>**ii.** Intent or recklessness
>**iii.** Causation
>**iv.** Damages—*severe* emotional distress
>**v.**

 b. Extreme and Outrageous Conduct
>**i.** This is conduct that transcends all bounds of decency.
>>**1. Slocum v. Food Fair Stores of FL**—Employee insults customer – NOT IIED

ii.   **distress alone suffices as extreme and outrageous if severe**
  1. <u>State Rubbish Collectors v. Siliznoff</u>—Trash collector threatened by Association
  2. <u>Harris v. Jones</u>—Coworkers ridiculed about speech impediment – distress must be severe
iii.   Conduct that is not normally outrageous may become so if:
  1. Continuous in nature
  2. Directed toward a certain type of
   a. Children, elderly, known supersensitive people
  3. Committed by a certain type of
   a. Common carriers, innkeepers

Infliction of Emotional Distress		
	Intentional	**Negligent**
Conduct Required	Extreme and outrageous conduct by the D	Subjecting P to threat of physical impact or severe emotional distress likely to cause physical symptoms
Fault Required	Intent to cause severe emotional distress or recklessness as to the effect of conduct	Negligence in creating risk of physical injury to P
Causation and Damages	D's conduct must cause severe emotional distress	D's conduct generally must cause tangible physical injury (i.e. miscarriage)
Bystander Recovery when Another is Physically Injured	P bystander must be present when injury occurs and be close relative of the injured person and the D must know these facts when he intentionally injures the other person or D must have intent to cause P distress	P bystander must be within the "zone of danger" created by D's negligent conduct – must be subjected to threat of impact. Modern trend allows recovery based on foreseeability factors

c. **Damages**
  i. Actual damages required; no nominal
  ii.   Physical injury not required
  iii.   More outrageous activity, less proof necessary
  Only Intentional Tort that REQUIRES damages
d. **Causation in Bystander Cases**
  i. <u>Taylor v. Vallelunga</u>
   1. ∏ witnesses father's beating by Δ
  ii.   When intentionally causes physical harm to 3rd party and ∏ suffers severe emotional distress because of it, may recover by showing *either* prima facie case

317

elements of IIED OR

      1. Present when injury occurred

      2. Close relative of injured person

      3. knew facts 1 and 2

IIED is a FALLBACK tort position. If other tort will allow recovery, use it instead

G. Trespass to Land

  a. Prima facie case

      i. Physical Invasion of 's ***real property***

      ii.   Intent

      iii.   Causation

  b. Physical Invasion

      i. <u>Dougherty v. Stepp</u>

         1. Δ surveyed land he thought was his, actually ∏'s – no damages but still trespass

      ii.   Invasion may be personal or object

         1. <u>Rogers v. Board of Road Com'rs</u>

            a. Δ failed to remove fence post on ∏'s land, ∏ runs it over with tractor and dies

         2. Throwing a baseball onto the land of another

      iii.   ***Intangible matter*** may be a case for nuisance.

         1. <u>Bradley v. American Smelting & Refining Co.</u>

            a. Particulate matter from Δ settles on ∏'s land – must cause **actual and substantial damages**

         2. Vibrations, odor

  c. Real Property

      i. Includes not only the surface, but also airspace and subterranean space for a reasonable distance

         1. <u>Herrin v. Sutherland</u>

            a. Δ shot at ducks over ∏'s land

  d. Potential s

      i. Anyone in actual or constructive possession of the land may maintain this action

H. Trespass to Chattels

  a. Elements of prima facie case

      i. An act by that ***interferes with plaintiff's right of possession*** in a chattel

      ii.   Intent

      iii.   Causation

      iv.   Damages

  b. Two Types of Interference

      i. Intermeddling

         1. Directly ***damaging*** the chattel

         2. <u>CompuServe Inc. v. Cyber Promotions</u>

            a. Junk mail inhibits server's ability to process mail

      ii.   **Dispossession**

         1. depriving of his lawful right of ***possession*** of the chattel

  c. Damages

      i. Actual Damages are required

         1. Not necessarily to chattel, but at least to possessory right

         2. <u>Gidden v. Szybiak</u>

            a. Dog bites girl outside of a store while she's riding on it – no dispossession

Trespass to Chattels v. Conversion		
	Trespass to Chattels	**Conversion**
Act by Defendant	An interference with P's right of possession of chattel (either intermeddling or dispossession)	An interference with P's right of possession so **serious** as to warrant that D pay the chattel's full value
Intent	Intent to do the act that brings about the interference	Intent to do the act that brings about the interference
Remedy	Recovery of actual damages from harm to chattel or loss of use (if dispossession, damages based on rental value)	Damage award of fair market value of chattel at time of conversion (i.e. force sale of chattel) may instead recover chattel (replevin)

I. **Conversion**
   a. Elements of a prima facie case
      i. Act by that *interferes with 's right of possession* in a chattel
      ii.   The interference is *so serious* that it warrants requiring to pay the chattel's full value
      iii.   Intent
      iv.   Causation
   b. **Acts of Conversion**
      i. Wrongful acquisition (theft)
      ii.   Wrongful transfer
      iii.   Wrongful detention
      iv.   Substantially changing, severely damaging, or misusing a chattel
   c. **Seriousness of Interference**
      i. The longer the withholding period and the more extensive the use, the more likely it is to be conversion
         1. LESS SERIOUS INTERFERENCES IS T to CHATTELS
   d. **Subject Matter of Conversion**
      i. Only tangible personal property and intangibles that have been reduced to physical form are subject to conversion
         1. **Pearson v. Dodd**
            a. Employees remove and copy files – ideas on paper are not subject to conversion unless they are intellectual property
         2. Promissory note
   e. **Potential s**
      i. Anyone with possession or the immediate right to possession of the chattel may maintain this action
   f. **Remedies**
      i. may recover *damages* (fair market value)
      ii.   *or possession* (replevin)

II. DEFENSES TO INTENTIONAL TORTS
    A. Consent
        a. 's consent to 's conduct is a defense
            i. MAJ: One *cannot* consent to a *criminal act*
        b. Express (Actual) Consent
            i. Not liable if expressly consents to 's conduct
            ii. Exceptions
                1. Mistake will undo express consent *if* knew of and took advantage of the mistake
            iii. **DeMay v. Roberts**
                1. Δ misrepresents himself while ∏ is delivering a baby
                2. Consent induced by fraud will be invalidated if it goes to an essential matter, but not a collateral matter
            iv. Consent obtained by duress will be invalidated unless the duress is only threats of future action or future economic deprivation
        c. Implied Consent
            i. *Apparent consent*
                1. **O'Brien v. Cunnard S.S. Co.**
                    a. Immigrant vaccinated by a ship doctor
                    b. That which a reasonable person would infer from custom and usage or 's conduct
                2. **Hackbart v. Cincinnati Bengals**
                    a. Normal contacts inherent in body-contact sports, ordinary incidental contact, etc.
                3. *Consent implied by law*
                    a. **Mohr v. Williams**
                    b. doctor operates on wrong ear of ∏
                    c. When action is necessary to save a person's life or some other important interest in person or property
        d. Capacity Required
            i. Individuals without capacity are deemed incapable of consent
                1. Incompetents, drunken persons, very young kids
            ii. This requirement differs from the rule for the intent element of intentional torts, where incapacity is no defense
                1. EVERYONE has the capacity to *commit* a tort, not everyone has capacity to *consent* to a tort
        e. Exceeding Consent Given
            i. If exceeds the scope of consent and does something substantially different, he may be liable

    B. Self-Defense, Defense of Others, and Defense of Property
        a. When discussing defense of self, others, or property, ask:
            i. Is the privilege available? Must be present or immediate future tort, past tort does not qualify
            ii. Is a mistake permissible as to whether the tort being defended against is actually being committed?
            iii. Was a proper amount of force used?
Keep your parties clear. The conduct of the was prompted by the commission/apparent commission of a tort by . **This tort is NOT AT ISSUE. The issue is whether 's response

itself constituted a tort against the or instead was privileged by one of these defenses.***

    b. Self Defense

        i. When a person ***reasonably believes*** that she is being/is about to be attacked, she may use such force as is reasonably necessary to protect against injury.

        ii. ***When is Self Defense available?**

            1. Need not attempt to escape.

                a. Modern trend imposes a duty to retreat ***before using deadly force*** if retreat can be done safely, unless in home.

            2. Self-defense is generally not available to the initial aggressor.

            3. Self-defense may extend to 3rd party injuries caused while defending herself.

                a. Actor may be liable if deliberately injures 3rd party in protecting herself.

        iii. **Is Mistake Allowed?**

            1. YES—A reasonable mistake as to the existence of danger is allowed

        iv. **How Much Force May Be Used?**

            1. May use only that force that reasonably appears to be necessary to prevent the harm; including ***deadly force.***

            2. If more force than is reasonably necessary is used, the defense is lost.

    c. Defense of Others

        i. When is Defense available?

            1. One may use force to defend another when the actor ***reasonably believes*** that the other person could hve used force to defend himself.

        ii. **Is Mistake Allowed?**

            1. YES—A reasonable mistake as to whether the other person is being attacked or has a right to defend himself is permitted.

        iii. **How Much Force May Be Used?**

            1. The defender may use as much force as he could have used in self-defense if the injury were threatened to him.

    d. Defense of Property

        i. When is Defense Available?

            1. <u>Katko v. Briney</u>

                a. ∏ robbing Δ? is shot with a spring gun

                b. May use reasonable force to prevent the commission of a tort against her real or personal property.

            2. A request to desist or leave must first be made unless it clearly would be futile or dangerous.

            3. Defense does not apply once the tort has been committed; however one may use force in ***hot pursuit*** of another who has tortiously disposed the owner of her chattels because the tort is viewed as still being committed.

            Defense of Property is NOT available against one with a privilege.** Whenever an actor has a privilege to enter on the land of another because of necessity, recapture of chattles, etc., that privilege will ***supersede the privilege of the land possessor to defend her property.

        ii. **Is Mistake Allowed?**

            1. Yes—A reasonable mistake is allowed as to whether an intrusion has occurred or whether a request to desist is required.

            2. A mistake is ***NOT*** allowed as to whether the entrant has a privilege (eg. Necessity) that supersedes the defense of property right, unless the entrant conducts the entry so as to lead to reasonably believe it is not privileged (such as refusing to say what the necessity is).

  iii. **How Much Force May Be Used?**

   1. Reasonable force may be used. However, one may ***not*** use force causing death or serious bodily harm unless the invasion of property also entails a serious threat of bodily harm.

   There is a common misperception that deadly force may be used to protect one's home. This is not strictly true. Many of the "home defense" cases are really self-defense cases. Thus, deadly force can only be used when a person, not just property, is threatened.

C. Reentry onto Land

 a. At common law, one could use force to reenter land only when the other came into possession tortiously. Under modern law, there are summary procedures for recovering possession of real property. Hence, resort to self-help is no longer allowed.

D. Recapture of Chattels

 a. The basic rule is the same as that for reentry of land at common law: when another's possession began lawfully (a conditional sale), one may use only peaceful means to recover chattel. Force may be used to recapture a chattel only when in hot pursuit of one who has obtained possession wrongfully, e.g. by theft

 b. **When is Defense Available?**

  i. Timely Demand Required

   1. A timely demand to return the chattel is first required unless clearly futile or dangerous.

  ii. Recovery Only from Wrongdoer

   1. The recapture may be only from a tortfeasor or some third person who knows or should know that the chattels were tortiously obtained.

   2. One may not use force to recapture chattels in the hands of an innocent party.

   3. Entry on Land to Remove Chattel

    a. On Wrongdoers Land

     i. When chattels are located on the land of the wrongdoer, the owner is privileged to enter on the land and reclaim them at a reasonable time and in a reasonable manner, after first making a demand for their return.

    b. On Land of Innocent Party

     i. Similarly, when the chattels are on the land of an innocent party, the owner may enter and reclaim her chattel at a reasonable time and in a peaceful manner when the landowner has been given notice of the presence of the chattel and refuses to return it.

     ii. The chattel owner's right of recapture supersedes the landowner's right to defend his property.

     iii. The chattel owner will be liable for any actual damage caused by the entry.

    c. On Land Through Owner's Fault

     i. If the chattels are on the land of another through the owner's fault there is no privilege to enter on the land.

      1. Letting cows wander

     ii. They may recover only through legal process.

 c. **Is Mistake Allowed?**

      i. No, generally no mistake regarding defendant's right to recapture the chattels or enter on the land is allowed.

      ii. However, *shopkeepers* may have a privilege to detain for a reasonable period of time individuals whom they reasonably believe to be in possession of shoplifted goods.

            1. <u>Bonkowski v. Arlan's Dept Store</u>

               a. ∏ detained for suspected shoplifting by Δ's security guard

   d. How Much Force May Be Used?

      i. Reasonable force, not including force sufficient to cause death or serious bodily harm, may be used to recapture chattels.

            1. <u>Hodgent v. Hubbard</u>- ∏ buys a stove from Δ on bad credit – use of force in hot pursuit

E. Privilege of Arrest

  a. Depending on the facts, the actor may have a privilege to make an arrest of a third person.

  b. Invasion of Land

      i. The privilege of arrest carries with it the privilege to enter another's land for the purpose of effecting an arrest.

  c. Subsequent Misconduct

      i. Although the arrest itself may be privileged, the actor may still be liable for subsequent misconduct

            1. Failing to bring the arrested party before a magistrate, unduly detaining the party in jail.

F. Necessity

  a. A person may interfere with the real or personal property of another when it is reasonably and apparently necessary to avid threatened injury is substantially more serious that the invasion that is undertaken to avert it.

  b. There are two types of necessity:

      i. Public—when the act is for the public good

            1. <u>Surocco v. Geary</u>

               a. Δ blows up ∏'s house to prevent the spread of a fire

      ii. Private—when the act is solely to benefit any person or any property from destruction or serious injury.

            1. <u>Vincent v. Lake Erie Transp. Co.</u>

               a. Boat damages a dock during a storm

               b. Under private necessity, the actor must pay for any injury caused

      Necessity is a defense ONLY to property torts

G. Discipline

  a. A parent or teacher may use reasonable force in disciplining children.

H. Justification

  a. Last resort – defense were it would be unfair to hold Δ liable but facts do not meet requirements of traditional defenses/privileges

      i. <u>Sindle v. NYC Transit Authority</u>

            1. Bus driver refuses to let destructive kids off bus. Takes them to the cops.

            2. May exceed the scope of consent but must be reasonable action to protect persons or property from damage

III. NEGLIGENCE
    A. PRIMA FACIE CASE
        a. Elements
            i. A *duty* on the part of *to conform to a specific standard of conduct* for protection of against an unreasonable risk of injury
            ii. A *breach* of that duty by
            iii. *Damage*
    B. DUTY OF CARE
        a. A duty of care is owed to all foreseeable s.
            i. <u>Lubitz v. Wells</u> - man leaves golf club in yard, son injures neighbor w/ it
                1. <u>TEST for Foreseeability</u>– **if it's likely to happen an individual must foresee that it could happen. If likelihood is remote, but seriousness of injury is great must foresee serious injury**
        b. The extent of the duty is determined by the applicable standard of care.
            i. Blyth v. Birmingham Waterworks – water main break during record frost
                1. Failure to do what a reasonable person would do and doing something that a reasonable person would not do
        c. When confronted with a negligence question, always ask:
            i. Was the foreseeable?
            ii. IF so, what is the applicable standard of care?
        d. Foreseeable/Unforeseeable s
            i. A duty of care is owed only to foreseeable s
            ii. A problem arises where breaches a duty to one and also causes injury to another (poss. unforeseeable) .
            iii. There are two possible outcomes: (**<u>Palsgraf</u>**)
                1. Cardozo View (MAJ)—Foreseeable Zone of Danger
                    a. -2 can recover ONLY if she can establish that a reasonable person would have foreseen a risk of injury to her under the circumstances
                        i. Located in the foreseeable zone of danger
                2. Andrews View (MIN)—Everyone is Foreseeable
                  a. -2 may establish the existence of a duty extending from to her by a showing that has breached a duty owed to -1.
        e. Foreseeable Harm
            i. <u>Gulf Refining Co. v. Williams</u> - defective bung cap on gas drum explodes
                1. <u>Threat of Serious Injury</u>- **the more serious the potential injury the less probable its occurrence need be before Δ will be held liable for not guarding against it**
        f. Specific Situations
            i. Rescuers
                1. A rescuer is a foreseeable where negligently put himself or a third person in peril
                  a. Danger invites rescue
            ii. Prenatal Injuries
                1. A duty of care is owed to a viable fetus.
                2. In cases of failure to diagnose a congenital defect or properly perform a contraceptive procedure:
                  a. No recover by child for "**wrongful life**"
                  b. Yes—the parents may recover damages in a "**wrongful birth**" or "**wrongful pregnancy**" action for
                        i. Any additional medical expenses

    ii.   Pain and suffering from labor

    iii.   No recovery of ordinary child rearing expenses

 iii. **Intended Beneficiaries of Economic Transactions**

   1. A 3rd party for whose economic benefit a legal or business transaction was made may be a foreseeable

    a. Ex. Beneficiary of a will

 iv. <u>**United States v. Carrol Towing**</u> – run away barge w/o an employee on board

   1. <u>**HAND BALANCING TEST**</u> - B< L x P

    a. <u>**B**</u> **– burden which the Δ would have had to bear to avoid risk**

    b. <u>**L**</u> **– gravity of the potential injury**

    c. <u>**P**</u> **– probability that harm will occur from Δ's conduct**

g. **Standards of Care**

 i. Basic Standard—The Reasonable Person

   1. <u>**Vaughn v. Menlove**</u>

    a. Dry hay bale of the Δ? catches fire – built to his best ability and his best knowledge – violates reasonable person standard

   2. An *objective* standard

   3. <u>**DeClair v. McAdoo**</u>

    a. Δ's tire blows out causing collision w/ ∏ - cannot escape liability simply b/c the Δ "doesn't know"

    b. One's conduct measured against what the average person would do

   4. <u>**Breunig v. American Family Ins.**</u>

    a. Insane Δ crosses hwy. median hitting ∏

    b. A 's *mental* deficiencies and inexperience are not take into account

    c. i.e. stupidity is no excuse

   5. <u>**Roberts v. State of Louisana**</u>

    a. Blind person knocks down ∏ man while walking

    b. "Reasonable person" is considered to have the same *physical* characteristics as

    c. REMEMBER one is expected to know one's physical handicaps and to exercise the care of a person with suck knowledge

     i. A blind person should not fly a plane

   6. <u>**Trimarco v. Klein**</u>

    a. Δ landlord installs glass shower door which shatters injuring ∏

    b. Evidence of custom or industry practice may be used as evidence of what a reasonable person would do under the circumstances

    c. Not conclusive evidence

 ii. **Particular Standards of Care**

   1. Professional

    a. A professional or someone with special occupational skills is required to possess

     i. The knowledge and skill

     ii. of a member of the profession or occupation

     iii. In good standing

     iv. in similar communities

    b. <u>**Boyce v. Brown**</u> – ankle trouble follows after a break

    c. <u>**Morrison v. MacNamara**</u> – man injured during lab testing

     i. Medical specialists are held to a higher, national standard of care

d. **Duty to Disclose Risks of Treatment**
    i. <u>**Scott v. Bradford**</u> – woman's hysterectomy goes awry
    ii.   A doctor has a duty to disclose the risks of treatment to enable a patent to make an informed consent
e. <u>**Heath v. Swift Wings Inc.**</u> – faulty takeoff leads to plane crash
    i. <u>**Expert testimony must be used to est.Δ as a professional who departed from all courses of conduct of that profession –unless it's something that could be known by law jurors**</u>
f. <u>**Hodges v. Carter**</u> – lawyers improperly serve insurance company
    i. <u>**Professionals who meet the standard of care are not liable for mere errors in judgment**</u>

2. **Children**
a. <u>**Robinson v. Lindsay**</u> - child driving a snowmobile injures another child
b. Children are held to the standard of a child of:
    i. *Like age*
    ii. education
    iii. *intelligence*
    iv. *and experience*
c. This is a *subjective* test
d. A child under 4 is generally without the capacity to be negligent.
e. Children engaged in adult activities may be required to conform to an "adult" standard of care

3. **Common Carriers and Innkeepers**
a. Held to a very high degree of care
    i. Liable for slight negligence
For higher common carrier/innkeeper standards to apply, the MUST be a passenger or guest

4. **Automobile Drivers**
a. A guest in an automobile is owed a duty of ordinary care
b. In the few guest statute states, one is liable to nonpaying passengers only for reckless tortious conduct

5. **Emergency Situations**
a. <u>**Cordas v. Peerless Transportation**</u> – taxi driver abandons car after being held at gunpoint
b. must act as a reasonable person would under the same emergency conditions
c. the emergency is NOT to be considered if it of 's own making

iii. **Owners and Occupiers of Land**
1. The extent of the liability of owners and/or occupiers of land depends on where the injury occurred and on the status of the
    a. Also applies to those in privity with owner/occupier
2. **Duty of Possessor to Those Off Premises**
a. There is no duty to protect one off the premises from *natural conditions* on the premises
b. There IS a duty for unreasonably dangerous *artificial* conditions or structures abutting adjacent land
c. One must carry on activities on property so as to avoid unreasonable risk of harm to others outside the property

In urban areas, the owner/occupier is liable for damage caused off the premises by trees on the premises, such as falling branches

   3. **Duty of Possessor to Those On Premises**
     a. In most states the duty owed a on the premises depends on the 's status as trespasser, licensee, or invitee

   4. **Attractive Nuisance Doctrine**
     a. <u>Chicago B &QR v. Krayenbuhl</u> – child injured by unlocked RR turntable – public good v public nuisance
     b. must show
       i. a dangerous condition on the land that the owner is or shouldbe aware of
       ii. the owner knows or should know children frequent the vicinity of the condition
       iii. the condition is likely to cause injury; is dangerous because of child's inability to appreciate risk
       iv. the expense of remedying the situation is slight compared with the magnitude of the risk

**the child does not have to be attracted onto the land by the dangerous condition NOR is the attraction alone enough for liability*

   5. **Modern Trends Rejects Status Rules**
     a. Strong MIN of stats reject the distinction between licensees and invitees and simply apply a reasonable person standard to dangerous conditions on land

  iv. **Negligence Per Se**
   1. A statute's specific duty may replace the more general common law duty of due care if:
     a. The statute provides for a *criminal penalty*
     b. The statute *clearly defines the standard* of conduct
     c. is*within the protected class*
     d. the statute was *designed to prevent the type of harm suffered* by
   2. <u>Osborne v. McMasters</u>- lady swallowed unlabeled poison and dies
     a. Specific conduct required by the statute substitutes for more general reasonable person standard
   3. **Excuse for Violation**
     a. Violation of some statutes may be excused where compliance would cause more danger than violation or where compliance would be beyond 's control
   4. **Effect of Violation or Compliance**
     a. <u>Martin v. Herzog</u> - car rounds curve hits buggy w/o lights
     b. <u>Stachniewicz v. Mar-Cam Corp.</u> – bar brawl and stampeded cause injury
       i. administrative regulation does not have same force as statute
     c. MAJ—an unexcused statutory violation is negligence per se
       i. Establishes first two requirements of prima facie case
       ii. A *conclusive* presumption of duty and breach of duty

          d. Even though violation may be negligence, compliance does not necessarily establish due care

    5. Rebuttable Presumption

        a. <u>**Zeni v. Anderson**</u> – nurse uses snow path instead of sidewalk and is hit by a car – snow path was customary

            i. Statute est. a rebuttable presumption - Δ can introduce evidence of due care to rebut the presumption of negligence

h. Duty Regarding Negligent Infliction of Emotional Distress

    i. The duty to avoid causing emotional distress to another is breached when creates a *foreseeable risk of physical injury* to , either by:

        1. Causing a threat of physical impact that leads to emotional distress

        2. Directly causing severe emotional distress that by itself is likely to result in physical symptoms

    ii. <u>**Thing v. LaChusa**</u> – man hits woman's son w/ car causing emotional distress

        1. Injury Requirement

            a. can recover damages only if 's conduct caused some *physical injury*

            b. While pure emotion distress may be insufficient, a severe shock to the nervous system that causes physical symptoms IS sufficient

            c. Physical Injury NOT required when

                i. An erroneous report of a relative's death

                ii. A mishandling of a relative's corpse

    iii. Zone of Danger Requirement

        1. If 's distress is caused by threat of physical impact, most courts require that the threat be directed at the or someone in her immediate presence

        2. a bystander outside the "zone of danger" of physical injury who sees negligently injuring another cannot recover damages for her own distress

        3. a strong modern trend allows recovery based on foreseeability factors rather than zone of danger if:

            a. and the person injured by are closely related

            b. was present at the scene, and

            c. observed or perceived the injury

Torts for emotional distress are not the only means of recovering damages for emotional distress. If physical injury has been caused by commission of another tort, can "tack on" damages for emotional distress as a "parasitic" element of his physical injury damages, without the need to consider the elements of the emotional distress torts

  i. Affirmative Duties to Act

    i. **L.S. Ayers & Co. v. Hicks** – boy gets fingers caught in escalator – duty to rescue may be owed where Δ controls the instrumentality causing the injury

    ii. Generally, one does not have a legal duty to act.

    iii. **(Hegel v. Langsom)** University co-ed becomes promiscuous and uses drugs. University not liable, only duty to keep safe in classroom and on campus. Not responsible for off campus responsibility.

    iv. Exceptions:

    v. Assumption of Duty by Acting

        1. One may assume a duty to act by acting

            a. One comes to aid, he must do so with reasonable care

        2. Exception: many stats have enacted ***Good Samaritan*** statutes, which exempt doctors, nurses, etc., from liability for ordinary, but not gross,

negligence
- **vi. Peril Due to 's Conduct**
    1. One has a duty to assist someone he has negligently or innocently placed in peril
- **vii. Special Relationship Between Parties**
    1. A special relationship may create a duty to act.
        a. Parent-child
    2. *Common carriers, innkeepers, shopkeepers,* and others that gather the public for profit owe duties of reasonable care to aid or assist their patrons.
    3. Places of public accommodation have a duty to prevent injury to guests by third persons.
    4. <u>Tarasoff v. Regents of U. of California</u>- man tells psychologist he's going to kill a woman, months later he kills her
        a. <u>**Therapists must have a relationship with the actor to be held to have a duty to act**</u> – not just the victim
- **viii. Duty to Control Third Persons**
    1. Generally there is no duty to prevent a third person from injuring another.
    2. An affirmative duty may be imposed, however, if one has the actual ability and authority to control a person's actions, and knows or should know the person is likely to commit acts that would require exercise of this control.

C. BREACH OF DUTY

a. Where 's conduct falls short of that level required by the applicable standard of care owed to the .
- i. Whether the duty of care has been breached in an individual case is a question for the trier of fact
- ii. Main problem is proof of breach

b. may use one of the following theories:
- **i. Custom or Usage**
    1. May be used to establish standard of care, but does NOT control the question of whether certain conduct amounted to negligence.
        a. Ex. Behavior may be custom in industry, but ct may find custom negligent
- **ii. Negligence per se (Violation of Statute)**
    1. Existence of a duty owed to the and breach thereof may be established as a matter of law by proof that violated an applicable statute
        a. Causation and damages must still be established by
- **iii. Res IpsaLoquitur**
    1. <u>Byrne v. Boadle –</u> man hit by falling barrel of flour
        a. Sometimes the very occurrence of an event may tend to establish a breach of duty
    2. must show:
        a. the accident causing the injury is a type that would not normally occur unless someone was negligent
        b. the negligence is attributable to
            i. this type of accident ordinarily happens because of the negligence of someone in 's position
        c. Can often be shown by evidence that the instrumentality causing the injury was in the exclusive control of the
        d. (**Larson v. St. Francis Hotel, McDougal v. Perry**—tire falls off

bottom of truck, strikes s car)
- e. must also establish freedom from fault on his part
3. **Effects of Res IpsaLoquitur**
   - a. Where RIL is established, has *made a prima facie case* and no directed verdict may be given for . can still lose if inference of negligence is rejected by the trier of fact.
   - b. Questions testing RIL often have the making a *motion for a directed verdict.* For these questions remember:
   - c. *Deny* 's motion for directed verdict if has established RIL or presented some other evidence of breach of duty (such as neg per se)
   - d. *Grant*'s motion if has failed to establish RIL and failed to present some other evidence of breach
   - e. Occasionally, may also move for a directed verdict. 's motion should always be *denied* except in the rare case where has established neg per se through violation of an applicable statute *and* there are no issues of proximate cause
4. **Ybarra v. Spangard -** Narrow Exceptions to Exclusive Control: if ∏ is unconscious in course of medical treatment all Δ's who had any control over his body/instrumentalities which might have caused injury may be called upon to meet inference of negligence by explaining their conduct

** PROOF OF BREACH: Slip and Fall Cases
   - ☐ **Jasko v. F. W. Woolwoth Co. -** Before there can be liability for injuries resulting from a dangerous condition it must be shown:
     - o Δ in control of the premises had actual knowledge of the condition and failed to correct it
     - o Δ had constructive knowledge of the condition and failed to correct it
   - ☐ When operating methods of a proprietor are such that dangerous conditions are continuous or easily foreseeable, logical basis for notice requirement dissolves

D. CAUSATION
   - a. Once breach is shown, must show that the conduct was the cause of his injury. For liability to attach, P must show *both* actual cause and proximate cause
   - b. **Actual Cause (Cause in Fact)**
     - i. **Kramer Service v. Wilkins** – glass injury is blamed as cause of cancer
       1. Before 's conduct can be considered a proximate cause of 's injuries, it must first me a cause in fact of the injury. Use these tests:
     - ii. **Perkins v. Texas and New Orleans RR -** car hit by negligent train
     1. **But For Test**
        - a. Act or omission is the cause in fact of an injury when the injury would not have occurred BUT FOR that act.
          - i. This test applies where several acts (each insufficient to be sole cause) combine to cause injury
     2. **Joint Cause—Substantial Factor Test**
        - a. Where several causes bring about injury, and any one alone would have been sufficient to cause the injury, 's conduct is the cause in fact if it was a substantial factor in causing the injury
        - b. **Here BOTH parties caused the harm.**
        - c. **Hill v. Edmonds -** car crashed into parked car on the highway
          - i. Each is responsible for the entire result even though his act alone may not have caused the injury

3. **Single Indivisible Injury Rule**
   a. **Summers v. Tice** - two hunters negligent 1 bullet injured ∏
   b. This test applies when there are two acts, only one of which causes injury, but it is not known which one.
   c. Burden of proof shifts to s, and each must show that his negligence is not the actual cause
   d. **Here BOTH parties negligent, only ONE caused harm-**

** **Rear View Mirror** - Δ's own negligence is not a but for cause of the ∏'s injury b/c even if the Δ had checked the mirror the ∏ would still not have been in view and the ∏ would still have been injured

** **Act of Nature** – if the intervening force is an act of nature that is truly extraordinary and unforeseeable act of nature merely produces the same result as the threatened by the Δ's negligent conduct the Δ may still be liable

c. **Proximate Cause (Legal Causation)**
   i. In addition to being cause in fact, 's conduct must also be the proximate cause of the injury. Even though the conduct actually caused 's injury, it might not be deemed to be the proximate cause. Thus the doctrine of proximate causation is a *limitation of liability* and deals with liability or nonliability for unforeseeable or unusual consequences of one's acts.
   ii. **General Rule—Scope of Foreseeable Risk**
      1. **Ryan v. New York Central RR** – RR woodshed fire spreads to surrounding houses – every person is liable for the consequences of his own acts but NOT remote damages
      2. A generally is liable for all harmful results that are the normal incidents of and within the increased risk caused by his acts. This is a *foreseeability* test.

Questions raising proximate cause issues will not require you to make a judgment call on foreseeability in a close case. If the answer turns on the proximate cause issue, the correct choice will almost always be phrased in "if" or "unless" terms. Otherwise the facts in the question will be so clear-cut that common sense will tell you immediately whether the harm that occurred was foreseeable

Proximate Cause Rules		
	Direct Cause Cases	Indirect Cause Cases
Foreseeable Harmful Result	D Liable liable unless intervening force is crime or intentional tort	D liable D
Unforeseeable Harmful Result	D not liable D not liable; Intervening force is Superseding	D not Liable

3. **Liability in Direct Cause Cases**
    a. Where there is an uninterrupted chain of events from the negligent act to 's injury, is liable for all *foreseeable harmful results,* regardless of unusual manner or timing. **(Wagon Mound 2)**
    b. is not liable for *unforeseeable harmful results* not within the risk created by 's negligence. Most harmful results will be deemed foreseeable in direct cause cases.**(Wagon Mound 1)**
4. **Liability in Indirect Cause Cases**
    a. **Bortolone v. Jeckovich** – car crash exacerbates ∏'s schizophrenia
    b. An affirmative intervening force comes into motion after 's negligent act and combines with it to cause 's injury
        i. Act of God, Act by a third person
    c. **Foreseeable Results Caused by Foreseeable Intervening Forces— Liable**
        i. **Derdiarian v. Felix Contracting** – Epileptic's car crashed into unprotected worksite
        ii. **Watson v. Kentucky and Indiana Bridge** - match ignites gas from a spill after RR cars derail
        iii. is liable where his negligence caused a foreseeable harmful response or reaction from a dependent intervening force or created a foreseeable risk that an independent intervening force would harm
        iv. **Common Dependent Intervening Forces**
        These intervening forces are *almost always foreseeable:*
            1. Subsequent medical malpractice
            2. Negligence of rescuers (**McCoy v. American Suzuki**)
            3. Efforts to protect the person or property of oneself or another
            4. Injuries caused by another "reacting" to s actions
            5. Subsequent diseases caused by a weakened condition
            6. Subsequent accident substantially caused by the original injury
        v. **Independent Intervening Forces**
        Are not a natural response or reaction to the situation created by the 's conduct may be foreseeable if's negligence increased the risk of harm from these forces:
            1. Negligent acts of third persons
            2. Crimes and intentional torts of third persons
            3. Acts of God
        vi. **Foreseeable Results Caused by Unforeseeable Intervening Forces— Usually Liable**
            1. Neg increased risk of a foreseeable harmful result
            2. Does not apply where the unforeseeable force was a crime or intentional tort by third party
        vii. **Unforeseeable Results Caused by Foreseeable Intervening Forces— Not Liable**
            1. Rare

viii.   **Unforeseeable Results Caused by Unforeseeable Intervening Forces— Not Liable**

    1. If results not within the increased risk created by 's negligence, deemed *superseding*

  5. **Unforeseeable Extent or Severity of Harm— Liable**

    a. **Eggshell-Skull Rule**

    b. takes as he finds him; is liable for all damages including aggravation of an existing condition, even if extent unforeseeable

E. JOINT TORTFEASORS

  a. **Apportionment Damages**

    i. **Causal** – one Δ cased a particular or identifiable share of the loss and should held to no more than that liability

    ii.   **Comparative Fault** – each Δ is held liable for a percentage of the ∏'s damages in proportion to that Δ's percentage share of the fault

    iii.   **Joint and Several Liability** - ∏ may sue each tortfeasor separately, sue both in a single action, obtain judgment against one alone and enforce it, obtain judgment against both and enforce it – may NOT collect more than one full compensation

      1. **Indivisible Injury** – where negligence of 2 or more persons concur in producing single, indivisible injury tortfeasors are jointly and severally liable although there was no common duty, design or concert of action

      2. **Divisible Injury** – where there are independent concurring acts that cause distinct and separate injury no joint and several liability

    iv.   <u>**Bruckman v. Pena**</u> – man's injuries exacerbated in 2nd car accident

      1. Jury must allocate btwn the two injures

    v.   <u>**Miche v. Great Lakes Steel Division**</u> – families harmed by pollutants from several companies emissions

      1. Indivisible – jury cannot reasonable apportion damages between the Δ's

F. DEFENSES TO NEGLIGENCE

  a. **Contributory Negligence**

    i. <u>**Butterfield v. Forrester** – Δ is required to specifically plead contributory negligence as an affirmative defense -</u> ∏ is held to same standard as Δ - reasonable person

    ii.   **Negligence** on the part of the that contributes to her injuries. Same standard of care as ordinary negligence.

    iii.   **No Defense to Intentional Torts**

      1. Not a defense to wanton and willful misconduct or intentional tortious conduct

    iv.   **Effect of Contributory Negligence**

      1. Completely barred 's right to recover at common law. Almost all Js now favor comparative negligence system

    v.   **Last Clear Chance—An Exception to Contributory Negligence (<u>Davies v. Mann</u>)**

      1. Permits to recover despite her contributory negligence

      2. Under rule, person with LAST CLEAR CHANCE to avoid accident who fails to do so is liable for negligence

      3. *'s rebuttal to the defense of contributory negligence*

        a. **Helpless Peril**

          i. Where is in helpless peril, will be liable if he knew/should have known of s predicament

   b. Inattentive Peril
    i. could have extricated himself if attentive
    ii. must actually have known of s predicament
   c. Prior Negligence Cases
    i. for last clear chance to apply, must have been able, but failed, to avoid harming at the time of the accident
    ii. If 's only neg occurred earlier, doctrine will not apply
  vi. **Imputed Contributory Negligence**
   1. Contributory negligence of a third party will be imputed to a (and bar her claim) only when the relationship between the 3ʳᵈ party and the is such that a court could find the vicariously liable for the 3ʳᵈ party's negligence
 b. Assumption of Risk
  i. may be denied recovery if she assumes the risk of any damage caused by 's act. must have:
   1. known of the risk
   2. voluntarily proceeded in the face of the risk
  ii. **Implied Assumption of Risk**
   1. Knowledge may be implied where the risk is one that an average person would clearly appreciate.
   2. may***not*** be said to have assumed the risk where there is no available alternative to proceeding in the face of the risk or in situations involving ***fraud, force, or an emergency.***
   3. Common carriers and public utilities may not limit their liability by disclaimer, and members of a class protected by statute will not be deemed to have assumed a risk.
   4. **Blackburn v. Dorta – MERGED IMPLIED WITH COMPARATIVE NEGLIGENCE**
  iii. **Express Assumption of Risk**
   1. **Seigneur v. National Fitness** – woman injured at gym fitness evaluation
   2. The risk may be assumed by an express agreement
  iv. **No Defense to Intentional Torts**
   1. Assumption of risk is not a defense to intentional torts, but it is a defense to wanton and willful misconduct.
  v. Primary – Δ was not negligent b/c he owed no duty or didn't breach a duty
  vi. Secondary – D owed duty but asserts affirmative defesne of assumption of risk
   1. Pure – reasonable conduct but nonetheless bars recovery
   2. Qualified – unreasonable conduct and bars recovery
**If the ∏'s conduct is unreasonable and places ∏in dangers this will be contributory negligence. If ∏'s conduct is reasonable and places ∏in danger the conduct is not negligent
 c. Comparative Negligence
  i. In comparative negligence states, 's contributory negligence is not a complete bar to recovery. Rather, the trier of fact weighs 's negligence and reduces damages accordingly.
   1. If 10% at fault, damages reduced by 10%
  ii. Pure: ∏ can recover some percentage from a liable Δ regardless of the extent of ∏'s own negligence
  iii. Modified
   1. Greater than 50% - ∏ barred from recovery when ∏ is more negligent than

Δ

  2. Less than or Equal to 50% - $\prod$ is not barred from recovery if $\prod$'s own negligence is less than or equal to Δ's negligence

  3. Slight - $\prod$ can recover where $\prod$?'s negligence is slight

 iv.   **Effect on Other Doctrines**

  1. Last clear chance is not used in comparative negligence jurisdictions. Most comparative negligence jurisdictions have abolished the defense of implied assumption of risk but have retained the defense of express assumption of risk.

  2. In most states, 's negligence will be taken into account even though 's conduct was "wanton and willful" or "reckless" but not if it was intentional.

Negligence Defenses				
	Contributory Negligence	**Implied Assumption of Risk**	**Pure Comparative Negligence**	**Partial Comparative Negligence**
Defined	P's own negligence contributed to her injury	P knew of a risk of injury and voluntarily assumed it	P's own negligence contributes to her injury	P's own negligence contributes to her injury
Effect	P's claim completely barred	P's claim completely barred	P's damage award reduced by percentage of fault attributable to her	P's damage award reduced IF her fault falls below the threshold level – otherwise P's claim is barred
Defense Negated by "Last Clear Chance" Rule	Yes	n/a	n/a	n/a
Defense Applies to "wanton or reckless tortious conduct"	No	Yes	Yes	Yes

IV. STRICT LIABILITY (LIABILITY WITHOUT FAULT)
A. PRIMA FACIE CASE

a. For strict liability, following elements must be shown:
   i. Existence of an **absolute duty** on the part of the to make safe;
   ii. **Breach** of the duty
   iii. The breach of the duty was the **actual and proximate cause** of the 's injury
   iv. **Damage** to the 's person or property

B. LIABILITY FOR ANIMALS

a. **Trespassing Animals**
   i. An owner is strictly liable for reasonably foreseeable damage done by a trespass of his animals.
b. **Personal Injuries**
   i. **Strict Liability for Wild Animals**
   ii. **No strict Liability for Domestic Animals**
      1. Unless owner has knowledge of that particular animal's dangerous propensities that are not common to the species
   iii. **Strict Liability Not Available to Trespassers**
      1. Generally no S/L in favor of trespassers in the absence of the owner's negligence.
      2. HOWEVER, a landowner may be liable on intentional tort grounds for injuries inflicted by vicious watchdogs.

C. ULTRAHAZARDOUS OR ABNORMALLY DANGEROUS ACTIVITIES

a. <u>Rylands v. Fletcher</u> - reservoir burst s and destroys mines- non natural use of the land
b. <u>Indiana Harbor RR v. American Cyanamid -</u> dangerous chemical spills out of train car – no S/L b/c it was not the transporting that was ultrahazardous it was the negligence that brought about the ultrahazardous harm
c. Three requirements for the app of S/L
   i. Activity must involve **risk of serious harm** to person or property
   ii. The activity must be one that **cannot be performed without risk of serious harm** no matter how much care is taken; and
   iii. The activity **is not commonly engaged in** the particular community
      1. Blasting, manufacturing explosives, etc.
   iv. Some courts also consider the value of the activity and its appropriateness to the location
d. Limitations
   i. <u>Foster v. Preston Mill -</u> blasting frightens minks who kills kittens - ∏ may only recover for the **type of harm that makes the activity ultrahazardous or abnormally dangerous**
   ii. <u>Golden v. Armory</u>- hydroelectric plant overflows during flood – **keep things on your land at your own peril – if they cause mischief you are S/L**
   iii. <u>Sandy v. Bushy</u> –Owners and keepers of domestic animals are not answerable for an injury done by them in a place where they have a right to be
      1. <u>P must prove:</u>
         a. Δ kept the animal
         b. Animal had vicious tendencies
         c. Δ had knowledge of the vicious tendencies
            i. Unless animals are in fact dangerous and owner has knowledge that the animals are vicious

S/L questions often include a statement in the facts or in an answer choice that the exercised reasonable care. REMEMBER that no amount of due care on the part of the will relieve him of liability in a strict liability situation

D. EXTENT OF LIABILITY
- **a. Scope of Duty Owed**
  - **i.** The duty owed is the absolute duty to make safe the normally dangerous characteristic of the animal or activity. It is owed to all foreseeable s.
- **b. Defenses**
  - **i.** In ***contributory negligence*** states, contributory negligence is no defense if has failed to realize the danger or guard against it.
  - **ii.** It is a defense if knew of the danger and his unreasonable conduct was the very cause of the ultrahazardous activity miscarrying.
  - **iii.** Assumption of the risk is a good defense in strict liability.
  - **iv.** Most ***comparative negligence*** states apply their comparative negligence rules to strict liability.

. **Products Liability**
- A. Basic Principles – P/L is the liability of a supplier of a defective product to someone injured by said product
  1. 5 Theories of Liability
     - a. Intent
     - b. Negligence
     - c. Strict liability
     - d. Implied warranties of merchantability and fitness for a particular purpose
     - e. Express warranty and misrepresentation
  2. **Strict P/L Prima Facie Elements**
     - **a. Knowledge that the D manufactured or sold product**
       - **i. The P must show that the D manufactured the item or placed it in the stream of commerce**
     - **b. Defect existed**
       - **i. The p must show that the product was defective**
     - **c. Causation**
       - **i. The P must show that the product and its defective aspects were the cause-in-fact and the proximate cause of the P's injuries**
     - **d. Defect existed when the D's hands**
       - **i. The P must show that the defect existed at the time the product left the D's hands**
  3. Types of Defects
     - a. Manufacturing Defects – if a product emerges from manufacturing different and more dangerous than products made properly
       - i. <u>**Rix v. General Motors -**</u> faulty brake system
         1. <u>**P must prove**</u>
            - a. <u>**Product was in a defective condition**</u>
            - b. <u>**Product was expect to and did reach the ultimate consumer**</u>
            - c. <u>**Defective condition in the product was proximate cause of injury to P**</u>
     - b. Design Defect – all products of a line are the same but have dangerous propensities
       - i. <u>**Prentis v. Yale Mfg. Co.**</u> –forklift power surge injures worker
         1. <u>**Pure Neligence Risk Utility Test -**</u>liability is predicated upon defective design, look to negligence of manufactures in designing product
     - c. Inadequate Warnings – manufactures failure to give adequate warnings of the risks involved in using the product – danger must not be apparent to users

i. __Anderson v. Owens-Corning__ - asbestos
    1. ∏ must demonstrate that Δ had actual or constructive knowledge of the potential risk or danger that caused the injury to ∏
    2. DEFENSE: Evidence of **State of the Art** was such that the Δ could not have known the risk

Products Liability Theories			
	__Negligence__	__Strict Liability__	__Implied Warranties__
Who Can Sue?	Any foreseeable P	Any foreseeable P	Purchaser and his family, household and guests
Who Can Be Sued?	Any commercial supplier (i.e. manufacturer, wholesaler, retailer)	Any commercial supplier	*Merchantability*: a merchant dealing in the kind of goods sold *Fitness for a Particular Purpose:* any seller of the goods
What Constitutes Breach?	Negligent conduct that results in the supplying of a defective product	The supplying of a defective product	*Merchantability*: sale of goods not generally acceptable or fit for ordinary purposes *Fitness for a Particular Purpose:* sale of goods not fit for purpose that seller knows or has reason to know of (and knows that buyer is relying on seller's judgment
What Damages can be Recovered?	Personal injury and property damage (no recovery for economic loss standing alone)	Personal injury and property damage (no recovery for economic loss standing alone)	Personal injury and property damage (recovery solely for economic loss permitted)
What	Assumption of	Contributory	Contributory

Defenses are Available?	risk and any contributory negligence	Negligence States: assumption of risk and unreasonable misuse (failure to discover or guard against defect is NOT a defense) Comparative Negligence States: any type of fault under state's comparative negligence rules	Negligence States: assumption of risk, unreasonable misuse, failure to give reasonable notice of breach Comparative Negligence States: any type of fault under state'

B. Proof of Defect
   a. Manufacturing Defect - D will be liable if P can show the product failed to perform as safely as an ordinary consumer would expect
   b. Design Defect - P must show that the D could have made the product safer w/o serious impact on product price or utility
   c. Non compliance with government safety standards will establish defect – compliance is evidence but not conclusory
   d. State of the Art – D will not be held liable for dangers not foreseeable at the time of marketing due to scientific or technological limitations
   e. Unavoidable unsafe product – manufacturers will not be held liable if the danger is APPARENT and there is no safer way to make the product (i.e. knives)
C. Defect must have existed when product left
D. Liability based on Negligence
   a. Duty of care owed to any *foreseeable plaintiff*
      i. Users, consumers and bystanders can sue if foreseeable P
      ii. Commercial suppliers can be held liable i.e. manufacturers, wholesalers and retailers. (Garage sales are not commercial suppliers)
   b. Breach of Duty is shown by
      i. Negligent conduct of the D that leads to
      ii. Supplying of a defective product
      iii. Proof – same as standard negligence case – P may invoke Res IpsaLoquitur
      iv. Retailers and Wholesalers can satisfy duty w/ a reasonable inspection
   c. Causation – intermediary in the chain's failure to discover a defect is not a superseding cause unless their conduct exceeds reasonable negligence
   d. Damages – physical or property injury must be shown
E. Defenses
   a. **Ford Motor Co v. Matthews** –tractor runs over man due to faulty switch
   b. **Misuse -** ∏'s misuse of a product will not prevent recovery IF the ∏'s abnormal and unintended use of his product was not reasonably foreseeable or should have been foreseeable to the Δ

    c. **Forseeability** – manufacture is not liable for injures resulting from abnormal or unintended use of the product if such use was not reasonably foreseeable

    d. **Failure to Discover Danger** – if the ∏'s contributory negligence lies in failing to inspect the product or otherwise failing to become aware of the danger this is NOT a defense for Δ

    e. **Unreasonable Exposure to Risk** –if ∏ learns of the risk and nonetheless voluntarily submits to the risk assumption of risk

    f. **Abnormal Use** – if ∏'s contributory negligence consists of abnormal use or misuse this MAY be a defense but depends on the degree of foreseeability of the use of the product

    g. **Independent Negligence** –if ∏'s contributory negligence is an independent concurring cause of the harm the ∏ will probably be able to recover if ∏ can show that the effect of the independent event was not foreseeable or bizarre that it should be considered a superseding act

F. Liability based on S/L

    a. Duty – D has a duty as a commercial supplier to supply safe goods

      i. Product must reach P w/o substantial alteration

      ii. Applies only to products not services

      iii. Any commercial supplier can be held liable – casual sellers will not usually be held liable (i.e. garage sales)

    b. Breach of Duty

      i. P must show product is defective – defect must make product unreasonably dangerous. Retailers may be liable even if no opportunity to inspect

    c. Causation

      i. Actual cause – P must show that the defect existed when product left D's control

      ii. Proximate Cause – same for negligence cases

    d. Defenses

      i. Contributory Negligence is no defense where P merely failed to discover the defect or guard against its existence or where misuse was foreseeable

      ii. Comparative negligence jurisdictions apply appropriate rules

    e. Disclaimers – irrelevant if negligence or S/L if personal injury or property damages occur

G. Implied Warranty

    a. Merchantability – whether goods are of average acceptable quality and are generally fit for the ordinary purpose for which the goods are used

    b. Fitness for a particular purpose – seller knows or has reason to know the particular purpose for which the goods are required and the buyer is relying on seller's skill and judgment in selecting goods

    c. Breach of Warranty - if product fails to live up to either (a) or (b) warranty is breached and D is liable

      i. P does not have to prove any fault by D

    d. Causation – actual and proximate cause as in negligence

    e. Defenses

      i. Assumption of risk

      ii. Failure to give notice of breach

      iii. Contributory negligence

H. Express Warranty

    a. Any affirmation of fact or promise concerning goods (i.e. claims or advertising)

      i. Anyone that is part of the bargain can sue

    b. Breach – P need only show that product didn't live up to advertisement

    c. Disclaimer will only be effective if consistent with the warranty

VI. Nuisance

A. Private Nuisance
  a. ***Substantial and unreasonable interference*** with another private individuals
  b. ***Use or enjoyment*** of property that he actually possess or has a right to immediate possession
  1. Substantial interference – interference that is offensive, involvement, or annoying to the average person in the community. Not substantial if it is result of P's hypersensitivity or specialized use of property
  2. Unreasonable Interference – based on intent or negligence – severity must outweigh the utility of D's conduct
     a. Balancing test – every person is entitled to use his own land in a reasonable way
** Nuisance questions will often flag the correct choice w/ a key term from the definition of nuisance. i.e. D is liable b/c the activity created a "substantial" or "unreasonable" interference w/ P's use of land
B. Public Nuisance
  a. An act that unreasonable interferes with the ***health, safety or property rights of the community***
C. Defenses
  1. Legislative authority – i.e. zoning ordinance – not absolute defense but is persuasive
  2. Conduct of Others – no one actor is liable for all damage caused by concurrence of his acts and others – i.e. ten steel mills are polluting a stream. Each is responsible for the pollution it creates
  3. Contributory Negligence – no defense unless P's case rests on negligence theory
VII. General Considerations for all Cases
  A. Vicarious Liability -one person commits a tortious act against a 3rd party and another person will be liable to the 3rd party for this act.
  1. Respondeat Superior – employer vicariously liable for employees tortious act if w/in the ***scope of his employment***
  2. Partners and Joint Venturers – each member of a partnership or joint venture is vicariously liable for tortious conduct of another member committed in ***the scope and course*** of the partnership or joint venture
  3. Parent/Child – parent is not vicariously liable for the tortious conduct of a child
     a. There are statutory exceptions to this
        i. Child acting as an agent for the parents
        ii. Parents may be held liable for her own negligence in letting child do something
  4. Tavern keepers
     a. C/L – no liability on venders of intoxicating beverages for injuries resulting from drunkenness
     b. Modern law – dram shop act – liability to 3rd party b/c of drunken patron's actions
  B. Multiple Defendants/ Parties
  1. Joint and Several Liability – 2 or more negligent acts combine to proximately cause an ***indivisible injury*** – each negligent actor is held jointly and severally liable. **If divisible injury** - each D is liable only for the damages they caused
     a. D acting in concert are held jointly and severally liable even if injury is divisible
     b. Statute of Limitations – many states have abolished joint liability either
        i. For D's less at fault that P OR
        ii. All D's regarding non-economic damages
           1. Liability in these cases is proportionate to D's fault
  2. Contribution and Indemnity – determine how joint tortfeasors allocate damages
** Generally for Contribution to apply both D's must have a miserable degree of culpability for the tort. Indemnity usually applies when one party is much more responsible than the other. Neither of these

doctrines affects P's amount of recovery, they only determine how much EACH D must pay

> a. Contribution - allows multiple D's to apportion responsibility and damages amongst themselves
>> i. Not applicable to intentional torts and D must be originally liable to P
> b. Comparative Contribution – contribution imposed in proportion to the relative fault of the various D's
> c. Equal Shares (Minority) – apportionment is in equal shares regardless of degree of fault
> d. Indemnity – shifting entire loss between or among tortfeasors. Only available:
>> i. By contract
>> ii. In vicarious liability situations
>> iii. Under strict products liability
>> iv. In some jurisdictions where there has been an identifiable difference in degree of fault

C. Wrongful Death – grants recovery for pecuniary injury resulting to the spouse and next of kin.

> a. A decedents creditors have no claim against reward

Deceased's contributory negligence reduces recovery in comparative negligence standard

Made in the USA
Coppell, TX
20 September 2021

62562867R10188